The Secret Doctrine of the Jews

SUNY series in Western Esoteric Traditions
____

David Appelbaum, editor

The Secret Doctrine of the Jews

Jewish Theosophists and the Kabbalah

BOAZ HUSS

Cover: The emblem of the Theosophical Society with the slogan of the Society in Hebrew, as it appeared in the publications of the early Israeli members of the Theosophical Society. Courtesy of the Theosophical Society.

Published by State University of New York Press, Albany

© 2025 State University of New York

Links to third-party websites are provided as a convenience and for informational purposes only. They do not constitute an endorsement or an approval of any of the products, services, or opinions of the organization, companies, or individuals. SUNY Press bears no responsibility for the accuracy, legality, or content of a URL, the external website, or for that of subsequent websites.

EU GPSR Authorized Representative:
Logos Europe, 9 rue Nicolas Poussin, 17000, La Rochelle, France
contact@logoseurope.eu

For information, contact State University of New York Press, Albany, NY
www.sunypress.edu

Library of Congress Cataloging-in-Publication Data

Name: Huss, Boaz, author.
Title: The secret doctrine of the Jews : Jewish theosophists and the kabbalah / Boaz Huss.
Description: Albany : State University of New York Press, [2025] | Series: SUNY series in western esoteric traditions | Includes bibliographical references and index.
Identifiers: LCCN 2025003549 | ISBN 9798855803877 (hardcover : alk. paper) | ISBN 9798855803891 (ebook) | ISBN 9798855803884 (pbk : alk paper)
Subjects: LCSH: Cabala—History. | Theosophy—Influence. | Theosophy—Relations—Judaism. | Judaism—Relations—Theosophy.
Classification: LCC BM525 .H87 2025 | DDC 296.1/609—dc23/eng/20250312
LC record available at https://lccn.loc.gov/2025003549

Contents

Illustrations

Preface and Acknowledgments

The library of Gershom Scholem, the eminent scholar of Kabbalah, now housed at the National Library in Jerusalem, is a treasure house for researchers of Kabbalah and related topics. During my graduate studies in the late 1980s, I spent many hours working in Scholem's library. When I lost focus on my work, I would browse the shelves at random, always discovering new and intriguing titles or interesting notes that Scholem jotted down in the margins of his books. One particular book that caught my attention was a translation of the *Idra Zuta*, one of the most revered sections of the *Zohar*, into Judeo-Arabic (i.e., Arabic written in Hebrew script), published in Pune, India, in 1887. The translation was prepared and printed by A. D. Ezekiel in his own publishing house. On the title page, Scholem had written: "This book is very rare as it was banned by the Rabbis of Baghdad, Jerusalem, and Hebron, who pronounced the translation of the secrets of the *Idra* into Arabic a sacrilege."

The little book intrigued me, and from time to time, I would pull it out for another look. What was the context of its printing? Who was A. D. Ezekiel, and what motivated him to translate the *Zohar* into Judeo-Arabic, thereby incurring the wrath of the rabbinical authorities?

Only many years later, while researching the history of *Zohar* translations, I found the clue to these questions. I noticed that Ezekiel, who was a member of the Iraqi Jewish community in India, published his Judeo-Arabic translation of the *Idra Zuta* the same year that the English occultist Samuel Liddell McGregor Mathers published an English translation in his book, *Kabbalah Unveiled*. Mathers translated the words *Idra Zuta* as "The lesser Holy Assembly," the same phrase that Ezekiel used in the English title page of his translation. This led me to wonder: Could there be any connection between the two translations? Was the Jewish printer from Pune associated with the same circles as the British esotericist Mathers?

A quick search in online resources, and a more thorough reading of Ezekiel's introduction to the *Idra Zuta*, as well as other books he published in his printing house, revealed that Ezekiel was, like Mathers, a member of the Theosophical Society. Ezekiel mentioned the society (which he referred to as "the Sufi Society from America"!), several times and affirmed that his interest in Kabbalah was stimulated by the importance it had in the teachings of the Theosophical Society.

Although I knew very little about the Theosophical Society at the time (my main area of research is history of Jewish Kabbalah), I found the story of A. D. Ezekiel's *Zohar* translation intriguing and decided to study it further. Since Ezekiel wrote the introduction to his book in the Baghdadi Judeo-Arabic dialect, which I found difficult to understand, I sought assistance from the late Prof. Sasson Somekh, a prominent Israeli scholar of modern Arab literature, who was born and raised in Iraq.

Prof. Somekh, who kindly helped me to translate Ezekiel's introduction, was not very surprised when I told him that the translator of the *Idra Zuta* was a Jewish Theosophist. His aunt and uncle, he told me, who lived in Basra in the 1930s, were also Jewish Theosophists.

Prof. Somekh referred me to the description of his Theosophist relatives in his memoirs, *Baghdad, Yesterday,* and to a short article in Hebrew, written in 1965 by Hayyim Yoseph Cohen, about the Jewish Theosophists of Basra. From these sources, I learned that Ezekiel was not a unique case and that about fifty years after he joined the Theosophical Society in India, a Jewish Theosophical group was established in Iraq. Like Ezekiel, the community in Basra, headed by Kadouri Ani (Prof. Sasson Somekh's uncle), faced opposition from the rabbinical authorities, who demanded that the Jewish Theosophists close their lodge. When they refused, they excommunicated them. Following the excommunication, Kadouri Ani and his supporters established their own Theosophically inspired Jewish community, which had its own synagogue, graveyard, and ritual slaughterer.

What a fascinating story! When I started exploring it, I discovered that the group in Basra was not the only Jewish Theosophical group that was active at that period. I learned that the foundation of the Basra group was stimulated by the creation of a Jewish Section of the Theosophical Society, the Association of Hebrew Theosophists. The association was founded in late 1925, during the Jubilee Congress of the Theosophical Society in Adyar. I later found that the Association of Hebrew Theosophists established branches in India, England, Holland, and the United States and that the American branch published a journal, *The Jewish Theosophist*. To my surprise and delight, I found some of the copies of this rare journal in Scholem's library.

At that point, it was clear to me that I had stumbled upon a fascinating new area of research. I had no way of knowing just how far this research would lead me, how many new friends I would make along the way, or how many years it would take before I could present the findings in this book.

The research for *The Secret Doctrine of the Jews* was supported by two generous grants of the Israeli Science Foundation: Kabbalah and the Theosophical Society (1875–1936) (774/10) and Western Esotericism in Israeli Society (2284/22). These grants allowed me to dedicate time to study the Jewish Theosophists and travel to Theosophical libraries and archives in the United States, Europe, and India. I am also grateful for the financial support provided by the Rector of Ben-Gurion University and the Dean of the Faculty of Humanities and Social Sciences for the publication of the book.

I would like to express my gratitude to James Peltz, editor-in-chief, Diane Ganeles, senior production editor, and the entire production team at the State University of New York Press for their meticulous work in the production and publication of this book.

This book could not have been written without the invaluable support of librarians, archivists, and fellow scholars. I am deeply grateful to Janet Kerschner, archivist of the Henry S. Olcott Memorial Library in Wheaton, Illinois; to Jaishree Kanan, the archivist of the Adyar Library and Research Center (ALRC) at the international headquarters of the Theosophical Society in Chennai; to Renger Dijkstra, the librarian of the Theosophical Society in the Netherlands; and to Rafa C. Sidor of the University College Library Special Collection in London. Their kindness and expert assistance during my visits and beyond have been invaluable.

I also wish to express my sincere thanks to the scholars and colleagues who took an interest in my work and provided relevant information and materials for my research. Julie Matos-Hall (Chajes), who collaborated with me as part of the Israeli Science Foundation project, shared her extensive knowledge of Blavatsky's and other early Theosophists' interest in Kabbalah and kindly read and commented on drafts of several chapters of my book. Pat Deveney, whom I first met at the beginning of my research, encouraged me to pursue my research and generously shared information he had gathered about Jewish Theosophists in the late nineteenth century. Alexandra Nagel provided materials she found on Jewish Theosophists in the Netherlands and offered translations of relevant documents. Marco Pasi supplied information about Jewish Theosophists in Italy and turned my attention to the first Jewish Lodge of the Theosophical Society, which was founded in Livorno in 1904. Chuang Chienhui helped me locate information on Jews active in the Shanghai and Hong Kong lodges. Karolina Maria Kotkowska (Hess), provided information on Jewish Theosophists in Poland and translated documents related to them. Shimon Lev shared his extensive knowledge of the Jewish Theosophist in South Africa, and Menashe Anzi contributed documents relating to the Jewish Theosophist in Basra and shared drafts of his lectures and articles on this subject. Sam Glauber offered substantial information on Jewish interest in Theosophy which he found in the Yiddish press in East Europe and the United Sates, as well as in other sources. Additional thanks go to Francesco Baroni, Hans-Jürgen Bracker, James Chiriyankandatha, Marc Demarest, Philip Deslippe, Michael Gomes, Mátyás Mervay, Victor Lal, Enrico Lucca, Leslie Price, Avi-ram Tzoreff, Agata Świerzowska, Okamato Yoshiko, and Yaakov Zamir for their generous assistance and sharing of information and documents. I would also like to thank Asher Benyamin, the administrator of the Goren-Goldstien Center of Jewish Thought, for his friendship and invaluable assistance over the years. Last, my profound gratitude goes to Ephrat for her unwavering support, encouragement, and love.

Introduction

In December 1925, the Jubilee congress of the Theosophical Society, the worldwide esoteric movement established in New York in 1875 by Helena Petrovna Blavatsky and Henry Steel Olcott, took place in Adyar, southern India. At this congress, twelve Jewish delegates, from Egypt, India, and Europe, came together to establish the Association of Hebrew Theosophists. The three aims of the nascent Jewish-Theosophical association were

- To study Judaism in light of Theosophy and Theosophy in the light of Judaism.

- To spread Theosophical teachings among the Jews.

- To undertake any other activity that could aid in the realization of the objects of the association.[1]

The Jewish Theosophical Association was established fifty years after the foundation of the Theosophical Society. However, Jews were actively engaged in the society since its inception. One of its founding members was Jewish, and many Jews played prominent roles in Theosophical lodges worldwide. Additionally, Jews became involved in some of the offshoots of the Theosophical Society, such as the Quest Society, the Anthroposophical Society, and Agni Yoga.

In 1904, the first Jewish Theosophical lodge was founded in Livorno (Leghorn), and by 1925, the Association of Hebrew Theosophists was established. The association opened sections in India, Poland, the Netherlands, Iraq, and the United States. It published several books by Jewish Theosophists and oversaw the publication of the journal *The Jewish Theosophist*. In Basra, Iraq, the members of the Jewish Theosophical lodge, who had been excommunicated by rabbinic authorities, opened an independent Jewish community that remained active for several years.

By the end of the 1930s, the Jewish sections of the Theosophical Society had become dormant. Nonetheless, many Jews continued to participate actively in the Theosophical Society. Since the 1930s, several Jewish Theosophists immigrated to Mandate Palestine, and after the foundation of the State of Israel, Theosophical lodges were established in Safed, Jerusalem, Tel Aviv, and Haifa.

Jewish followers of the Theosophical Society were interested in reconciling their Jewish identity with their Theosophical convictions. As we have seen, the stated goals of the Association of Hebrew Theosophists were "to study Judaism in light of Theosophy and Theosophy in the light of Judaism, and to spread Theosophical teachings among the Jews." Kabbalah played a central role in the endeavors of the Jewish Theosophists to reconcile Theosophy and Judaism. Jewish Theosophists published many articles and books on Kabbalah, translated Kabbalistic texts, and offered innovative, Theosophical interpretations of Kabbalah. The Jewish Theosophists aspired to revitalize and spiritualize Judaism through a return to Kabbalah and to create a liberal Jewish mystical movement based on Theosophical principles. The centrality of Kabbalah within a modern Jewish liberal movement was unique at the time. By the late nineteenth century, knowledge of Kabbalah was restricted in westernized Jewish cultures and was prevalent mostly among traditional Jews in Eastern Europe, the Middle East, and North Africa. Jewish Theosophy offered a unique attempt to create a modern, liberal form of Judaism that embraced Kabbalah and presented Jewish mysticism as the central component of the Jewish tradition.

The endeavors of Jewish Theosophists to advance a mystical liberal reform of Judaism had limited success in the late nineteenth and early twentieth centuries. However, a spiritual liberal reform of Judaism, much like that suggested by the Jewish Theosophists, has been offered with much more success by Jewish renewal and neo-Kabbalistic movements since the late twentieth century. The Jewish Theosophists can be seen as the early precursors and heralds of Jewish renewal movement and New Age Kabbalah.

Despite the considerable number of Jews who joined Theosophical lodges worldwide, the prominent roles played by some within the Theosophical Society, and the impact of Jewish Theosophy on modern perceptions of Kabbalah, very little research has been dedicated to the Jewish adherents of the Theosophical Society. Hayim Cohen addressed the Jewish Theosophists in Basra and their excommunication in an article published in 1965, while

David Sagiv discussed this topic in his 2004 monograph on the Jewish community in Basra.[2] In recent years, several studies were dedicated also to other Jewish Theosophists. In the framework of my research of the Jewish Theosophists, which was funded by the Israeli Science Foundation, I have published studies on A.D. Ezekiel, the Jewish Theosophists from Pune, on Jewish Theosophists' perceptions of Kabbalah, and on the Association of Hebrew Theosophists and their missions to the Jews and gentiles.[3] Expanded versions of these articles are incorporated in the present monograph. Shimon Lev contributed a study on the Jewish Theosophist supports of Gandhi in South Africa,[4] while Alexandra Nagel explored the Association of Jewish Theosophists in the Netherlands.[5] Further insights into the Jewish Theosophists in Basra were provided by Menashe Anzi in his article on Theosophy and anti-Theosophy in Basra, and by Sasha Rachel Goldstein in her PhD dissertation on Baghdadi Jewish Networks in Hashemite Iraq.[6]

This book offers the first comprehensive study of Jewish followers of the Theosophical Society. It presents a detailed examination of the global history of Jewish Theosophists, exploring their ideologies, activities, and relations with the Jewish communities from which they originated, as well as their interactions with non-Jewish fellow Theosophists. The book aims to underscore the role of Jewish Theosophists within the Theosophical Society and explore their impact on modern Jewish culture, particularly, their influence on the development of modern perspectives and forms of Kabbalah.

This book begins with a brief sketch of the Theosophical Society. The first chapter examines the foundation of the society in New York in 1875, the major ideas and principles of the movement, the relocation of the founders to India in 1879, and the subsequent global history of the society. The chapter also explores the institutional structure of the Theosophical Society, the religious subgroups affiliated with it, and some of the major schisms that the society underwent.

The following three chapters examine the involvement of Jews in the Theosophical Society, as well as in some of its offshoots, spanning the initial fifty years of the society, up to the foundation of the Association of Hebrew Theosophists. The second chapter delves into some of the prominent Jewish followers of the Theosophical Society in the late nineteenth century. The chapter explores their activities within the society and examines how they negotiated between their Jewish identity and their commitment to Theosophy. The Jewish followers of the Theosophical Society discussed in the chapter include David Etienne de Lara, the Jewish founding member of the Theosophical Society; Leon Hyneman, the Freemason journalist, author, and editor from Philadelphia; and his daughter, the author, poet, and essayist Alice Hyneman-Rhine. Other early Theosophists of Jewish origins that are discussed in the chapter are A. D. Ezekiel, a member of Baghdadi community in India, who, under the impact of Theosophical ideas, decided to translate Kabbalistic texts to Judeo-Arabic; Fredrich Eckstein, an intellectual and occultist who served as the first president of the Theosophical lodge in Vienna; Rabbi Herman van Staveren, who was one of the founding members of the Theosophical Society in Wellington, New Zealand; and Naphtali Herz Imber, the famous Jewish Zionist poet, who was affiliated with the society during his years in the United States.

During the last decade of the nineteenth century and the early decades of the twentieth century, the Theosophical Society underwent significant developments. The founders of the society passed away, and Annie Besant became its international president. During this period, the society underwent several schisms, and some offshoots of the society, such as the Quest Society, the Anthroposophical Society, and the Agni movement were founded. Notwithstanding these events, the Theosophical Society grew under the leadership of Annie Besant and reached its peak in the late 1920s. As the Theosophical Society's global dispersion and public visibility grew, many Jews were drawn to it and joined its national sections all around the world.

The third chapter of the book explores the activities of Jewish followers of the Theosophical Society in the first two decades of the twentieth century in different countries around the globe, including Italy, Poland, England, the United States, China, India, South Africa, and Egypt.

The fourth chapter discusses Jewish Theosophists who joined some of the major offshoots of the Theosophical Society. The chapter examines the involvement of Rabbi Moses Gaster in the Quest Society, founded in 1909, by G. R. S Mead, the former secretary of Blavatsky, who departed from the British Section of the society. Additionally, it explores the participation of Jewish Theosophists in the Anthroposophical Society, founded by Rudolf Steiner, the former president of the German Section, who separated from the Theosophical Society in 1912. Last, the chapter examines the Jewish members of the inner group of Agni Yoga, established in the United States by Russian Theosophists Nicholas and Helena Roerich in 1920.

As mentioned earlier, the Association of Hebrew Theosophists was established in 1925, during the Jubilee congress of the Theosophical Society. The association, active for several years, established branches in India, Holland, Iraq, England, Poland, and the United States. The American branch, which was especially active, published a journal titled *The Jewish Theosophist.*

The fifth chapter of the book examines the events leading to the foundation of the Jewish Association and explore the establishment and activities of its Indian, English Dutch, and Polish Sections. It also covers the activities of the American Section of the association and discuss *The Jewish Theosophist*, published by the American branch.

In 1927, a Jewish Theosophical branch associated with the Association of Hebrew Theosophists was established in Basra, Iraq. The rabbinical authorities opposed the Jewish Theosophists in Basra and ordered them to leave the Theosophical Society. Refusing to comply, the rabbis excommunicated the group, sparking widespread attention and a heated debate in both Jewish and Theosophical circles. The excommunicated Theosophists established an independent Jewish community known as "Sincere Jews," which operated until 1936, when the excommunication order was rescinded.

Chapter 6 explores the foundation of the Jewish Theosophical Lodge in Basra, the ensuing controversy over the Jewish Theosophists and their excommunication, the reactions and debates surrounding the excommunication, the formation and activities of the independent Sincere Jews community, and the eventual annulment of the decree against them.

The branches of the Association of the Hebrew Theosophists stopped their activities in the mid-1930s, and the Jewish Theosophical community in Basra dissolved in 1936. During World War II, many of the European Jewish Theosophists perished in the Holocaust. Others emigrated to the Land of Israel before and after the war. Following the 1948 Israeli Arab Jewish war and the foundation of the State of Israel, Jewish Theosophists from Arab countries also left their countries, and some of them immigrated to Israel. Some of the Jewish Theosophists who immigrated to Israel contacted and met each other, and beginning in the early 1950s, Theosophical lodges, whose members were predominantly Jewish, were established in Safed, Tel Aviv, Jerusalem, and Haifa.

Chapter 7 discusses the establishment of the Theosophical lodges in Israel, examining the social and cultural background to the Israeli Theosophists. The chapter explores the activities and publications of the Israeli Theosophical lodges, as well as their efforts to reconcile their Jewish and Israeli identity with their Theosophical convictions.

The next two chapters of the book examine the relations and interactions of Jewish Theosophists with the Jewish communities from which they originated, as well as with non-Jewish fellow Theosophists. The eighth chapter considers the Jewish identity of Jewish Theosophists and their connections to other contemporary Jewish movements and trends. It explores the aspiration of Jewish Theosophists to propagate Theosophy among Jews, and to reform Judaism through Theosophy. It delves into the critiques voiced by Jewish Theosophists against other forms of Judaism, particularly Rabbinic and Orthodox Judaism. highlighting their endeavors to spiritualize Judaism. Additionally, it addresses the opposition that Jewish Theosophists encountered within Jewish and Israeli communities and their responses to these criticisms.

Chapter 9 discusses the anti-Jewish and antisemitic attitudes of some of the leaders and members of the Theosophical Society and examines the ways in which Jews responded to these biases. It also explores the aspiration of Jewish Theosophists to elevate the standing of Judaism among their fellow Theosophists and to enrich Theosophy with Jewish spiritual traditions.

Kabbalah played a central role in the attempts of Jewish adherents of the Theosophical Society to harmonize Judaism and Theosophy. Jewish Theosophists regarded Kabbalah as representing the secret doctrine of the Jews, a perennial knowledge essentially identical with the teachings of the Theosophical Society.

The tenth and concluding chapter of the book provides an in-depth exploration of how Jewish adherents of the Theosophical Society perceive and interpret Kabbalah, offering an analysis of the contexts and significance of Jewish-Theosophical engagement with Kabbalah. The chapter begins with a brief discussion of the interest of non-Jewish Theosophists, especially Blavatsky, in Kabbalah. It then explores the fascination of Jewish Theosophist with Kabbalah, delving into their sources of knowledge, perspectives, and interpretations of Kabbalah. The chapter also examines the Jewish Theosophical endeavors to revive Kabbalah. It concludes with a discussion of the relations between Jewish Theosophy and the academic study of Kabbalah and the impact of Jewish Theosophists on modern forms and perceptions of Kabbalah.

Chapter 1

The Theosophical Society

On the evening of September 7, 1875, a small group of people, interested in Spiritualism and occultism, gathered in a small apartment in 46 Irving Place in New York City, the residence of a recent émigré of Russian origins, Helena Petrovna Blavatsky (1831–1891), to hear a lecture by George H. Felt (1831–1906) on "The Egyptian Cabala." The day after, the group reconvened, and one of the participants, Colonel Henry Steel Olcott (1832–1907), suggested establishing a society dedicated to the study of esoteric topics. His suggestion was accepted by the group, and the Theosophical Society was inaugurated on November 17, 1875.[1]

One of the participants in these early meetings who took part in the foundation of the Theosophical Society was a Jewish scholar of Sephardic origins, David Etienne de Lara (1796–1879).[2] In the following years, many more Jews joined and were active in the society, and in 1925, a Jewish Theosophical Association was founded. The interest that the founders of the Theosophical Society discovered in Kabbalah continued also in later years, notwithstanding the growing interest of the Society in Buddhism and Hinduism. Many of the Jews who became active in the Theosophical Society wrote about Kabbalah and emphasized its resemblance and compatibility of Jewish Kabbalah and the values and teachings of the society.

The following chapters of this book will discuss in detail the Jews who joined and were active in the Theosophical Society, the ways they negotiated their Jewish identity and their Theosophical convictions, and their perceptions and interpretations of Kabbalah. Before delving into an examination of the vicissitudes of Jewish Theosophy, I would like to present a brief sketch of the Theosophical Society and its historical development.

The Theosophical Society and Its Founders

As mentioned above, the Theosophical Society was founded in New York in the autumn of 1875. The leaders of the newly founded society, which soon became the largest and most influential modern esoteric movement, were Helena Petrovna Blavatsky, who became the primary theorist and charismatic leader of the society, and Henry Steel Olcott, who served as the first president. Blavatsky was born Helena Petrovna von Hahn, in Ekaterinoslav (now Dnipro), Ukraine, to an aristocratic German Russian family. In 1849, at the age of eighteen, she married Nikifor Blavatsky, vice governor of Yerevan province in Armenia but left him just a few months afterward. After leaving her husband, Blavatsky traveled for the next twenty-four years. She claimed that during these years she met and studied with her mysterious spiritual masters or "mahatmas" in the Far East. Very little reliable information is known about her life during these years. In 1873, she arrived in New York, traveling from Paris via Odessa and Eastern Europe. In 1874, she met the American lawyer and journalist Henry Steel Olcott in Chittenden, Vermont, where he was investigating Spiritualistic phenomena.[3]

Henry Steel Olcott was born to a Presbyterian family in Orange, New Jersey, in 1832. He was educated at Columbia University and worked as an agricultural correspondent for *The New York Tribune.* He served in the Union army during the Civil War and later worked as a lawyer, specializing in insurance, revenue, and fraud. In 1874 he became interested in Spiritualism, and during his investigations of the séances of the Eddy brothers in rural Vermont, he first met with Blavatsky.[4]

The small group from which the Theosophical Society emerged included also other people who were interested in occultism and Spiritualism: Emma Hardinge Britten (1823–1899), a former English actress who became a famous trance medium and historian of Spiritualism; William Quan Judge (1851–1896), an Irish American lawyer, who later became the leader of the American branch of the society, and the above-mentioned George H. Felt, a mechanical engineer, inventor, and freemason. In October 1875, the group met in Britten's apartment to elect officers and draw up the bylaws of the society. On 17 November, Olcott gave his inaugural address as the president of the Theosophical Society.[5]

In its initial stages in New York, the members of the Theosophical Society were interested in occult training, conjuring elemental spirits, astral travel, and means of achieving immortality. They developed a system of Masonic-like degrees and encouraged temperance and fasting, as well as some form of sexual abstinence.[6] The original objectives of the society included studying "the esoteric philosophy of ancient times" and "collecting and diffusing knowledge of the laws which govern the universe." The founders declared that "the society has no dogmas to enforce and no creed to disseminate" and that the qualifications for membership are not dependent on race, sex, color, country, or creed.[7] Later, the principals of the society were formulated as they are known today: "to form a nucleus of the Universal Brotherhood of Humanity, without distinction of race, creed, sex, caste or color; to encourage the study of comparative religion, philosophy and science; and to investigate unexplained laws of Nature and the powers latent in man."[8]

From its beginning, the Theosophical Society was interested in different religious and esoteric traditions: first, in Western esoteric, ancient Egyptian, and Kabbalistic doctrines and later, in Hinduism and Buddhism. As a movement, Theosophy encouraged the comparative study of religion and integrated into its teachings concepts and themes derived from a large variety of contexts. Unlike other esoteric movements, the Theosophical Society included many non-Christian and non-Western members from the outset. These members participated in Theosophical adaptations and interpretations of their traditions. Despite these interpretations being offered by adherents of the traditions themselves, they were many times predicated on a Western esoteric perspective and rooted in orientalist discourse.[9]

During the early period of the Theosophical Society, Emma Hardinge Britten, who later rejected Theosophy, but then was still one of the most active members of the movement, prepared two books that appeared in 1876, *Art Magic*, and *Ghost Land*.[10] These were followed by Blavatsky's first major work, *Isis Unveiled*, which was published in 1877 and soon became a bestseller. The work, of over thirteen hundred pages, was divided into a volume on science and a volume on theology. Blavatsky wrote the book in a state of semitrance and claimed that it was written through, rather than by her. The book, which contained innumerable quotations from a variety of sources on comparative religion, occultism, Kabbalah, and contemporary science, included diverse doctrines, such as the solar and phallic origin of all religions, the superiority of ancient Eastern and Egyptian knowledge, the preexistence and future evolution of the human soul, and the existence of an ancient universal wisdom religion, guarded by adepts through the generations.[11] Blavatsky claimed that she was in touch with such adepts, to whom she referred also as masters or brothers, and later, Mahatmas. The adepts were perceived to be evolved human beings, who had reached the highest states of occult knowledge and spiritual enlightenment. The adepts, or Mahatmas, especially Masters Morya and Koot Hoomi, communicated also with Olcott and other leading Theosophists.[12]

The Move to India and Later History of the Theosophical Society

In 1877, the founders of the Theosophical Society contacted Dayananda Saraswati (1824–1883), the founder of the reform Hindu movement Arya Samaj (Aryan Society), and for a few years, the two societies merged.[13] Following the merger (that ended in 1882), Blavatsky and Olcott decided to move to India. After a short visit in London, where a branch of the Theosophical Society was recently founded, they arrived in Bombay in February 1879. There, they founded a periodical, *The Theosophist*, which was edited by Blavatsky and became the central organ of the Theosophical Society. The founders of the society were also interested in Buddhism, and already in New York, corresponded with Buddhist leaders in Ceylon (today, Sri Lanka). In May 1880, Blavatsky and Olcott traveled to Ceylon and made a formal profession (*pansil*) of Buddhism. Olcott became an ardent supporter of the Sinhalese Buddhists. In 1881 he composed a Buddhist catechism, which contributed to the revival of modern Buddhism in Sri Lanka.[14]

In 1882, the Theosophists moved to Adyar, a neighbourhood in Madras (today, Chennai) in South India, and established there the international headquarters of the Theosophical Society. The move to India marked a change in the interests and nature of the society. The new society had a more intellectual and less practical orientation than the earlier one,[15] and Hinduism and Buddhism became more prominent in the teaching than Western occultism, Egyptology, and Kabbalah.

Following the move to India and the founders' visit to Ceylon, many Indians and Sinahlese joined the Theosophical Society.[16] Most prominent among them were the Hindu scholars Tallapragada Subba Row (1856–1890) and Damodar K. Mavalankar (1857–1885?) and the Sinhalese Buddhists Hikkaduwe Sumangala (1827–1911) and Anagarika Dharmapala (1864–1933). Members of the English colonial community in India also joined the Theosophical Society. A prominent new member of the society was Alfred Percy Sinnett (1840–1921), an English civil servant and journalist with an interest in Spiritualism. Between 1880 and 1885, Sinnett exchanged letters with Blavatsky's secret masters, Koot Hoomi and Morya, the letters often arriving mysteriously, such as falling from the ceiling. Sinnett's correspondence with the Mahatmas formed the basis of his work *Esoteric Buddhism* (1883), another early Theosophical work that became a best seller.[17]

Another member of the English colonial community who joined the Theosophical Society was Allan Octavian Hume (1829–1912). Hume, a retired senior officer in the Indian Civil Service, who joined the society in 1879, was also a recipient of letters from the Mahatmas. Hume, who later distanced himself from Blavatsky and the Theosophical Society (following the Coulomb affair and the investigation of the Society for Psychical Research), was one of the initiators and founders of the Indian National Congress.[18]

In 1884, Emma Coulomb, the former housekeeper of Blavatsky, published a series of letters she claimed were written by Blavatsky that implicated the latter in forging the Mahatma letters and other supernatural phenomena. A report of the Society of Psychical Research, which was written by Richard Hodgson, corroborated Coulomb accusations and caused much damage to Blavatsky's reputation.[19]

Following the Coulomb affair and the Hodgson report, Blavatsky left India in 1885, traveling to Würzburg, Bavaria, where she began writing her second major work, *The Secret Doctrine: The Synthesis of Science, Religion, and Philosophy*. Blavatsky claimed that the book, which was published in 1888, was based on translations of verses from a secret text, the Book of Dzyan. *The Secret Doctrine*, which is more than fifteen hundred pages and divided into two volumes, dealing with "cosmogenesis" and "anthropogenesis," presents Theosophical doctrines on the emanation of the worlds, the nature of higher beings, and the evolution of humanity through a series of root races and subraces.[20]

Blavatsky spent her later years in London. There, she launched, together with the English Theosophist Mabel Collins (1851–1927), a new periodical, *Lucifer*, and founded the Esoteric Section of the Theosophical Society. During that time, G. R. S. Mead (1863–1933), who later became a scholar of Gnosticism, Hermeticism, and early Christianity, joined the society and became Blavatsky's private secretary. Another important recruit of the Theosophical Society who became very close to Blavatsky and joined the Esoteric Section, was Annie Besant (1847–1933). Besant, a renowned freethinker and social reformer joined the society following a review she was asked to write on *The Secret Doctrine*. Blavatsky died in Besant's home on May 8, 1891.[21] Olcott, who stayed in India and Ceylon, continued to serve as the president of the Theosophical Society and the editor of *The Theosophist* and wrote his memoirs, *Old Diary Leaves*. He died in 1907.

Annie Besant, who moved to India, succeeded Olcott as the president of the society and occupied that position until her death in 1933.

Under the leadership of Besant, the Theosophical Society spread the world over, and the number of its lodges and membership grew steadily. Besant, who supported the Indian national and anticolonial movement, was one of the founders of the Home Rule movement. She was elected as president of the Indian National Congress in 1917 and was arrested for her activities in support of Indian home rule.[22]

In 1909, Annie Besant became the legal guardian of Jiddu Krishnamurti (1895–1986), the fourteen-year-old Indian boy who was identified by Charles Leadbeater as suitable to become the world teacher. Krishnamurti and his younger brother, Nityananda (1898–1925), were put under the care of Leadbeater, who prepared Krishnamurti for his role as the world teacher, the new manifestation of Christ and Lord Maitreya. Annie Besant became dedicated to the proclamation of the advent of the world teacher and founded the Order of the Star in the East for this purpose. The new order attracted many followers, who swelled the membership of the Theosophical Society, which reached its peak in 1928, with more than fifteen hundred lodges and forty-five thousand members. However, in 1929 Krishnamurti denounced his role as the world teacher and distanced himself from the teachings of the Theosophical Society. The numbers of lodges and members declined, and in the early twenty-first century, its international membership was around thirty thousand.[23]

The Esoteric Doctrines of Blavatsky and the Theosophical Society

The teachings of the Theosophical Society are largely based on the writings of Blavatsky, especially *Isis Unveiled*, published in 1877, and *The Secret Doctrine* published in 1888. Other Theosophists, such as Emma Hardinge Britten, Alfred Percy Sinnett, Allan Octavian Hume, Mable Collins, Annie Besant, and Charles Webster Leadbeater also contributed to the occult teachings of the society.

Blavatsky's writings are based on a large variety of sources, including Western occultism, Kabbalah, Hindu and Buddhists traditions, contemporary scientific theories, and historical, archeological, and comparative religious studies. Blavatsky's ideas changed over the years, and the doctrines presented in her writings, as well as of other Theosophical leaders, are complex and sometimes seem contradictory. In the following, I will present a short overview of some of the major concepts and tenets of the Theosophical Society, especially as they are presented in Blavatsky's later writings.[24]

Blavatsky claimed that her teachings were based on an ancient universal-wisdom tradition, the Secret Doctrine, or Theosophy,[25] that underlies all religions: "The esoteric philosophy . . . reconciles all religion, strips every one of it outward, human garments, and shows the root of each to be identical with that of every other great religion."[26] Theosophists hold that the ancient wisdom, which unites religion, philosophy, and science (as suggested by the subtitle of *The Secret Doctrine*), is guarded by a brotherhood of ageless adepts, the masters, or mahatmas, who conveyed it to Blavatsky and other leading Theosophists. Some aspects of the ancient-wisdom tradition were preserved in the esoteric teachings of the ancient religions. However, they can be understood only through the lens of the teachings of modern Theosophy. Blavatsky asserted in the preface to *The Secret Doctrine* that the aim of her work was "to rescue from degradation the archaic truths which are the basis of all religions, and to uncover, to some extent, the fundamental unity from which they all spring."[27] In her first book, *Isis Unveiled*, Blavatsky declared that the unveiled ancient wisdom will become the universal religion of the future: "Be this as it may, the religion of the ancients is the religion of the future. A few centuries more, and there will linger no sectarian beliefs in either of the great religions of humanity. Brahmanism and Buddhism, Christianity and Mahometanism will all disappear before the mighty rush of facts."[28] Theosophy asserts the existence of an ineffable, impersonal, ultimate reality, which is the source of all material and spiritual realms. In *The Secret Doctrine*, Blavatsky identified the ultimate reality with the Neoplatonic "One," the Hindu *parabrahman*, and the Kabbalistic Ein-Sof. The divine reality reveals itself through periods of activity and rest. According to Blavatsky, the universe, which emanated from the ultimate reality

> manifests periodically, for purposes of the collective progress of the countless lives, the outbreathings of the One Life; in order that through the Ever-Becoming, every cosmic atom in this infinite Universe, passing from the formless and the intangible, through the mixed natures of the semi-terrestrial, down to matter in full generation, and then back again, reascending at each new period higher and nearer the final goal; that each atom, we say, may reach through individual merits and efforts that plane where it re-becomes the one unconditioned All.[29]

The human soul, which is a divine spark of consciousness that emerged from the universal soul that emanated from the ultimate reality, will finally return to its source, after a long and complex process of reincarnation.

A central concept of Theosophy is the septenary (seven-fold) structure of the human physical and spiritual constitution. According to this concept, Human beings are divided into seven principals, four lower physical elements and three, higher, spiritual elements.[30] In the *Key to Theosophy*, Blavatsky summarizes the seven "principals in man," which are referred to by Sanskrit terms:

> The Higher Self is Atma, the inseparable ray of the Universal and One Self. It is the God above, more than within, us. Happy the man who succeeds in saturating his inner Ego with it! The Spiritual divine Ego is the Spiritual soul or *Buddhi*. . . . The Inner, or Higher "Ego" is *Manas,* the "Fifth" Principle, so called, independently of Buddhi. . . . The Lower, or Personal "Ego" is the physical man in conjunction with his lower Self, i.e., animal instincts, passions, desires, etc. It is called the "false personality," and consists of the lower Manas combined with Kama-rupa and operating through the Physical body and its phantom or "double." The remaining "Principle" "*Pranâ*," or "Life," is, strictly speaking, the radiating force or Energy of Atma—as the Universal Life and the One Self.[31]

Blavatsky developed a complex theory concerning seven different stages, or "root races," through which the human souls reincarnated and develop. In the first stage, the ethereal, human beings do not have a distinct physical body. The second root race, the hyperborean, who lived in the far North, had fluid bodies and reproduced by dividing their bodies in half. In the third stage, tall human beings, who were governed by kings, inhabited the lost continent of Lemuria. The fourth root race, who resemble present-day human beings, resided in Atlantis. When Atlantis submerged, some of its inhabitants migrated to other continents and became the present, Aryan root race. The fifth, Aryan, root race is further subdivided into seven cultural epochs, or subraces. The first five of them are the Hindu, Arabian, Persian, Celtic, and Teutonic, which will be followed by two future subraces. In the distant future, following the end of the Aryan root race, two more root races will appear.[32]

The notions of reincarnation and karma, which became very central to the teaching of the Theosophical Society, were developed by Blavatsky and her followers during the 1880s. Previously, in *Isis Unveiled*, Blavatsky taught a theory of postmortem ascent to higher worlds, which she called "metempsychosis."[33] In her later works, especially *The Secret Doctrine*, Blavatsky claimed that the human spirits or monads, go through a long and circular process of evolutionary reincarnations, over millions of years, through the different root races, until they finally become fully spiritualized and reunited with their Divine source. Between death and rebirth, the soul finds rest in the intermediate state of Devachan, a blissful period in which it absorbs its past life.[34] The process of reincarnation is governed by the law of karma, which determines into which body the monad, who retains it individuality through its various reincarnations, is reborn. In the *Key to Theosophy*, Blavatsky defined karma as "the law of cause and effect, or ethical causation. . . . Karma neither punishes or rewards, it is simply the one Universal Law which guides unerringly, and, so to say, blindly, all other laws productive of certain effects along the grooves of their respective causations."[35]

According to Blavatsky, humanity reincarnates in similar stages of development. However, there are some individuals who went through more advanced evolutionary development and surpass in their spiritual development the rest of present-day humanity. These spiritually advanced individuals are the masters, or mahatmas, who reside in highly spiritual locations and guide humanity from there. Besides the mahatmas, there are other beings of higher spiritual development, which are referred to by Blavatsky as "manus," *dhayan-cohans*, and *maha-chohans*.[36] The second-generation leaders of the Theosophical Society, especially Leadbeater in his *The Masters and the Path*, published in 1925, offered further elaborated theories concerning the cosmic hierarchy and evolutionary progress of the masters and other higher spiritual beings. Leadbeater and Besant assigned a place in the spiritual hierarchy also to Jesus, who, according to them, gave his body to Christ, whom they identified as one of the masters of wisdom.[37] The second generation leaders of the Theosophical Society presented this idea in the framework of the millenarist theory they developed concerning Jiddu Krishnamurthi, the Indian boy whom Leadbeater and Besant identified as an incarnation of Christ and Lord Maitreya and proclaimed to be the future world teacher.[38]

The Institutional Structure and the Religious Subgroups of the Theosophical Society

The basic group within the Theosophical Society is a *lodge*, a term adopted from Freemasonry. As the society grew, lodges were organized in national sections, whose representatives served on a general council under the international president, who was (and still is) elected by the members of the society. Apart from national sections and regional lodges, several other subgroups were active within the framework of the society or affiliated with it. Following her move to London, Blavatsky established the Esoteric Section within the society. The Esoteric Section (later, the Esoteric School) founded for the purpose of a deeper study and practice of Theosophy, is open only to members of the Theosophical Society who were active for a couple of years and who fulfill certain requirements and restrictions (such as vegetarianism and avoidance of alcohol and drugs). As the Esoteric Section required strict secrecy of its members, little is known of its activities and membership, although Blavatsky's instructions to the members of the section were later published.[39] As mentioned above, in 1911, Annie Besant founded, in Benares (today, Varanasi) the Order of the Star in the East, to prepare the world for the arrival of the world teacher. The Order of the Star of the East was an independent organization, but most of its members were also fellows of the Theosophical Society.

Apart from the Esoteric Section and the Order of the Star of the East, several other groups were established within the framework of the Theosophical Society or were affiliated with it. In 1880, soon after Blavatsky and Olcott arrived in Sri Lanka and declared themselves Buddhists, they opened the Buddhist Theosophical Society in Colombo, in cooperation with several prominent Buddhist monks. The Buddhist Theosophical Society played an important role in the Sri Lankan Buddhist revival and opened English-language Buddhist schools in the island (by 1898 they were sixty-three schools affiliated with the Theosophical Society in Sri Lanka).[40] However, notwithstanding it's educational success, the Buddhist Theosophical Society had only one lodge, in Colombo, and its activities were restricted to Sri Lanka.

Another religious organization that was affiliated with the Theosophical Society was the Liberal Catholic Church, which was established in the second decade of the twentieth century by two prominent Theosophists, Charles Webster Leadbeater (1857–1934) and James Ingal Wedgwood (1883–1951). Wedgewood, who joined the Old Catholic Church of Great Britain, a small Anglo-Catholic church that branched from the Old Catholic Church in Holland, was consecrated bishop of the church in 1916. In turn, he consecrated Leadbeater a few months later, in Australia. The two Theosophical bishops renamed it the Liberal Catholic Church and created liturgy that reflected Theosophical ideas. The Liberal Catholic Church reached the peak of its activity in the 1920s and 1930s and operated in close ties with the Theosophical Society and its leaders in that period.[41]

In 1923, at the annual convention held in Benares (today, Varanasi), a Theosophical Muslim League was founded, with the support of Curuppumullage Jinarajadasa (1875–1953), the vice president of the Theosophical Society. The president of the league, which later changed its name to the Theosophical Society Muslim Association, was Nawab A. Hydari of Hyderabad.[42] H. C. Kumar, a Theosophist who was active in the Muslim Theosophical association and wrote the reports on its activity, lectured in the following years extensively on Islam and Sufism, from a Theosophical point of view, and encouraged formation of Theosophical study groups on Islam in different locations in India. In the Jubilee congress of the Theosophical Society, held in Adyar in December 1925, a foundation stone for a mosque was laid by the members of the Muslim association.[43] As we shall see later, it was at that convention the Association of Hebrew Theosophists was founded, and a foundation stone of a synagogue was laid at the Adyar compound. In the 1927 annual convention, three main goals for the Theosophical Muslim association were suggested—to study Islamic religion in the spirit of comparative religion and to place the result before the public, to carry into effect the resolution of the 1926 Theosophical convention regarding the restoration of harmony between Hindus and Muslim communities in India, and to collect funds for the completion of the Adyar mosque.[44] As mentioned, another subgroup that operated within the Theosophical Society was the Association of Hebrew Theosophists, which will be discussed in detail in the following chapters.

Schisms and Offshoots

The Theosophical Society underwent several schisms, and several Western esoteric movements originated or were inspired by it.[45] In 1886, most of the American Section broke off from the rest of the society, following a dispute between William Quan Judge and the leaders in the Adyar international headquarters. After Judge's demise, the leadership of the new branch passed to Katherine Tingley (1847–1929). The headquarters of the organization (which preserved the name *Theosophical Society*) was first based in Point Loma and later moved to Pasadena, were it is still located today.[46] Other schisms in the society occurred in the first decade of the twentieth century, following Annie Besant's support and reinstatement of Charles W. Leadbeater, notwithstanding the allegations concerning his inappropriate sexual relations with boys.[47] Following the Leadbeater affair, the general secretary of the India Section of the Theosophical Society, Upendranath Basu (1864–1940), resigned his post in 1909, and established the Independent Theosophical League, with headquarters in Benares. Although the Independent Theosophical League challenged Besant authority, Besant agreed to accept it as an autonomous section of the Society, with local branches in England, France, and Italy. The most active branch of the new organization was the Italian branch, which, under the leadership of Decio Cavlari (1863–1937), separated from the Italian Section of the Theosophical Society in 1910. The Italian Section of the league, whose main organ was the journal *Ultra*, was especially active in the 1920s and included several leading esotericists among its ranks, including Julius Evola (1898–1974) and the Jewish psychoanalyst Roberto Assagioli (1888–1964).[48]

Another schism that followed the Leadbeater affair occurred in 1909, when G. R. S. Mead (1863–1933), the English scholar and esotericist, who was the private secretary of Blavatsky in her final years, resigned from the Theosophical Society, followed by about seven hundred fellows of the British Section. Mead, who opposed Besant's leadership of the society and the reliance on the supernatural authority of the mahatmas in the society's internal affairs, established a new movement, the Quest Society, which attracted many prominent scholars and artists who were interested in esoteric and religious studies. The Quest Society, which can be seen as a forerunner of the famous Eranos conventions in Ascona, Switzerland, was active until the early 1930s.[49]

In 1912, Rudolf Steiner (1861–1925), the charismatic leader of the German Section of the Theosophical Society since 1902, left it with his followers and established the Anthroposophical Society. The dissociation from the Theosophical Society was consequent upon Steiner's preference of a European, Christian esotericism over the Eastern orientation of the society and his rejection of Annie Besant's proclamation of Krishnamurti as the new world teacher and reincarnation of Christ.[50] Steiner established the headquarters of the new society in Dornach, Switzerland, where it still operates. The Anthroposophical Society was based on the teaching of Steiner that integrated Theosophical, Christian esoteric, and German idealist themes. Under the leadership of Steiner, Anthroposophy developed several practical fields, which included Waldorf education, Anthroposophical medicine, biodynamic agriculture, and eurhythmy. Gradually, the Anthroposophical Society grew into a highly successful international movement, and today, it is larger and more influential than its parent society.[51] Another significant movement derived from Theosophy is the Arcane School, which was founded by Alice A. Bailey (1880–1949) in 1923, following her leaving (or expulsion from) the American Section of the society.[52] The last offshoot that should be mentioned is the Agni Yoga Society (also known as Living Ethics), which was established in the 1920s in New York by the former Russian Theosophists, the painter Nicholas Roerich (1874–1947) and his wife, Helena Roerich (1879–1955).[53]

A devastating blow to the Theosophical Society occurred when Krishnamurti denounced his role as the world teacher. Following his brother's death in 1925, Krishnamurti begun to distance himself from some of the teaching of the Theosophical Society. In 1929, he dissolved the Order of the Star, disassociated himself from the role of the world teacher, and famously declared that truth is a pathless land that cannot be approached by any religion or sect.[54] Krishnamurti continued to teach his individualistic spiritual message and became one of the most influential spiritual teachers of the twentieth century.[55]

Krishnamurti's dissolution of the Order of the Star brought about a decline in the society's membership. Other factors, including the economic depression of the 1930s and World War II and its aftermath, contributed to the decline of membership and cultural influence of the society. However, the Theosophical Society, which is still active today, had a very significant impact on many twentieth-century new religious alternative spiritual movements and on the emergence of New Age culture.

The Theosophical Society had a considerable impact on modern Judaism. From its very beginning, Jews were attracted to the society and joined its ranks, as well as some of its offshoots, especially, the Anthroposophical Society. Jews played an active role in the Theosophical Society, served as officers of many Theosophical sections and lodges, gave lectures, and wrote articles and books inspired by Theosophical ideas. In 1925, a Jewish Theosophical movement, the Association of Hebrew Theosophists, was founded and was active, in several locations around the world for several years.

The following chapters of this book are dedicated to the Jewish Theosophists and their impact on the Theosophical Society and on modern Jewish culture. I will begin, in the next chapter, with a discussion of the Jewish founding member of the Theosophical Society, David Etienne de Lara, as well as some other prominent Jewish fellows of the early society.

Chapter 2

Jewish Followers of the
Early Theosophical Society

In the very early beginning of the Theosophical Society, several Jews became interested in its teaching, and some of them joined its ranks. Although the number of Jewish fellows of the society in the late nineteenth century was very small, some of them played important roles in different sections and lodges of the nascent society. As mentioned in the previous chapter, one of the founding members of the society was a Jewish scholar of Sephardic origins, David Etienne de Lara. In the following two decades, other Jews from different locations around the world became interested in Theosophy, and some of them joined the society. In this chapter, I will discuss some of the prominent Jewish followers of the Theosophical Society in the late nineteenth century: David Etienne de Lara, the Jewish founding member of the society; Leon Hyneman, the Freemason journalist, author, and editor from Philadelphia and his daughter, the author, poet, and essayist Alice Hyneman-Rhine; A. D. Ezekiel, a member of the Baghdadi community in India, who, under the impact of Theosophy, translated Kabbalistic texts to Judeo-Arabic; Dr. Adolf Grünhut, a Jewish medical doctor and a Spiritualist from Budapest; Fredrich Eckstein, an intellectual and occultist who served as the first president of the Theosophical lodge in Vienna; Rabbi Herman van Staveren, who was one of the founding members of the Theosophical Society in Wellington, New Zealand; Rabbi Doctor Max Samfield, who was the first president of the Theosophical lodge in Memphis, Tennessee; and Naphtali Herz Imber, the famous Jewish Zionist poet, who was affiliated with the Theosophical Society during his years in the Unites States.

As we will see in this chapter, the early Jewish Theosophists came from diverse geographical areas and from different social and cultural backgrounds. However, most of them were Western acculturated and proficient in European languages. Many of them were Freemasons. Most of them had a strong Jewish identity and were involved in Jewish religious, cultural, and national activities.

Etienne David de Lara, the Jewish Founding Member of the Theosophical Society

In his memoires, "Old Diary Leaves," Olcott mentions that among the founders of the Theosophical Society was "Mr. de Lara . . . a learned and most loveable old gentleman, of Portuguese Hebrew extraction, for whom H. P. B. [Helena Petrovna Blavatsky] and I felt a great affection and who remained an F. T. S. [Fellow of the Theosophical Society] until his death, which occurred two or three years later."[1]

The Jewish founding member of the Theosophical Society was Etienne David de Lara (1796–1879), who was born in Amsterdam and immigrated as a young person to England.[2] In England, he worked as a teacher of languages and published two grammar books, a *Key to the Spanish Language* (1823) and a *Key to the Portuguese Language* (1825). In the 1930s, he taught at the Liverpool Mechanic's Institution. In an advertisement for a lecture series on "the dramatic literature of France, Germany, Spain and Italy" given in Manchester in 1838, he was presented as "Monsieur D. E. de Lara, Professor of Continental Languages and Literature in the Royal, the Mechanics' the Literary, Scientific and Commercial Institutions, the High School and Academy of literature and science, Liverpool."[3] De Lara, who was described by Bill Williams as "a man of grandiose pretensions and inconsiderable talent," was involved in the schism that divided the Jewish congregation in Manchester in 1844, and gave the first public speech on the occasion of the opening of the New Synagogue.[4] His speech, in which he declared that the Jewish religion was "free from dogmas, doctrines, or superstitions. It is not founded upon belief at all," was published under the title "The Termination of the Mosaic Economy, as described by a Modern Jew," in the London journal of Jewish converts, *The Voice of Israel.*[5]

De Lara immigrated to the United States in the early 1850s and resided first in Boston and then in New York. He taught European languages (French, Spanish, German, Italian, Portuguese, and Dutch)[6] and gave lectures on various topics, including a serious of lectures on the political, social, and moral conditions in Russia, delivered in Boston in 1853,[7] and a lecture on "Russian Serfdom and American Slavery" delivered at the Jewish Touro Literary Institute in New York in 1856.[8]

In 1857, de Lara was involved in a public dispute with two Jewish converts to Protestantism, Gideon Robert Lederer (1804–1879) and Dr. Ephraim Epstein (1829–1913).[9] Dr. John Thomas (1805–1871), the founder of the Christadelphian movement, who was involved in the dispute,[10] related that de Lara "boldly and justly" disputed the claims of the converts and that "his acumen and arguments were too astute for their treatment, so that they were put to shame before the Jews they sought to proselyte."[11]

Between 1873 and 1876, de Lara lectured at various venues[12] and published extensively in *The New Era*, the Jewish reform periodical, published and edited by Rabbi Raphael D. C. Lewin. De Lara articles included a series on the "Defense of Our National System of Education against the Attacks of the Catholic Press" and a series on "Freemasonry, Judaism and Christianity," as well as a poem entitled "The Cat, or Art and Nature."[13] De Lara, who was a Freemason, claimed that while Freemasonry harmonizes with genuine Judaism and Christianity, it is incompatible with "the vagaries of Hasidism" and the "speculations of Cabalists."[14] As we will see in the following, later Jewish Theosophists had a much better opinion of Kabbalah and Hasidism.

During this period, de Lara became acquainted with the English Freemason and Socialist Charles Sotheran (1847–1902), who introduced him to Olcott and Blavatsky.[15] Sotheran, who immigrated to New York in 1874, was active in the Liberal Club and the American Socialist Labor Party, published articles in *The New Era* and was one of the founding members of the Theosophical Society.[16] Interestingly, Olcott wrote that Sotheran introduced him and Blavatsky to the daughter of de Lara, the poetess "Alice B. Rhyne."[17] It seems that Olcott confused de Lara and his daughter, Victoria de Lara Fibel, and the Jewish Freemason friend of Blavatsky, Leon Hyneman and his daughter Alice Hyneman-Rhine. Both Victoria de Lara-Fibel and Alice Hyneman-Rhine (who later married Charles Sotheran) became fellows of the Theosophical Society.

De Lara, who is recorded as member number 25 of the Theosophical Society,[18] participated in its first meeting, which took place at Blavatsky's residence in New York on September 7, 1875, and read a paper in the second meeting.[19] As mentioned above, his daughter, Victoria de Lara-Fibel (1873–1920), also joined the nascent society.[20] According to Olcott, de Lara remained a member of the Theosophical Society until his death, in 1879, the year that the founders of the society moved to India.

Two other Jewish supporters of the early Theosophical Society in America were Leon Hyneman and his daughter, Alice Hyneman-Rhine (whom, as we saw above, Olcott confused with E. D. de Lara and his daughter).

Leon Hyneman (1808–1879), the son of a Jewish immigrant from Holland, was a prominent member of the Jewish community of Philadelphia. He was one of the managers of the American Jewish Publication Society and was active in the Hebrew Relief Association. Hyneman was a prominent Freemason journalist, author, and editor. He was one of the founders of the Masonic Shekinah Lodge in Philadelphia and a member of the Grand Lodge of Pennsylvania. He was the editor of the weekly Masonic journal, the *Masonic Mirror* (which was subsequently absorbed by the *American Keystone*) and the author of several books on Freemasonry.[21]

Blavatsky mentioned Hyneman in *Isis Unveiled* as "our venerable friend" and cited from his *Ancient York and London Grand Lodges*.[22] In an interview published in the New York Herald in 1891, Charles Sotheran mentioned that Leon Hyneman was one of the "notable group of white haired and patriarchal scholars" who were friends and frequent visitors of Blavatsky. He describes him as "the venerable and erudite Leon Hyneman, whose 'Origins of Freemasonry,' *History of Freemasonry in England*, and 'Fundamental Principals of Science' established his reputation as one of the ripest and most accurate scholars in America."[23]

Notwithstanding his friendship with Blavatsky, Hyneman did not join the Theosophical Society. However, his daughter, the author, poet, and essayist, Alice Hyneman-Rhine, joined the society in 1877.[24] Hyneman-Rhine (1840–1919) was a member of the Society of American Authors, a Socialist, and a women's rights activist. She published articles on women's work, Jewish issues, and other topics in journals such as *Arena, Popular Science Monthly*, and *The North American Review* and edited a volume on the Niagara Park. Following the death of her first husband, she married, in 1893, the above-mentioned Theosophist and Socialist, Charles Sotheran.[25]

A. D. Ezekiel, the Jewish Theosophist from Poona

In 1879, Blavatsky and Olcott moved to India and established the headquarters of the Theosophical Society, first in Bombay (today Mumbai), and later in Adyar, near Madras (today, Chennai). The Theosophical Society attracted to its ranks many Indians of diverse communities. One of them was Abraham David Salman Hai Ezekiel (A. D.) Ezekiel (d. 1897), a member of the Jewish Baghdadi community of Poona (today Pune), who joined the society in 1882.[26]

A. D. Ezekiel was a member of a prominent family of the Indian Jewish Baghdadi community. The Baghdadis (a term that refers not only to Jews who emigrated from Baghdad itself) were Jews who came to India in the nineteenth century from Iraq and other Middle Eastern communities and established thriving communities in Calcutta, Bombay, and Poona.[27] His father, David Hai Ben Ezekiel Mazlia, was a member of the Beit David benevolent Society in Bombay, and the owner of a large collection of books and manuscripts.

In January 1882, Ezekiel joined the Poona branch of the Theosophical Society.[28] He was well acquainted with Blavatsky and Olcott, who resided in his home during their visits to Poona.[29] In his memoires, Olcott gave a colorful description of his stay in Ezekiel's household in 1885:

> I passed on to Poona with our colleague the late Mr. Ezekiel,
> a member of the great family of the Sassoons and an ardent

Figure 2.1. A. D. Ezekiel standing, first on the right. Sitting in the middle are Madame Blavatsky and Colonel Olcott. *Source: The Theosophist* 124 (November 2002): 40. Courtesy of the Theosophical Society.

Kabbalist. At his house I met a Rabbi Silbermann of Jerusalem and his wife. [. . .] He wore the Oriental costume as also did Mr. Ezekiel senior, who lived in the other half of the little house. [. . .] The old gentleman and I were sitting together one day, he was watching me so closely that I thought something must be wrong about my dress, but he soon undeceived me. Beckoning me mysteriously into his bedroom, he took from a press a complete Jewish costume [. . .] and asked me to put them on. When I had done so, he led me by the hand along the verandah to the adjoining rooms, intimating that he was going to pass me off as a Jew. Entering into the spirit of the joke, I gravely saluted the Jerusalem family after the Eastern fashion. [. . .] The aged Rabbi [. . .] saluted me with great respect, [. . .] He then began putting me a lot of questions in Hebrew, and refused to believe that I was a mere Gentile, when young Ezekiel, laughing heartily at his bewilderment, told them who I was. [. . .] His wife [. . .] looked me over most scrutinisingly, and confirmed her husband in his belief of my Hebraic origins. "Why" said she to the maid, "who can deny it? See, has he not the *shekinah*?" meaning the shining aura the *tejas* as the Hindus call it. Both the Ezekiels were immensely amused at the success of the old gentleman's trick.[30]

Ezekiel was involved in the events surrounding the controversy over the Theosophical Society that erupted in 1884 and 1885, after the publication of incriminating letters Blavatsky allegedly wrote to her former aid, Emma Coulomb, and the critical report written by Richard Hodgson for the Society for Psychical Research (SPR). In one of the letters, dated October 24, 1883, Blavatsky tells of a meeting A. D. Ezekiel arranged for her with his wealthy cousin, Jacob Sassoon, asking Coulomb to fabricate a message from the mahatmas to secure a donation from Sassoon:

Whether *something* succeeds or not I must try. Jacob Sassoon, the happy proprietor of a crore of rupees, with whose family I dined last night, is anxious to become a Theosophist. He is ready to give 10,000 rupees to buy and repair the head-quarters, he said to Colonel (Ezekiel his cousin arranged all this) if only he saw a little phenomenon, got the assurance that the *Mahatmas* could hear what was said, or give him some *other sign of their existence (?!!)*. Well, this letter will reach you the 26th, Friday, will you go up to the Shrine and ask K. H. (or Christopholo)[31] to send me a telegraph that would reach me about 4 or 5 in the afternoon, same day worded thus: "Your conversation with Mr. Jacob Sassoon reached Master just now. Were the latter even to satisfy him still the doubter would hardly find the moral courage to connect himself with the Society.

"Ramalinga Deb."

If this reached me on the 26th even in the evening—it will still produce a tremendous impression.[32]

The publication of the Coulomb letters and the Hodgson report, which received worldwide attention, was a very serious blow to the Theosophical Society, causing a great stir among its followers. In a letter printed in the *Times of India*, Ezekiel denied the charges made by Emma Coulomb:

In one of the letters my name has been mentioned, and you will allow me to make a few observations. I know in detail all the particulars of Madame Blavatsky's last visit to Poona. Some of the particulars have inaccurately been put into the alleged letter. The telegram referred to therein was not at all meant, even in the most distant way, to suggest the possession of phenomenal powers by Madame Blavatsky, and she never attempted to put before me or Mr. Sassoon the telegram in any such light. On carefully reading this paper I can plainly see that Madame Blavatsky could not have written the letter, much less have called for the telegram.[33]

Notwithstanding his defense of Blavatsky, Ezekiel was skeptical concerning some of the supernatural phenomena related with the Theosophical Society, especially the mysterious appearance of letters from the mahatmas. Dr. Franz Hartmann declared in his statement to the SPR committee that "Mr. Ezekiel is a great sceptic, and he made me promise that if any occult phenomena should happen after my return to headquarters, I would let him know it."[34] Ezekiel's skepticism concerning the wondrous appearance of the mahatmas' letters is mentioned in Coulomb's pamphlet. According to Coulomb, Ezekiel, who was present at Blavatsky's apartment when a letter fell from the ceiling, shared with several fellows of the society his suspicion that it was pulled down by some device.[35] Hodgson wrote that

Ezekiel confirmed Coulomb's account and that he also told him about a communication he received from a mahatma that corroborated Hodgson's suspicions of Blavatsky.[36] Ezekiel asked Hodgson not to publish the details of this event. However, later, Hodgson disclosed that it concerned a question that Ezekiel sent to the Mahatma Koot Hoomi, in Judeo-Arabic, concerning an interpretation of a Kabbalistic text: "[. . .] When Mr. A. D. Ezekiel, Theosophist of Poona, prepared a question in the Arabic language and in Hebrew characters, and submitted it to the mahatma, he received a reply that showed complete ignorance of his question. His question concerned the interpretation of a specific portion of the Kabbala, and not the slightest reference was made to this in the reply which he received."[37] Ezekiel himself tells of his skepticism in a letter he wrote to the editor of *The Times of India* after the publication of Coulomb's letters:

> Madame Blavatsky and several others knew but too well what an inveterate doubter I am regarding these phenomena and she must have been a thorough simpleton, and not the clever imposter she is represented to be if she called for the telegram to make a "tremendous impression" as alleged. It was only through me that she could hope to make any impression regarding the telegram upon Mr. Sassoon, but she knew my nature too well to expect anything out of me.[38]

According to Coulomb's account, Blavatsky was infuriated by Ezekiel's skepticism. Coulomb claimed that Blavatsky ignored Ezekiel when she passed through Poona in February 1884:

> On route to Bombay the party was met at Poona by Mr. Khandalvala [. . .] and by Mr. Ezekiel also a Fellow of the Society. This last gentleman uttered a cry of joy when he saw the train stop saying: "Oh, here is Madame." But when she heard his voice she told me in a loud whisper and in French: "*Ne laissez pas entrer ce C [. . .] de juif; Je ne veux pas le voir. Qu'il aille au diable! Dites lui que je dors*" [Do not let that [. . .] of a Jew come in. I will not see him. Let him go to the devil ! Tell him that I am sleeping].[39]

Blavatsky, in her comments on Coulomb's account, denied she had said that but admitted she did not want to see Ezekiel because of his treacherous behavior: "It is true I did not want to see him & told so to Khandalavala & others. But that was because Mme C. had told me that he had behaved treacherously that he pretended to believe, and then told his friends I was a swindler."[40]

Notwithstanding his skepticism and the tension with Blavatsky, Ezekiel remained a member of the Theosophical Society and as we saw above, defended Blavatsky after the publication of the Coulomb letters.

A. D. Ezekiel's Interest in Kabbalah and His Publication Ventures

A. D. Ezekiel related that the interest and knowledge of Kabbalah in the Theosophical Society, which he described to the members of his community as "the Sufi Society" from America, prompted him to study Kabbalah. In the introduction to one of the texts he published in Judeo-Arabic, he wrote: "Ten years ago some people came from America who called themselves the Sufi Society. [. . .] I met them and joined their society five years ago. I have seen from their writings that much of their movement was based on our Kabbalah. I desired to understand the wisdom of Kabbalah, and asked people to direct me to the books of this knowledge."[41] In July 1887, Ezekiel published in *The Theosophist* a story entitled "The Kabbalist of Jerusalem." The story tells of a friend of Ezekiel, Rabbi Jacob,[42] a merchant from Jerusalem, a skeptic who did not believe in magic, the future life, or the kabbalah. Yet, through a chance meeting in India with a mysterious woman with supernatural psychic powers (identifying herself as Sarah, a Jewess born in Constantinople), he becomes interested in Kabbalah and Theosophy. In his quest for occult knowledge, relates Ezekiel, Rabbi Jacob met with a medium in Paris, and later, after a long search, with an old kabbalist from the Beth-El synagogue in Jerusalem:

> He saw before him a thin-faced, white-bearded old man, clad in a ragged national costume, and squatted upon a mat in the darkest corner of the synagogue [. . .] [H]is appearance was not that of one asleep, but rather of one whose attention was fixed upon an inner world. A holy calm seemed to have settled over him, and this internal beatitude made Rabbi Jacob think he saw upon his face and round his head that Shechina, or soul shine, which is believed to appear upon the face of the true seer.[43]

The Beth-El kabbalist agrees to teach him kabbalah, only after he will make a pilgrimage to hidden kabbalistic masters in Tunis. The story ends with the old kabbalist's declaration that "the doctrines promulgated by the Theosophical Society are identical with those taught by the Kabbalists of our race."[44]

At the same year the story was published, Ezekiel opened a printing press, in which he printed several Kabbalistic texts translated into Iraqi Judeo-Arabic. The first publication, printed in December 1887, was a translation of highly revered text from the *Zohar*, called the *Idra Zuta* (the small assembly), which he printed together with the Aramaic original, line on top of line.

Ezekiel dedicated his translation of the *Idra Zuta* to the philanthropist Mazal Tov, the wife of the wealthy merchant Elijah David Joseph Ezra, from Calcutta (today Kolkata). In his introduction, Ezekiel declares that he does not intend to reveal the secrets of the *Zohar*, but only to explain the literary meaning of its words for those who read the *Zohar* without understanding its meaning (he is referring to the custom of the ritualistic reading of the *Zohar* on special occasions, which was common in Jewish communities).[45]

The translation of the *Idra Zuta* into Jewish Arabic stirred a fierce controversy. On January 5, 1888, Rabbis of Baghdad published a letter objecting to the translation in the Calcutta Judeo-Arabic newspaper *Jewish Gazette Paerah*.[46] On 24 February 1888, a letter signed by Rabbi Raphael Meir Panigel, the Sephardic chief rabbi (*Haham Bashi*) of Palestine, and his son in law (who later succeeded him) Rabbi Yaacov Shaul Eliashar, was published in the Jerusalem Hebrew newspaper *Havatzelet*. The rabbis of Jerusalem decreed that Jews are not allowed to read the translated *Idra* and that they are obliged to keep and hide the translations in a place where no foreign hand can reach them. Furthermore, they decreed that Ezekiel must try to collect all the printed volumes and conceal them.[47] A similar decree was signed by Rabbi Elijah Mani and four other rabbis of Hebron.[48] The most important rabbinic authority in Baghdad at the time, Rabbi Yosef Hayyim (known as the "Ben Ish Hai" 1835–1909), who was asked about the matter, wrote a comprehensive response in which he justified the decree against the translation of the *Idra*.[49]

Ezekiel did not recoil in the face of his being denounced by the great rabbinic authorities of his time. He published several letters in the *Jewish Gazette Paerah* defending his translation and attacking his opponents[50] and sent a letter to Rabbi Panigel (dated 20 July 1888) in which he defies his ban, and defends his translation.[51] Ezekiel wrote that in his opinion, it is not only not forbidden to translate the *Idra*, but rather it is: "a religious

Figure 2.2. *The Lesser Holy Assembly*, A. D. Ezekiel's Press, Poona, 1887. Courtesy of the National Library of Israel collections. Public domain.

IDRA ZUTA

OR

THE LESSER HOLY ASSEMBLY

TRANSLATED

FROM THE

ARAMAIC CHALDEE

INTO

ARABIC (IN HEBREW CHARACTERS)

BY

ABRAHAM DAVID EZEKIEL

FIRST EDITION.

All rights reserved.

Registered under Act XXV of 1867.

Poona:

PRINTED AT A. D. EZEKIEL'S PRESS.

1887.

Price to Subscribers   Rs. 3 per Copy.
  ,, to Non-Subscribers ,,   5   Do.

obligation (*mizvah*) to study and teach and write and translate it into Arabic, which is the accustomed language amongst us." He cited a passage from the sixteenth-century Kabbalist Hayyim Vital to the effect that it is a *mizvah* to reveal the kabbalistic secrets of the *Zohar* as this revelation will bring forth redemption and adduces several examples of kabbalistic texts written in foreign languages or translated into them. Ezekiel wrote, defiantly, that Panigel's decree did not achieve its goal, but on the contrary, enhanced the sales of the book, which was now out of stock. Ezekiel concludes his letter by requesting Panigel to withdraw his decree and asserting his independence from the rabbinic authorities: "Thus, I request his highness that if the truth be with me, he should publish in *Havazelet* that it [the translation of the *Idra*] is permitted, and furthermore, that it is a *mitzvah* to read in it. [. . .] And my master and Rabbi should also know that the sages and Rabbis of Baghdad have written to the dignitaries of India concerning this affair, thinking they had authority over me. Praise God, I am a free person, and they don't have power over me."[52] During the months of the controversy over the printing of the translation of the *Idra Zuta*, Ezekiel continued his printing venture, including the publication of other kabbalistic texts, translated into Judeo-Arabic. Yet, he did not print any other *Zoharic* texts.

In February 1888, Ezekiel published an *Introduction to the Kabalah*, the only English text he published in his printing press. The book is a reprint of an article entitled "Introduction to the Cabalah," published in London in two volumes in 1845 and 1846, respectively, in the *Voice of Israel*, propagated by "Jews who believe in Jesus of Nazareth as the Messiah," edited by the convert Reverend Ridley Haim Herschell. The "Introduction to the Cabalah" was an English translation of excerpts from the book on Jewish sects by the Jewish scholar Peter Beer, published in German in two volumes in 1822 and 1823, respectively.[53]

All the other books that Ezekiel printed that year were in Judeo-Arabic and addressed to the Jewish Baghdadi community. In April 1888, he published *Natural Philosophy*, a textbook on physics for school children.[54] During that year, he also produced translations of *Song of Songs*, and of *The Book of Creation (Sepher Yetzirah)*, a fundamental work of the kabbalistic tradition (which was also of much interest to the Theosophists),[55] as well as two Arabian tales, *Dewan El Mathee* and *Dewan El Rahban*.[56] In October 1888, he published a translation of the first part of Yosef Ergas' *Shomer Emunim* (an early eighteenth-century Lurianic kabbalistic text, written in the form of a disputation). Ezekiel dedicated this book to the editor of the *Jewish Gazette Paerah*, Elijah Moshe Dweck ha-Cohen, and to other members of "our group" in India and other places, who stood by him in his struggle to "overthrow the yoke of the priestcraft" during the controversy over the publication of the *Idra Zuta*.

A month later, in November 1888, Ezekiel printed *The Sermon of True Faith* (*Drush be-Inian ha-Emunah ha-Amitit*). The sermon is a summary of *Drush Boker le-Avraham,* written by the seventeenth-century Sabbatean theologian Michael Cardozo.[57] In the introduction, Ezekiel writes that he had decided to translate and print this short work because he found that it could be beneficial to understanding the kabbalistic books he had already published and those he intended to publish in the future. Here too Ezekiel refers to the controversy against him. He says that since he had translated the *Idra*, many people started studying kabbalah, and many urged him to print more kabbalistic books. Yet, the translation of *The Sermon of True Faith* was the last kabbalistic text Ezekiel translated and printed. Possibly, he succumbed to the pressure of the rabbinic authorities or gave up his printing venture for other reasons.

Ezekiel continued to be active in the Theosophical Society for the rest of his life. In 1892, his name appears in a list of members of the Indian branch of the Theosophical Society on a notice concerning a prospective lecture tour by Annie Besant.[58] In July 1897, *The Theosophist* announced: "We regret very much to record the departure from this life of brother A. D. Ezekiel [. . .] a very old and well known member of the Poona Branch."[59]

Ezekiel dedicated his translation of *Shomer Emunim* to the members of "our group" who stood by him in his fight with the rabbis. Probably, he is referring to other Jews of his community that joined the Theosophical Society. Indeed, names of several other Jews from the Jewish Baghdadi community in India appear on the Theosophical Society general register in the 1880s, including Samuel Abdulla Ezekiel, probably, Abraham David's brother, from Bombay, an employee of David Sassoon's company, who joined the society in 1883.[60] As we shall see in later chapters, in the early twentieth century, Jews from the Baghdadi community and from other Jewish communities in India joined the Theosophical Society and took part in the foundation of the Association of Hebrew Theosophists.

Jewish Theosophists around the Globe:
Adolf Grünhut, Friedrich Eckstein, Herman van Staveren, and Max Samfield

In the last decades of the nineteenth century, Theosophy continued to spread around the globe. During this period, several Jews from Europe,

New Zealand, and the United States joined the Theosophical Society, and some of them played important roles within it.

Dr. Adolf Grünhut (1826–1906), a Jewish medical doctor and a Spiritualist from Budapest, joined the society in 1876, a year after its founding.[61] Grünhut became interested in animal magnetism when he served as a military surgeon during the 1848 through 1849 Hungarian revolution and war of independence. Later, following his encounter with the medium Baroness Adelma von Vay (neé Countess Adelaide von Wurmbrand-Stuppach, 1840–1925), he became interested in Spiritualism. Grünhut founded, together with Adelma von Vay and her husband, Baron Ödön (Edmond) von Vay, the Budapest Association of Spiritual Investigation (Szellemi Búvárok Pesti Egylete) and edited the Spiritualist journals *Reflexionen aus der Geistwerk, Reformierende Blätter* and *Égi Világosság*.[62]

The connection between Grünhut and the leaders of the Theosophical Society was probably made through Adelma and Ödön von Vay.[63] Grünhut

Figure 2.3. Friedrich Eckstein. *Source:* Wikimedia Commons. Public domain.

was the first Hungarian member of the Theosophical Society. However, he was not very active in it, and the Hungarian Section of the society was not established until 1906, the year Grünhut died.

Another prominent Jewish follower of the Theosophical Society in its early period was Friedrich Eckstein (1861–1939), who joined its ranks in 1887.[64] Eckstein, a son of a wealthy Austrian Jewish family, was a central figure in literary, philosophic, artistic, and occultist circles in Vienna. Eckstein was part of the small Viennese vegetarian milieu and of the circle of Engelbert Pernerstorfer (1850–1918), which included many assimilated Jews, who were looking for alternatives to bourgeois liberalism.[65] Eckstein, who was the personal secretary of the composer Anton Bruckner and a close friend of Sigmund Freud,[66] became acquainted with the leaders of the Theosophical Society through the German occultist and Theosophist Franz Hartmann (1838–1912). Following his meeting with Blavatsky, during her visit in Europe in 1886, Eckstein established the Theosophical lodge in Vienna and was appointed the president and general secretary of the Austrian Section of the society.[67] Other prominent figures in the Viennese Theosophical circle were the occultist, women rights activist, and vegetarian Marie Lang (1848–1934) and her husband, lawyer Edmund Lang (1860–1918), who was born to a Jewish family (he was the son of the Jewish industrialist Leopold Lang and the grandson of Isaak Löw Hofmann von Hofmannsthal) and converted to Protestantism.[68] Another participant in the meeting of Eckstein and Lang's circle was Rudolf Steiner, the future leader of the German Section of the Theosophical Society and the founder of Anthroposophy. Steiner had a close relationship with Eckstein, who introduced him to occultism and Theosophy.[69] In a letter to Eckstein, dated November 1890, Steiner wrote that meeting him was one of the two most important events in his life.[70]

Eckstein came from an assimilated Jewish family and was estranged from his Jewish roots. Painter, writer, and feminist Rosa Mayreder (1858–1938), who was also affiliated with the Viennese Theosophical circle, related in a letter to Steiner that their mutual friend Eckstein (to whom she referred by his nickname, *Eck*), who was opposed to Orthodoxy, and especially, Jewish Orthodoxy, was enraged by the observance of Kosher restrictions at his sister's wedding.[71] Ernst Müller (1880–1954), a Jewish Anthroposophist from Vienna (he will be discussed in the chapter 4 in more detail), related that Eckstein, whom he met in the 1930's, had complex relations to Judaism. According to Müller, Eckstein had much interest in Jewish Kabbalah as well the role that Judaism played in Western culture.

However, he had little interest in modern Jewish nationalism, and he disapproved of Martin Buber, as well as of the Hasidic movement, which he regarded as a popular dilution of the Kabbalah. Müller related that in his last years, Eckstein worked on a book about the Jewish influence on European culture and spent much time in the library of the Jewish community in Vienna.[72]

As we have already seen in this chapter, several Jews joined the early Theosophical Society in the United State, India, and Europe. Another location in which a Jewish Theosophist played an important role was New Zealand. In 1889, Rabbi Herman van Staveren (1849–1930) and his wife, Miriam (nee Barnett, 1857–1930), joined the Wellington lodge, which was chartered a year previously, and among its founders was Sir Harry Albert Atkinson, the prime minister of New Zealand.[73] Herman, whose father was also a rabbi, was born in the Netherlands and was educated in Antwerp and London. He was ordained as a rabbi in 1868 and traveled to New Zealand in 1877 to serve as the minister of the Wellington Jewish community. He served as the rabbi of the congregation for fifty years and was involved in benevolent work both in the Jewish congregation and in the wider community. He was active in the formation of the Jewish Philanthropic Society and served as the chairperson of the Wellington Hospital Board. Apart from his affiliation with the Theosophical Society, van Staveren was a member of the Waterloo and Hinemoa Masonic lodges.[74]

Another rabbi and Freemason who joined the Theosophical Society in the late nineteenth century was Rabbi Max Samfield (1844–1915) from Memphis Tennessee. Samfield was born in Marksteft, Bavaria, and earned a doctorate in philosophy at Julius University in Duerzburg. Following his ordination as a reform rabbi in 1867, he emigrated to America, where he served as a rabbi in Shreveport, Louisiana. In 1871, he moved to Memphis and served as the rabbi of congregation B'nai Israel for more than forty years. Samfield founded and served as the editor of a Jewish weekly, the *Jewish Spectator*. He was very active in various associations and charities, including the Tennessee Society for the Prevention of Cruelty to Animals, the United Charities, and the Young Men's Hebrew Association. Samfield was also active in the Masonic lodges in Louisiana and Tennessee, as well as in B'nai B'rith (Sons of the Covenant), the Jewish fraternal association, which was inspired by Freemasonry.[75] Samfield, who joined the Theosophical Society in December 1890, served as the president of the Memphis lodge, which was chartered the same year.[76]

Naftaly Herz Imber, the Zionist Poet, and His Interest in the Theosophical Society

Beside the Jewish fellows of the Theosophical Society that were discussed above, and several other Jews who joined the society in the late nineteenth century,[77] there were other Jews who found interest in Theosophy and were influenced by the writings of Blavatsky and other Theosophists. I would like to conclude this chapter with a short discussion of the interest of the famous Jewish Zionist poet Naftaly Herz Imber (1856–1909) in Theosophy and the impact that Theosophical ideas had on his interest and perception of Kabbalah.

Naphtali Herz Imber, who was born in Zloczów, Galicia (today, in Ukraine), traveled as a young man to Romania, where he became familiar with the ideas of the early Zionist group Hovevei Zion (Lovers of Zion) and where he probably wrote the first version of the poem "Hatikva" (The

Figure 2.4. Naftali Herz Imber. *Source: By-Paths in Hebraic Bookland*, by Israel Abrahams (Philadelphia: Jewish Publication Society of America, 1920), 360. Wikimedia Commons. Public domain.

hope) that eventually became the anthem of the Zionist movement, and later, of the State of Israel. Imber continued his travels and arrived in Istanbul, where he met the English writer, politician, and occultist Laurence Oliphant (1829–1888), who hired him as his secretary. Laurence Oliphant was engaged at the time in his plan to obtain concessions from the Turkish government for Jewish settlement in the northern part of Palestine.

In 1882, Imber arrived in Palestine with Laurence Oliphant and his wife, Alice le Strange (1846–1886), where he remained for five years. Notwithstanding his excessive drinking, eccentric behavior, and contacts with Christian missionaries, Imber became renowned as a Hebrew poet, and his song "Hatikva" became popular in the new Zionist colonies (moshavot). In 1886, he published his first book of poems, *Barkai* (The Light of Dawn or The Morning Star), which he dedicated to Laurence Oliphant. After leaving Palestine, Imber resided in London for five years, where he gave lectures for Zionist organizations and published articles in the Jewish press. In 1891, he emigrated to the United States, where he wandered through different locations, until his death from health problems related to his excessive drinking, in New York in 1909. Imber, who was interested in Kabbalah and esotericism, published a booklet entitled *The Keynote to Mystic Science* in 1894 in Indianapolis, and in 1895, during his stay in Boston, he published the first and last issue of a journal entitled *Uriel: A Monthly Journal Devoted to Cabbalistic Science*. In his last years, Imber worked on several articles and translations from the Talmud, the Zohar, and other sources, which were published after his death as *Treasures of Two Worlds*.[78]

Imber probably became acquainted with Theosophy during his residence in Palestine, at the home of his patrons, Laurence and Alice Oliphant. In 1883, Sinnett's *Esoteric Buddhism* reached the Oliphants' residence in Haifa and stimulated much interest among their friends. Laurence Oliphant, who related that he had met Blavatsky and Olcott in New York and was asked to join their movement, was very critical of the book and of the Theosophical Society in general.[79]

When Imber reached the United States, in the early 1890s, he contacted members of the Theosophical Society. In Indianapolis, he met two "prominent Theosophists," Judge Macbride and Dr. Atkinson,[80] who helped him to publish *The Keynote to Mystic Science*. According to Imber, during his stay in Boston, in 1893, George D. Ayers, who was at the time president of the Boston Theosophical Society,[81] and Rabbi Solomon Schindler tried to form a society that would enable him to translate the *Zohar*.[82] In 1895, Imber attended the Theosophical Convention in Boston, in which Annie

Figure 2.5. *Uriel: A Monthly Magazine Devoted to Cabbalistic Science*. Source: Wikimedia Commons. Public domain.

Besant, the president of the society, accused the general secretary of the American Section, William Q. Judge, of forging letters from the mahatmas (a charge that created the schism between the Adyar-based Theosophical Society and the later Pasadena-based society).[83] Imber was in touch with Theosophists also during his travels in California. According to a report in the *San Francisco Call* from April 1896, more than half of the audience that came to hear him lecture on Kabbalism at Temple Emanuel was composed of "Gentile Theosophists."[84]

Imber was ambivalent toward Theosophy. He described the Theosophical Society as "an organization that lives more in the past than in the present."[85] In relating his impressions from the 1895 convention in Boston, he wrote that he had "never witnessed a more disgraceful convention."[86] In an interview with *The San Francisco Call* in 1896, Imber said: "I am opposed to Theosophy, as it is a misconception of the truth . . . Mme. Blavatsky was misled—willfully or otherwise I do not know—but she failed in her effort to secure the truth."[87]

Notwithstanding his criticism, he regarded Blavatsky as one of the "great ones" who walked in the line of Occultism and thus suffered the "purgatory of slander and crucifixion caused by the mob, who cannot and never will understand nobility."[88] In an article entitled "Madame Blavatsky Unveiled," he exclaimed: "All respect to Madame Blavatsky. Shut your mouths ye scandalmonger and slanderers, for this alone is proof how great was Madame Blavatsky! Indeed she did more for the elevation of mankind than many of the ministers, for she was the preparer of a new age."[89] Yet, Imber claims that "she was only a pointer—as some may be able to point out the way to a city in which they themselves be strangers."[90] In his "History of Mysticism—The Mahatma of the Essenes," Imber is more critical of Blavatsky and claims that she based her ideas of the mahatmas on the principles of Jewish Hasidim: "Madame Blavatzsky (!), the founder of the Theosophists, was a shrewd Russian woman, familiar with the ways and doing of the Mahatmas or 'Good Jews,' as are all the Russians, and she must have taken her cue from some 'Chasid' (a pious Jew, who believes in the occult power of the Mahatmas)."[91] Imber criticized Blavatsky's references to Kabbalah in *Isis Unveiled* and *The Secret Doctrine*, saying that she could never have read nor understood Kabbalistic texts.[92] Imber saw a similarity between Theosophy and Kabbalah but declared the latter's superiority: "Cabbala . . . is older than and superior to Theosophy, as the latter mentions the former, while the Cabbala does not mention the latter."[93] Despite his criticism, Imber was influenced by the ideas of Blavatsky and employed Theosophical terminology in his exposition of Kabbalah, referring to the Hasidim as the "Jewish Theosophists" and to Talmudic, Kabbalistic, and Hasidic masters as "Mahatmas."[94]

Chapter 3

Jewish Theosophists around the Globe

The Theosophical Society underwent significant developments during the last decade of the nineteenth century and the early decades of the twentieth century. In 1891, Blavatsky passed away. Annie Besant, who joined the society in 1889 and was Blavatsky's closest confidant in her last years, became more and more influential in the Theosophical Society. In 1907, following Olcott's death, she was elected as the international president of the society. During that period, the society underwent several schisms and crises, which included the controversies over Charles W. Leadbeater's sexual misconduct, the resignation of G. R. S. Mead and his followers from the British Section, and the secession of Rudolf Steiner and his followers. Notwithstanding these events, the society grew under Besant's leadership and reached its peak in the late 1920s. During her long presidency, the nature of the society changed considerably. Besant promoted the revival of Hinduism and became involved in the struggle for Home Rule in India. Besant became dedicated to the proclamation of Krishnamurti as the new manifestation of Christ and Lord Maitreya, and the advent of the new World Teacher became central in the Theosophical Society and its affiliated Order of the Star in the East.

As the Theosophical Society's global dispersion and public visibility grew, many Jews were drawn to it and joined its national sections all around the world. In this chapter, I would like to examine some of the activities of Jewish followers of the Theosophical Society in the first two decades of the twentieth century, which eventually brought about the establishment of the Association of Hebrew Theosophists in 1925. The chapter will focus on some countries around the globe where Jewish Theosophists were especially active.

Jewish Followers of the Theosophical Society in Italy and the Foundation of the Jewish Lodge in Livorno

In 1904, *The Theosophical Review* announced that "a group has been formed of Italian Jews, students and admirers of the works of the Rabbi Benazmozegh . . . Rabbi Cerrigo Lates [*sic*!] the president of the group, was a pupil of Rabbi Benamozegh, and works zealously for Theosophy, which embodies the ideas already familiar to him."[1]

Rabbi Elijah Benamozegh (1823–1900), whose disciples founded the Theosophical group in Livorno, was a renown Jewish philosopher and Kabbalist, who served as the rabbi of Livorno for many years. Benamozegh, whose parents immigrated to Livorno from North Africa, wrote many articles and books, including an extensive Torah commentary in Herbew, *Em La-Mikra*, published in 1862 through 1865. His major theological book, *Israel and the Nations*, which was edited by his disciple Aimé Pallière, was published posthumously in French in 1914.[2] In his writing, Benamozegh presented a unique Jewish-universalistic philosophy, which was based on modern Western philosophical, as well as Jewish Kabbalistic ideas. Benamozegh was interested in Freemasonry and in the Christian Theosophy of Jacob Boehme and his followers. The term *Theosophy* and the identification of Kabbalah as a form of Theosophy were central to his thought.[3] In the last years of his life, Benamozegh became aware of the ideas of the Theosophical Society and acknowledged the resemblance between his ideas and those of the "modern Theosophical schools."[4]

The founder and president of the Jewish lodge in Livorno was Rabbi Dr. Arrigo Lattes (1879–1918). His father, Rabbi Guglielmo Lattes (1857–1928), who was a pedagogue, author, and journalist, was a disciple of Rabbi Elijah Benamozegh (1823–1900).[5] Arrigo, who was a teacher at the rabbinical college in Livorno and like his father, a follower of Benamozegh,[6] joined the Theosophical Society in the early twentieth century. In 1904, he established a Theosophical lodge in Livorno and served as its president.[7] The secretary of the Livorno lodge was Salvatore Attal (1877–1967), also known as Soter, an engineer, esotericist, and a disciple of Benamozegh. Attal, who later became a supporter of the Fascist Party, was persecuted during the World War II because of his Jewish origins, and following the war, he converted to Catholicism. Like Benamozegh, Attal was very interested in Kabbalah. In 1908, he published a book entitled *Esoterismo Biblico*,[8] in which he suggested reconciling religion, science, faith, and philosophy through the Kabbalah and asserted the Jewish Kabbalistic sources of Christianity. Attal relied on the *Zohar*, on Christian Kabbalistic sources, on the philosophy of Benamozegh, the Kabbalah scholarship of Sylv (Samuel) Karppe, and the writings of Western esotericists such as Fabre d'Olivet, Éliphas Lévi, and Papus.[9]

Decio Clavari, the general secretary of the Italian Section at the time, emphasized the similarities between Benamozegh's teaching and those of the Theosophical Society, in his report on the Livorno lodge:

> Theosophy and its teachings are not a new language for them, for they are all students and admirers of the philosophical and theological works of the great rabbi Elia Benamorzegh [*sic*] who, several years before the Theosophical Society was founded, was writing about Theosophy and speaking of reincarnation, as he had discovered it in the Talmud. The President of the group, Rabbi Arrigo Lattes, was a pupil of Elia Benarmozegh [*sic*], and he is spurred on to work ardently for the Theosophical cause by devotion to his master and admiration for our doctrines, which are partly a confirmation of ideas already familiar to him.[10]

In 1904, Arrigo Lattes published, together with Rabbi Alfredo Toaff, a monthly magazine entitled *Lux, rivista mensile per il pensiero e per la vita ebraica* (Lux, a monthly magazine for Hebrew thought and life). Theosophy may have had some impact on the magazine,[11] which had a Zionist orientation and was influenced by Benamozegh's ideas.[12] However, the journal did not last for long, and only ten issues were published in 1904. The Livorno lodge also did not last for long and was dissolved in 1905.[13]

Jews were active also in other lodges of the Italian Section. The renown expert on Semitic languages, Giorgio Levi della Vida (1886–1967), frequented the headquarters of the Theosophical Society in Rome in his youth.[14] Cesare Augusto Levi (1856–1927), the director of the Museum of Torcello, who was a historian and antiquarian and was interested in magnetism, hypnosis, and the nature of dreams, served as the president of the Fulgentia Adriatica Lodge in Venice between 1904 and 1906.[15]

Roberto Assagioli (1888–1974), the famous Italian psychoanalyst, esotericist, and parapsychologist, was also affiliated with the Theosophical Society. Assagioli, who came from an upper-middle-class Jewish family from Venice, was introduced to Theosophy by his mother, Elena Kaula (1863–1925). Before the First World War, Assagioli was close to esoteric and Theosophical circles in Florence. After the war, Assagioli collaborated with Decio Calvari, the former general secretary of the Italian Section, who established the Italian Independent Theosophical League. Assagioli served as the vice president of the league and edited the league's official organ, *Ultra*. At the same time, Assagioli developed a method he called "psychosyntesis" that combined Theosophic ideas and humanistic psychology and emphasized the spiritual and holistic aspects of human psychology. Assagioli served also as the Italian representative of the Arcane school of Alice Bailey. Assagioli participated, together with Bailey, at the summer schools that were convened in Ascona in the early 1930s by Olga Fröbe-Kapteyn (1881–1962), Dutch Theosophist and follower of Jung (these summer schools were the forerunners of the famous Eranos meetings). After World War II, during which he was imprisoned for a short period, Assagioli became active also in the United States, and his psychosynthesis had a considerable influence on American transpersonal psychology and the New Age movement.[16]

Jewish Theosophists in Poland

Jews in Poland also found interest in the teachings of the Theosophical Society and in some cases, joined its ranks. Hillel Zeitlin (1871–1941), Jewish journalist, author, and scholar from Warsaw, was acquainted with Theosophical literature, which had, as suggested by Israeli scholar Oz Bluman, a considerable impact on his interest in Eastern religions, esotericism, and mysticism.[17] Zeitlin, who called for a mystical, Hasidic-inspired revival of Judaism, studied Kabbalah with the circle of Kazimierz Stabrowski (1869–1929), a Polish painter who founded the first lodges of the Theosophical Society in Poland.[18] Bluman suggests the possibility that Wanda Dynowska, the founder of the Polish branch of the Theosophical Society, visited Zeitlin in his home.[19] However, Zeitlin criticized Jewish youth that joined the Theosophical Society.[20]

A prominent figure who was affiliated with the Theosophical Society in Poland was the Jewish pediatrician, author, and educator Henryk Goldschmidt, also known as Janusz Korczak (1878–1942).[21] According to the memoirs of Hanna Rudnianska (b. Rotwand, 1924–2003), Korczak belonged to a Theosophical circle in Warsaw and participated in the summer schools of the Polish Theosophical Society in Mężenin. Korczak was also a member of the Co-Masonic order Le Droit Humain, to which many Polish Theosophists, including the general secretary of the Polish Section, Wanda Dynowska (1888–1971), belonged.[22]

Another person of Jewish Polish extraction who was affiliated with the Theosophical Society and became a friend of Krishnamurti was Maurice Frydman (also known as Bharatananda, 1901–1976), an electronic engineer and spiritual seeker, who probably encountered Theosophy during his visits in Western Europe. In 1935, Frydman traveled to India and became a disciple of Ramana Maharshi and a follower of Gandhi. In India, Frydman collaborated with Wanda Dynowska, who by then had taken the name *Umadevi*, the former general secretary of the Polish Section of the Theosophical Society, with whom he founded, in Madras (today, Chennai), the Indian Polish Library.[23]

Another Polish Theosophist of Jewish origins was Eugenia Steinberg, who served as the president of the Sattva Lodge in Łódź, which was founded in 1923.[24] It is likely that other Jews were also members of the lodge. Ewelina Karaś (1895–1965), a prominent Polish Theosophist, wrote in a report on the activities of Polish lodges in 1924/5: "In Łódź there were many Jews among the members. The revival movement is alive among them. Two circles are established: a Jewish one for Poles who want to meet Jews, Polish (apparently for studying Poland) for Jews wishing to meet Poles. Apart from that there is an inner circle standing above the nations."[25] Later, in 1926, the Jewish lodge Judaizm Istotny (essential Judaism) was chartered, which probably took the place of the Sattva Lodge. Eugenia Steinberg served as the president of the lodge, and M. Steinberg (possibly Moses Steinberg, Eugenia's husband) as its secretary.[26] The Jewish lodge, whose establishment was probably connected to the foundation of the Association of Hebrew Theosophists,[27] which will be discussed in chapter 5, was active for several years. Another Jewish Theosophical lodge was active in Warsaw in 1927. The only information about it that I was able to locate, is an announcement concerning a public lecture held by the lodge: "Theosophy and the Problem of Jewish Life."[28] This lodge was likely also affiliated with the Association of Hebrew Theosophists.

The Anglo-Jewish Theosophists

England was one of the largest sections of the Theosophical Society, and after the early twentieth century, several Jews became active in the English Theosophical lodges.

One of the most prominent Anglo-Jewish Theosophists was Samuel Levi Bensusan (1872–1958). Bensusan, who came from an affluent

Sephardic Jewish family, was a famous author of his time, best known for his stories about the Eastern Essex marshland where he had resided since the early 1900s. Bensusan, who came from an observant family, was active in the Sephardic Jewish community in London and edited the Zionist *The Jewish World* between 1897 and 1899. In his short autobiographical article "How I Became a Member of the T.S.," Bensusan relates that he became estranged from Jewish practice and found interest in Buddhism, Hinduism, and Confucianism.[29] Probably around 1919, he joined the Theosophical Society.[30] Since that year, he published more than two hundred articles, letters, and book reviews in Theosophical journals.[31] He was the literary advisor of the Theosophical Publishing House and the editor of the new series of *The Theosophical Review*, between 1925 and 1928.[32] Bensusan recruited the prominent rabbi, scholar, and Zionist activist Moses Gaster, who will be discussed in more detail in the following chapter, to publish in *The Theosophical Review*.

Joshua Abelson (1873–1940) was another Anglo-Jewish scholar who was affiliated with the Theosophical Society in England and was interested in Jewish Mysticism. Abelson, who was born in Merthyr Tydfil, Wales, was ordained as a rabbi at Jews College in London and earned his PhD at University College London in 1911. He served as a rabbi in Cardiff (1895–1899) and Bristol (1899–1907). Later, he was the principal of the rabbinical Aria College in Portsmouth (1907–1920) and the senior minister of the United Hebrew Congregation of Leeds (after 1920).[33]

Abelson was interested in Theosophy and gave lectures and published articles in Theosophical frameworks. In 1905, he published in *The Theosophical Review* an article about the Talmud and Theosophy, which was based on a lecture he gave in the Bristol lodge of the Theosophical Society.[34] In the lecture, which deals not only with the Talmud, but also with other Jewish sources, especially Kabbalah, Abelson describes some ideas which he regards as shared by Judaism and Theosophy. Nonetheless, he asserts that he is not an expert in Theosophy.[35] In 1912, he published "Rabbinical Mysticism" in *The Theosophic Review*.[36] In 1913, his book *Jewish Mysticism* was published as the third volume in the Quest series of G. R. S. Mead, who wrote the introduction to the book.[37] Following the publication of the book, Abelson gave lectures on Jewish mysticism in several Theosophical lodges.[38] Abelson was connected with the English branch of the Association of Hebrew Theosophists, and in 1927, he gave a lecture to the Manchester group of the association.[39] Abelson was castigated in the Jewish press for his involvement in the Theosophical Society, which was described as "inimical to Judaism."[40]

Similar to other Jewish Theosophists, Abelson was very much interested in Kabbalah and other Jewish trends he identified as part of the Jewish mystical tradition.[41] Apart from his *Introduction to Jewish Mysticism* and his article on rabbinical mysticism mentioned above, in 1912 he published *The Immanence of God in Rabbinical Literature*, a book that was based on his doctoral thesis,[42] as well as several articles in the *Jewish Chronicle* that are related to Jewish mysticism, including "Swedenborg and the Zohar"[43] and "Occult Thought in Jewish Literature."[44] In the 1930s, Abelson published reviews of Israel Regardie's *The Tree of Life* and of Dion Fortune's *The Mystical Qabbalah*.[45] Abelson was involved in the publication of first comprehensive translation of the *Zohar* into English by the Soncino Press in 1931 and wrote the introduction to the translation (which was prepared by Maurice Simon, Harry Sperling, and Paul P. Levertoff).[46]

Another Theosophist of Jewish origins who was active in England (and later in the United States) and was very much interested in Kabbalah—although he lacked the scholarly expertise and rabbinical training of Abelson—was Elias Gewurz (1875–1947).[47]

Figure 3.1. Elias Gewurtz. *Source: Beautiful Thoughts of the Ancient Hebrews* (New York, 1924). Courtesy of the National Library of Israel collections. Public domain.

Gewurz (sometimes spelled Gewurtz, or Gewirz) was born in Dembitz (Dębica), in southeast Poland, to a wealthy and learned family. He received traditional Jewish education in the Yeshiva but became interested in modern literature and in the ideas of the Jewish enlightenment, and joined the small Zionist circle of the town.[48] When he was about twenty years old, following an unsuccessful marriage (his observant wife asked for a divorce because of his free thinking), Gewurz left Dembitz for London.[49] In 1902, he published a small booklet celebrating King Edward's coronation, *The Coronation of King Edward VII and the Jews*, in three languages—German, Yiddish, and English.[50] The same year, Gewurz was baptized. Although rumors about his conversion reached his hometown,[51] Gewurz never mentioned this in his writings and did not identify himself as a Christian. As we will see later, one of his books was published by a Jewish publishing company and was introduced by a prominent Jewish American Reform rabbi.

Gewurz, who presented himself as an expert in esoteric Judaism and Kabbalah, joined the Theosophical Society in the first decade of the twentieth century. In 1914, the Dharma Press announced, "The publishers have secured Mr. Gewurz's services as editor and collaborator. He has devoted the last ten years to the study of Qabbalah and to research in its original Hebrew-Chaldaic literature."[52] Together with his disciple, Leonard Bosman, who was probably the owner of the Dhrama Press, Gewurz published a book entitled *The Cosmic Wisdom as Embodied in the Qabbalah and in the Symbolical Hebrew Alphabet.*[53] The author's perception of Kabbalah in this book, as well as in other publications of Gewurz and Bosman, was based mostly on Theosophy and on the ideas of the eighteenth-century French esotericist Fabre d'Olivet, to whom they dedicated their work. The same year, Gewurz published "Qabalah," in *The Theosophist*, an article in which he asserted the antiquity of Kabbalah and the similarity between Kabbalah and Theosophy: "The immortal merit of the Qabalistic writings is their freedom of dogma and from all sorts of limitations in regard to race, creed or colour: their antiquity is proved by the greatest scholars to antedate the most ancient teachings of the East."[54]

A year later, Gewurz resettled in the United States. His involvement with the Theosophical Society there and his later publications about Kabbalah will be discussed later.

Gewurz was the teacher of one of the most active Anglo-Jewish Theosophists, Leonard Alexander Bosman (1879–1936).[55] Bosman was born in 1879 in East London to a Jewish family who had immigrated from Holland some years before. He was married and had three daughters. Apart from that, very little is known about his life, his education, and occupation.[56]

Bosman joined the Theosophical Society in 1909. He founded several Theosophical lodges and served as the president of the Hackney lodge in London. He was also very interested in Freemasonry, and joined Co-Masonry, the form of Freemasonry that also admitted women and to which many Theosophists belonged.[57] Since 1910, he published many articles and books on esotericism, Freemasonry, Theosophy, and Kabbalah.[58] Several books by Bosman (some of them, written together with Gewurz) were published by Dharma Press.[59]

Bosman related that he came from a "fairly Orthodox" background. Like Bensusan, he related that he became interested in Theosophy following an estrangement from his Jewish heritage:

> The writer, brought up in fairly orthodox surroundings from which, he and the whole of a large family, later fell away because of the lack of reality behind the too rigid forms and customs, turned almost with contempt from Religion to become agnostic and nearly atheistic in his darkness. In later years, however thanks to the Light shewn (!) him in a peculiar manner, he was attracted to the Theosophical Society and there found the Light of Judaism which had long eluded him in Judaism as taught by those to whom he was sent for guidance.[60]

Notwithstanding his estrangement from Jewish Orthodoxy, Bosman did not lose his interest in Judaism. As he relates, through Theosophy, he discovered the light of Judaism, which was concealed in the traditional Jewish upbringing he received. The light of Judaism that he found in Theosophy was the Kabbalah. Bosman devoted many of his lectures, articles, and booklets to Kabbalah as he understood it. Bosman's (as well as Gewurz's) ideas on Kabbalah were inspired by Theosophical ideas and by the esoteric system of Fabre d'Olivet. In 1913, Bosman published *The Mysteries of the Qabbalah*, which was dedicated to his teacher, Elias Gewurz, and was to be the first of the Esoteric Studies series. The publishers, most probably Bosman himself, expressed the hope that "the unsurpassed beauty of the Qabbalistic gems strewn about plentifully in this series may find admirers among Theosophical students." The second book in the series was *The Cosmic Wisdom*, mentioned above, which Bosman published together with Gewurz.

In his writings, Bosman argued that Judaism could be reconciled with Theosophy and that the reconciliation between the two could be achieved through Kabbalah, which was essentially identical with the teaching of the Theosophical Society. In his book *The Music of the Spheres*, published in 1914, Bosman declared, "But verily, the Secret Doctrine of the Jews is Theos-Sophia and nothing but Theos-Sophia, and hence it is a matter of perfect simplicity to reconcile the two teachings that emanate from One source."[61] Bosman continued to suggest a connection between the *Zoharic* text *Sifra Dezniuta* and the mysterious Book of Dzyan, one of the alleged sources of Blavatsky's *Secret Doctrine*: "The inner teaching of Judaism is the same as that offered in the *Secret Doctrine*, the very name of the Book of Dzyan from which the *Secret Doctrine* was taken and the Qabbalistic work called the Book of Dzyaniouta being similar in construction and purpose."[62]

As we shall see later, Bosman became active in the Association of Hebrew Theosophists, and his *A Plea for Judaism* was one of the few books published by the Hebrew Association. Bosman was also interested in psychic research, and in the 1930s, he was one of the founders of a Jewish Society for Psychical Research.[63] Bosman continued to publish and lecture in Theosophical frameworks until his death in 1936 at fifty-eight.

Finally, before turning to examine the American Jewish Theosophists, it should be mentioned that in the second decade of the twentieth century, two interesting and influential esotericists of Jewish origins, Michael Houghton (born Horowitz, also known as Michael Juste, 1897–1961) and his friend Hyman Raphael Hurst, who later was known as Paul Brunton (1898–1981), became active in the Theosophical Society.[64] Michael Houghton, a poet and occultist, described the experiences of Hurst (*David* in the book) and himself in the Theosophical Society in the book *The White Brother: An Occult Autobiography*, which he published in 1927 under the name *Michael Juste*.[65] Houghton and Hurst left the Theosophical Society after a few years.[66] Houghton became associated with Aleister Crowley, founded the famous occult bookstore Atlantis, and later became the editor of *The Occult Observer*. Hurst traveled in 1930 to India, where he met Ramana Maharshi and described his experience in India in his influential book *A Search in Secret India*, which he published under the name *Paul Brunton*. Although both came from Jewish backgrounds, they were estranged from their Jewish roots, and as far as I know, they did not express much interest in Judaism or Kabbalah.[67]

Jewish Theosophists in America

As mentioned above, Elias Gewurz, Bosman's teacher, left England in 1914 and resettled in the United States. For a time, he resided in Fairfax, California, and had connections with a circle of occultists who were interested in Theosophy, Buddhism, Sufism, and Kabbalah. According to Samuel Lewis, who was a member of this circle, Gewurz was engaged in translating the *Zohar* and Fabre d'Olivet's *The Hebrew Language Restored* into English.[68]

Gewurz was active in Theosophical circles in the United States and published several books and articles. In 1918, he published *The Hidden Treasures of the Ancient Qabalah*, which was based on lectures he gave in 1915 for the Krotona Lodge of the Theosophical Society in Hollywood. In the same year, Gewurz published *The Diary of a Child of Sorrow*, which he says he wrote in Las Palmas, in the Canary Islands, in 1914. Both books were printed by the Yogi Publication Society, an occult publishing company based in Chicago.[69] In 1922, the Yogi Publication Society printed a book entitled *The Mysteries of the Qabalah*, "written down by the seven pupils of E. G., and prepared for publication by one of them." The book, dedicated to "Elias Gewurz, my teacher," is a reprint from the *Esoteric Studies* that were published earlier in London, by Dhrama Press. Gewurz also published several articles in Theosophical journals.[70] In 1924, his *Beautiful Thoughts of the Ancient Hebrew* was published by the Bloch Publishing Society, the oldest Jewish publishing house in the United States, affiliated with the Reform movement. Martin A. Meyer (1879–1923), the rabbi of the reform synagogue Emanuel in San Francisco, and a Professor of Jewish studies at the University of California[71] wrote the introduction to the book, in which he praises Gewurz: "The author and compiler of this little book, Mr. Elias Gewurz, has specialized in a field little cultivated by the modern Jew. He is a master of the Hebrew language and of the mystical literature which the Jew has produced during the centuries past."[72] Gewurz himself declares in the preface to the book that the volume included "precious gems of poetical prose," which he collected from the Talmud, Midrash, and Kabbalah. The book includes many citations from Jewish sources. However, almost all these citations are fabrications that cannot be found in the sources Gewurz cites (similar fabrications can be found in earlier writings of Bosman and Gewurz). Gershom Scholem, who noted Gewurz's fabrications, expressed his puzzlement over this in a letter he sent to Samuel Lewis in 1948: "I have never understood the mind of this author in putting out this book, not a single quotation of which is authentic. His quotations have nothing to do with what is contained actually in the source he mentions, and I would appreciate it very much if you have an explanation of this kind of modern pseudepigraphy."[73]

Gewurz resided in different locations in Southern California until his death in San Bernardino in 1947.[74] As far as I know, *Beautiful Thoughts of the Ancient Hebrews* was his last publication.

As mentioned above, Gewurz was in touch with a circle of Californian esotericists who were interested in Kabbalah, Sufism, Zen Buddhism, and the teaching of Fabre d'Olivet. According to Samuel Lewis, who was a member of this circle, Gewurz resided in the building that housed the Sufi center, Kaaba Allah, which was established by Ada Martin in the 1920.[75] Both Ada Martin and Samuel Lewis, who were of Jewish origins, were members of the Theosophical Society.

Ada Martin (1871–1947), known as Murshida Rabia Martin, was the first American follower of the Sufi teacher Inayat Khan (1887–1927) and the founder of the Kabba Allah in Fairfax, California.[76] Martin, who was born to Jewish parents who immigrated from Russia, joined the Theosophical Society, and in 1910, she gave a lecture at the Golden Gate Lodge titled "The Century of the Child."[77] Murshida Ada's disciple, Samuel Lewis (1896–1971), who later became known as Sufi Sam, was also active in the Theosophical Society.[78] Lewis, who was born to an affluent Jewish American family (his father, Jacob, was the vice president of the Levi Strauss company) became acquainted with Theosophy at the age of eighteen, at the Palace of Education in the 1915 world's fair held in San Francisco.[79] He probably met Ada Martin in the framework of the Theosophical Society. It is interesting to note that according to Lewis, his first question to Martin was about Kabbalah:

In November 1919 he is walking on Sutter Street; he sees a display of books. He is unaware of how but soon he is upstairs facing a little dark-haired lady. She is Jewish. "You can explain the Kabbalah?" he asks. "Yes, and all religions." "What is Sufism?" "Sufism is the essence of all religions. It has been brought to the West by Hazrat Inayat Khan." The woman is Murshida Rabia A. Martin, Inayat Khan's senior disciple, and his first appointed Murshida.[80]

Although Lewis related that he was disappointed with the teaching of the Theosophical Society because they have proven to be only intellectual,[81] he kept his contacts with the society after becoming a disciple of Inayat Khan.

Another prominent Theosophist of Jewish origins who was active in the United States in the early twentieth century was the suffragist and political activist Pauline Perlmutter Steinem (1864–1940). Steinem (the grandmother of the American feminist activist Gloria Steinem), whose father was a cantor, was born in Poland and raised in Bavaria, where she was trained as a teacher. She immigrated to the United States and settled in Toledo, Ohio, where she founded a vocational school, served on the Toledo Board of Education, and was active in several Jewish organizations. She was active in the suffragist movement and served as the head of the Ohio Woman's Suffrage Association and as the president of the Toledo Council of Women.[82] Steinem became a devoted Theosophist and served as the publicity agent

Figure 3.2. Pauline Perlmutter Steinem. *Source:* "For the Woman Who Reads," *Labor Digest* (November 1909): 19. Wikimedia Commons. Public domain.

of the Harmony Lodge of the Theosophical Society in Toledo.[83] Steinem's commitment to women's rights was related to her Theosophical convictions. In her public statement, "Why I am a Suffragist" she asserted, "I believe in woman suffrage because I believe that the perfect equality of men and women is founded on Divine Wisdom. Divine Wisdom, or in the Greek term, Theosophy, teaches first of all the brotherhood of man without distinction of race, creed, color, or sex."[84]

Many other Jews joined Theosophical lodges in the United States in the first decades of the twentieth century. As we shall see later, some of them became active in the American Section of the Association of Hebrew Theosophists, which became the largest section of the Jewish Theosophical association.

Before turning to discuss Jewish Theosophists in Asia and Africa, I would like to note that Jews also joined the Theosophical Society in South America. One of the Jewish Theosophists who was active in South America was the journalist and author Pedro (Pinchas David) Sprinberg (1886–1974). Sprinberg (sometimes spelled Shprinberg) was born in Bessarabia and immigrated with his parents to Argentina in 1903. Sprinberg, who resided in Buenos Aires and Rosario, and later moved to Montevideo, Uruguay, was a Zionist and an anarchist. He published extensively in Yiddish and Spanish, founded the first Yiddish anarchist newspaper in Argentina, *Leben Un Freiheit* (Life and freedom), and edited the Yiddish journal *Shtarlen* (Rays). In Montevideo, he edited the first Yiddish daily newspaper in Uruguay, *Urugvayer Tog* (Uruguay Day), and founded, together with his wife, Catalina Stoliar, the Jewish radio station Hora Cultural Israelita.[85]

Sprinberg joined the Argentinian Section of the Theosophical Society in 1918. He was a member of the Hypatia Lodge in Rosario, and between 1930 and 1931, he served as the president of the Dharma Lodge in Buenos Aires. In 1925, he edited the special edition of the Theosophical journal *Theosofia en el Plata* that was published in Rosario to celebrate the Jubilee of society.[86] Sprinberg published articles on Theosophy in the Yiddish press and signed some of his articles with the penname *Theosoph*.[87] In 1965, Sprinberg visited Israel and met with Israeli Theosophists.[88]

Jewish Theosophists in China

In a letter to the editor published in the Jewish newspaper published in Shanghai, *Israel's Messenger*, in 1927, a member of the Jewish community in Shanghai, who signed as *Lover of Truth*, attacked the Theosophical Society and the Jews who joined it: "There are some Jews in Shanghai who are leading the local branch of The Theosophical Society, but not one of them is ever seen in his house of worship, and none has been known studying the philosophy of Judaism. They read the ill compiled and plagiarized books of Blavatsky."[89] The *Lover of Truth* mentions by name only one of the Jewish Theosophists—Alex Horne, the author of a pamphlet titled *Spiritualizing Unspiritual Judaism.*

Alex Horne (originally Horenstein) was one of the founders of the first Theosophical lodge in China, the Saturn Lodge in Shanghai (later known as the Shanghai Lodge), in 1919.[90] Horne was born in Odessa, Russia, and immigrated, with his parents, to China. He became the president of the Shanghai Lodge in 1923 and edited its journal, the *Saturn Lodge Monthly.*[91] Frieda Horne, Alex's sister, and Dora Horne (née Stone), his wife, were also members of the lodge.[92]

Between 1923 and 1924, Horne gave a series of lectures on Curuppu- mullage Jinarajadasa's *First Principals of Theosophy*, at the Shanghai Lodge.[93] In May 1923, the *North China Herald* gave a detailed report on a lecture given by Horne titled "Various Accounts of the Creation," in which he mentioned the Kabbalists, who understood that the creation in the Bible was performed by Elohim, or Creative power, and not by the supreme God.[94] Horne published several articles in Theosophical reviews, including "The Chinese Jews of K'ai-Feng-Fu," published in *The Theosophist* in 1925.[95] In the article, Horne notes the importance of ritual in keeping a race together as an individual entity and says that it is especially important for Jewish Theosophists to bear this in mind:

> Theosophy is liable to give them such an insight into the myster- ies of their religion that the observance of their tradition would seem futile and unnecessary. Perhaps for them it is so. But for the race as a whole it appears to be still a great and powerful unifying force, and for the sake of the race it would seem that even a Theosophist should keep to his tradition as much as he can, for in this way does he contribute to the preservation of the organism of which he is a member and which undoubtedly has an important role to play in the cultural and spiritual world.[96]

In 1926, Horne moved to San Francisco, where he became active in the Pacific Lodge of the Theosophical Society. Horne continued to be interested in Judaism, and to advocate for a Jewish spiritual-Theosophical revival. As we will see in chapter 5, Horne, who suggested in 1926 to form "a league of Jewish Theosophists,"[97] became active in the American Section of the Association of Hebrew Theosophists and his above-mentioned pamphlet, *Spiritualizing Unspiritual Judaism* was published by the Hebrew Association.[98]

As mentioned, Horne's wife, Dora, and his sister, Frieda, were also members of the Shanghai Lodge. Another Jewish member was Dr. Fredrick Reiss (b. Samuel Reisz, 1891–1981). Dr. Reiss, a renown Hungarian-born dermatologist, who was trained in Budapest and other European capitals, immigrated to Shanghai in 1922, where he set up the Department of Dermatology at the Central National University in Shanghai.[99] Reiss joined the Shanghai Lodge of the Theosophical Society and represented the lodge as a physician to the Jewish Communal Association.[100] Reiss was also a Freemason, and in 1933 he established the German-speaking Masonic lodge Lux Orientis in Shanghai.[101] Reiss was sympathetic to Zionism. He visited Palestine in 1933 and returned full of admiration for the Yishuv (the Jewish residents of Palestine).[102] In 1941, just before Pearl Harbor, he left China for the United States and continued his career as a dermatologist.

Jews were also active in the Hong Kong lodge of the Theosophical Society. David Sassoon Gubbay (1886–1931), who was born in Hong Kong to an affluent Jewish Baghdadi family[103] and was employed by the Sassoon company, became interested in Theosophy at the end of the first decade of the twentieth century. In 1910, Gubbay sent Annie Besant a letter in which he apologized for his previous criticism of Besant and Leadbeater and requested to enroll as a member of the society.[104] Gubbay became active in the Hong Kong lodge, which was founded in 1923, and served as its vice president.[105]

David Sassoon Gubbay's brother, Charles Sassoon Gubbay (1867–1941), who was employed in the Sassoon company in Shanghai and served as the president of the Jewish Communal Association there, was also interested in Theosophy. Although he did not join the society, he published a letter in April 1932 in *Israel's Messenger* in which he expressed his support of the Jewish Theosophists in Basra (which will be discussed in the following chapters). In the conclusion of the letter, he wrote, "Eastern Jewry is crying for the spiritual and is seeking this understanding in the teaching of Theosophy, and why not, when Theosophy is able to bring the thinkers of Eastern Jewry nearer to the understanding of the spiritual which is denied to them in the synagogues and in the Talmud Torahs. . . . I am not a Theosophist, but am appreciative of the efforts of these thinkers and seekers who are groping to find the way to God."[106]

Jewish Theosophists in India

In the previous chapter, I discussed A. D. Ezekiel, who was active in the Theosophical Society in India in the late nineteenth century. Other Indian Jews joined the society in the early twentieth century. One of them was N. E. David, who probably resided in Karachi. I have not been able to find any biographical information about David, who published several articles in the *The Theosophist* in 1907 and 1908.[107] In 1909, David participated in the convention of religions in Calcutta, which was organized by the Vivekananda Society. David was one of the three lecturers representing Judaism in the convention (the others were M. E. D. Cohen and I. A. Isaac, who may have also been a Theosophist). David's lecture (as well as those of Isaac and Cohen) was published in the proceedings of the convention.[108]

In his articles, David distinguished between the Jews, or Hebrews, and Israel. He argued that Israel "is not a national dynasty, but rather a peculiar community of spiritual people who have taken up the 'Path,' having no worldly-mind men among them, and caring little for earthly possessions and worldly enjoyments"[109] The Jews, or Hebrews, on the other hand, are a nation that is in possession of the "true faith of Israel," which was followed by their forefathers and which is preserved in Jewish scriptures.[110] David maintains that "Israelitism" is a universalistic religion that holds the core ideas and values of Theosophy and argues that the idea of Karma and reincarnation, as understood in Theosophy "forms the very corner-stone of the teaching if Israelitism, and are as old as the cardinal principles of that faith."[111] According to David, the Jews believed and taught these doctrines in days of old, "but in the present time day . . . they have lost sight of the true spirit of these grand truths."[112] He argues that "innumerable instances . . . prove beyond the shadow of doubt that our religion, even in its exoteric teaching, does not only *express* 'the truth of universal brotherhood,' but insists most emphatically on the practice of universal love by everyone in a most willing and liberal spirit."[113] After citing the final part of the Jewish prayer "Aleinu le'shabeiach" (We should praise): "And the Living One shall be king all over the earth, in that day shall the Living One be one and His name One," David exclaims, "How sublime! How Theosophical! What a spirit of unselfish brotherhood and love to thus supplicate Heaven thrice daily throughout one's life."[114]

In the early twentieth century, Dr. Jacob E. Solomon (originally, Warsulkar 1884–1941), a member of the Bene Israel community, one of the three Jewish communities in India (the others are the Baghdadi and Cochin communities),[115] joined the Theosophical Society. Solomon, who was born in Pune but resided most of his life in Ahmedabad, was a physician and a municipal councilor and was awarded by the government the Kaiser-i-hind and Jubilee medals for his public service. He was active in the Bene Israel community and served as the secretary of the Ahmedabad branch of the India Home Rule League.[116]

Solomon, who was also a Freemason, joined the Theosophical Society in 1912, and both he and wife, Sarah (née Ezekiel), were active in the Ahmadabad lodge of the society. During his army service in Iraq in World War I, Solomon established the Dar-es-Salaam Theosophical lodge at the military area in Basra and served as its president.[117] In the 1920s, he returned to India and served as the secretary of the Ahmedabad lodge.

There is some evidence that Solomon stood at the head of a group of Jewish Theosophists in Ahmedabad in the second or third decade of the twentieth century. In an article published in *The Theosophist* in June 1931, Curuppumullage Jinarajadasa cites Solomon: "In Ahmedabad I was beaten in the Synagogue and excommunicated for protesting the unrighteous actions of the leaders; we formed a separate community and had prayers in my hall. After seven years we were honorably taken back."[118] According to scholar Margaret Chatterjee, the Ahmedabad Bene Israel Synagogue excommunicated Solomon because of his Theosophical activities, and this action was condemned by the All-India Israelite League.[119] I have not found any other information concerning the excommunication of Solomon or of the existence of a separate community of Jewish Theosophists in Ahmedabad. As we will see later, Solomon was one of the founders of the Association of Hebrew Theosophists. He continued to be active in the Theosophical Society also in later years, and in 1936, he published in *The Theosophist* an article entitled "My Experience in Healing."[120]

Another Jewish Theosophist who was active in India was S.S. (Sulman Samuel) Cohen (1895–1980). Cohen was the eldest of eleven children of a poor family from Basra, Iraq. As a young man, he traveled to India, where he worked as a shop assistant and was trained as an accountant. In Mumbai, Cohen joined the Theosophical Society, and at Annie Besant's request, he moved to the headquarters of the society to Adyar. Cohen lived there for more than five years during the 1920s and studied at the Theosophical Brahmavidya Ashram. He became acquainted with the other leaders of the society, including Charles Webster Leadbeater and Jiddu Krishnamurti.[121] Later, Cohen became one of the founders of the Association of Hebrew Theosophists and was involved in the controversies over the Jewish Theosophical group in Basra. In October 1933, Cohen published a letter in the *Theosophist* in which he expressed his indignation over the support of Prof. Johannes Maria Verweyen (1883–1945), the former general secretary of the Theosophical Society in Germany, of Hitler and the Nazi regime.[122]

In 1936, after reading Paul Brunton's *A Search in Secret India*, Cohen visited Ramana Maharshi in Tiruvannamalai and became his devotee. Cohen published several books about Sri Ramana and his teachings. He resided for many years in Ramanashram, where he died in 1980. Cohen did not cut off his contacts with the Theosophical Society, and he continued to be interested in Jewish affairs. In 1942, he sent a letter to the editor of *The Theosophist* in which he criticized him for ignoring Polish cooperation with the Nazi regime and its persecution of the Jews.[123] In 1951, Cohen expressed his identification with Judaism and his sympathy for the recently established State of Israel in a couple of publications in the journal *India and Israel*.[124]

Apart from Jews from the Baghdadi and Bene Israel communities, there was also one member of the Cochin Jewish community who joined the

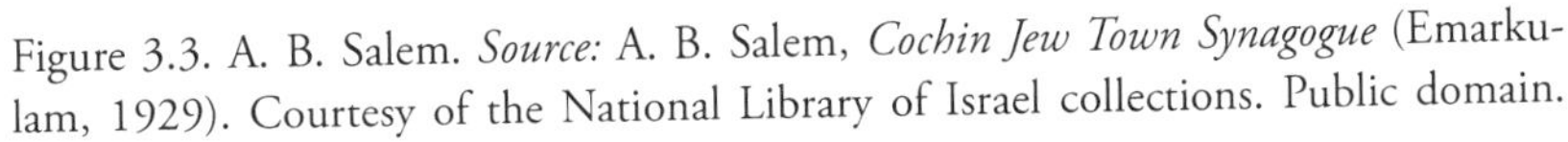

Figure 3.3. A. B. Salem. *Source:* A. B. Salem, *Cochin Jew Town Synagogue* (Emarkulam, 1929). Courtesy of the National Library of Israel collections. Public domain.

Theosophical Society.[125] It was A. B. (Abraham Barak) Salem (1882–1967), who was known as "the Jewish Gandhi." Salem was born to a poor family of the lowest caste of the Kerala Jewish community. He was the first of his caste to receive university education and the first Cochin Jew to receive a law degree. He served as a government official and as an advocate, and he was active in the Mahajana Sabha (All-People's Association) and in the Indian National Congress. Salem was also a Trade Union organizer and worked for the social reform of the Jewish Cochin community. He was an observant Jew and a Zionist. Later, in 1954 and 1955, he played an important role in the emigration of the Jewish community to Israel, although he himself stayed in Cochin.[126] Salem joined the Theosophical Society and attended the Jubilee congress, in which the Association of Hebrew Theosophists was founded. At the library of the headquarters of the society in Adyar, there is a copy of the book Salem published in 1929 on the Cochin Synagogue,[127] with a dedication to Annie Besant, dated November 11, 1930.

Jewish Theosophists in South Africa

Several Jews, most of them friends and supporters of the Indian leader Mohandas Karamchand Gandhi (1869–1948), played an important role in the history of Theosophy in South Africa. One of the founders, and the first president, of the first South African Theosophical lodge, was Lewis Walter Ritch (1868–1952), who arrived at South Africa from England in 1889 and worked as a business manager.[128] Ritch was a supporter of the Indian struggle in South Africa and a friend of Gandhi, whom he first met in 1895. In a letter published in *The Theosophist* in 1896, Ritch mentioned "the pluck and persistence of my Indian friend, Mr. Gandhi, Barrister at Law, a gentleman who has for a long time past been fighting the Indian battle in Natal, almost single-handed."[129] In 1905, Ritch returned to England to study law and served as secretary of the South African British Indian Committee. After he returned to South Africa in 1911, he worked as a lawyer in Gandhi's law firm in Johannesburg.

Ritch was connected to the Jewish community in South Africa and England. In a letter to the *South African Jewish Chronicle* from 1908, Ritch told how during the Yom Kippur (day of atonement) service he attended in London, "my thoughts turned to South Africa, my home for seventeen years, and the refuge of many thousands of prosperous co-religionists escaped from Russia's red terror. And there too, in the Transvaal, I saw the picture of a persecuted people, an Eastern people, albeit not my own, oppressed, reviled, despoiled."[130] Ritch continues and criticizes the Jewish community for not joining the struggle against racism in South Africa.

Ritch was interested in Theosophy already before his arrival to South Africa.[131] In the mid-1890s, he organized a small Theosophical circle that met near Johannesburg. In a report on the Theosophical activities in South Africa, published in *Lucifer*, in September 1894, Ritch wrote, "The last two weeks Herbert Kitchin[132] and the undersigned held small informal meetings some seven miles from Johannesburg explaining the general principals of Theosophy. . . . A little more patience and perseverance, and we shall be able to tender still another branch of the Theosophical Society."[133] The lodge was indeed established (it received its charter in 1899), and Ritch served as its president. Ritch introduced Gandhi to other members of the Theosophical Society in South Africa, many of them Jewish. Gandhi, who became acquainted with the society during his studies in London, participated in meetings of the Johannesburg lodge and gave several lectures to its members.[134] However, later he became critical of the occult interests of the Theosophical Society and objected to Ritch's involvement in it. In a letter Gandhi wrote to Dr. Pranjivan Mehta, dated May 8, 1911, Gandhi wrote that although the Theosophical rule of universal brotherhood appealed to him, he had no sympathy for its search for occult powers. Gandhi refers to Ritch's activities in the Theosophical Society (as well as to other of his Theosophist friends, including Polak and Kallenbach, whom I will discuss later): "Ritch was a theosophist. He urged me to become a member. Not only did I not become one, I helped him to be free from that humbug. Polak is a Theosophist, but he stays miles away from the practices and writings of Theosophists. The same is true of Kallenbach."[135] It seems that indeed, Ritch ceased his involvement in the Theosophical Society in later years. Nonetheless, in the 1913 report of the South African Section of the Theosophical Society, Ritch is mentioned as one of the members of the section who are among the leaders of the Indian cause in South Africa.[136]

Hermann Kallenbach (1871–1945), who was mentioned in Gandhi's letter, was born in Lithuania and studied architecture in Berlin. He immigrated to South Africa in 1896 and joined the Johannesburg lodge of the Theosophical Society. He met Gandhi in 1903 or 1904 and became his closest friend. In later years, Kallenbach became a Zionist and tried, unsuccessfully, to secure a supportive statement for the Zionist cause from Gandhi. After his death in 1945, Kallenbach' s ashes were brought to Israel and buried in Kibbutz Degania.[137]

Figure 3.4. Gandhi, Sonia Schlesin, and Hermann Kallenbach, 1913. *Source:* Wikimedia Commons. Public domain.

Another Jewish Theosophist who was a friend and supporter of Gandhi was Gabriel Isaac (1874–1914). Isaac, who was born in Leeds and immigrated to South Africa at the end of the nineteenth century, was an ardent Theosophist and a vegetarian. He joined the Theosophical lodge in Johannesburg and was an enthusiastic follower of Gandhi and a supporter of the Indian cause in South Africa. In 1913, Issac was arrested for his participation in the Satyagraha struggle. He died in 1914, shortly after his release from jail.[138]

Isaac's friends and Gandhi supporters Henry and Millie Polak were also active in the Theosophical Society. Henry Salomon Leon Polak (1882–1959) was born in Dover, England, to an affluent Jewish family (his mother was a scion of the Sephardi de Sola Pool family).[139] In 1903, he traveled to South Africa and worked there as a journalist and, later, as an attorney.[140] He and his wife, Millie (who wasn't Jewish), became staunch supporters of Gandhi. In 1909, Polak published his first book, *The Indians of South Africa.*[141] In 1916, he returned to England, where he worked as a solicitor.

Figure 3.5. Henry Salomon Leon Polak. *Source: Indian Opinion*, 1914. Public domain.

The Polaks continued to support Gandhi and the Indian national cause, and both Henry and Millie published books about Gandhi.[142]

Polak, who heard a lecture of Annie Besant before his journey to South Africa, joined the Johannesburg lodge of the Theosophical Society in 1905.[143] In 1910, he published an article in *The Theosophist* concerning the treatment of Indians in South Africa. Polak criticized local Theosophists for not standing on the side the Indians, attacked a certain principal member of the South African Theosophical Society for his support of race segregation, and condemned a lodge that did not permit non-European membership.[144]

Polak continued to be active in the Theosophical Society after his return to England. In 1926, he served as the vice president of the St. John's Wood lodge and later as the treasurer and the general secretary of the English Section.[145] He published several articles in Theosophical journals, the last one in 1957. Although he was not involved in the establishment of the Association of Hebrew Theosophists, he contributed funds for the founding of a synagogue at the Adyar headquarters of the Theosophical Society, which was initiated by the association.[146] Polak was also interested in Spiritualism and he was one the founders of the Jewish Society of Psychic Research, which was active in London in the interwar period.[147]

Polak connected his support of the Indian cause in South Africa to his Jewish origins and to his Theosophical convictions. Polak related that in his address to the South African court in 1913, when he was charged with aiding the Indian cause, he pointed out "that my own Jewish people had suffered from religious and racial persecutions throughout the centuries, and that when I discovered that the Indians were being similarly persecuted on racial and religious grounds, it was impossible for me to hold aloof. I felt that, as a Theosophist, I must take my stand by the side of those who were being degraded in this way and for no fault of their own save that of race, color and religion."[148] Like Ritch, Polak criticized the Jews of South Africa who did not learn the lesson of the persecution of the Jews. In a letter published in the *Jewish Chronicle* in 1911, Polak wrote, "Unfortunately, many of our co-religious in South Africa appear never to have learnt this foremost lesson of the age long persecution of the Jewish people . . . [A]s soon as they set a foot on South African soil, they do not hesitate to join in the hue and the cry against the disinherited residents of the subcontinent."[149]

Finally, before moving to discuss the Jewish followers of some of the offshoots of the Theosophical Society, I would like to mention the activities of Jewish Theosophists in Egypt. A few Jewish Theosophists were active in the Egyptian Section after it received its charter in 1917.[150] Joseph Haim Perez, the owner of the firm J. H. Perez & Co and the president of the Cairo stock exchange between 1925 and 1929,[151] was one of the founders of the Egyptian Section. Between 1917 and 1948, Perez served as the president of the French-speaking lodge, Hikmat-el-Kadim, in Cairo (which was founded in 1908) and as the general treasurer and the general secretary of the Egyptian Section.[152] As we will see in chapter 5, Perez was also one of the founders and first treasurers of the Association of Hebrew Theosophists. In 1948, Perez's firm and property were put under custodianship, following the steps taken by the Egyptian government against Jewish firms and businesses.[153] Perez, who was on vacation in Switzerland at the time, informed Curuppumullage Jinarajadasa, the president of the Theosophical Society, of the recent events in Egypt.[154] Perez suggested to Jinarajadasa that he not refer to him as the presidential agent in Egypt in the publications of the society and to change the address of the Egyptian Section, which was at Perez's address at the time. Perez was hesitant to suggest another candidate instead of him as the presidential agent because "amongst the two or three members which might be chosen, all are Jews and Jews are just now considered outcasts in Egypt."[155] Jinarajadasa accepted Perez's suggestion, and he did not appoint another presidential agent to Egypt.

Another prominent Jewish member of the Egyptian Section was Theo (Theophile) Levi (1877–1969). Levi, a banker from Cairo, who published book reviews in Jewish journals,[156] served in the 1920s as the acting general secretary of the Theosophical Society in Egypt and as the secretary of the Hikmet-el-Kadim Lodge.[157] Levi was still active in the Egyptian Section in the 1940s.[158] Following the Israeli Arab War, he also left Egypt and emigrated to Switzerland.

Chapter 4

Jewish Followers of the
Offshoots of the Theosophical Society

In the first decades of the twentieth century, the Theosophical Society underwent several schisms and crises. In 1909, following the controversies over allegations of sexual misconduct by Charles W. Leadbeater, G. R. S. Mead, the former secretary of Blavatsky, and some of his followers, left the British Section of the society and established the Quest Society. A few years later, in 1912, Rudolf Steiner, the president of the German Section, who objected to the Annie Besant's declaration of Krishnamurti as the new world teacher, broke away from the Theosophical Society and established the Anthroposophical Society. In 1920, the Russian Theosophists Nicholas and Helena Roerich, who resided at the time in the United States, seceded from the society and founded the Agni Yoga movement.

Several Jews who were affiliated with the Theosophical Society in the early decades of the twentieth century followed Mead, Steiner, and Roerich and joined the offshoots of the society. In this chapter, I would like to discuss some of the Jewish Theosophists who joined the Quest Society, the Anthroposophical Society, and the Agni Yoga movement.

Rabbi Moses Gaster and the Quest Society

Rabbi Moses Gaster (1856–1939) was an important scholar of Romanian folklore and Jewish studies who was expelled from Romania in 1885 because of his Zionist activities. Gaster moved to England, where he was appointed the *hacham* (chief rabbi) of the Spanish and Portuguese congregation and

Figure 4.1. Portrait of Moses Gaster. *Source: Ost und West*, nr. 8–9/1904. Wikimedia Commons. Public domain.

served as principal of Lady Judith Montefiore College and as the president of the English Zionist Federation.[1]

In 1925, Samuel Levi Bensusan, the Anglo-Jewish Theosophist who was discussed in the previous chapter, recruited Gaster to publish in *The Theosophical Review*, which he took on editing at the time. Gaster accepted Bensusan's invitation and published "The Divine Name and the Creative Word" in the first volume of the new series.[2] He continued to publish articles and book reviews in the following volumes.[3] In 1928, Gaster was invited to give a lecture at the Jewish Lodge of Theosophists.[4] I do not know whether Gaster accepted the invitation or if he had any other connections with the Jewish Lodge of Theosophists (which will be discussed in the following chapter).

Although Gaster published in *The Theosophical Review*, he did not become a member of the Theosophical Society and seems to have had some reservations about it.[5] Gaster had closer connections with the Quest Society, which was founded by G. R. S. Mead in 1906, after the latter left the Theosophical Society. Gaster, who became acquainted with Mead in the 1920s, took part in the Quest Society's meetings, gave lectures, and published an article ("A Gnostic Fragment from the Zohar") in *The Quest*, the society's journal.[6] In 1925, Gaster became the president of the Quest Society and gave a presidential address entitled "The Quest Universal."[7]

Gaster was interested in Jewish esotericism and published several articles about the Kabbalah and the *Zohar* (one of them, as mentioned above, was published in *The Quest*). His interest in Kabbalah was formed before he became acquainted with the Theosophical Society and the Quest Society. It was probably his scholarly interests in Jewish esotericism and his favorable stance to Kabbalah that prompted his connections with them.[8]

Jewish Followers of Rudolf Steiner and the Anthroposophical Society

Rudolf Steiner, the charismatic leader of the German Section of the Theosophical Society, who rejected Annie Besant's proclamation of Krishnamurti as the new world teacher, left the Theosophical Society in 1912 and established the Anthroposophical Society. The doctrines and activities of the new society were based on Steiner's unique amalgam of Theosophy, Christian Esotericism, and German idealist philosophy. Most of the members of the German Section of the Theosophical Society, including its Jewish members, followed Steiner and joined the Anthroposophical Society.

Two central figures in the German Section of the Theosophical Society who had Jewish origins were Adolf Arenson (1855–1936) and his friend and son-in-law, Carl Unger (1878–1929). Arenson, who was born to a Jewish family with Sephardic roots in Altona, was a businessman and a music composer. He joined the Theosophical Society in the early twentieth century together with his wife, Deborah, née Piza. He was active in the Stuttgart Theosophical lodge, served on the board of the German Section, and became very close to Rudolf Steiner, who appointed him as a subwarden in the esoteric school of the society. Arenson took part in the publication of Steiner's lectures and composed music for Steiner's mystery dramas. Following the split of the German Section from the Theosophical Society, Arenson joined the Anthroposophical Society and headed the Stuttgart branch. He published several books, including one on the "Sermon on the Mount," one on the childhood story of Jesus, and a guide through

Steiner lecture cycles, which served for many years as a major study aid for Steiner's teachings.[9] Notwithstanding his commitment and interest in Anthroposophical Christology, Arenson was proud of his Jewish Sephardic heritage and asserted that esoteric Judaism was compatible with esoteric Christianity.[10] According to the Russian author and Anthroposophist Andrej Belyj (1880–1934), Arenson was interested in Kabbalah and attempted to "integrate modern music with the thousand-year tradition of Jewish Gnosis" in his compositions for Steiner's mystery plays.[11]

Dr. Carl Unger (1878–1929) was born in Bad Cannstatt. His grandfather was a mathematics professor, and his father, a banker. Unger studied mechanical engineering and opened a machine tool factory. He joined the Theosophical Society in 1903 and met Steiner for the first time in 1904. He was active in the Stuttgart lodge, the German Section, and the esoteric school of the society, together with his friend Adolf Arenson, whose daughter Auguste he married in 1907. He lectured extensively in Germany and Switzerland and published several books. After Steiner's separation from the Theosophical Society, Unger joined the Anthroposophical Society, became one of its central leaders, and served on its central board. In January 1929, just before delivering a lecture in Nuremberg, he was shot and killed by a mentally disturbed fellow member of the Anthroposophical Society.[12]

Among the Jewish Theosophists who became followers of Steiner were also artists Richard Pollack-Karlin (1867–1943) and his wife, Hilde Pollack Kotanyis (1874–1943). Richard, who studied art in Prague, was a friend of Friedrich Eckstein and joined the Blue Lotus Theosophical lodge, which was founded by Gustav Meyrink. He was first a follower of the German occultist Alois Mailänder (1844–1905) and later became a follower of Rudolf Steiner. In 1912, Richard married Hilda Kontányi, an artist who was born to Jewish parents in Vienna and was also interested in occultism and Theosophy. Richard and Hilda joined the Anthroposophist Society and in 1914 relocated to headquarters in Dornach, where they were part of the group of painters who decorated the first Gothenaum. Richard, who was very interested in Christian mysticism, was affected by stigmata (bodily signs corresponding to the crucifixion wounds of Christ). Richard and Hilda returned to Prague in the early 1920s and were active in the Anthroposophical circle there. In 1943, they were deported by the Nazis to Theresienstadt concentration camp and murdered the same year in the Treblinka extermination camp.[13]

Berta Fanta's Circle in Prague

Many of the Jewish followers of Rudolf Steiner and Anthroposophy in Prague were affiliated with the German-speaking Theosophical circle in Prague, which met at the salon of the Jewish intellectual Berta Fanta (1866–1918).[14] Berta Fanta (née Sohr), who came from a well-off, assimilated Jewish family and was married to the wealthy Jewish pharmacist Max Fanta (1858–1925), held a philosophical salon, which first met at the Café Louvre and later, at the Fantas' residence. Fanta became interested in Hinduism, Spiritualism, and Theosophy in the first decade of the twentieth century.[15] Her sister, Ida Freund (1868–1931), a feminist and a Spiritualist, as well as Fanta's daughter Else (1886–1969) and Else's husband, the philosopher and Zionist activist Samuel Hugo Bergmann (1883–1975), shared Fanta's esoteric and Theosophical interests.[16] In 1912, Fanta and her sister formed a new lodge of the German Section of the Theosophical Society in Prague. (The other lodges in Prague belonged to the Bohemian Section of the society. The first lodge in Prague, the Blue Star Lodge, was opened in 1891.)[17] The German-speaking lodge, which included twenty-one members, was later named by Rudolf Steiner the Bolzano Lodge, to commemorate the philosopher from Prague and to honor Hugo Bergmann, who published a book about him.[18] Later, following Rudolf Steiner's separation from the Theosophical Society, the lodge joined the Anthroposophical Society,[19]

Steiner, who visited Prague several times and gave lectures to the Theosophical circles and the larger public, visited Fanta's Salon and lectured to its members, which included Hugo Bergmann, Max Brod, Franz Kafka, and Albert Einstein. Else Bergmann recalled these lectures in her diary: "Steiner's lectures were crowded, and all the intellectuals were electrified by Steiner's novel impulses. I remember noticing during the lectures, how Franz Kafka's eyes lightened and sparkled, and a delighted smile brightened his face."[20] Although Kafka criticized Steiner's lectures in his diaries, he made a private appointment with him in which he told him of his clairvoyant experiences and discussed his attraction to and fear of Theosophy.[21] Albert Einstein, however, was less impressed by Steiner.[22]

Hugo Bergmann, a young philosopher who was active in the Jewish student organization in Prague and was also interested in Kabbalah (he translated passages from the *Zohar* together with his friend Ernst Müller), became interested in Theosophy, through Berta Fanta. On December 18, 1918, while watching over the body of his deceased mother-in-law, he wrote

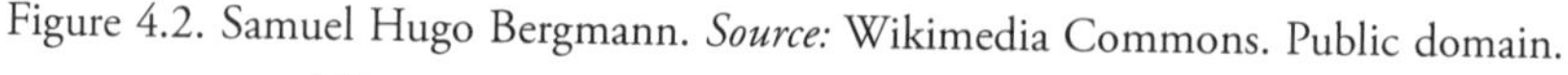

Figure 4.2. Samuel Hugo Bergmann. *Source:* Wikimedia Commons. Public domain.

in his diary: "How much, Mama, did we experience together in theosophy! At first, I laughed at you. Then you won me over and we went [to lectures], together, and I defended the old view against your growing skepticism."[23] Bergmann met Steiner for the first time in 1910 and received spiritual exercises from him.[24] He attended Steiner's public lectures in Prague, participated in a closed circle of Steiner followers during his studies in Berlin in 1912, and watched the performance of one of Steiner's mystical plays in Munich.[25] Steiner, from his side, read Bergmann's anthology of Torah translations, *Worte Mosis*, which was published in 1913, and lauded it in a lecture he gave in 1914.[26] However, Steiner did not regard Bergmann's Zionist convictions and activities favorably. In a lecture he gave in 1924, in which he explained his objections to Zionism, Steiner recalled a conversation he had before World War I, with "a distinguished Zionist friend"—referring, most probably, to Bergmann—who aspired to travel to the Land of Israel to establish the Jewish State. Steiner recalled that he told him that such a particularistic national project was not suitable for the time.[27] During the war, in which Bergmann participated as an officer, Bergmann continued to read Steiner's writings and to correspond with him.[28] In 1919, previous to his immigration to Palestine, Bergmann visited Steiner in the Anthroposophical headquarters in Dornach, Switzerland.[29] Later that year, Bergmann traveled to London, where he served as the head of the cultural department at the Central Zionist office. In a letter he sent to Steiner from there, Bergmann related that he attended lectures at the London Theosophical Society.[30]

Under the impact of Hugo Bergmann, Berta Fanta became interested in Zionism and planned to immigrate to Palestine with her daughter and son-in-law. However, she died of a heart attack in 1918, before she could fulfill her plan. Her sister, Ida Freund, became an ardent Anthroposophist and, like some other Anthroposophical Jews, converted to Christianity. In 1925, she founded the Anthroposophical Christian Community (Christengemeinshcaft) in Prague.[31]

Hugo Bergmann immigrated to Palestine in 1920 and served as the first director of the Hebrew University Library in Jerusalem. In 1935, he was elected as the first rector of the Hebrew University. Although he never joined the Anthroposophical Society, he continued to be interested in Steiner's teaching throughout his life.[32] After his immigration to Palestine, he wrote a few articles on Steiner's ideas (one of them was published in the festschrift in honor of Gershom Scholem). He was in contact with the Anthroposophical circles in Israel and wrote the introduction to the Hebrew translation of Steiner's *How to Know Higher Worlds*, which was published in 1960.[33] Notwithstanding his admiration of Steiner, he also expressed doubts about his teaching and criticized his followers.[34] Nonetheless, he recognized that Steiner had a great impact on his life and on his thought and believed Steiner was "one of the great teachers of humanity."[35]

Ernst Müller and His Interest in Kabbalah

In the second chapter, I discussed the activities of Friedrich Eckstein in the Austrian Section of the Theosophical Society in the late nineteenth century. Another Jewish scholar who became active in the Theosophical Society in Vienna in the early twentieth century was Ernst Müller (1880–1954), who became a lifelong follower of Rudolf Steiner and Anthroposophy.

Müller, whose father was a doctor, and both his grandfathers served as rabbis, was born in Misslitz (now Miroslav, Czech Republic) and later moved with his family to Vienna. Although his first intention was to become a rabbi, his interests turned to philosophy, physics, and mathematics. In

1897, he met Theodore Herzl and became an active Zionist. He published articles in the Zionist paper *Die Welt*, edited by Martin Buber, and became a close friend of Samuel Hugo Bergmann, who shared his interests in Western esotericism and Kabbalah. In 1907, Müller traveled to Palestine, where he took a teaching position at the recently founded Hebrew Gymnasium in Jaffa. He stayed in Palestine for only two years and had to leave because he contracted malaria. After his return to Vienna, he found a position as the librarian of the Jewish community of Vienna. He worked there (with an interval during the First World War) until the library was closed by the Nazis. In 1939, he escaped to England and lived in London in great poverty until his death in 1954.[36]

Müller became interested in Spiritualism and occultism as a student in Vienna, and in 1899, he attended a lecture of the Theosophist Franz Hartmann, together with his brother Edmund, who became active in the Theosophical Society. After his return from Palestine, Ernst Müller also joined the society. In 1910, he met Rudolf Steiner and attended his lectures. In 1911, during his visit to Prague, he attended another series of lectures by Steiner, which were held in the Theosophical circle of Berta Fanta, the mother-in-law of the above-mentioned Samuel Hugo Bergrman. Steiner made a very strong impression on Müller. He became his lifelong follower and joined Steiner when he left the Theosophical Society and founded the Anthroposophical Society.

Under the impact of Buber's writing on Hasidism and the influence of Steiner's teachings, Müller became interested in Kabbalah. In 1909, during his stay in Palestine, he visited, the "Kabbalistic" town Safed, together with the author Shmuel Yosef Agnon. Later, during his stay in Prague in 1911, he began to study the *Zohar*, together with Hugo Bergmann, at the home of Berta Fanta. In 1913, Bergmann and Müller published translations of *Zohar* excerpts in German in the volume *Vom Judentum*, which was published by the Zionist student association in Prague.[37] Müller published further translations of *Zoharic* articles in Buber's journal *Der Jude* between 1913 and 1920.[38] In 1920, he published a book about the *Zohar* and its teachings (*Der Sohar und Seine Lehre*), and in 1932, he published an anthology of *Zoharic* articles translated into German.[39] In 1928, he published a German translation of Isaac Luria's hymns for the Sabbath meals.[40]

In 1924, under the impact of Steiner's teaching and spiritual exercises, Müller published an article in *Der Jude* on the biblical story of creation, in which he tried to show the unity of form and content inherent in the Hebrew words of Genesis.[41] Müller further presented his Anthroposophical-inspired ideas of the mystical meaning of the Hebrew language, in a series of articles that he published in Jewish and Anthroposophical journals between 1928 and 1934.[42] During this period, Müller organized Anthroposophical study groups, in which several young Jews, some of them affiliated with the Zionist youth movement, participated.[43]

In 1939, following the Anschluss, Müller escaped from Vienna to London, where he lived in poverty but continued his work on Anthroposophy and Jewish mysticism and kept in touch with other Jewish Anthroposophists who fled from Germany and Austria, including some who immigrated to Palestine. In 1946, he published a monograph entitled *A History of Jewish Mysticism.* The book, in which he presents his ideas concerning the history and nature of Jewish mysticism, was written originally in German and translated to English by Maurice Simon, an Anglo-Jewish scholar who took part in the publication of the Soncino English edition of the *Zohar.* In 1952, two years before he passed away, Müller published an autobiographical account of his spiritual itinerary, in which he discussed the relation between Judaism, Christianity and Anthroposophy and expressed his aspiration to bring Judaism and Christianity together.[44]

The Jewish Followers of Nicholas and Helena Roerich

Finally, before turning to the next chapter, which will discuss the foundation of the Association of Hebrew Theosophists, I would like to discuss the American Jewish followers of the Russian Theosophists Nicholas and Helena Roerich, the founders of the Agni Yoga Society (also known as Living Ethics), one of the largest offshoots of the Theosophical Society.

The Russian symbolist artist Nicholas Roerich and his wife, Helena, became interested in Theosophy, as well as in Spiritualism, occultism, and Eastern religions in the early twentieth century.[45] After they left Russia in 1918, they traveled in Scandinavia and then stayed in London, where they officially joined the Theosophical Society.[46] In 1920, they moved to New York, where they stayed for three years before continuing their travels in Europe and India.

During that period, a circle of followers and admirers gathered around Nicholas and Helena, who became the inner circle of the emerging Agni Yoga movement. Most, if not all, of the members of the inner circle were of Jewish origins. They included the journalist Frances Ruth Grant (1896–1993), the daughter a German Jew who immigrated from Germany to Albuquerque,

New Mexico; Zina (Zinaida) Lichtman (née Shafran, 1889–1983) and her husband, Maurice Lichtman (1887–1948), both talented musicians who were born at Kamenetz-Podolsk (in western Ukraine), studied in Vienna, and immigrated to New York in 1912, where they opened the Lichtman Piano Institute; Esther Lichtman (1892–1990), Maurice's sister, who was also a musician; Sophia Shafran (1871–1954), Zina's mother; Nettie Horch (née Silverstein, 1896–1991), a school friend of Ruth Grant, who was born in New York to Jewish immigrants from Russia; and Nettie's husband, Louis Levi Horch (1889–1979), a successful Wall Street exchange broker of Jewish German descent who was born in New Orleans.[47]

The members of the inner circle accepted Nicholas and Helena Roerich as their gurus, studied with them, practiced automatic writing, participated in séances, and received messages and instructions, especially through Helena, from Master Morya, one of Blavatsky's mahatmas, who first manifested himself to Helena by the name *Allal-Ming*. They accompanied the Roerichs in their travels, supported them financially, and helped them

Figure 4.3. Left to right, sitting: Esther Lichtmann, Sina Lichtmann, Nicholas Roerich, Nettie Horch, Frances Grant; standing: Louis Horch, Sofie Shafran, Svetoslav Roerich, Maurice Lichtmann, Tatiana Grebenshchikova, Georgii Grebenshchikov, December 7, 1924. *Source:* Nicholas Roerich Museum, New York. Used with permission.

establish their main institutes and propagate their teachings. Ruth Grant was one of the founders and later, one of the vice presidents of the Nicholas Roerich Museum, which was established in 1923. Grant, who received the esoteric name *Modra* from Morya, lectured and published articles on the teaching of Roerich, translated his works to English,[48] and in 1936, published *Oriental Philosophy*, which was illustrated by Nicholas Roerich.[49] Maurice and Zina Lichtman, whose esoteric names were *Avirah* and *Radna*, founded the Master Institute of United Arts with Nicholai and Helena, which was opened in 1921 and became the headquarters of the Agni Yoga movement. Maurice also served as the second vice president of the Roerich Museum.

Louis Horch, who received the esoteric name *Logvan*, was the main financial supporter of the Roerichs. He bought the building at 310 Riverside Drive that housed the Master Institute, funded the travels and expeditions of the Roerich family, and served as the president of the Roerich Museum. He also translated into English the first book of the Agni Yoga, which was based on Morya's revelations to the circle, *Leaves of Morya's Garden*.[50] However, in 1935, a rift was created in the circle. Louis and Nettie Horch and Esther Lichtman (who received direct messages from Master Morya) challenged Helena's supreme authority and severed their connections with the Roerichs. Louis Horch ousted Nicholas and Helena from the board of trustees of the Roerich Museum, took legal control of it, and sued Roerich for the money he advanced to him.[51] In the late 1930s, Ruth Grant also distanced herself from Helena and Nicholas.[52] Maurice and Zina Licthman remained faithful to their gurus, and Zina (who divorced Maurice in 1939 and married the jazz musician Dudley Fosdik) continued to be active in the Agni Yoga Society until her death in 1983.

Nicholas and Helena Roerich tried to propagate their teachings, through their Jewish followers, to the wider Jewish community. According to Helena's diary notes, Master Morya suggested translating *Leaves of Morya's Garden* into Hebrew in February 1922 (as the diaries were written in Russian, *Hebrew* probably meant Yiddish).[53] Later, in December 1922, Morya dictated that the book be published in Russian, English, "Hebrew," and German.[54] Horch was assigned to publish the English translation, and the Lichtmans, the "Hebrew" translation (and later, a German one). The Yiddish translation was published in 1926 under the title *Bleter Fun M's Gorten*.[55]

In March 1922, the Roerichs started a short-term association with Boruch Rivkin (the penname of *Baruch Abraham Weinrib*, 1883–1945), a Yiddish journalist and literary critic who was interested in spiritualism and parapsychology. Rivkin, who was born in Latvia and emigrated to the United

States in 1911 and began publishing a Yiddish weekly, *Nature and Miracle* (נאטור און וועגדער). The weekly, that stopped appearing after a few months, aimed to shed light on the "hidden powers in men, that determines their life and destiny," considering "the new life philosophy" that Rivkin identified as "new Hassidism." In the fifth issue of *Nature and Miracle*, published in April 1922, Rivkin published a Yiddish translation of an article by Nicholas Roerich, "The Redemptive Art," which he said was written especially for *Nature and Miracle*.[56] The article was followed by an announcement of the editor that the brilliant Russian painter would contribute articles, poems, and reproductions of his paintings to the newspaper. Rivkin added that *Nature and Miracle* shared the same belief as Roerich—a messiah of sorts—that redemption comes through art.[57] In the sixth and last issue of the weekly, which was accompanied with a reproduction of a painting by Roerich, Rivkin published a Yiddish translation of Leonid Andreyev's article, "The Realm of Roerich,"[58] and an article entitled "The Messiah Will Come in a Play, on September 27, 1931," in which he tells of his meeting with Roerich and of the messianic prophecy he received from Roerich's invisible teacher.[59] According to Rivkin, the invisible teacher (whom he compares to Socrates's daemon and to Rabbi Joseph Karo's heavenly teacher) informed him that he and Roerich would meet again, in Russia, on September 27, 1931, on "the date of the great holiday of the spirit" (יום טוב פון דעם גייסט גרויסען). Rivkin related that this prophecy was declared fifteen minutes after the meeting started, following his explanation that the goal of *Nature and Wonder* was to prepare the Jews for the coming of the messiah. Rivkin included in his article a song that Roerich sent him after the visit, entitled "Mount Moriah," which alludes to the name of Master Morya. Rivkin does not mention explicitly the name of Roerich's invisible teacher but relates that he is a living human being who resides in Tibet and is the reincarnation of all the great teachers of humanity.

The cooperation with Rivkin is mentioned a few times in the diary of Helena Roerich. According to Helena, Master Morya suggested approaching Rivkin on March 1922.[60] At the end of April, following Rivkin's publications on Roerich in *Nature and Wonder*, Morya said, "We rejoice at Rivkin's deed; We need to remember the day of the magazine's release; You must be able to judge Rivkin by his spirit."[61]

Although the publication of *Nature and Wonder* stopped, Rivkin continued to be in touch with Roerich and his followers. In a letter that Nicholas sent from Vichy to his to his followers in New York, in June 1923, he wrote, "It's a pity we can't read the Jewish newspapers—I feel there must be something good there. Regards to Rivkin—let him hold out."[62]

Nicholas and Helena Roerich assigned their Jewish followers a role in their "grand plan" to establish a messianic, Euro-Asian "New Country" under the leadership of the masters.[63] According to entries from Zina Lichtman's diary from 1924, Maurice Lichtman was commissioned to contact his parents in Kamenets-Podolsk, to prepare the Jews for the "New Country." According to Zina, the Roerichs planned for Maurice, Zina, and Esther Lichtman to travel to their hometown and for Maurice to publish a book of his essays and Helena Roerich's writings in Hebrew (probably, meaning Yiddish) under the pen name *Bolshem* (i.e., Baal Shem, master of the name, the Hebrew appellation given to wonder workers, the most famous of them, the founder of the Hasidic movement, Israel Baal Shem Tov). In these essays, Maurice was to call upon the Jews to take a role in the practical work in the "New Country."[64]

Nicholas and Helena Roerich's Jewish followers played an important role in the formation of Agni Yoga, and Jews were given a central place in the esoteric-political plan of the Roerichs. The attempts of the Roerichs and their Jewish followers to reach a wider Jewish audience did not seem to have a great success. However, it is interesting to note that in 1930, the American diplomat William R. Castle told the British ambassador in Washington that Roerich was "backed in a remarkable manner by the whole Jewish community of New York."[65]

Chapter 5

The Association of Hebrew Theosophists

In the preceding chapters, we observed that Jews have been part of the Theosophical Society since its inception in 1875. As the Theosophical Society expanded and gained prominence during the late nineteenth and early twentieth centuries, Jews were actively engaged in Theosophical lodges and national sections worldwide. Moreover, Jews also played a significant role in various offshoots of the Theosophical Society, including the Quest Society, Anthroposophy, and the Agni Yoga movement. In some instances, Jewish followers of Theosophy established their own lodges or Theosophical circles, where the majority, if not all, of the members were Jewish. These include the Livorno lodge, founded by a follower of Rabbi Elijah Benamozegh, the Theosophical circle of Berta Fanta in Prague (which later aligned with the Anthroposophical Society), the inner circle of the Agni Yoga movement in New York, and possibly, a group of Jewish Theosophists in Ahmadabad.

In the mid-1920s, several Jewish Theosophists, in different locations, suggested forming a Jewish association withing the framework of the Theosophical Society. In 1925, during the Jubilee congress of the society, several Jewish delegates founded the Association of Hebrew Theosophists. Later, the association opened branches in India, Holland, Iraq, England, Poland, and the United States. The American branch, which was especially active, published a journal for several years, *The Jewish Theosophist*. However, the different branches of the Association of Hebrew Theosophists ceased their activities in the 1930s. In this chapter, I will examine the foundation of the Association of Hebrew Theosophists, the various branches of the association, and its main activities.

The Foundation of the Hebrew Association

On December 6, 1925, J. H. Perez, a Jewish businessman and the general secretary of the Theosophical Society in Egypt embarked on board the SS *Pilsna* at Port Said, on his way to the Jubilee congress of the Theosophical Society in Adyar. During the voyage to India, Perez met three other Jewish Theosophists, who were among the seventy-seven delegates on board—M. Cohen, from Sofia, Bulgaria; Gaston Polak, the general secretary of the Belgian Section of the Society;[1] and Pia Muller, a Jewish Theosophist from Trieste, Italy. In his article "A Short History of the Foundation of the AHT," Perez wrote: "It was at the second or the third meeting that the idea came to us to create an Association of Hebrew Theosophists, and on the spot, before reaching Bombay, we had a kind of official meeting with regular minutes during which the 'baby Association' was conceived."[2]

Soon after reaching Adyar, Perez met with Samuel Suliman Cohen, originally from the town of Basra, in Iraq, who was studying at the time at the Theosophical Brahmavidya Ashrama in Adyar. Perez related the Cohen asked him to give a lecture on Judaism at the third annual meeting of the Congress of Religions, which was held at Madras at the same time. Perez wrote that he was not able to deliver the lecture and offered Cohen to present it.[3] Yet, it was another Jewish delegate, Abraham Barak Salem, a member of the Jewish community in Cochin, who finally gave the lecture. On Friday, January 1, 1926, Salem noted in his diary: "went over to see Madame Muller, Cohen, Peretz, Polak & others . . . Motored with Adyar friends to the Universal Religious Conference & lectured on 'Judaism' to a crowded hall in the Triplicane Hindu High School Swami Shradhananda presided."[4]

Perez noted that "the lecture was a cause of bringing the group of four Jews of the SS *Pilsna* in contact with another group of half a dozen other Jews from various parts of India and Mesopotamia."[5] These included, apart from Cohen and Salem, Dr. Jacob E. Solomon, from Ahmedabad; his wife, Sarah Solomon; E. I. Bashi and E. M. Joseph, Baghdadi Jews from Bombay; and A. Isaac, from Poona.[6]

Perez related that the group of Jews from India and Iraq "also caught the thought which had come to us on board and was planning a Jewish association. The actual Association of Hebrew Theosophists came to life from the combination of the aspirations of both groups."[7] Albert Schwarz, the treasurer of the Theosophical Society (and Annie Besant's lawyer), who resided in Adyar, probably also took part in the decision to establish the association. The Jewish delegates who met in Adyar elected Gaston Polak as the president of the association, M. Cohen as the secretary, and J. H. Perez as the treasurer.[8] The first activity of the nascent association was to lay a foundation for building a synagogue at the Adyar compound. Annie Besant, the president of the Theosophical Society, laid the foundation stone, and A. B. Salem conducted the ceremony, in Hebrew.

Annie Besant wrote of the foundation of a Jewish association in the editorial ("On the Watch Tower") of the February 1926 issue of *The Theosophist*:

> It is very interesting to notice the signs that Theosophy is more and more attracting members of the great religions. Last month we printed a proposal from the Christian Mystic lodge for the formation of a T. S. Christian league; now we have a suggestion for an association of Hebrew Theosophists. I welcome all such ideas, for the study of each religion by its own members can only make them value it more, and also help them to feel how much

Figure 5.1. The founders of the Association of Hebrew Theosophists. Left to right: J. H. Perez, Cairo; Gaston Polak, Brussels; S. Solomon, Ahmedabad; Pia Muller, Trieste; M. Cohen, Sophia; A. B. Salem, Cochin; Mr. E. M. Joseph, Bombay; Dr. Jacob E. Solomon, Ahmedabad; A. Isaac, Poona; S. S. Cohen, Adyar; E. I. Bashi, Bombay. *Source: The Jewish Theosophist* 1, no. 4 (July 1927): 4. Courtesy of the National Library of Israel collections. Public domain.

Figure 5.2. J. H. Perez. *Source: The Jewish Theosophist* 1, no. 4 (July 1927): 1. Courtesy of the National Library of Israel collections. Public domain.

Figure 5.3. S. S. Cohen. *Source: The Jewish Theosophist* 1, no. 2 (December 1926): 3. Courtesy of the National Library of Israel collections. Public domain.

they have in common with other faiths. . . . Mr. G. Polak, of Brussels, Belgium, is the president of the Hebrew Association, Mr. S. S. Cohen, Theosophical Society Adyar, is the secretary, and Mr. A. Schwarz, the treasurer.[9] The foundation stone of a Hebrew synagogue was laid in the Headquarters estate in December 1925, and there should be some Hebrew resident to take charge of it when it is built.[10]

In April 1926, the founders of the Association of Hebrew Theosophists announced its foundation in *The Theosophist* and in *The Messenger* (the journal of the American Theosophical Society).[11] They reported on the foundation of the association at the Jubilee congress and stated its objects:

1. To study Judaism in the light of Theosophy and Theosophy in the light of Judaism

2. To spread Theosophical teachings among the Jews

3. To undertake any other activity which could aid in the realization of the objects of the Association.[12]

According to the founders, "The Association proposes to bring to light all the hidden spiritual riches of the Jewish religion. A profound study of this last in the light of Theosophy will undoubtedly lead to the increase of Theosophical information in this field, while this same study will help the Jews to understand their own religion."[13]

In the editorial to the April 1926 issue of *The Theosophist*, Besant wrote again about the foundation of the Association of Hebrew Theosophists and expressed her hope that its foundation would enable the Jews to recognize the world teacher in his second coming:

I am very glad to welcome the association; it would be indeed splendid if some of the Nation which ignorantly rejected the World Teacher when He came to them using the body of a Jewish disciple as His vehicle, should welcome Him on his return 2000 years later. Who knows what word He may have for the ancient people to whom He came on his previous visit, when He manifested Himself in Palestine. Will he lift them up again among the nations of the world? St. Paul looked forward to such a revival of his people and likened it to "life from the dead."[14]

As we shall see later, the anti-Jewish and Christological ideas expressed in Besant welcome announcement stimulated attacks from Jewish circles against the Association of Hebrew Theosophists. In November 1926, Besant published another message to the Hebrew Theosophists, this time avoiding any mention of the Jews ignorant rejection of Christ and the second coming of the world teacher:

> Friends: It is a great happiness to me to see members of the great Hebrew race enriching Theosophy with contributions from their ancient Faith. Much wisdom in enshrined in their occult treaties, and European philosophy and metaphysics owe much to the subtle genius of the Hebrew Nation. Great have been its sufferings in the past, but the greater will be its gifts in the future to the human race. Step forward, then, Brothers, and take your rightful place among the Nations. Israel has a future and a work to accomplish therein.
>
> Last year I had the pleasure of laying the foundation stone of the Hebrew Synagogue on the Theosophical Society's estate at Adyar, and in our daily Act of Worship a Hebrew Theosophist chanted a Hebrew prayer. Your faith has thus its first place among the faiths of the world, each of which is erecting its temple in that Home of Divine Wisdom.[15]

Raising funds for the building of the Adyar synagogue became one of the central activities of the Association of Hebrew Theosophists. A special committee was established for it (consisting of the founding members of the association). In April 1926, S. S. Cohen, the secretary of the committee, published, in the *Adyar Bulletin*, an appeal for support to build the synagogue (whose costs were estimated to be 20000 RS, 1000 of which were donated by the founders of the association).[16] Further appeals were published in the following year.[17] The American Section of the of the Association of Hebrew Theosophists also established an Adyar synagogue committee.[18] Plans for the proposed synagogue were published,[19] as well as lists of the donations to the Adyar synagogue fund.[20] In spite of these efforts, the Hebrew Theosophists were not able to raise sufficient funds for building the synagogue. In the 1927 general report of the Theosophical Society, S. S. Cohen wrote, "The funds of the Adyar Synagogue are still very low, making it impossible for us to start the building."[21] The synagogue has still not been built.

In 1926, the newly established association published *The Plea for Judaism*, a book by the Anglo-Jewish Theosophist Leonard Bosman. In the book, Bosman relates to the foundation of the Hebrew association and to its mission to spread Theosophy to the Jews and to revivify Judaism through bringing back its deeper, unmaterialistic, truths: "Having found the Light, he (i.e, the author, Bosman), in company with other Jewish Theosophists, is anxious to share it with his compatriots. Hence the new movement, founded within the Theosophical Society, to revivify Judaism by seeking to bring back to it the deeper truths so long overshadowed by materialistic wanderings."[22] Some other books and pamphlets, as well as a journal, which will be discussed in detail in the following, were published by the American Section of the Association of Hebrew Theosophists. There were also plans, reported by S. S. Cohen, to finance a publication of a Hebrew translation of Krishnamurti's "At the Feet of the Master."[23]

The founders of the Association of Hebrew Theosophists invited Jewish members of the Theosophical Society to join the association and to form local Jewish Theosophical groups. In their first appeal to members of the Theosophical Society, they wrote, "We appeal to Jewish Theosophists all over the world to join us and to organize themselves in every country, forming small committees which will be responsible for collecting subscriptions for the Synagogue, and which will undertake to work through the medium of the local press and in other ways for the realization of the object of the Association."[24]

Members of the Association of Hebrew Theosophists organized meetings of Jewish members during Theosophical conventions. In the December 1926 convention in Benares, several Jewish members met and "resolved unanimously to support *The Jewish Theosophist* and the synagogue fund, to appeal for collection of books on Jewish literature, philosophy, religions, history, etc., for a library which must be attached to the Adyar synagogue for the use of the Hebrew Theosophists students who will come to Adyar in the course of time to study deeply the Jewish literature in the light of Theosophy."[25]

In the summer of 1927, about forty Jewish Theosophists and representatives of the Hebrew association from Italy, Austria, Czechoslovakia, Poland, Romania, Egypt, Holland, Belgium, France, and England participated in the camp congress of the Order of the Star that took place in Ommen, Holland. The Jewish members met and heard a lecture by Gaston Polak, the president of the Association of Hebrew Theosophists, about the genius and the mission of the Jew to the world. The participants in the meeting decided to arrange a conference of the Hebrew association in Brussels, Belgium, in July 1928.[26] However, it seems that the plan did not materialize.

The Association of Hebrew Theosophists nominated national representatives in different countries and encouraged the establishment of local sections of the associations. According to a report published in December 1927,[27] the Association of Hebrew Theosophists had national representatives in India (Rueben Ani), Egypt (J. H. Perez), Belgium (Gaston Polak), Bulgaria (M. Cohen), England (S. I. Heiman), America (Henry C. Samuels), and Austria (Miss Schlam).[28] The Association of Hebrew Theosophists' directory, published in January 1930, also records representatives in France (Leon Benzimbra),[29] Italy (Pia Muller), Poland (Moses Steinberg), Czechoslovakia (Oscar Beer), Hungary (Elizabeth Kortesz) and Romania (Tuna Schoenberg).[30]

In the 1927 report on the Association of Hebrew Theosophists, sent by the secretary of the association to the president of the Theosophical Society, S. S. Cohen reported on the establishment of national sections and study groups of Jewish Theosophists in America and England and on the slow progress of establishing such a section in India. Cohen expressed the hope that following the meeting of Jewish Theosophists in the Star Congress at Ommen, more national sections would be founded. Indeed, during this period, Jewish Theosophical groups were also formed in Poland and Iraq. In the following, I will discuss the American Section, which became the largest and most active section of the Association of Hebrew Theosophists, and in the next chapter, I will discuss the Jewish Theosophical group in Basra, Iraq, which was excommunicated by rabbinic authorities and established an independent Jewish Theosophical community. Before turning to examine the American Section of the Association of Hebrew Theosophists and its activities, I would like to examine the sections in India, England, Holland, and Poland.

The Indian Section of the Association of Hebrew Theosophists

Indian Jews were active in the Theosophical Society from its very early years in India, and several Indian Jews were active in the foundation of the Association of Hebrew Theosophists. Following the Jubilee congress in Adyar, an Indian Section of the Hebrew association was founded. The president of the Indian Section was the lawyer I. J. Samson from Bombay (who was not among the founders of the association). Samson was a member of the Bene

Israel community who set up a law practice in Bombay in the beginning of the twentieth century and in 1926 was appointed as an additional judge of the Bombay court of small causes. Yet, he did not receive a permanent appointment in the court because of his political activities. In 1924, he joined the Theosophical Society (probably under the influence of his nephew Jacob Solomon of Ahmadabad), became a vegetarian, a follower of Gandhi, and an advocate of the *swadeshi* (buy Indian) movement.[31]

The vice president of the Indian Section of the Association of Hebrew Theosophists was Jacob Solomon, from Ahmadabad, who was one of the original founders of the association. Reuben E. Ani, a member of the Baghdadi community in Bombay, was the treasurer and secretary of the section.[32]

In July 1927, the officers of the Indian Section published "A Message to Jews in India," urging them to join the Hebrew association:

> Dear Brothers. Now it is high time to begin to work for a cause so dear to our heart. Many, many years have gone by since the Theosophical Society was sent by the Masters of wisdom to bless the world by its teachings. But our Jewish people in India held themselves in the background, where they remained unknown for about half a century. Now all the barriers have fallen down. All limitations have dropped before the tremendous uplifting influence of the Jubilee Convention of the TS. . . . [T]he birth of the Association of Hebrew Theosophists was the outcome. It was born to serve our Society, to serve our race—to serve our Society by enriching it with the Jewish thoughts which have been evolving for many centuries from the ancient scriptures of our prophets, and ages of old: to help our race by bringing them to the light of Theosophy, by returning their narrow orthodoxy to a rational broad-mindedness, adorned with intelligent spirituality—a spirituality tinged by the high philosophical conceptions of the races and cultures other than their own.[33]

According to the report of Reuben Ani, published in December 1927, members of the Indian Section of the Hebrew association in Bombay met twice a week for study and discussion.[34] In August 1929, Dr. Wolfgang Von Weisl, the Jewish-Austrian journalist and Zionist activist, reported in his "Indian Travel Sketches," published in *The Reform Advocate*: "Perhaps half the members of the local Zionist group in Bombay . . . are also members of the theosophical movement, and many of them—something totally incomprehensible from the Jewish religious standpoint—are even member of the 'Order of the Star,' that is to say, believers in the so-called new world-savior, Krishnamurti."[35] The Indian Section of the Association of Hebrew Theosophists was active in Bombay at least until 1931.[36] However, the number of Jewish Theosophists in Bombay dwindled by then. In July 1931, the editor of the Bombay Zionist journal, *The Jewish Advocate*, estimated that "although there are a negligible number of theosophists amongst the Jews it would appear that there are very remote chances of this cult spreading much further."[37]

Jewish Theosophists from Karachi also joined the Indian Section of the Association of Hebrew Theosophists. However, in a report presented to the president of the Theosophical Society in December 1927, S.S. Cohen complained, "Progress is very slow on account of its small membership. Large numbers of Theosophist Jews in Karachi and elsewhere have not yet chosen to join us and help us in our movement."[38] Jewish Theosophists in Karachi donated to the Adyar synagogue in 1927,[39] and in 1928, L. Solomon, a Jewish Theosophist from Karachi, published on behalf of the Indian Section of the Hebrew association a booklet by N.E. David, *Karma and Reincarnation in Judaism*.[40] The group in Karachi, headed by L. Solomon was still active in 1930.[41]

The Jewish Lodge:
The English Section of Association of Hebrew Theosophists

Samuel Isaac Heiman, an Anglo-Jewish Theosophist,[42] wrote in the first issue of *The Jewish Theosophist* (the journal of the American Section of the Association of Hebrew Theosophists) that through the years he had thought of doing something to "theosophise Judaism" but that other Jewish fellows of the Theosophical Society in England were apathetic to the idea. But now, he said,

> The news of the forming of the AHT (I think "Jewish" might have been used instead of Hebrew), leave me with no doubt as to the work that we might do. . . . We had our national TS convention last week in London, and I tried whilst up in London to get into touch with Jewish FTS [Fellows of the Theosophical Society]. The Jews to whom I spoke, despite their

previous indifference, seem now to be keen on doing something, and I am hoping a British section of the Association may be formed.[43]

In December 1926, Heiman announced that a section of the Hebrew association was formed in England: "A section of the above Association has been formed in England for the purpose of studying Theosophy in light of Judaism, and Judaism in the light of Theosophy. The Association is composed of members of the Jewish faith who desire to come together for the study of religious truths and to share the results of this study with others. In particular they desire to study Theosophy and Mysticism especially as they are revealed in and affect Judaism."[44] The section, which was titled "The Jewish Lodge," was chartered on October 28, 1927.[45] Heiman was its president, and Mrs. E. Hymans, its treasurer.[46]

In December 1927, S. S. Cohen wrote, based on a report sent to him by Heiman, that the number of members of the Association of Hebrew Theosophists in England had risen from nine to thirty, that study groups were organized in London and Manchester, public lectures were delivered, and a library of the section was opened.[47] The editorial of *The Jewish Theosophist* from the same month reports on the activities of the two groups in England and mentions that the Manchester group organized a public lecture by Dr. Joshua Abelson.[48]

A flyer of the Jewish Lodge, from early 1928, stated that: "The Jewish Lodge has as its special work the encouraging of the study of teachings and philosophy contained in the Kabbalistic and mystic literature of the Jews, together with those in modern Theosophic literature."[49] According to the flyer, the lodge held several study and discussion meetings every month and organized public lectures. The lectures planned for early 1928 included "The Angeles in Literature and Symbolism," by Miss Regina M. Bloch,[50] "Philo-Judaeus, Jewish Theosophist," by David Freeman, and "Some Popular Jewish Views on the Soul," by Dayan Rev. L. Mendelson.[51]

Later that year, Samuel Heiman invited the famous Jewish scholar Moses Gaster, whose connections to the Theosophical Society were discussed in the previous chapter, to give a lecture at the Jewish Lodge.[52] I do not know if Gaster accepted the invitation. The Jewish Lodge was active at least until early 1930. According to a report given in the January 1930 issue of the *Jewish Theosophist*, the Jewish Lodge of the Theosophical Society continued to meet every Sunday evening.[53]

Figure 5.4. Flyer of the Jewish Lodge, London, 1928. *Source:* UCL Special Collections. Used with permission.

In February 1928, a columnist of the *Jewish Chronicle*, who signed by name *Mentor*, discussed, in an article entitled "Strange Faiths," the "Jewish Branch of the Theosophical Society," whose members "relied largely for their inspiration upon the mysticism of the Kabbalah."[54] Although the author accepted that Theosophy can be traced back to Judaism, he argues that Theosophy is an alien faith that is fundamentally opposed to Jewish teaching. *Mentor* relates to the announcement concerning Dayan Mendelson's lecture for the Jewish Lodge and advises him to reconsider his decision.[55] S. I. Heiman wrote a response to *Mentor*, in which he claimed that Theosophy is not alien to Judaism and that some of the greatest sons of Israel have been students and exponents of "the ancient wisdom, or theosophy."[56]

Vereeniging voor Joodsche Theosofen: The Dutch Section of Association of Hebrew Theosophists

Jews have also been active in other European sections of the Theosophical Society since the end of the nineteenth century.[57] In 1926, a Dutch Section of the Association of Hebrew Theosophists, Vereeniging voor Joodsche Theosofen (The Association of Jewish Theosophists) was established.[58] The foundation of the Dutch Section was announced in August 1926, in an article published in the Dutch Theosophical journal, *De Theosofische Beweging*.[59] According to the article, which was probably written by Louis Vet, the president of the section, the purpose of the Jewish association was to study Theosophy in light of Judaism and Judaism in light of Theosophy: "Judaism, illuminated by theosophy, holds many treasures of wisdom that can contribute to the uplifting of humanity in general, but especially for the Jews, who nowadays lack this knowledge."[60] In 1927, Vet published in the same journal a translation of Annie Besant's message to the Hebrew Theosophists, which was discussed above.[61] The establishment of the Dutch Section was announced in *The Jewish Theosophist* in July 1927.[62]

The president of the Dutch Association of Jewish Theosophists was Louis Vet from Utrecht. Louis Vet (1876–1963) was a schoolteacher in the Jewish community. Later, he and his sister Clara (who was also a fellow of the Theosophical Society) ran a bookshop in Utrecht, which was founded by their father, Moses Vet. The secretary and treasurer of the association was Ré Levie (1865–1943), from Bloemendal. Ré (Rebekka) Levie, a piano and English teacher and a women's suffrage activist, joined the Theosophical Society in the first decade of the twentieth century.[63] Similar to other Jewish Theosophists, Levie became interested in Kabbalah. She initiated a Theosophical Kabbalah study group in Amsterdam in 1905, gave lectures on Kabbalah, and discussed the study of Kabbalah by Theosophists at the European Theosophical Congress in Paris in June 1906.[64] Other members of the association were Cato Adelina Nijburg-Lorjé (1879–1959), from Amersfoort; her sister-in-law, Rosalie (Rosa) Lorjé-Wolf (1873–1942), from Amsterdam; Delphina Lena Levie (1890–1943), the younger half-sister of Ré Levie, who was the secretary of the Wahana Theosophical Lodge; Sara Gerarda Cohen (1875–1930), from Amsterdam; Bertha Cohen (1859–1943), who had been active since 1902 in the Dutch Theosophical Society; Gertrude Themans-Godschalk (1875–1957), from Deventer; and Abraham (Bram) Klein (1868–1943) from Amersfoort.[65]

As Alexandra Nagel observed, objections to the foundation of a Jewish Section within the Theosophical Society were voiced by the Dutch Jewish Theosophist Herman van Praag in an article entitled "Again a New Sect?" ("Weer een nieuwe secte?") in the *De Theosofische Beweging*.[66] Van Praag objected to the formation of a separate Jewish Section and called for unity between Christians and Jews within the framework of the Theosophical Society that aspired to create a nucleus of human brotherhood without distinction of race, religion, or creed. Vet answered to Van Praag's criticism, arguing that the aim of the Jewish Section was not to create another Jewish sect, but rather to encourage Jews to join the Theosophical Society, to introduce Jewish wisdom to Theosophy, and to collect funds for the building of the Adyar synagogue.[67] Another Dutch Theosophist, Johannes H. Kengen, from Utrecht, who was an ordained priest of the Theosophical Liberal Catholic Church also responded to Van Praag's objections. Kengen approved of the foundation of the Jewish Section, noting that the national revival of the Jewish people in Palestine also required a religious revival that could not come from Jewish Orthodoxy. The advent of the expected world religion through the Theosophical Society as suggested by Annie Besant in *Evolution and Man's Destiny*, writes Kengen, requires a purification and spiritualization of the existing religions. Kengen compares the role of the Jewish Theosophical Association to that of the Liberal Catholic Church and hopes that the Jews will be sent a "great occultist" who will advance an occult reformation of Judaism, similar to what Leadbeater has done to Christianity and Krishnamurti to Hinduism.[68]

The Dutch Section of the Association of Hebrew Theosophists was active only for a few years. In 1927, Vet published two short updates on the section in the *De Theosofische Beweging*.[69] The January 1930 issue of *The Jewish Theosophist* listed Vet as the national representative of the Association of Hebrew Theosophists in Holland.[70] In 1931, in a letter to the editor of the Dutch Theosophical journal, Vet wrote about the persecution of the Jewish Theosophists in Basra, Iraq (which will be discussed in the next chapter).[71]

In his report, Vet included a letter he had sent to the chief rabbis in the Netherlands concerning the events in Iraq. In 1932, Vet gave a radio talk on the "world bond" between Jewish Theosophists and the Jewish people and delivered a lecture on Kabbalah in the Theosophical lodge in The Hague.[72]

In his account of the foundation of the Association of Hebrew Theosophist, J. H. Perez relates that the founders of the association heard that the thought of establishing an association of Jewish Theosophists had reached "receptive" minds in America and Poland and that "action followed the reception of the thought."[73] The activities in Poland probably refer to the Jewish Lodge in Łodź, "Judaizm Istotny," that was chartered in 1926, headed by Eugenia Steinberg and her husband, which was discussed in chapter 3.[74] I would like to turn now to the activities of the Association of Hebrew Theosophists in America.

The American Section of the Association of Hebrew Theosophists

In May 1926, an announcement entitled "Jewish Theosophists and Star Members—Attention," was published in the American Theosophical journal, *The Messenger*:

> In view of the extraordinary period in the world's history, owing to the immediate Coming [*sic*] of the World-Teacher, we, members of the Theosophical Society and the Order of the Star in the East, who are of the Jewish race, feel that an effort must be made to present to the Jewish people our beliefs about the Coming [*sic*], the existence of the Great White Lodge, Reincarnation and Karma, from an angle best suited to their historical background, and their traditions, and link these truths with the work of the great sages as given in the Midrashim, Mishna, Talmud, and the Kabala. We therefore appeal to all Theosophist and Star members of the Jewish antecedents to present suggestion of ways and means of procedure, and to form some sort of an association of an auxiliary nature to the Theosophical Society and the Order of Star in the East.[75]

The announcement, which does not mention the foundation of the Association of Hebrew Theosophists (although it was announced in the previous issue of *The Messenger*), was signed by three Jewish American fellows of the Theosophical Society: Henry C. Samuels of Seattle, the president pro tem of the suggested Jewish Auxiliary Association; Louis B. Ball of Long Beach, California, the secretary pro tem; and Ephraim Silberman of Milwaukee, the publicity agent pro tem.

A month before this announcement, Alex Horne, the Jewish Theosophist who moved from Shanghai to San Francisco, published in *The Theosophist* an article entitled "Theosophy and Modern Judaism." Horne, who was probably unaware at the time of the initiative of his fellow Jewish Theosophists in America and of the establishment of the Association of Hebrew Theosophists in Adyar, wrote that "it is time that Theosophically-minded Jews the world over banded themselves together for service of their co-religionists, for the purpose of bringing out the highest, the noblest the most beautiful and inspiring truths that Judaism has to offer, to the end that that is mission may be perpetuated and its purpose achieved."[76] Horne expressed the hope that perhaps "a league of Jewish Theosophists will in time be formed, for the centralization of this work" and asked Jewish Theosophists who were working for a similar purpose to make contact with him.

Soon after the publication of these announcements, the American initiators of the Jewish Auxiliary Association joined the Association of Hebrew Theosophists and established its American Section. Later, Alex Horne also joined the section. In May 1926, letters from the "Association of Hebrew Theosophists, American Section, an Auxiliary to the Theosophical Society and the Order of the Star in the East," signed by Ephraim Silberman were sent to Theosophical lodges in the United States.[77]

In the letter, the pro tem officers of the section observed that the Theosophical Society had neglected the study of Judaism: "During the fifty years of the existence of the TS much has been done in the study of and comparison of the different religions, particularly Buddhism, Hinduism and Christianity and to attract the members of these faiths into the TS and its auxiliaries. Judaism alone, of the great world religions has been left out, and up to the present no literature of any importance on the Jewish religion from a Theosophical point of view has been produced." To fill this need and in light of the coming of the world teacher, the American Jewish Theosophists decided to band together "for the purpose of bringing Theosophy and the Message of the Coming to Jews and to translate the ancient Wisdom in terms that are familiar in Jewish tradition by linking these truths with the Jewish mystical teachings." The officers of the section

Figure 5.5. Letter from the Association of Hebrew Theosophists, American Section, sent to the Washington Theosophical lodge. *Source:* The Theosophical Society in America Archives. Used with permission.

… in the … … … ill wait daily for ᵗhis Coming."
(12th Article of the Jewish Faith)

An Auxiliary to The
Theosophical Society
and
The Order of the
Star In The East

Assoc… Hebrew Theosophists

American Section

Milwaukee, Wis.,
May 20, 1926

PRESIDENT,
Henry C. Samuels
323 - 15th Ave. No.
Seattle, Wash.

SECY.-TREAS.
Louis B. Ball
1031 Bennett Ave.
Long Beach, Cal.

Washington Lodge, T. S.,
Washington, D. C.

Fellow Theosophists:

During the fifty years of the existence of the T. S. much has been done in the study and comparison of the different religions, particularly Buddhism, Hinduism and Christianity and to attract the members of these faiths into the T. S. and its auxiliaries.

Judaism alone, of the great world religions has been left out, and up to the present no literature of any importance on the Jewish religion from a Theosophical point of view, has been produced.

In order to fill this need and because of the Coming of the World Teacher, we, Theosophists of the Jewish race feel it is our duty to band ourselves together for the purpose of bringing Theosophy and the Message of the Coming to Jews and to translate the Ancient Wisdom in terms that are familiar in Jewish tradition by linking these truths with the Jewish mystical teachings.

Although our task is great and delicate, we have reason to believe our undertaking will be very successful because the American Jew is liberal and a great number of the East European Jews are natural mystics.

There is no reason why more of the people who in the past made such valuable contribution to occultism, witness, the Kabalah, the mysticism of the Essenes and Hassidism should not be influenced to enter the ranks of the Theosophical Society.

We would consider it a great favor if your Lodge would instruct the Secretary to send us the names and addresses of your Jewish members that we may get in touch with them for the purpose of enlarging our organization and be prepared to do publicity work among Jews before Mrs. Besant comes to America.

We thank you for your co-operation.

Theosophically yours,

ASSOCIATION OF HEBREW THEOSOPHISTS
American Section

Silberman

Publicity Agent.
P. O. Box 657

P. S. Kindly send names and addresses to Mr. Louis B. Ball, 1031 Bennett Avenue, Long Beach, California.

asserted that this undertaking would be successful because "the American Jew is liberal and a great number of the East European Jews are natural mystics. There is no reason why more of the people who in the past made such valuable contribution to occultism, witness, the Kabalah, the mysticism of the Essenes and Hasidism should not be influenced to enter the ranks of the Theosophical Society." The letter ended with a request for the names and addresses of Jewish members of the American lodges, to get in touch with them and enlarge the organization.[78]

The founders of the American Section drafted a constitution that contained ten articles. Later, they published some of them in the journal they founded, *The Jewish Theosophist* (which will be discussed in detail below).[79] The constitution included the objects of the Association of Hebrew Theosophists: "to study Judaism in light of Theosophy and Theosophy in the light of Judaism and to spread Theosophical teaching to the Jews." It further declared:

> The Association recognizes all religions to be the mean to an end—the attainment of Theo-sophia—divine wisdom—and proclaims Judaism to be the means most suitable to the Jewish people. It shall therefore be the aim of the Association to search for and bring out the divine wisdom underlying the Jewish revelation throughout the ages and to make present day Judaism a channel through which ever more and more of the divine wisdom may reveal itself to the heart and mind of man.

According to the constitution, full membership was open to Jewish fellows of the Theosophical Society, and non-Jews could join as associate members.

In December 1926, the American Section announced that the temporary officers of the section were nominated for reelection, with the addition of a vice president, Mrs. W. B. Rubin (1886–1969, also known as Bozena Brydlova), from Milwaukee.[80]

Before turning to examine the activities of the American Section, and especially, the journal it published, *The Jewish Theosophist*, I would like to present the officers of the section and some of the members who were most active in it.

The central figure in the American Section of the Hebrew association was Henry Cohen Samuels (1886–1965), who founded the section, served as its president, and edited its journal. Samuels was born as Henry Cohen Katz in Grodno, Belarus, to Samuel and Gitel (Gertrude) Katz. He immigrated with his parents to England and then, in 1907, to the United States.[81]

In "A History of the Jewish People," published in 1950, Samuels writes that he was brought up in "a strictly Jewish or Hebrew Orthodox home and community."[82] Samuels resided in Milwaukee, Wisconsin, and later, in Spokane and Seattle, Washington, where he worked as a dental mechanic. In 1919, he joined the Theosophical Society and later became active in the Besant Lodge in Seattle, which was established in 1922.[83] As we have seen, Samuels was one of the founders of the American Section of the Association of Hebrew Theosophists. Between 1926 and 1932, he served as its president and edited *The Jewish Theosophist*. His wife, Dora (1892–1980), was also active in the section.[84] Apart from his activities in the Association of Hebrew Theosophists, Samuels was also connected with the Liberal Catholic Church (LCC), a church affiliated with the Theosophical Society that was founded by J. I. Wedgwood and C. W. Leadbeater. According to the 1926 Seattle city directory, Samuels served as the secretary of the local Liberal Catholic Church.[85] It seems that Samuels did not see a conflict between his activities as a Jewish Theosophist and his connection with the Liberal Catholic Church. In an article published in *The Jewish*

Figure 5.6. Henry C. Samuels, editor of *The Jewish Theosophist* and president of the Association of Hebrew Theosophists. *Source: The Jewish Theosophist* 1, no. 2 (December 1926): 3, 1. Courtesy of the National Library of Israel collections. Public domain.

Theosophist, in which he responds to accusation of the Jewish press that the Association of Hebrew Theosophists was leaning toward Christian beliefs, Samuels declares that those who seek to understand the purpose of life and gain happiness "cannot afford to entertain the least resentment against Jesus or any other teacher."[86] Nonetheless, he adds that acceptance of the Theosophical knowledge concerning Christ's nature, as the knowledge of any other facts, "can never make a Jew less Jewish."[87]

During the period in which he served as the president of the American Section of the Hebrew association and as the editor of *The Jewish Theosophist*, Samuels published a modern Jewish prayer book and a booklet entitled *Krishnamurti the Jew*.

Samuels's *Morning Prayer: For Individual and Congregational Jewish Worship*, published in 1928,[88] offers a Theosophical inspired adaptation of the Jewish prayer service. Samuels, who signed the book with the initials *FTS* (Fellow of the Theosophical Society), added to the passages taken from traditional Jewish prayer service (cited in Hebrew and in English translation), prayers that he himself composed, as well as passages from the writings of Krishnamurti and the English Theosophist Mable Collins, a passage from the Liberal Catholic Church liturgy, and several Christian hymns. In one of the prayers he composed, Samuels praises the "great Elder Brother, a son of our own race and kin, Jesus, the Master, who in his great agony held fast to the works of Thy light and love."[89]

In *Krishnamurti the Jew: A Presentation from the Jewish Point of View*,[90] Samuels included excerpts from the writings of Krishnamurti and an article on Krishnamurti by N. E. B. Ezra, the editor of *Israel Messenger*, the official journal of the Shangahi Zionist federation.

Samuels continued to be active in the Theosophical Society in Seattle after the Association of Hebrew Theosophists was dissolved, and *The Jewish Theosophist* stopped appearing. He continued to identify himself as a Hebrew Theosophist and continued publishing books and articles, mostly on questions regarding Judaism and Zionism.[91] In these writings, Samuels developed a unique Christian-Jewish perspective inspired by Theosophy. Samuels claimed that Judaism is just a fraction or denomination of the larger Hebrew faith, which is "fully Christian": "There are obviously three principal faiths in the one Christian religion, namely Hebrew, Catholic and Protestant. In each faith there is a definite belief in Christ (the World Teacher, Emanu-El, etc.). And in each faith there are differing beliefs, views, and expressions about the Christ or the World teacher—and likewise of the Deity."[92] According to Samuels, the Hebrew faith and Jewish religion should be distinguished from the Judaic national group: "The term 'Jewish' refers to a religious community in the world regardless of nationality and race, while the term 'Judea' refers to a state, which historically has a rightful place in Palestine, among the other states there. The term 'Hebrew' refers to a particular faith in the world . . . and the Jewish community is one of several elements in the Hebrew faith, just as a denomination is in the Protestant faith."[93]

I turn now to the other officers of the American Section of the Association of Hebrew Theosophists. Bozena Brydlova, the vice president of the American Section, was born as Bozena Bess Bredle in Iowa, in 1886.[94] Brydlova, who was a teacher and a playwrite, lived in Omaha, Nebraska, with her first husband, the wealthy investor Charles (Chas) Grotte (1868–1927).[95] Following her divorce from Grotte in 1919, Brydlova resided first in New York and later in Hollywood, where she joined the Theosophical Society. She also studied with Shri Yogendra, the founder of the Yoga Institute,[96] and developed a theory of the occult significance of numbers, which she presented in her book, *10 Unveiled: The Brydlovan Theory of the Origin*

Figure 5.7. Bozena Brydlova, vice president of the Association of Hebrew Theosophists (American Section). *Source: The Jewish Theosophist* 1, no. 3 (April 1927): 11. Courtesy of the National Library of Israel collections. Public domain.

of Numbers, published by a Masonic press in 1922.[97] In 1925, Brydlova, married the Jewish attorney, lawyer, and political activist William B. Rubin (1873–1959), from Milwaukee.[98] She joined the Milwaukee lodge of the Theosophical Society and became active in the Association of Hebrew Theosophists. She served as the vice president of the Jewish association and published several articles in *The Jewish Theosophist*.[99] Like many other Jewish Theosophists, Brydlova found interest in Kabbalah and dedicated one of her articles to "The Ancient Kabbalah." Kabbalah, according to Brydlova, is "that almost forgotten store of learning, that flower of Hebrew Spiritualism."[100] In her article "A Plea for the Humble," Brydlova called for the resurrection of Kabbalah, which, she affirmed, contains teaching identical with that of Christian Science and Theosophy:

> Why these countless ages, has the Jew been so blind as to have ignored the priceless pearls of his forefathers in his terrific struggle for material recognition?
>
> Why has the Jew left it to the Gentile to dig up the Jewels of his faith and to bring them back to life in a beautiful modern setting? Why has Christian science, the teaching of which are those of the Kabbalah, been left to the Gentile to discover?
>
> Why has the reincarnation, or transmutation, been left to Theosophy for reinstatement? The Kabbalah is based upon reincarnation and reincarnation affirms the brotherhood of Man.[101]

In 1927, Brydlova published two booklets, *Flame of Fog* and *A Sinners Sermon*, in the Theosophical Press.[102] After her separation from Rubin, Brydlova moved with her daughter back to Los Angeles, where she married the journalist and film writer Herbert Hartwell Van Loan. She died in Los Angeles in 1969.

The treasurer of the American Section of the Association of Hebrew Theosophists was Louis Benjamin Ball (1884–1965), from Long Beach California. Ball was born in Russia and immigrated to the Unites States in 1898 (before moving to California, in 1918, he resided in New York).[103] Ball, who had a tobacco and candy wholesale business, joined the Theosophical Society, probably in the 1920s, and became active in the Association of Hebrew Theosophists. Ball continued to be active in the Theosophical Society also after the dissolution of the Jewish association. He served as the president of the Long Beach Theosophical lodge and published many letters to the editor and articles in Theosophical journals, especially in *The*

American Theosophist.[104] The last letter he published was in January 1965, a few months before he passed away.[105]

The publicity agent of the American Section of the Association of Hebrew Theosophists was Frank Ephraim Silberman from Milwaukee, Wisconsin. Silberman (1897–1989), who was born in Russia, became a member of the Milwaukee Theosophical lodge in 1922. His sister, Miss Gertrude E. Silberman, was also a member. Later, in 1936, Silberman married Dorothy Esther Jacobs, who was also a Theosophist, and the couple moved to California. Frank Silberman was the uncle of the actor Jerome Silberman (Gene Wilder).[106] Wilder was introduced to the Theosophical Society by his aunt when he was a teenager and was active in the society for a short while.[107]

Apart from the officers of the American Section of the Association of Hebrew Theosophists, other Jewish Theosophists were active in the section and contributed articles to its journal. One of the members of the section was L. E. (Lazar) Blochman (1856–1946), from Berkeley, who was born in San Francisco to a Jewish-observant family.[108] Blochman was an accountant and teacher who eventually became a landowner and entered the oil business and had an interest in fruit and tree culture, weather forecasting, and astronomy. He and his wife, Ida Twitchell, whom he married in 1888, advocated women suffrage, vegetarianism, and pacifism and were active in the temperance movement. Blochman, who was interested in astrology, spiritualism, and esotericism,[109] joined the Theosophical Society in the late nineteenth century[110] and later became active in the Hebrew association. He published articles in *The Jewish Theosophist* on Jewish and occult conception of heaven, on the aura, and a prayer to the "Infinite source of Holiness."[111] Blochman dedicated part of his essay on the Jewish conception of heaven to the Kabbalah, which, according to Blochman, "most resembles the Theosophical presentation of today."[112]

As mentioned above, Alex Horne, the Jewish Theosophist who moved from Shanghai to San Francisco, advocated the establishment of a league of Jewish Theosophists previous to the foundation of the American Section of the Association of Hebrew Theosophists. Horne joined the section after its foundation and contributed some articles to *The Jewish Theosophist*, including "Judaism and Theosophy" (a response to criticism raised by the editor of the *Israel's Messenger*),[113] and "suggestions for reading courses on Judaism and Theosophy."[114] In 1926, the American Section of the Association of Hebrew Theosophists published his book, *Spiritualizing Unspiritual Judaism.*[115]

Horne published articles also in other Theosophical journals. His publications included a report on the Association of Hebrew Theosophists and an appeal for Jewish Theosophists to join the association,[116] an article on "Theosophy and Modern Judaism,"[117] and reviews of books related to Kabbalah and Jewish Philosophy.[118] In 1928, the Theosophical Press in Wheaton, published his *An Introduction to Esoteric Judaism*.[119] Horne was involved in the controversy around the Jewish Theosophists in Basra (which will be discussed in the following chapter). Horne continued to publish many articles and book reviews in Theosophical journals in later years, some of them related to Jewish questions. In 1939, he published in *The Theosophist* an article about the persecution of the Jews in Germany.[120] In March 1948, following the 1947 UN resolution to end the British Mandate and to establish a Jewish and an Arab State in Palestine, Horne published an enthusiastic article in *The American Theosophist* entitled "After Two Thousand Years." He explained the return of the Jews to their homeland from a Theosophical perspective and wrote in the conclusion of the article, "[A] people dispersed to four corners of the earth . . . are coming back from their harvest of suffering laden with a new experience, to contribute to world culture a new note, and perhaps to forge for future generations—who knows? a new sub race."[121]

In 1927, the American Section established an Adyar synagogue committee[122] and advocated the formation of local groups of Association of Hebrew Theosophists in the United States. The officers of the American Section published in the second issue of *The Jewish Theosophist* detailed instructions on how to form such local groups and suggested that they meet for study and discussion, collect funds for the Adyar synagogue, and circulate *The Jewish Theosophist*.[123] The American Section of the Association of Hebrew Theosophists put up booths at the annual conventions of the Theosophical Society in 1926 and 1927 to recruit new members.[124]

A branch of the American Section of the Association of Hebrew Theosophists, which was established in New York by Solomon L. Flatow and Morris D. Rosenbaum, held regular public meetings during 1926 and 1927. Lectures were presented to the branch by Botzena Brydlova, Alvin J. Baker ("Reincarnation in Judaism"), Beatrice Wood ("Invisible helpers"), and F. Milton Willis ("The Star of David").[125] In 1930, the group held a meeting at the Federation building in New York. The president of the group was Morris D. Rosenbaum, and its secretary, Jennie Wilson.[126] In 1932, Rabbi Hayim Yehuda Leib Auerbach, the head of one of the major Kabbalistic Yeshivot in Jerusalem, Shaar ha-Shamayim, gave a lecture at the New York branch.[127] This is the only case I am aware of, in which a traditional Orthodox Kabbalist co-operated with Jewish Theosophists. The lecture of Auerbach was announced in the April–June 1932 issue of *The Jewish Theosophist*: "New York Jewry are honored with the presence of Rabbi Cha-im Yuda Lieb Auberbach [*sic*], principal of the Sha-ar Hasoma-im Yeshiva in Jerusalem (a Kabbalistic institution). Rabbi Auerbach delivered a lecture titled "The Soul" under the auspices of the New York branch of the Association of Hebrew Theosophists, which is headed by Mr. Morris D. Rosenbaum. The lecture was well attended and appreciated, and the rabbi was gratefully welcomed."[128] Jennie Wilson, the secretary of the branch, describes her meeting with Auerbsch, whom she describes as "the Dean of Cabala University of Jerusalem," in a letter to the editor entitled "The Ancient Wisdom in Palestine," published in the April 1932 issue of *The World Theosophy Magazine*:

> Last March, a celebrated Jewish Scholar and Cabalist came to New York from Jerusalem. . . . The writer was fortunate to come in contact with the famous Rabbi Auerbach, to explain to him the ideals and aims of the Theosophical Society and hopes of the Association Hebrew Theosophists. The existence of the Society was new to him, but when some of the teachings were mentioned, especially re-incarnation, his face lighted up in recognition. "You mean Gilgal" he said. Then he proceeded to give me the following information about his university.[129]

The Jewish Theosophist

The most important contribution of the American Section of the Association of Hebrew Theosophists was its journal, *The Jewish Theosophist*, which was edited by the president of the section, Henry C. Samuels, and printed in Seattle. The first issue of the journal (that was intended to be a quarterly) was published in September 1926. It was followed by five more issues, published between 1926 and 1928. Another, unnumbered, issue was published in January 1930. In 1932, the second and last volume appeared in three issues. According to the title page of the first issue, *The Jewish Theosophist* was "devoted to the study of Judaism in the light of Theosophy and Theosophy in the light of Judaism." Beneath the title appeared the emblem of the Theosophical Society and a depiction of the Tablets of Law inscribed with Hebrew letters. The 1930 unnumbered issue carried the title: *The Jewish Theosophist: A Newer Magazine*. The second volume of the journal published

Figure 5.8. *The Jewish Theosophist* 1, no. 4 (July 1927). Courtesy of the National Library of Israel collections. Public domain.

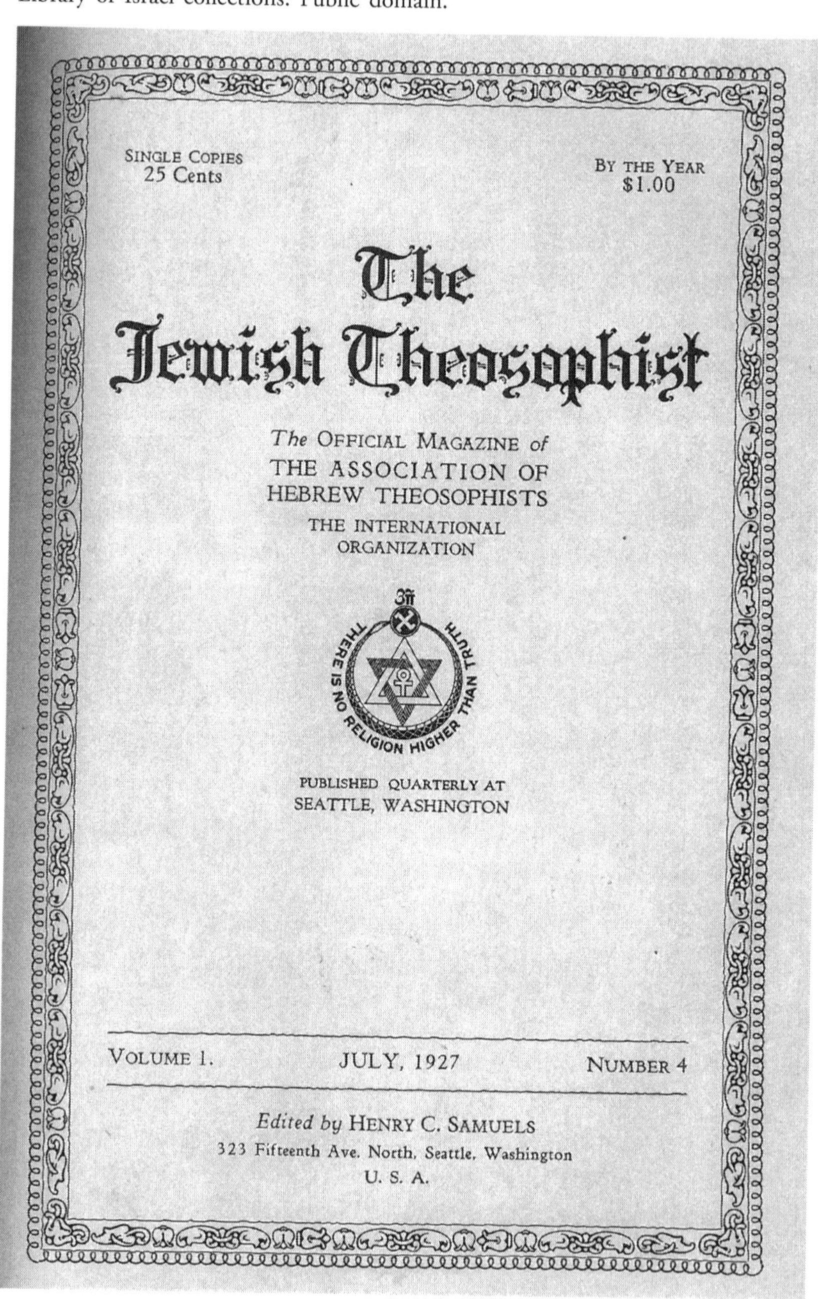

in 1932 (with the subtitle, *a Newer Magazine, Filled with Life and Interest*) carried beside the emblem of the Theosophical Society and the depiction of the Tablets of Law, a pentagram in which the word *Zion*, in Hebrew, was inscribed. According to the first issue of the 1932 volume: "The Jewish Theosophist is international in scope and is directed to the practical side of life. It deals primarily with progressive and constructive thought, presenting various interesting subjects that are appealing and up to the times. It is a Jewish magazine of recreation and education, dealing with things we really wish to know."

The Jewish Theosophist published a large variety of articles, poems, reviews, reports, letters, and editorials. Some of the articles discussed issues related to the Theosophical Society, such as information on the Order of the Star in the East and the schedule of Annie Besant's American lecture tour,[130] as well as extracts from the writing of leaders of the society, such as Jinarajadasa's, "Practical Religion" and Leadbeater's "The Idle Word" and "The Raising of Humanity."[131] It discussed topics of general interests to Theosophists, such as a report of the 1932 Parliament of Religions,[132] Jewish issues, such as the meaning of Jewish holydays[133] and events related to Jews in America and Zionism, such as the Henri Ford 1927 apology for his antisemitic activities, the fifteenth Zionist congress, held in 1927 in Basle, and Dr. Nahum Sokolov's statement conceding Arab-Jewish relations in Palestine.[134] Many articles dealt with the foundation and activities of the Association of Hebrew Theosophists, and with the establishment of the Jewish Theosophical community in Basra, Iraq, and the rabbinic ban against it (which will be discussed in detail in the next chapter). Other articles dealt with questions related to Judaism and Theosophy, such as Botzena Brydlova Rubin's "Why Every Jew Should Join the Association of Hebrew Theosophists";[135] "The Jewish Theosophist—A Paradox" signed by "Sophia;"[136] Lila B. Allebach's "Our Task as Hebrew Theosophists";[137] and Alex Horne's "Judaism and Theosophy."[138] *The Jewish Theosophist* also published a message from Annie Besant to the Hebrew Theosophists, which was mentioned above,[139] as well as an article by C. Jinarajadasa, the vice president of the Theosophical Society at that time, entitled "The Message of Judaism."[140] A large number of articles were dedicated to Jewish esotericism, Kabbalah, and Hasidism. These included the following: Annie Besant, "Schools of Initiation Amongst the Hebrews," which was based on her book *Esoteric Christianity*;[141] Bozena Brydlova, "The Ancient Kabbalah";[142] Rabbi Leonide Stambalchek, "Hasidism—One of the Jewish Aspects of Theosophy";[143] H. Blumenfeld, "Theosophy and Kabbalah";[144] and Pia Muller, "The Chassidim."[145]

The last issue of *The Jewish Theosophist* was published in December 1932, when the American Section of the Association of Hebrew Theosophists stopped its activities. Nonetheless, as we have seen, many of the members of the Hebrew association continued to be active in the Theosophical Society and continued to express their opinions concerning Theosophy and Judaism. As we have seen above, the other sections of the Association of Hebrew Theosophists also ceased activity around the same period. However, one Jewish Theosophical group that was active in Basra, Iraq, and was affiliated with the Hebrew association, continued to be active for a few more years. In the next chapter, I would like to discuss the Jewish Theosophists in Basra, the controversy around them, and the independent community they founded following their excommunication.

Chapter 6

"Sincere Jews"

The Jewish Theosophists in Basra

In 1935, The Jewish historian and geographer Abraham Jacob Brawer (1884–1975) visited the Jewish community in Basra, the port city located on the Shatt al-Arab in southern Iraq. Brawer wrote of his impressions:

> A strange phenomenon exists in this community: A Theosophical group, which has recently emerged there, amongst the merchants who travel to India. Theosophical societies and groups exist today in the metropolises of West Europe amongst the people who are tired of materialistic culture, and who seek after God. I wished to become acquainted with the Jewish Theosophists and enquired about them. I was told by my informants that they were expelled from the Jewish Community and were forced to establish their own synagogue, and if I am not mistaken, also their own cemetery. Every Saturday and Holiday they gather for prayer and Torah reading. They circumcise their sons according to Jewish law, and they are careful to observe Shabbat.[1]

The Jewish Theosophical group in Basra was indeed unique. The Jewish members of the Theosophical Society in Basra encountered opposition and were excommunicated by the rabbinic leaders of Iraqi Jewry. The foundation of the Jewish lodge in Basra and the excommunication of its members stirred a fierce controversy in the Jewish world and were reported in the Theosophical press. The Jewish Theosophists and their supporters, who called themselves "Sincere Jews," established their own community, which was active for almost ten years, until the ban on the group was canceled. In this chapter, I will discuss the history of the Jewish Theosophists of Basra and the establishment of the Sincere Jews community, the struggle against the Iraqi Jewish Theosophists, and the controversies it stimulated.[2]

The Foundation of the Jewish Theosophical Lodge in Basra

A Theosophical lodge, Dar-es-Salaam, was established at the military area in Basra in 1915, after the British conquest of the town in World War I. The lodge was founded by Dr. Jacob E. Solomon, the Jewish Theosophist from Ahmadabad, whom we encountered already in the previous chapters. Solomon served in the British Army at the time. After his return to India, he was one of the founders of the Association of Hebrew Theosophists.[3]

Kadouri Elijah Ani (d. 1955), who participated in the meetings of the lodge, related that the headmaster of the Alliance Israélite Universelle (AIU) school, was the secretary of the lodge, and among the members of the lodge were several British officers.[4] According to Ani, Rabbi Heskel (Ezekiel) Sassoon, the chief rabbi of Basra, was present at the opening ceremony of the lodge.[5] However, after the end of war, the lodge ceased its activities.

In 1928, a new Theosophical lodge was founded in Basra. At the head of the new lodge stood Kadouri Ani. Ani, a prominent member of the Jewish Basra community, was born in Baghdad and studied at the AIU school there. In 1915, after the British conquest of the town, he moved to Basra, and in 1929, he was elected as the head of the Jewish community Lay Council (el Majlis el Gasmani).[6] He was also active in the Masonic lodge in Basra.[7]

As mentioned above, Ani participated in the meetings of the first Theosophical lodge in Basra. His interest in Theosophy was renewed in 1926, after he visited his brother and business partner, Reuben Ani, who was a member of the Theosophical lodge in Bombay and of the Indian Section of the Association of Hebrew Theosophists. According to a letter found in Adyar archives, Kadouri Ani established the Basra Lodge that was attached to the India Section of the Theosophical Society, on February 7, 1928.[8] Ani reported that initially, the lodge included four Jewish members, two Muslims, and one Christian.[9] However, it seems that later it included only Jewish members.

Figure 6.1. Kadouri Ani, the head of the Jewish Theosophists in Basra. *Source:* Ezekiel Zvi Kalzel, "Theosophy and Kosher Meat," *Ha-Doar Hayom* (January 21, 1936). Courtesy of the National Library of Israel collections. Public domain.

At first, the Theosophical group met at the house of Kadouri Ani and his wife, Rosa (d. 1978), but as the number of fellows increased the Theosophists moved their activities to an apartment in the center of the Jewish neighborhood next to the community's synagogues and schools. In

1931, there were about thirty Jewish members in the Basra Lodge. Although a small number of the community (there were about seven thousand Jews living in Basra at the time),[10] the Jewish Theosophists were influential and affluent members of the Jewish community—merchants, lawyers, bankers, and engineers, many of them graduates of the AIU school.[11]

The Controversy and Excommunication of the Jewish Theosophists

Initially, the Jewish Theosophists did not encounter opposition, and the acting chief rabbi (Hacham Bashi) of Basra, Heskel (Ezekiel) Sassoon (d. 1941) approved of their activities.[12] Yet, in early 1931, several members of the Jewish community who opposed the activities of Ani and his group began a campaign against them. The opposition to Ani and the Jewish Theosophists was related to political struggles within the Lay Council of the community. Ani, who was standing at the time at the head of the Lay Council, claimed that he discovered that the former head of the Lay Council, Jacob Murad Noah (d. 1933), embezzled community funds. According to Ani and his followers, the opposition against the Jewish Theosophists was organized by the supporters of the former head of the council.[13]

The detractors of the Theosophists appealed to the rabbis of Baghdad, to the chief rabbi of the United Kingdom, Rabbi Joseph Hertz (1872–1946), and to Rabbi Dr. Leo Jung (1892–1987) and Rabbi David de Sola Pool (1885–1970), of the Rabbinical Council of the Union of Orthodox Jewish Congregations of America.[14] In his reply, Rabbi Hertz wrote that the Theosophical teachings are foreign to Judaism and urged the Basra community to distance themselves from the Theosophical Society.[15] Similarly, Rabbis Jung and Pool wrote in a cable they sent to the chief rabbi of Basra that Theosophy undermines the foundations of Jewish faith and practice. The rabbis included in their cable reference to several biblical verses, including Deuteronomy 13:7–9, that decrees that idolaters should be put to death.[16] In another letter that Rabbi Jung sent, he warned the Jews of Basra not to lose themselves in the "unprofitable mazes of Theosophic thought."[17]

On March 21, 1931, the rabbinical court in Baghdad issued a circular against the Jewish Theosophists, which was read by Rabbi Heskel Sassoon in the main synagogue in Basra. The circular, which was based on the letter of Rabbi Hertz and some other sources, stated that the Theosophical Society "appears to hold a new belief which in some respect differs from the Jewish faith." The circular called the members of the community to take extreme actions against the Basra Theosophists:

> You are therefore enjoined before everything else to have the Lodge of this Society removed away from the vicinity of the Grand Synagogue and to notify all those who bear the name of Israel to keep away from this religion which is against the belief of Israel since its foundation up to now. Further, all members of this Society are not entitled according to the Law, to participate in all religious matters and thereby influence others to change their old religion for a new one. Furthermore, no members of this Society are entitled to be elected to the Jewish Lay Council, nor be wardens nor agents nor leaders. You are therefore charged with the execution of these [our] orders in consonance with the Holy Law and to apply this order in connection with the entire Holy congregation.[18]

As a response, Kadourie Ani wrote a letter to Rabbi Heskel Sassoon, which was published in the Arabic Section of *The Times of Mesopotamia*, on March 28. In the letter, Ani writes that Sassoon has "strayed in directions which are against the Holy Jewish Faith, truth and freedom of thought." He goes on to say, "Theosophy is not a religion, as you have alleged, but is a philosophical society—the Jewish Kabbalah itself." He wonders why the Jewish Theosophists in Basra are attacked, while "the majority of Jews in the West and East, as well as in the new world, who are members of this Society, have received neither advice nor warning against it from the Rabbis of London, or those of France or America or other quarters." Furthermore, he claims that Sassoon previously encouraged the Theosophists and that he was present at the opening of the first Theosophical lodge in Basra and gave it his blessings. He concludes his letter to Sassoon with a threat to resort to legal steps: "You are therefore requested to withdraw your Circular, or else we shall be compelled to resort to legal steps to have the truth revealed."[19]

The circular was not withdrawn, and the hostility between the fractions escalated. On Saturday, April 11, 1931, Rabbi Sassoon gave a sermon against the Theosophists. That evening, a mob attacked the Theosophical Club and tore down its signboard, threw stones at Ani's house, and chased after some of the Jewish Theosophists. The police intervened, and seven people were arrested.[20] Rabbi Sassoon requested that the governor of the district (the Mutasarrif) close the Theosophical lodge, according to an Ottoman law that houses of worship of different denominations should not be in the same street. Yet, his appeals were rejected.[21] He also filed a defamation case against Kadouri Ani (on account of his open letter published on March 28), which was tried by the district magistrate of Basra, who dismissed the case. According to the report in the *Times of Mesopotamia*, five hundred Jews from both parties were present inside and outside the court.[22]

In May 1931, one of the main opponents of the Jewish Theosophists, Isaac Said Nathan, an English teacher who was born in Yemen and studied in India before settling in Iraq,[23] published *The New Religion in Basra and the Response to It* (الدين الجديد في البصرة والرد عليه).[24] The pamphlet, published in Arabic and addressed not only to Jews, but also to Muslims and Christians, was written in response to articles published by Ani in the Arabic Section of the *Times of Mesopotamia*. Nathan criticized the Theosophists' reliance on Hinduism and Buddhism, accused them of atheism and of rejecting the basic principles of faith and moral conduct of the monotheist religions, and attacked the use of Ouroboros (a serpent swallowing its own tail) in the emblem of the Theosophical Society. Nathan claimed that the Theosophists rejected private property and that money and women were shared freely between them, "like water and air."[25] The Jewish Theosophists sued Nathan because of his allegations against their moral conduct. Nathan was found guilty and charged with a fine, which was paid by his Jewish and Muslim supporters.[26]

The controversy reached its peak when Rabbi Heskel Sassoon gave a notice to all Jewish Theosophists to resign from the society, or they would be excommunicated. As they refused, a *herem* (decree of excommunication) was issued on May 20, and read in Basra's synagogues: "As our final notice to the Theosophical Society has expired on Tuesday, henceforth according to the judgment given by the Rabbis of Baghdad, those who are affiliated to the above Society are excluded from the congregation of Israel in circumcision, marriage, and burial, and other matters relating to the community and all the religious affairs of Israel. Furthermore, people who will go to visit them in their lodge will be accused of being affiliated to the Society."[27]

The Reactions to the Excommunication

The events in Basra caused a sensation and were covered in the local press (specifically, the bilingual *Times of Mesopotamia*[28]); in the Jewish press, especially in the Zionist papers of Shanghai and Bombay, *Israel's Messenger* and *The Jewish Advocate*;[29] and in Theosophical journals, especially, *The Theosophist*. In the following months, Jewish detractors and defenders of the Jewish Theosophists debated the excommunication and the compatibility between Theosophy and Judaism.

Some members of the Jewish communities in Shanghai and Bombay supported the actions taken against the Theosophists. According to an article published in *Israel's Messenger*, "The case of Khadoory Sasoon (!) and his treacherous conduct against his own people, had added a bad and sad chapter in the modern history of the Baghdad Jewish community. Today the whole community is seething with unrest, and drifting like a ship without a compass."[30] In a letter to the editor of *The Jewish Advocate*, a member of the Jewish community in Bombay by the name of A. Menashe approved of the excommunication and asserted that the rabbis of Iraq had taken the right step according to Jewish Law.[31] Nayim B. Samuel, another member of the community, supported the excommunication and blamed the Theosophists for establishing a liberal section of Judaism that was contrary to the teaching of the Torah and for disturbing the efforts to build a Jewish homeland in Palestine.[32]

However, some of the opposers of the Jewish Theosophists objected to the excommunication. In letters sent to the editor of *The Jewish Advocate*, N. Hillel and David I. Sargon (the brother of the editor of *The Jewish Advocate*) denounced the excommunication, although they emphasized that they were not affiliated with the Theosophical Society and advised against joining it.[33] N. E. B. Ezra, the editor of *Israel's Messenger*, expressed his reservations about the Jewish Theosophists: "We are not at all in sympathy with Jews throwing themselves into the arms of Theosophy, or any other new cults, in order to advance in life." However, he condemned the Iraqi rabbis for issuing the decree against them: "The decree of excommunication issued by the Rabbinical authorities in Iraq is to be greatly deplored and should be withdrawn immediately. We cannot help saying that they have not acted in the best interests of Judaism: On the contrary, they have kindled a spark which is likely to spread far and wide and render infinite harm to our sacred cause."[34]

The Jewish Theosophists and their supporters condemned the excommunication and rebuffed the accusations against them. Reuben Ani, the secretary of the Bombay Section of the Association of Hebrew Theosophists (and Kadouri Ani's brother), published several articles and letters in the months following the excommunication. In the August 1931 issue of *The Jewish Advocate*, Rueben E. Ani published a letter in which he attacked

Rabbi Jung and Rabbi Pool for implicitly calling for the execution the Jewish Theosophists. Ani claimed that the motives for the conflict were not "religious fanaticism" but rather "rank materialism," alluding to the conflict around his brother's election to the Lay Council of the community. Ani reports also of a meeting held in Baghdad between rabbis, representatives of the community, and the Iraqi minister of the interior in an attempt to withdraw the decree of excommunication.[35] In September 1931, he sent a letter to the editor of *Israel's Messenger* and attached to it a petition signed by one hundred members of the Basra community in support of Kadouri Ani. He declared the compatibility of Theosophy and Judaism and wrote that by following the main goals of the Association of Hebrew Theosophists (to study Theosophy in the light of Judaism and Judaism in the light of Theosophy), the Jewish Theosophists "become not less but more Jewish minded than they were before."[36] Reuben Ani also addressed the charges of Rabbi Jung against Theosophy and said that by referring to Deuteronomy 13:6–9 in the cable he sent to the chief rabbi of Basra, Jung implied that the Jewish Theosophists should be put to death. He wondered why Rabbi Jung attacked the Jewish Theosophists of Basra while ignoring the American Jewish Theosophists and blamed him for arousing the fanaticism of the ignorant masses in Basra. Reuben Ani repeated these arguments in a letter he published in the October issue of *The Jewish Advocate*.[37]

The leaders of the Theosophical Society and the members of the American branch of the Association of Hebrew Theosophists were also interested in the events in Basra and supported Ani and his followers. In June 1931, *The Theosophist* published several documents and articles under the title "The Persecution of Hebrew Theosophists."[38] These included a letter that Annie Besant, the president of the Theosophical Society, sent to Kadouri Ani on April 30, following his request to clarify that Theosophy is not a religion. In her letter, Besant ascertained that "persons of every faith can belong to the Theosophical Society, without leaving the religion in which they have been born."[39] As mentioned in the previous chapter, the events in Iraq were mentioned also in the Dutch Theosophical journal *De Theosofische Beweging*.[40] A year later, *The Jewish Theosophists* published several articles on the events in Basra. Henry Samuels, the editor of the journal, published "Fighting the Light (the Story of a Modern Excommunication—*Herem*)."[41] In the article, Samuels attacked Rabbis Jung and Pool and the rabbis of Iraq and declared: "I affirm with all vehement of my soul that in this action and attitude those Rabbis neither represent Judaism nor the Jew, but a darkness which still besets some of our people."[42] Samuels also published an open letter addressed to N. E. B. Ezra, the editor of *Israel's Messenger*, in which he thanked him for condemning the excommunication of the Jewish Theosophists in Basra. Nonetheless, he rejected Ezra's criticism against Jewish Theosophists and asserted the compatibility of Judaism and Theosophy: "Every Jewish Theosophist, I feel certain, will testify that through Theosophy and the work of the Theosophical Society he has come closer to Judaism the Beautiful and to all that is true and noble in our people."[43]

The Jewish Theosophists approached European Jewish leaders, asking for their support. S. S. Cohen, one of the founders of the Association of Hebrew Theosophists (who resided at the time in Kandy, Ceylon), wrote an open letter to Chayim Weitzman, the head of the World Zionist Organization, which was published in the June issue of *The Jewish Advocate*. Cohen asserted that the reasons for the opposition to the Jewish Theosophist were related to control of Basra's Lay Council: "But the true inward reasons are deep rooted and purely material. The local Rabbis thought if they could only get rid of the Theosophist members in the Lay Council, the affairs and especially the finance of the community will be left in their hands and in those of their confederates to do with them as they please."[44] Cohen, who describes the rabbis of Basra as "primitive, uneducated, half literate, religious autocrats" concludes his letter to Weitzman asking him to act for the annulment of the excommunication:

> The Jewish Theosophists in Basra who have lived all these years in peace and in perfect harmony with their co-religionists and within the fold of the Jewish Congregation as true worshipers of the God of Abraham are now excommunicated to die of starvation in disgrace. It is up to you then and other influential co-religionists to save them, and in saving them to save the Jewish race from the opprobrium brought down on it by the discreditable activities of the Rabbis of Iraq in mischievous collaboration with Dr. Jung from America. Will you not rise to the occasion and cause the Excommunication to be withdrawn?"[45]

On June 20, Kadouri Ani sent a letter to Sylvian Lévi (1863–1935), the prominent French-Jewish Indologist, who served as the president of the Société des Etudes Juives and served on the board of the AIU. Ani attached the letter sent by S. S. Cohen to Weitzman and asserted that the persecution of the Jewish Theosophists was related to the election to Basra's Lay Council. Kadouri asked Levi to write a letter to Basra's chief rabbi asserting that Theosophy is not a new religion and that the excommunication should be annulled.[46]

Sincere Jews: The Jewish Theosophical Community in Basra

However, notwithstanding the efforts of the Jewish Theosophists to annul the decree against them and the objections to the excommunication, even by some of the detractors of the Theosophists, the Jewish Theosophists were banned by the rabbis of the community. Soon after the decree was issued, the rabbis refused to circumcise the newborn son of one of the Jewish Theosophists.[47]

As a response, the Jewish Theosophists and their supporters founded their own Jewish communal institutions. In the summer of 1931, they purchased a plot for a cemetery and opened their own synagogue.[48] An important step taken by the Theosophists against their opponents was to appoint their own ritual slaughterer and to sell meat slaughtered by them to the members of the Jewish community, without the community tax (Gabila). As the price of the Kosher meat sold by the Jewish Theosophists was cheaper, members of the community preferred to buy from them, and the revenues of the community's committee were reduced.[49]

The Jewish Theosophists also appealed to the district governor, requesting that he dismiss the chief rabbi for his actions against them, but their appeal was refused. They also sued the head of the lay community, Jacob Murad Noah, for embezzling the community funds, but the proceedings stopped following Noah's death in 1933.[50]

By the end of 1932, the Jewish Theosophists were calling their new community "Sincere Jews."[51] Interest in the new community and disputes between the supporters and detractors of the Sincere Jews continued in the following years. Isaac Said Nathan, one of the main detractors of the Jewish Theosophists, who published a pamphlet in Arabic against Theosophy in the height of the controversy in Spring 1931, published another pamphlet following the foundation of the Jewish Theosophical community. In the second pamphlet, entitled, *The Upright Guide* (الدليل الصالح), Nathan repeated his accusations against Theosophy, referred to anti-Theosophical literature in English, and published an Arabic translation of Rabbi Jung's letters.[52] During 1932 and 1933, S. S. Cohen and Rabbi Jung continued to debate about the Jewish Theosophists on the pages of *Israel's Messenger*.[53] In March and April 1933, letters were exchanged between Elias S. Levy, from Shanghai, who defended the Sincere Jews, and N. E. B. Ezra, who criticized them.[54]

Rabbi Yehuda Fetaya (1859–1942), a leading Kabbalist from Baghdad, referred to the Jewish Theosophists in Basra in his book *Minhat Yehuda*, published in Baghdad in 1933. In his discussion of God's curse on the serpent (Genesis 3:14), Fetaya wrote that he heard that there are great and wise people in our times who are enticed by the serpent and justify it because its advice to eat from the tree of knowledge was beneficial and saved humanity from ignorance. "I also heard that these people claim to be faultless Jews," continues Fetaya, "that they have not left the fold, Heaven forbid, that they do not do anything wrong, but only strive to enter the wisdom of truth (i.e., Kabbalah B. H.), to understand the secrets of the higher world; because of that, they study from the Hindus, who worship the serpent, because the serpent worshiping Hindus are known to also have esoteric knowledge."[55] Although Fetaya does not mention explicitly the Jewish Theosophists, it is clear that he is referring to what he has heard about them from their opponents.[56] Fetaya expresses his dismay from the rumors about the Jews who worship the serpent and study esoteric knowledge from the Hindus. However, he ponders whether the rumors are slander. Alluding to the financial and political disputes that underlie the Basra controversy, he suggests that the renegade Jews are not sincere in their belief in "this new faith of the Serpent" but are motivated by economic reasons. He concludes his discussion with a call for the dissenting Jews to repent from their evil ways and return to the fold.[57]

During this period, attempts were made to reconcile the two factions in Basra. In March 1934, a delegation of the Jewish community from Baghdad, headed by Chief Rabbi Sassoon Kaduri, arrived in Basra to try to settle the dispute. However, Kaduri Ani refused to negotiate with the delegation before the *herem* was withdrawn.[58] Following his failure, Rabbi Kaduri appealed to court against the Jewish Theosophists, accusing them of causing financial damage to the Basra's community committee through selling cheap Kosher meat.

Further, unsuccessful attempts at reconciliation were made during the next year. Finally, at the end of 1935, a settlement was reached, with the help of Sir Eliezer Kaduri, the wealthy Jewish philanthropist from Shanghai. In February 1936, a delegation from Baghdad, headed by Rabbi Sassoon Kaduri, arrived at Basra. On February 24, 1936, the Baghdad rabbinic court announced that the excommunication was annulled.[59]

After the annulment of the excommunication, the Basra Jewish community was united again. It is unclear if the Theosophical lodge continued its activities. In 1945, Kadouri Ani and his family immigrated to Palestine, and he passed away there in 1954.[60] As we shall see in the next chapter, his wife, Rosa Ani, became active in the Israeli Theosophical Society.

Chapter 7

Theosophy in Israel

In 1953, Dr. Isaac S. Cohen, the presidential agent of the Theosophical Society in Israel reported that the members of the first Theosophical lodge in Israel decided to reestablish the International Association of Hebrew Theosophists.[1]

As we have seen in the previous chapters, the branches of the Association of the Hebrew Theosophists stopped their activities in the mid-1930s, and the Jewish Theosophical community in Basra dissolved in 1936. During World War II, many of the European Jewish Theosophists perished in the Holocaust. Others emigrated to the Land of Israel before and after the war. Following the 1948 Israeli-Arab Jewish war and the foundation of the State of Israel Jewish Theosophists from Arab countries also left their countries, and some of them immigrated to Israel.

Some of the Jewish Theosophists who immigrated to Israel contacted and met each other. As Cohen stated in his 1953 report, some of them aspired to revive the Association of Hebrew Theosophists. The attempts to revive an international Jewish Theosophical association failed. Yet, as we shall see in this chapter, the Israeli Theosophists established several lodges, whose members were predominantly Jewish, and the connection between Judaism and Theosophy was a central issue for the Israeli Theosophists.

The Foundation of the First Theosophical Lodges in Israel

In 1951, several Jewish Theosophists, who emigrated to Israel, met and decided to establish an Israeli Section of the Theosophical Society. Dr. Isaac

S. Cohen, who was appointed the presidential agent of the society in Israel, wrote of the decision in a letter he sent from Tel Aviv to the general secretary of the Theosophical Society in Toronto. In the letter, which was published in *The Canadian Theosophist*, Cohen wrote: "The Section is composed of members who immigrated here from Europe, North Africa and Asia. At our first meeting we unanimously decided to continue the Theosophical work that every one of us was conducting in his country of origin and to constitute this Section."[2]

In 1953, Cohen sent the first yearly report on Theosophy in Israel, in which he announced the establishment of one lodge in Israel and the plan to establish another one. According to the report, there were nineteen fellows of the society in Israel. Their meetings were rare because of transportation difficulties in the young state. Cohen reported that a committee of four members was assigned to translate into Hebrew Blavatsky's *Key to Theosophy* and Besant's *The Ancient Wisdom*. As mentioned above, Cohen aspired to reestablish the Association of Hebrew Theosophists. He stated that the objects of the new association were to raise funds for the construction of the Adyar synagogue; to supply the Adyar Library with books on Jewish religion, mysticism, and occultism; and to offer comparative studies of Judaism, Theosophy, and world religions.[3] In August 1954, the Israeli Theosophical Association, Israel branch, headed by Dr. Isaac Cohen, was officially registered in Tel Aviv.[4]

Berthe (Masha) Dominic (1897–1986), a Jewish Theosophist from Romania, who immigrated to Israel in 1949, described in the memorial book for the Israeli Theosophist Chana Mor (1924–1975) the events that led to the establishment of Theosophy in Israel, without mentioning Cohen's involvement:

When I arrived in Israel in 1949, I had to write to Mr. Jinarajadasa, the then president of the intern. Theosophical Society, the reason why I left my theosophical duties and went from my communist native country. His answer was that he is sure I will organize in two years time a Theos. Society in Israel as well. At that time there came most of the people who escaped from the Concentration camps, and other who came from all corners of the world, with many spoken languages. A period of many difficult tests and sorrows. How could I think to be able to interest people in Theosophy in such a tense time?[5]

A couple of years after her arrival, Chana and Pinchas Mor, Jewish The-osophists who immigrated from Germany and resided in Safed, contacted Dominic: "I then received a postcard from family Mor advising me that they will like to meet me. Could I think this was the Message of fulfilment of what Mr. Jinjaradasa wrote to me, as two years have elapsed? Family Mor arrived from Safed, we began to talk about Theosophy . . . and in fact, after two-three months we had in Israel the first branch of the Theosophical Society."[6] According to a timeline of the Israeli Theosophical Society, published in 1976, Berthe Dominic met with Chana and Pinchas Mor on May 1953 and decided to establish a Theosophical lodge at the home of the Mor family in Safed. Chana Mor was appointed chairperson, Pinchas Mor, secretary, and Baruch Albera, vice president. A month later, Martin Mashler, from Nahariya, joined the initiative, and two months later, in July 1953, the Galilea Lodge in Safed received its charter from Adyar.[7] (It is interesting to note that Isaac S. Cohen is not mentioned at all in this timeline.) In June 1953, the group published the first issue of its newsletter (*Mitteilungsblatt*) in German.[8]

The Israeli Lodges of the Theosophical Society

According to the June 1954 issue of the Israeli Theosophical newsletter, two lodges were active in Israel at the time—Lodge Galilea in Safed, chaired by Chana Mor, and Lodge Covenant in Tel Aviv, chaired by Berthe Dominic.[9] The two lodges, as well as a small Theosophical group that was active in Jerusalem, are mentioned in the 1955 annual report of the Israeli Theo-sophical Society.[10]

In November 1954, the newly elected international president of the Theosophical Society, Sri Ram, appointed Hans Zeuger, who resided at the time in Jerusalem, as the new presidential agent in Israel in the place of Dr. Isaac Cohen.[11]

Hans Zeuger (1903–1983), who was also appointed as the link officer of the Huizen Center for Israel,[12] joined the Austrian Section of the Theo-sophical Society in 1919. In 1932, he immigrated to Palestine. He worked in the administration of the British mandate and took part in the 1948 Jewish-Arab war. He was the chairperson of the Israeli Vegetarian Society, an astrologer, parapsychologist, poet, and activist for Jewish-Arab dialogue. He first resided in Jerusalem, and later, in Moshav (agricultural settlement), Tal Shahar, where he cultivated fruit trees and beehives.[13]

In the following years, several other lodges were opened in Israel. In 1956, Lodge Moriah was established in Jerusalem. The meetings of the lodge were first held at the home of Mrs. Orthal, and later, in the house of Rosa Ani, the widow of Kadouri Ani, the founder of the Jewish Theosophical lodge in Basra, who immigrated to Israel in 1945.[14] In 1957, a second lodge was established in Tel Aviv, Lodge Harmony, whose meetings took place in Café Raphael.[15] The lodge was presided over by Ilse Fischer, who was a former member of Lodge Covenant.[16] Ilse Fischer (1897–1981), born Ilse Patak, in Brno, immigrated to Palestine in 1939 and lived with her first husband, Dr. Rudolph Fischer, in Nahariya. Ilse, who later remarried twice (first with Dr. Fritz Hahn and then with Mr. Belilowsky), returned to Europe in the late 1960s and resided in Constance. Ilse was also interested in Anthroposophy, and in 1954, she visited Ernst and Frieda Müller in London. She was also a graphologist, and in 1974, she published a book on graphology, parapsychology, and Kabbalah.[17]

In 1958, Lodge Emmanuel was established in Haifa.[18] It was presided over by Heinrich Srebrow (1896–1976), a civil engineer and a Freemason who emigrated to Palestine from Bulgaria in 1935.[19] In 1962, a second lodge, Lotus, was established in Haifa. Its first president was E. Kudjoe Mawudeku, a visiting student from West Africa.[20] In 1965, a third lodge, Hallelujah, was established in Tel Aviv. According to a journal report from 1964, which carried the title "Old People and Women Are Attracted to Theosophy," there were approximately one hundred members of the Theosophical Society in Israel at the time.[21]

After 1963, there were attempts to create a federation of lodges in Israel and form a national section. However, the attempts failed because of disagreements between the different Theosophical groups.[22] The Israeli lodges became attached directly to the international headquarters of the society in Adyar, and the function of presidential agent was canceled. After 1968, annual reports were sent separately by the presidents of the different lodges.

Lodge Galilea, which was closed in 1963, was reestablished in 1968 under a new name, Bsorat ha-Galil (Galilee's message).[23] Lodge Moriah in Jerusalem, and Lodge Hallelujah in Tel Aviv stopped being active in the late 1960s. Lodge Lotus in Haifa, whose charter was canceled in 1966,[24] became active again in 1972, under the presidency of Raphael Bornstein.[25] In 1977, under the presidency of Varda Ben-Yizhak (who was previously active in Lodge Bsorat ha-Galil), it changed its name to Morya Lodge.[26] Lodges Covenant and Harmony in Tel Aviv and Lodge Emmanuel in Haifa continued to be active in the 1970s. In 1973, a new, Russian-speaking lodge, Lodge Blavatsky, was founded in Tel Aviv by immigrants from the Soviet Union.[27]

By the end of the 1970s, the activities of the Israeli Theosophists declined, and most lodges closed. In 1980, there were only two active lodges, both in Tel Aviv—Covenant Lodge, headed by Berthe Dominic, and Harmony Lodge, headed by Hans Zeuger.[28] Harmony Lodge was closed following Zeuger's demise in 1984. The only lodge that continued its activities was Covenant Lodge, which was headed since 1984 by Abraham Oron.[29] Oron presided over the Israeli Theosophical Society until 2019, when he was replaced by Bracha Alron.[30]

The Israeli Theosophists and Their Activities

In 1951, Isaac Cohen, the first presidential agent of the Theosophical Society in Israel, reported that the members of the Israeli Section of the Theosophical Society were immigrants from Europe, North Africa, and Asia. While most of the early Israeli Theosophists were immigrants from Europe (Germany, Austria, Romania, Hungary, and Yugoslavia), there were also some who came from the Middle East and North Africa. I have already mentioned that the meetings of the Jerusalem lodge were held in the house of Rosa Ani, who immigrated to Israel from Iraq in 1945. Salomon (d. 1959) and Rachel (d. 1973) Sicsu, who immigrated from Morocco, and resided in Kibbutz Ze'elim in the Negev, were also active in the Israeli Theosophical Society. Before his immigration, Salomon was active in the Zionist movement in Casablanca. He was the link officer of the Dutch Theosophical "Huizen Center" for Morocco and a member of the French Section of the Theosophical Society.[31]

Initially, most of the members of the different lodges were immigrants and only later did Israeli-born members join the Israeli lodges. At first, the meetings of Covenant, Harmony, and Galilea Lodges were held in German, and the first publications of the Israeli Theosophists were in German. Later, meetings were held also in Hungarian, English, Russian, and Hebrew.

Israeli Theosophists were interested and active in other alternative movements, such as vegetarianism, parapsychology, Freemasonry, and pacifism. As mentioned above, Hans Zeuger, the presidential agent of the Theosophical Society in Israel and the president of Harmony Lodge was active in the Israeli Vegetarian Society. The Morya Lodge in Haifa also had contacts with the Israeli vegetarian movement.[32] Yehuda Carmeli, who was active in Bsorat Ha-Galil Lodge, was one of the founders of the

Israeli vegetarian village, Amirim, where annual conferences of the Israeli Theosophical Society had been held since the early 1970s. Abraham Lissod (originally, Lisavoder, 1901–1993), a member of the Covenant Lodge, was a vegetarian, a yoga practitioner, a Gandhian, and a pacifist and was active in the movement for Israel-Arab friendship.[33]

Some of the Israeli Theosophists had connections with Anthroposophy. Yehuda Carmeli used to travel from Amirim to Tel Aviv to study with the Anthroposophical group headed by Benno Wolkowitz.[34] Chana Mor and Hans Zeuger gave lectures at the Oneg Shabat circle of Erich Bloch, who was affiliated with the Israeli Anthroposophical circles, and Bloch, in turn, gave a lecture to the members of the Covenant Lodge.[35]

Israeli Theosophists were also affiliated with the Israeli parapsychological groups. Magrot Klausner (1905–1975), the Berlin-born Israeli theater and film producer and founder of Israel Motion Picture Herzelia Studios, who was a member of the Harmony Lodge, and in 1970, participated in the Theosophical annual convention in Adyar, was one of the founders of the Israeli Parapsychological Society.[36]

Hans Zeuger delivered lectures to the circle that met at the Klausner home since the late 1950s and joined the board of the Israeli Parapsychological Society in 1970. In 1976, after Klausner's demise, he was elected as its president.[37] Some Israeli Theosophists were also Freemasons. Heinrich Srebrow, the president of Lodge Emmanuel in Haifa, was a Freemason, and joint meetings of Theosophists and Freemasons were held in the lodge.[38]

Some Jewish Israeli Theosophists were interested in forming a connection with the Israeli Arab population and (after 1967) with Palestinians from the occupied territories. In the 1959 annual reports, Hans Zeuger wrote, "Most valuable contacts were made . . . with members of the Arab sector of our populations which might lead to promising developments in the near future. It is of utmost importance that the message of Theosophy should reach the minority groups in our country."[39] In 1976, Berthe Dominic reported that Covenant Lodge hosted Arab students from the occupied territories and searched for people who could translate Theosophical writings into Arabic.[40] The connection with the Arab students was interrupted because of the political situation, but they were renewed again in 1978.[41] Notwithstanding these connections, I am not familiar with any Palestinians who became members of the Israeli Theosophical Society.

The activities of the Israeli Theosophical lodges consisted of study groups, lectures, and celebrations of special Theosophical dates, such as White Lotus Day (the anniversary of Blavatsky death) and Annie Besant's

Figure 7.1. Margot Klausner, member of the Harmony Lodge and founder of the Israeli Parapsychological Society. *Source:* Society Dan Hadani Collection / National Library of Israel / The Pritzker Family National Photography Collection. Wikimedia Commons. Public domain.

birthday. Sometimes, some of the lodges met for joint activities. In July 1969, a weeklong seminar was initiated by the Israeli composer and conductor Issak Tavior (originally, Vichodetz, b. 1943) and his wife, Liora, members of Bsorat Ha-Galil Lodge. The seminar was held at their home in Tirat Yael (today, Hemdat Yamim), near mount Meron.[42] In October 1970, the first summer school of the Israeli Theosophists took place in the vegetarian village Amirim, in the upper Galilee. The initiator of the summer school was Soshana (Rosa) Lusting, who organized the event together with Yehuda Carmeli and Varda Ben Yitzchak. The activities included lectures by Berthe Dominic, Chana Mor, Yehuda Carmeli, and Shoshana Lustig, as well as daily meditations under the direction of Dominic.[43] Further summer schools were held in Amirim in 1973 and 1974.[44]

The Publications of the Israeli Theosophists

From the beginning of their activities, in 1953, the Israeli Theosophists published newsletters and journals. The first newsletter, entitled *Theosophische Gesselschaft Adyar Israel, Mitteilungsblat*, edited by Chana Mor, was issued in German by Galilea Lodge.[45] Between 1956 and 1965, the newsletter was edited by Hans Zeuger and entitled "Theosophie in Israel." A Hebrew title, *Theosophia be-Israel* (Theosophy in Israel), was added, and the words in the emblem of the Theosophical Society, printed on the front cover, included the slogan "There is no religion higher than truth" in Hebrew. The issues of the newsletter include articles in German, French, and English, as well as some passages in Hebrew.[46]

In 1965, Galilea Lodge started issuing a journal entitled *Teosophia ba-Foal* (Theosophy in Action).[47] In 1968, the renewed Bestorat ha-Galil Lodge began publishing the journal *Theosophia*, edited by Varda ben-Yitzchak, which included articles in Hebrew, English, and German.[48] In 1976, members of the lodge published a booklet in memory of Chana Mor, which included several of Mor's lectures on general Theosophical themes and on Jewish and Israeli issues. In 1988, the Israeli Theosophical Society began publication of *Or* (Light), in Hebrew.

The publications of the Israeli Theosophists include articles concerning Theosophy and other topics, such as yoga, the New Age, and Kabbalah. Many of the articles were reprinted from other Theosophical journals and books, and some were written by Israeli Theosophists.

The Israeli Theosophists regarded as their mission introducing Theosophy to the Israeli public. In the 1971 annual report, Hans Zeuger wrote:

> As in previous years, we considered it our duty to study the Ancient Wisdom not only within the rather limited circumference of our little group but tried to bring the message of Theosophy to the Israel public at large. Thanks to these continued endeavors, Parapsychology and Astrology are now widely known and willingly accepted in our country. Gratifying opportunities are thus at hand to infuse theosophical ideas—the Oneness of life, Reincarnation, Life after Death, Karma, the Educational Purpose of Suffering, etc.,—into the consciousness of our nation.[49]

For this purpose, Israeli Theosophists endeavored to translate Theosophical texts into Hebrew.[50] As mentioned above, in the first annual report on

Figure *7.2. Theosophie in Israel: Mitteilungsblatt,* 1959. Courtesy of the National Library of Israel collections. Used with permission of the Theosophical Society in America.

Theosophy in Israel, from 1953, Isaac Cohen said that a committee of Israeli Theosophists was charged to translate Blavatsky's *Key to Theosophy* and Besant's *The Ancient Wisdom.*[51] Since 1956, short excerpts from Krishnamurti's *At the Feet of the Master* were published in Hebrew, in the volumes of

Theosophie in Israel. In 1971, the translation of the whole book, edited by Pinchas Mor, was published by Lodge Bestorat Ha-Galil.[52] During the early 1970s, the lodge published other translations of Theosophical texts: Charles W. Leadeater's *Life after Death*, translated by Abraham Lisod; Geoffrey Hodson's, *The Yoga of Life*, translated by Aliza Nahor; and Mabel Collins's *Light on the Path*, translated by Anva Kantor.[53] In 1981, the Theosophical Society in Israel published Ernst Wood's *Concentration and Character Building—Practical Course*, translated by Lily Bentav.[54] Since the late 1990s, the Israeli Theosophical Society published translations of Blavatsky and Besant's works, most of them rendered by Anva Kantor.[55]

Theosophy and Judaism

The Israeli Theosophical lodges that were established in Israel did not define themselves as Jewish lodges. Nonetheless, almost all the Israeli fellows of the Theosophical Society in Israel were Jewish, and like Jewish Theosophists in other countries, they found interest in questions relating to Judaism and Theosophy. Many of them believed that as Jewish Theosophists they had a mission not only vis-à-vis Israeli society, but also relating to Judaism and the Jewish people. As I mentioned earlier, the first presidential agent in Israel, Isaac Cohen, aspired to reestablish the Association of Hebrew Theosophists, to raise funds for construction of the Adyar synagogue (as far as I know, later Israeli Theosophists did not find interest in the construction of such a synagogue), and to offer comparative studies of Judaism, Theosophy, and world religions.[56] Chana Mor, one of the founders of Theosophy in Israel, wrote in a paper she gave in 1953 (in German), on the occasion of the foundation of the Galilea Lodge:

> Our tasks in Israel are enormous. We take part in a very hard karma of the Jewish people. The aims of the Theosophical Society are to investigate the still unexplained laws of nature and the soul powers latent in Man. Hence, I regard it as one of the aims of the theosophists in this land, to investigate the duties and place of the Jews in the Great Plan of development, and with the help of this knowledge, to elevate the karma of the Jews.[57]

Chana Mor found interest in the connection between Judaism and Theosophy and offered a Theosophical-inspired explanation to the Passover

Seder (in Hebrew).[58] In the framework of this paper, Mor referred to Kabbalah. Like many other Jewish Theosophists, she asserted the proximity between Theosophy and Kabbalah: "In the Bible, there is the exoteric, and the esoteric. The Kabbalah deals in the esoteric aspect. Kabbalah is a very important part of Theosophy—to some extent, it is based on it. There are concepts in Theosophy which are taken from the Kabbalah. Dealings with the Kabbalah exist since the appearance of the Jews and of the Bible. Nonetheless, the knowledge that is called Kabbalah—and Theosophy—is more ancient."[59] Other Israeli Theosophists also found interest in Kabbalah. The first issues of the newsletter of the Israeli Theosophists included excerpts and translations from the *Zohar* and from the writings of Gershom Scholem and Martin Buber.[60] Lectures about Kabbalah and Hasidism were presented in meetings of Israeli lodges in the 1970s,[61] and many articles about Kabbalah were published in *Or*, especially in the 1990s.[62]

As mentioned earlier, the Israeli Theosophical Society is still active in Israel today. Nonetheless, there is currently only one Theosophical group active. In 2005, the president of the Israeli Theosophical Society, Abraham Oron, succinctly explained the reason for the decline of attendance in the Israeli lodges activities, an explanation that holds true the for global decline of the Theosophical Society: "Attendance to the lodge activities decreased, probably due to the great expansion of groups offering lecture on Buddhism, the Kabbalah and various new age subjects."[63]

Chapter 8

"To Spread Theosophical Teachings among the Jews"

Jewish Theosophists and the Jewish World

In May 1926, Jewish members of the Theosophical Society published an announcement in *The Messenger*: "We, members of the Theosophical Society and the Order of the Star who are of the Jewish Race, feel that an effort must be made to present the Jewish people our beliefs about the Coming, the existence of the Great White Lodge, Reincarnation, and Karma, from and angle best suited to their historical background and their traditions, and link these truths with the work of the great sages as given in the midrashim, Mishna, Talmud and Kabala."[1] Many other Jewish Theosophists believed they had a mission to the Jews outside the Theosophical fold, and one of the aims of the Association of Hebrew Theosophists was "to spread Theosophical teachings among the Jews."[2] Jewish Theosophists aspired to initiate a spiritual reform of Judaism through the spreading of Theosophy among the Jews. However, as we have already seen in previous chapters, they faced opposition from other Jews, who denounced Theosophy as incompatible with Judaism.

This chapter explores the aspiration of Theosophists of Jewish descent to propagate Theosophy within their community and to reform Judaism through Theosophy. It examines their critiques of other forms of Judaism, particularly Rabbinic and Orthodox, highlighting their endeavors to "Spiritualize Judaism." Additionally, it addresses the opposition they encountered within their communities and their responses to these criticisms. Before turning to examine these issues, I would like to consider the question of their Jewish identity and their connections to other contemporary Jewish movements and trends.

"What Kinds of Jews?"

In 1926 Henry C. Samuels, the president of the American Section of the Association of Hebrew Theosophists, raised a question concerning the Jewish identity of the members of the association:

> It is of course to be expected that many should wonder just what the AHT is and what kinds of Jews are those who belong to it. Correspondence that we receive indicates that some think of us as an association of Jewish mystics, some as reformed Jews and some as Orthodox Jews. There is really much truth in all those expressions, for the fact is that the organization is an association of Hebrew Theosophists, composed of Jews of all phases and elements in Judaism.[3]

The members of the association, as well as those Jews who joined the Theosophical Society prior to the foundation of the Hebrew association, came from different geographical areas and ethnic backgrounds and had diverse religious affiliations. As we have seen in the previous chapters, the Association of Hebrew Theosophists had sections in India, England, Holland, Iraq, and the United States. Jewish Theosophists included Ashkenazy and Sephardic Jews, Iraqi Jews, and Indian Jews from the Cochin and Bene Israel communities. However, Jewish Theosophists did not come from all "phases and elements" of Judaism. Most of them in Europe, the United States, India, South Africa, Iraq, and Israel were predominantly middle-class, Western-acculturated people proficient in European languages. There were several rabbis and scholars who were affiliated with the Theosophical Society, such as Arrigo Lates, who headed a Jewish Theosophical group in Livorno; Joshua Abelson, the liberal Anglo-Jewish Orthodox rabbi and scholar; Edward L. Israel, a Reform rabbi and social activist from Baltimore; and Moses Gaster, scholar of Jewish studies and chief rabbi of the English Sephardic community. Other Jewish Theosophists came from traditional Orthodox homes, but many of them became estranged from rabbinic Judaism. Most Jewish Theosophists, however, did not receive traditional Jewish education and did not adhere to Jewish Orthodox practice.

Regardless of the degree of their adherence to Jewish religious practice, many of the Jewish Theosophists had a strong sense of national identity. Many of them were sympathetic to Zionism, and some were active in Zionist organizations. *The Jewish Theosophist*, the journal of the American Section of the Association of Hebrew Theosophists, expressed much interest and sympathy with Zionism. In its report on the Fifteenth Zionist Congress held in 1927 in Basel, the journal stated: "Jews the world over are now celebrating the 10 anniversary of the Balfour Declaration which restored to the Jew his national existence, and it has realized for him a hope that has not waned in the centuries of our 'Goluth.' "[4] The first two issues of *The Jewish Theosophist* cited a poem by Jewish national poet and Zionist activist Hayyim Nachman Bialik. The title page of the second volume of *The Jewish Theosophist*, published in 1932, carried a pentagram in which the word *Zion* was inscribed in Hebrew beside the emblem of the Theosophical Society.

S. S. Cohen, who was one of the founders of the Association of Hebrew Theosophists and later became a follower of Sri Ramana (without severing his contacts with the Theosophical Society), expressed his identification with Judaism and his sympathy for the recently established State of Israel in a couple of articles he published in 1952, in the journal *India and Israel*.[5]

Following the rise of Nazism and the vicissitudes of World War II and its aftermath, several Jewish Theosophists emigrated to Palestine. Although some of them were not initially committed to Zionism, most of the Israeli Theosophists identified with the Zionist endeavor and with the State of

Figure 8.1. Title page of *The Jewish Theosophist* 2 (1932). Courtesy of the National Library of Israel collections. Used with permission of the Theosophical Society in America.

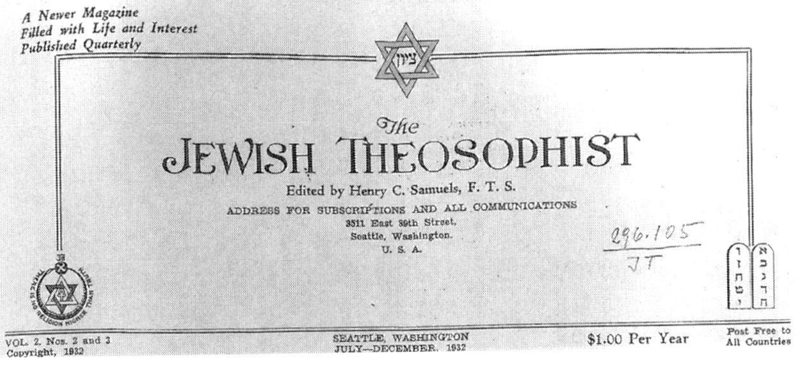

Israel. However, as we saw in the previous chapter, some of them were active in pacifist and interreligious activities.

Bringing Theosophy to Jews

In a letter sent to the Washington lodge in May 1926, the officers of the American Section of the Association of Hebrew Theosophists presented themselves and their mission: "We, Theosophists of the Jewish race feel it is our duty to band ourselves together for the purpose of bringing Theosophy and the Message of the Coming to Jews and to translate the Ancient Wisdom in terms that are familiar in Jewish tradition by linking these truths with the Jewish mystical tradition."[6] According to the letter, the aim of the Jewish Theosophists was "to do publicity work among Jews" and influence them to join the Theosophical Society: "There is no reason why more of the people who in the past made such valuable contribution to occultism, witness, the Kabbalah, the mysticism of the Essenes, and Hasidism should not be influenced to enter the ranks of the Theosophical Society."

Indeed, many Jewish Theosophists worked "to spread Theosophical teachings among the Jews," as stated in the second of the three aims of the Association of Hebrew Theosophists. Lila B. Allebach described the Hebrew Theosophists as follows: "The handful of men who at the call of the 'Masters' are assembled to carry forward the work of Universal Brotherhood among those of our ancient faith."[7] Alex Horne stated, "Too long have we drunk of the well of knowledge without making some attempt to share our inspiration with the rest of our co-religionists. Now that attempt is made and it is the privilege of every Jewish Theosophist to take a hand in the work of spreading the light, and the spiritual comfort and strength that go with it."[8] Similarly, in a later period, the Israeli Theosophists regarded as their mission introducing Theosophy to the Israeli public. In the 1971 annual report, Hans Zeuger wrote:

> As in previous years, we considered it our duty to study the Ancient Wisdom not only within the rather limited circumference of our little group but tried to bring the message of Theosophy to the Israel public at large. Thanks to these continued endeavors, Parapsychology and Astrology are now widely known and willingly accepted in our country. Gratifying opportunities are thus at hand to infuse theosophical ideas—the Oneness of life,

Reincarnation, Life after Death, Karma, the Educational Purpose
of Suffering, etc.,—into the consciousness of our nation.[9]

The Jewish Theosophists believed that introducing Theosophical ideas
to the Jews could offer them a better understanding of their own religion. Ré
(Rebekka) Levie, a Jewish Theosophist from the Netherlands who initiated
in 1905 a Kabbalah study group in Amsterdam, expressed her hope that the
study group will elevate the opinion of Jews of their own religion, "especially
the more developed youth, who now turn away from their religion with
defamation and contempt, because they think it is inferior."[10] Gaston Polak,
the general secretary of the Belgian Theosophical Society and the president
of the Association of Hebrew Theosophists, explained that the first declared
aim of the association—to study Judaism in light of Theosophy—"will help
the Jews to understand their own religion."[11] Similarly, Bozena Brydlova/
Mrs. Rubin wrote that Theosophy "will assist the Jew in becoming a better
Jew, inasmuch as it will aid him in understanding his own religion better."[12]
Chana Mor, one of the founders of the Israeli Theosophical Society, declared
in a paper she gave in 1953:

> Our tasks in Israel are enormous. We take part in a very hard
> karma of the Jewish people. The aims of the Theosophical Society
> are to investigate the still unexplained laws of nature and the
> soul powers latent in man. Hence, I regard it as one of the aims
> of the theosophists in this land, to investigate the duties and
> place of the Jews in the Great Plan of development, and with
> the help of this knowledge, to elevate the karma of the Jews.[13]

Jewish Theosophists were interested to spread Theosophical teaching
among their Jewish brethren. As Hebrew became the official and dominant
language in Israel, Israeli Theosophists initiated translations of Theosophical
texts into Hebrew.[14] In the first report on Theosophy in Israel, in 1953,
Isaac Cohen said that a committee of Israeli Theosophists was charged to
translate Blavatsky's *Key to Theosophy* and Besant's *The Ancient Wisdom.*[15]
Following that, the Israeli Theosophists published many texts by Blavatsky,[16]
Besant,[17] Krishnamurti,[18] Charles W, Leadbeater,[19] and other Theosophists.[20]

Theosophists were also interested in forming Jewish Theosophical
religious practices. Indeed, the first action of the Association of Hebrew
Theosophists was to lay the foundations for a synagogue in the Adyar compound. Annie Besant laid the foundation stone, and A. B. Salem conducted

Figure 8.2. Plan of proposed synagogue at Adyar. *Source: The Jewish Theosophist* 1, no. 4 (July 1927): 2. Courtesy of the National Library of Israel collections. Public domain.

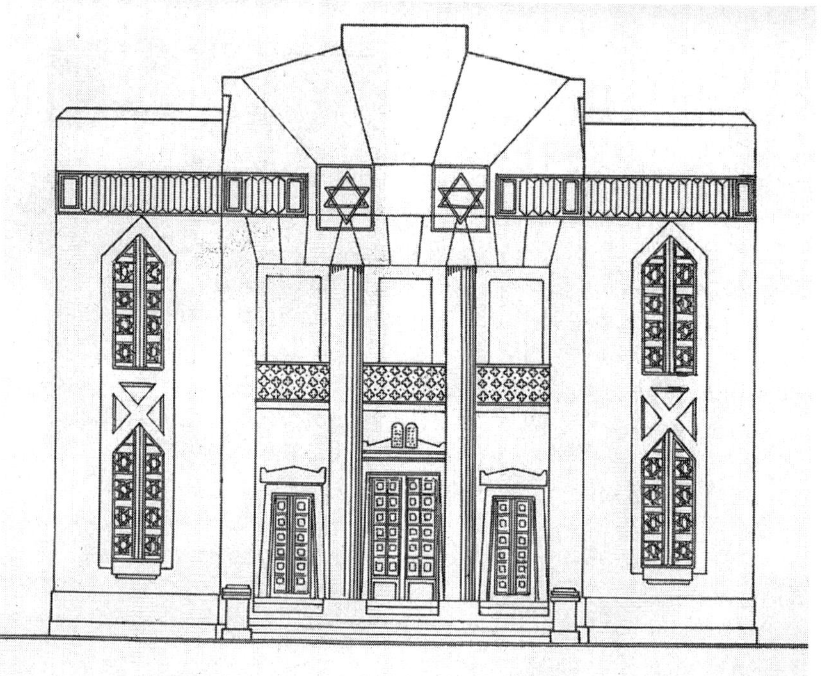

the ceremony in Hebrew.[21] The plans for the proposed synagogue were published, and efforts were made in subsequent years to secure funds for its building.[22] However, the synagogue was never built. Other Jewish Theosophists suggested forming a "synagogue on Theosophical lines" in cities with large Jewish populations.[23] The founders of the Association of Hebrew Theosophists were interested in creating Theosophically inspired prayers for the use in the Adyar synagogue. In a letter published in the first volume of *The Jewish Theosophist*, S. S. Cohen wrote, "It will also be desirable to prepare, with the help of the rabbis in America, a form of prayer book in Hebrew to be used in our Adyar Synagogue. You know that Jewish prayers nowadays are very dry from the spiritual standpoint and lack any sense of high aspiration. If we could give them a Theosophical tone in connection with the Jewish traditional ritual, it would be highly appreciated."[24] Similarly,

Samuel Isaac Heiman, the president of the Jewish lodge in London, suggested revising the Jewish prayer book, changing the ritual at the synagogue, and forming a ritual for the Jewish youth similar to that of the Theosophical youth order, the Round Table.[25]

In 1928, Henry C. Samuels, the president of the American Section of the Association of Hebrew Theosophists and the editor of *The Jewish Theosophist*, published a modern Jewish prayer book, *Morning Prayer: For Individual and Congregational Jewish Worship*. Samuels did not present the prayer book as a Jewish Theosophical prayer book but rather, as a "a modern comprehensive and applicable order of service, for individual and congregational Jewish worship." However, Samuels (who added the initials *FTS* to his name) compiled a Theosophical-inspired Jewish prayer service. In the introduction to the book, he declared that the aim of the service was "to inspire us towards noble conduct and ideal expression in so far as we develop the capacity to realize our own higher selves, the God within us, and the many great and beneficent things in life."[26] According to one of the prayers composed by Samuels, the rabbi, holding the closed Torah scrolls, should recite: "We join in praise and gratitude to the Holy Ones, the Elders, the Teachers and the Saints of all people and in all ages by whose devotion and sacrifice the gifts of Thy truths are known for the enlightenment of all Thy Children."[27]

The book, which is mostly composed of traditional Jewish prayers (brought in Hebrew with English translations) as well as prayers written by Samuels, includes several Theosophical passages: "The River" by J. Krishnamurti (which Samuels suggests can be employed in place of a sermon),[28] an excerpt from "At the Feet of the Master,"[29] and "Three Great Truths," by Mable Collins, at the end. The prayer book opens with "Holy, Holy, Holy," by the English bishop and hymn writer Reginal Heber (1783–1826),[30] and includes several other Christian hymns,[31] as well as the "Act of Faith" taken from the liturgy of the Theosophical Liberal Catholic Church.[32] One of the prayers mentions the "great Elder Brother, a son of our own race and kin, Jesus, the Master, who in his great agony held fast to the works of Thy light and love."[33]

"Spiritualizing Unspiritual Judaism"

In 1926, the American Section of the Association of Hebrew Theosophists published a booklet entitled *Spiritualizing Unspiritual Judaism*, written by

תפלת שחרית

Morning Prayer

A modern, comprehensive and applicable order of Service, for individual and congregational Jewish worship.

❧

THE NEW SYNAGOGUE PRESS

Route 1, Box 830 B.

SEATTLE, U. S. A.

Figure 8.4. Alex Horne, *Spiritualizing Unspiritual Judaism* (Association of Hebrew Theosophists, American Section, Seattle, 1926). Courtesy of the National Library of Israel collections. Public domain.

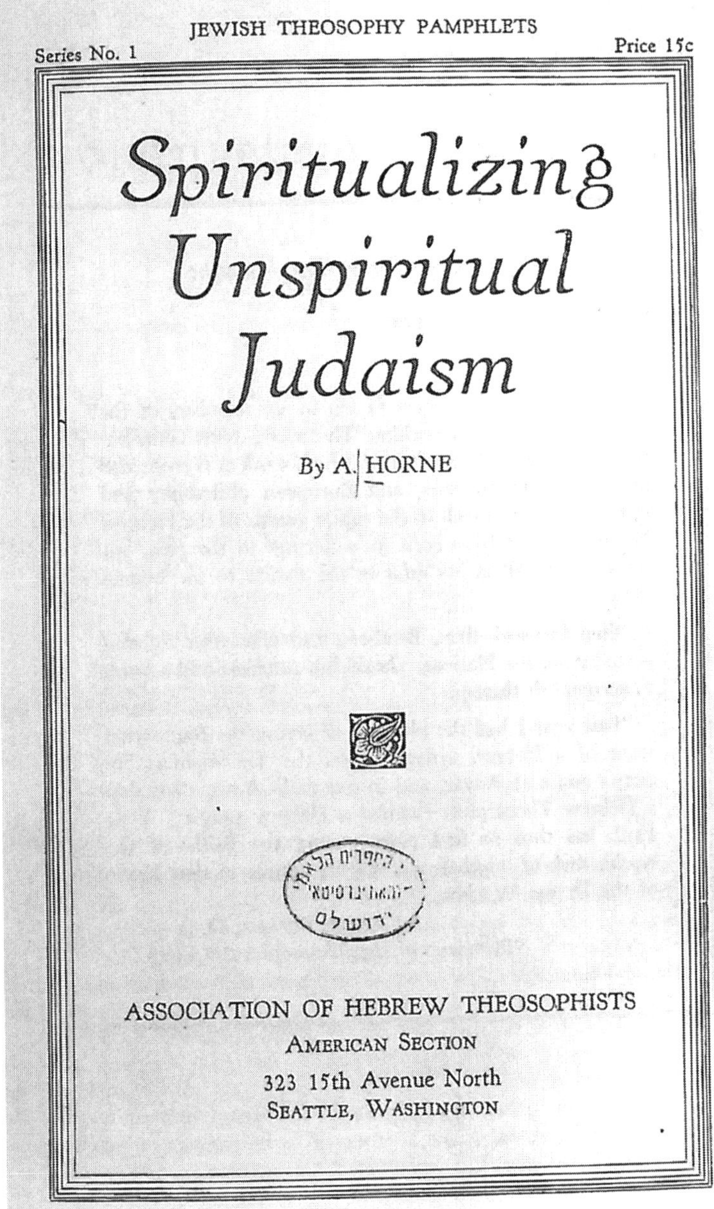

Alex Horne, the Jewish Theosophist who recently relocated from Shanghai to San Francisco. Horne, like many other Jewish Theosophists, believed that Judaism could be revived and spiritualized through Theosophy. Many Jewish Theosophists accepted the negative image of Judaism—especially rabbinic—as dogmatic, materialistic, and bereft of spirituality and vitality. Thus, for instance, Leonard Bosman, the Anglo-Jewish Theosophist who came from a Jewish observant background, wrote in his booklet, *A Plea for Judaism*, that he fell away from Jewish Orthodoxy "because [of] the lack of reality behind the too rigid forms and customs."[34] Bozena Brydlova/Mrs. W. B. Rubin, the vice president of the American Section of the Association of Hebrew Theosophists, wrote in an article published in 1926, "The Talmud . . . in our modern days seems dreadfully useless and unpractical with its laws that were established to govern conditions which we have long outgrown."[35]

Jewish Theosophists were especially critical of Orthodox Judaism. However, some of them were also critical of liberal Jewish trends. In *Spiritualizing Unspiritual Judaism*, Alex Horne wrote, "Present day Judaism, in both its Orthodox and Liberal branches, has failed to take stock of the spiritual and intellectual needs of the modern Jew."[36] In an article entitled "Theosophy and Modern Judaism," Horne asserted that "the Orthodox Jew keeps to the letter of the law and fails to see its mystic meaning. The Liberal Jew disregards the letter but fails likewise to seek its spirit."[37] Horne is sympathetic to the endeavor to re-form Judaism and detach it from the bonds of the past when they cease to have present-day significance. Yet, he is critical of "the liberal Jew" because he "cannot be made to realise that in doing this he throws overboard at the same time much that has a spiritual significance, simply because he had not been trained to perceive spiritual interpretations."[38] Horne's criticism was clearly aimed at the rejection and disparagement of Kabbalah and Hasidism by the Reform and Conservative Jewish movements of his time.

Horne, who criticized both Orthodox and liberal Judaism for lack of a mystical spirit, believed that Theosophy could satisfy the spiritual yearnings of the modern Jew without estranging him from his own religion. Horne argued that Jews had left Judaism to enter the ranks of Christian Scientists, New Thought, and Catholicism because of mystical cravings that could not be fulfilled within contemporary Judaism. According to Horne, these spiritual and mystical yearnings could be satisfied without leaving Judaism in the framework of the Theosophical Society: "The same yearnings, again, have brought some to the T.S., but here, fortunately, instead of estranging them from their race, as the other religious bodies have done, they have been encouraged rather to seek for the beauties in their own faith, and have no doubt been inspired to go back and work among their own people, and share with them the inspiration, the joy, of their newly acquired outlook on life and the universe."[39]

Theosophists of Jewish descent regarded the Theosophical-inspired reinterpretation of Jewish culture as a means for a spiritual reformation of Judaism. As we have seen, Jewish Theosophists were critical of rabbinic Judaism and regarded contemporary Judaism as materialistic and unspiritual. They believed that spreading Theosophy to the Jews and interpreting Judaism in the light of Theosophy would provide a way of "spiritualizing unspiritual Judaism." In his book, Alex Horne called for "a spiritualized Judaism, that will in fact form the foundation of a real, vital, soul inspiring religion—one that will be not merely a compromise between a half-hearted acknowledgment of one's religious inheritance and the attempt to make that acknowledgment as easy and comfortable as possible, but a religion in the true and fullest sense of the word—a channel through which may pour the spiritual aspirations of the people, and instrument that will instruct and elevate."[40] In another place, Horne explained that, because of the materialism modern Judaism had fallen to, "it needs a reviving breath, a fresh inspiration, a spiritualizing influence. All this we are in a position to give it."[41]

Lilla B. Allebach emphasized the reformative task facing Jewish Theosophists: "Our task should be to re-interpret the faith as to bring it into consonance with the conditions of a new environment and not permit ourselves to look upon the old type of Judaism as ultimate and binding and attempt to incrustate it in a shell of permanence."[42] According to the officers of the Indian Section of the Association of Hebrew Theosophists, the task of the association was "[t]o help our race by bringing them to the light of Theosophy by turning their narrow orthodoxy to a rational broad-mindedness adorned with intelligent spirituality—a spirituality tinged by the high philosophical conceptions of races and cultures other than their own."[43]

As mentioned earlier, many Jewish Theosophists had a strong sense of Jewish national identity and were supportive of the Zionist movement. Some of them regarded the Theosophically inspired spiritual reform of Judaism as necessary for a Jewish national revival. Thus, Alex Horne wrote in *Spiritualizing Unspiritual Judaism*, "We have too long made the mistake of regarding a nation or a race as nothing more than a political or social unit. We must now realize that a race is a spiritual entity, whose soul is that undefinable yet unmistakable something which vivifies the physical form, keeps it alive

and stamps it with the definite characteristic we so easily recognize as we
scan the pages of history. To feed that national soul requires spiritual aspiration."[44] In later years, Israeli Theosophist Chana Mor asserted that one
of the aims of the Theosophists in Israel was to use the understanding of
the duties and place of Jews in the "great plan of development" to elevate
the karma of the Jews.[45]

Jewish Opposition to Theosophy

Jewish Theosophists faced opposition from other Jews, who denounced
Theosophy as incompatible with Judaism

Already in the late nineteenth century, the Jewish Arabic translation
of a section from the *Zohar*, by the Jewish Theosophist from Pune, A. D.
Ezekiel, stimulated strong objections from leading rabbis from India, Iraq,
and Palestine. The Sephardic chief rabbi of the Land of Israel, Raphael Meir
Panigel, and his son-in-law (who later succeeded him), Rabbi Yaacov Shaul
Eliashar, declared in a letter that was published in the Hebrew newspaper
Havatzelet,

> Our soul has grieved to hear that the two *Idrot*, *Idra Rabba* and
> *Idra Zuta*,[46] were printed in the Arabic language in the town
> of Poona, a town in India. Who would believe such bad news?
> Who would not be upset and outraged by such a great sacrilege
> (*hilul ha-Shem*); whose hair will not stand on end when he sees
> such an evil thing, that the hidden secrets reach the hands of
> the multitude and the ignorant. [. . .] Woe is us! How did the
> holy Torah become, God forbid, a scorn and derision for the
> nations! How did villains come and profane it! [. . .] Woe is
> us! How was such a great profanation committed in our days![47]

The rabbis from Jerusalem decreed that the translation of the *Idra* should
be banned:

> We are thus obliged to decree in the power of the Divine Presence
> (*Shechina*) which never left the Wailing Wall, and in the power of
> the holy *Torah*, that no son of Israel should be allowed to read
> the above mentioned printed *Idrot*, in other languages, under
> any circumstance. Furthermore, every person called by the name

of Israel, has the obligation to keep and hide the translations in a place where no foreign hands can reach them, and eliminate them from the world.[48]

The decree against Ezekiel's translation was endorsed by the rabbis of Hebron and by leading rabbinic authority in Baghdad Rabbi Yosef Hayyim, the *Ben Ish Hai*.[49]

It is not clear whether these rabbis were aware that Ezekiel was a member of the Theosophical Society. However, his attempt to introduce Kabbalah to wider sectors of the Jewish population beyond the rabbinic elite—an objective inspired by his Theosophical convictions—was not acceptable to the rabbinic establishment.[50]

Jewish Theosophists were criticized, and sometimes persecuted, also in later periods. Jacob E. Solomon of the Bene Israel Indian community reported that he and other Jewish Theosophists in Ahmedabad were persecuted by the leaders of the community in the early decades of the twentieth century: "In Ahmedabad I was beaten in the Synagogue and excommunicated for protesting the unrighteous actions of the leaders; we formed a separate community and had prayers in my Hall. After seven years we were honorably taken back."[51]

Alex Horne was attacked following the publication of his pamphlet *Spiritualizing Unspiritual Judaism*. The editor of the *Israel Messenger* stated in his review of the booklet that "to join the rank of Hebrew Theosophists, and adopt Theosophy, the Jew actually slaps nolens volens, his own Judaism, the fountain head of all that is spiritual and uplifting in life."[52] In the following issue of the *Israel Messenger*, a reader who signed "Lover of Truth" wrote to the editor: "Dear Mr. editor. Mr. Horne, whose brochure was reviewed in your last issue, is doing a great disservice to his religion by calling the Jews unspiritual, and I would suggest to him to lift his eyes from the mist of modern Theosophy and look at the glorious sunshine of Judaism."[53]

The foundation of the Association of Hebrew Theosophists and its various branches at the end of the 1920s provoked negative reactions in the Jewish world. *The Jewish World* weekly newspaper in London denounced the foundation of the "sect" of Jewish Theosophists. The author of the report was worried about the pretense of Jewish Theosophists being loyal and true Jews and expressed his hope that eventually they would leave Judaism.[54] The author was especially suspicious of the Christological nature of the belief in the coming of the world teacher and condemned Annie Besant's message to the Jewish Theosophists in which she expressed her hope that the Jews would welcome the world teacher, "whom they ignorantly rejected when he first came to them."[55] Besant's statement was also denounced by the *Jewish Ledger* of New Orleans, which regarded it as proof that Jewish Theosophists (which were described as an "absurd cult" and an "abnormality") cannot be "strict adherents of the Jewish faith and unquestionable believers in the Unity of God."[56]

The Jewish lodge that was founded in London in 1926 was criticized in an article entitled "Strange Faiths" that was published in the *Jewish Chronicle*. The author of the article, who signed "Mentor," argued that Theosophy is an alien faith that is fundamentally opposed to Jewish teaching.[57] In another article, in which he reiterated his claim that there is a gulf between Judaism and Theosophy, Mentor cited Annie Besant's above-cited address to the Hebrew Theosophists. In it, Mentor concludes that it will not be long before the Jewish Theosophists will find themselves drawn altogether outside Judaism.[58]

The American Section of Hebrew Theosophists was criticized in an article entitled "Jewish Defection," which was published in the St. Louis Jewish journal, *The Modern View*, in 1931.[59] Although the Jewish Theosophists were denounced in the article as defectors, the main criticism was directed against their aspiration to revive Kabbalah and Jewish mysticism. The author of the article admitted that "there have long been in existence mystical and esoteric teachings among our people." However, he regarded these teachings as "abnormal and unhealthy": "What is primarily wrong with such a movement as Hebrew Theosophy is therefore the fact that it concentrates its effort and attention upon the preservation, or as it terms it, revival, of an abnormal and unhealthful phase and condition of Judaism, to the neglect of the normal, rational, and reasonable phases and conditions of Jewish lore and Jewish learning."[60]

As we have seen in previous chapters, the Jewish Theosophists in Basra, Iraq, encountered fierce opposition. One of their opponents, Isaac Said Nathan, published a pamphlet entitled *The New Religion in Basra and the Response to It*, in which he criticized the doctrines and the moral conduct of the Theosophists.[61] Nathan wrote that the esoteric teachings of the Theosophical Society "were based on sophisticated deception, that exploits mentally weak people, through magic and charms."[62] He asserted that the teachings of the Theosophical Society, which are based on a mixture of books from various ancient religions, especially Buddhism, contain "inner contradictions, insanity and confusion"[63] that repel knowledgeable scholars. He further claimed that the Theosophists deny the existence of God and do not believe in any religion, revealed scripture, or prophet. They reject all the obligations that monotheistic religions require, are not obliged to ethical and moral behavior, and spread licentiousness between young people and women. "Money and women in this society," he wrote, "are shared by all, like water and air."[64]

The local detractors of the Jewish Iraqi Theosophists appealed to the rabbinic authorities in England and the United States and asked for their opinion and advice concerning the Theosophical Society and its Jewish adherents. The chief rabbi of the British Empire, Rabbi Joseph Hertz, wrote in his response, "Whilst there are certain resemblances between the Jewish Kabala and some aspects of Theosophy, Theosophical teaching is, as a rule, foreign to Judaism, and sometimes against the very fundamentals of our faith. I would strongly urge brothers in Basra to abstain from affiliation with the Theosophy movement."[65]

Similarly, Rabbi Dr. Leo Jung of the Rabbinical Council of the Union of American Orthodox congregations asserted,

> Jews do not need Theosophy. In the Torah they are taught a philosophical life, not a mystic nothingness. Theosophy leads Jews away from their solid duties with which our lord has crowned us. I would certainly warn my brothers against the surrender of their religious identity, which is inevitable as they lose themselves in the unprofitable mazes of theosophic thought. . . . Theosophy is a malady of the weak. It is a punishment of ignorance. It is not a religion for men. It robs women of their grace and strength. It deprives youth of its moral stamina.[66]

Based on the letters they received, the rabbinical court in Baghdad issued a circular in which they stated that Theosophists hold to a new belief that differs from the Jewish faith and called the members of the community to take actions against them. The rabbis called for the removal of the Theosophical lodge from the vicinity of the synagogue and prohibited the Theosophists in participating in religious and lay affairs of the community.[67]

The acting chief rabbi of Basra, Rabbi Heskel Sassoon, gave a sermon against the Theosophists that stimulated members of the community to attack the Theosophical lodge and the home of its president, Kadouri Ani.[68] Finally, Rabbi Heskel issued a decree that excluded the Jewish members of the Theosophical Society from participating "in circumcision, marriage, and burial, and other matters relating to the community and all the religious affairs of Israel."[69]

Some members of the Jewish communities in Shanghai and Bombay supported the actions taken against the Theosophists.[70] Nayim B. Samuel of Bombay applauded the rabbis for "separating the rotten apples from the good ones." Samuel was especially opposed to the liberal stance of the Jewish Theosophists: "Theosophy, to my mind aims at establishing a liberal section of the Jews contrary to the teaching of the Torah." Furthermore, he argued that the Theosophists disturbed the efforts to build a Jewish homeland in Palestine. Hence, "in excommunicating those that are affiliated to the Theosophic society the rabbis of Basra have removed a serious impediment that would have obstructed us Jews, on our way towards the realization of a peaceful homeland in Palestine."[71]

The editor of *Israel Messenger*, N. E. B. Ezra, on the other hand, opposed the excommunication of Theosophists. Nonetheless, he accused them of detaching themselves from the Jewish congregation: "Mr. Ani and his friends had donned the costumes of beggars in the home of aliens, in the hope of snatching crumbs of bread from other tables when their own table lacks nothing by way of satisfying their hungry souls."[72]

In the following years, as the various sections and lodges of the Association of Hebrew Theosophists ceased to be active, Jewish Theosophists did not receive public attention. The Theosophical groups and lodges, which had been active in Israel since the 1950s, also received very little public attention and did not encounter much criticism or opposition. However, in an article published in the journal *Kol ha-Ir* in 1989, the reporter, who met with a group of Israeli Theosophists, observed, "The members of the group were cautious and suspicious. They all explained that they were afraid of harassment by religious [i.e., Jewish Orthodox]) circles and the malice of the press."[73]

Responses to the Criticism

Theosophists of Jewish descent rejected the accusations raised against them, responded to their detractors, and sometimes attacked them in return. A. D. Ezekiel, whose translation of the *Idra Zuta* to Jewish Arabic was banned by Jewish rabbinic authorities in Iraq and Palestine, published several letters in *The Jewish Gazette Paerah* defending his translation and attacking his opponents.[74] In a letter he sent to the chief rabbi (*Haham Bashi*) of Palestine, Rephael Meir Panigel, Ezekiel wrote, defiantly, that Panigel's decree did not achieve its goal but on the contrary, enhanced the sales of the book.

Ezekiel concluded his letter by requesting Panigel to withdraw his decree and asserted his independence from the rabbinic authorities: "The sages and Rabbis of Baghdad have written to the dignitaries of India concerning this affair, thinking they had authority over me. Praise God, I am a free person, and they don't have power over me."[75] Ezekiel continued to publish translations of Kabbalistic texts and discussed openly his affiliation with the Theosophical Society in his introduction to the translation of the first part of Yoseph Ergas's *Shomer Emunim*, which he published in 1888. Ezekiel dedicated the translation to Elijah Moshe Dweck ha-Cohen, the editor of the *Jewish Gazette Paerah* and to other members of "our group" who stood by him in his struggle to "overthrow the yoke of the priestcraft."[76]

Members of the Association of Hebrew Theosophists rejected the accusations that they had distanced themselves from Judaism. A person who wrote under the pseudonym *Sofia* acknowledged in an article entitled "Jewish Theosophy—A Paradox," published in 1926, that the ideas of the Theosophical Society may seem at first sight distant from Jewish ideas. Yet, she wrote,

> Be not too sure that because you do not readily recognize a thought as Jewish it is necessarily un-Jewish; do not insist that all of the truth manifests itself in present day Judaism, and that, because an idea is not today openly advocated from the pulpit it is necessarily untrue. Keep your mind open: study and reflect, and it will gradually be shown to you that fundamental principles of modern Theosophy conform to the spirit of the teachings promulgated by the Jewish mystics and sages of old.[77]

Samuel Isaac Heiman, the president of the English Section of the Association of Hebrew Theosophists, wrote a response to the accusation of Mentor, which was published in the *Jewish Chronicle* and was discussed above. Heiman claimed that Theosophy is not alien to Judaism and that some of the greatest sons of Israel have been students and exponents of "the ancient wisdom, or theosophy." Furthermore, Heiman argues that because Theosophists are not bound to any common faith, they cannot be accused of adhering to a faith that is alien to Judaism.[78]

Following the excommunication in Basra in 1931, Jewish Theosophists attacked the rabbis who issued the ban. S. S. Cohen, one of the founders of the Association of Hebrew Theosophists who originally came from Basra, described the rabbis of Basra as "primitive, uneducated, half literate, religious autocrats."[79] The American Jewish Theosophist Henry C. Samuels published an article entitled "Fighting the Light (the Story of a Modern Excommunication)," in which he attacked the rabbis who issued the ban: "I affirm with all vehemence of my soul that in this action and attitude those rabbis neither represent Judaism nor the Jew, but a darkness which still besets some of our people."[80]

Theosophists of Jewish background confronted biases and rejection not only from leaders and members of the Jewish community but also from some of their fellow Theosophists, who held racist and anti-Jewish prejudices. In the following chapter, I will examine the confrontation of the Jewish Theosophists with the negative attitude to Judaism of some of the leaders and members of the Theosophical Society.

Chapter 9

Jewish Theosophists Facing Anti-Judaism and Antisemitism within the Theosophical Society

In her article "Why Every Jew Should Join the Association of Hebrew Theosophists," Bozena Brydlova praised the Theosophical Society for its tolerance toward the Jews: "Theosophists draw no distinction between race, creed, sex, caste or color. Therefore the Jew enters the organization with no feeling of timidity of misgiving."[1] Brydlova argued that Theosophy would improve the image of Judaism and the attitude of the Gentiles to the Jews: "Hence Theosophy will tend to make the Gentile see the Jew in his true light and to endow Judaism with its rightful heritage . . . [I]nstead of persecuting the Jew because of his religion, the Theosophist hails him with welcome, because he brings into the society a grand old faith that is worth studying and heeding."[2] The tolerant, universalistic stance of the Theosophical Society, which called for a universal brotherhood of humanity without distinction of race, creed, sex, caste, or color attracted many Jews, who joined Theosophical branches all around the world. Yet, albeit the tolerant stance of the society and its declaration of universal brotherhood, a negative image of Judaism and antisemitic expressions could be found among many of its founders and followers. The Jewish followers had to face not only rejection and criticism from their Jewish brethren but also anti-Jewish biases from some of their fellow Theosophists.

In this chapter, I will discuss the anti-Jewish and antisemitic expressions of some of the leaders and members of the Theosophical Society and examine the ways that Jews responded to these expressions and their aspiration to elevate the standing of Judaism among their fellow Theosophists and to enrich Theosophy with Jewish spiritual traditions.

Anti-Jewish and Antisemitic Attitudes within the Theosophical Society

Helena Blavatsky, the founder of the Theosophical Society, expressed several times a negative stance toward Jews and Judaism.[3] Blavatsky wrote in *The Secret Doctrine* that while Jews were acquainted with sorcery and maleficent powers, they knew little of real divine occultism because their national character was "averse to anything which had no direct bearing upon their own ethnical, tribal and individual benefits."[4] According to Blavatsky, gross realism, selfishness, and sensuality were "the idiosyncratic defects that characterize many of the Jews to this day."[5] Blavatsky emphasized the chasm between Aryan and Semitic religious thought and declared, "There was a day when the Israelite had beliefs as pure as the Aryans have. But now Judaism, built solely on phallic worship, has become one of the latest creeds in Asia, and theologically a religion of hate and malice towards everyone and everything outside of itself."[6] In *The Key to Theosophy*, Blavatsky expressed the idea that universal truth could be found in all religions except Judaism: "What is also needed is to impress men with the idea that, if the root of mankind is one, then there must also be one truth which finds expression in all the various religions—except in the Jewish, as you do not find it expressed even in the Kabala."[7]

Privately, Blavatsky used blatant antisemitic expressions. In a letter to James Ralston Skinner from 1887, which was recently discovered by Jeffery D. Lavoie, Blavatsky repeated her opinion that the Jews have not given or preserved any real esoteric knowledge and added that she doesn't like the Jews "for the harm they [have] done the world and their grasping, selfish, hideous egotism. . . . The most commercial, money making grasping nation the world over."[8] According to Emma Coulomb, Blavatsky called A. D. Ezekiel, the Jewish Theosophist from Pune, *"con de juif."*[9]

Other Theosophical leaders expressed similar anti-Jewish opinions. J. D. Buck (1838–1916), the founder of the Theosophical lodge in Cincinnati, wrote in his article "The Cabbalah" that the key to the secret wisdom of the Kabbalah was lost from Judaism, which had become "a close corporation for commercial speculations and mutual protection."[10] Annie Besant, who became the president of the Theosophical Society in the early twentieth century, also expressed a bias against the Jews. Although she accepted the establishment of the Association of Hebrew Theosophists with enthusiasm, her letter of welcome to the Jewish Theosophists chided the Jews for ignorantly rejecting the world teacher when he appeared in the body of Christ and expressed the hope that in his second coming, he would lift the Jews back among the nations:

> I am very glad to welcome the association. It would indeed be splendid if some of the nation which ignorantly rejected the World Teacher when he came to them, using the body of a Jewish disciple as his vehicle, should welcome Him on his return two thousand years later. Who knows what Word He may have for the ancient people to whom He came on His previous visit, Will He lift them back among the nations of the world? St. Paul looked forward to such a revival of his people and likened it to "life from the dead."[11]

Rudolf Steiner, the general secretary of the German Section of the Theosophical Society in the early twentieth century, and later, the founder of Anthroposophy, also expressed negative opinions of Judaism and was opposed to Zionism.[12] In a review of Robert Hamerling's antisemitic book *Homunkulus*, which Steiner published in 1888 (before he joined the Theosophical Society), Steiner described Hamerling's critics as "oversensitive Jews" and asserted that "Jewry as such has long since outlived its time. It has no more justification within the modern life of peoples, and the fact that it continues to exist is a mistake of world history whose consequences are unavoidable. We do not mean the forms of the Jewish religion alone, but above all the spirit of Jewry, the Jewish way of thinking."[13] Steiner opposed Zionism, and in an article published in 1897, he declared that he regarded the leaders of the Zionist movement as worse than the "harmless" antisemites: "Much worse than the anti-Semites are the heartless leaders of the Jews who are tired of Europe, Herzl and Nordau. They exaggerate an unpleasant childishness into a world-historical trend. They pretend that a harmless squabble is a terrible roar of canons. They are seducers and tempters of their people."[14] Steiner's negative approach to Judaism continued after he joined the Theosophical Society and later, after he left it and founded the Anthroposophical Society. Like Blavatsky, Steiner regarded the Jews as materialistic and nonspiritual. In a lecture he delivered in March 1924, a year before he passed away, Steiner asserted that "the Jews have a great gift for materialism, but little for recognition of the spiritual world, because out of the whole world beyond this earth they venerated only the moon."[15]

Steiner developed Blavatsky's theories of the "root races" and the superiority of the Aryan root race. He asserted that the Jews' historical mission was to prepare the way for Christ and that after the fulfillment of this mission, there was no justification for the continuing existence of Judaism.[16] Steiner advocated the assimilation of the Jews and the cessation of Jewry as a people. In a lecture titled "The Essence of Judaism," which he delivered on May 1924, he suggested "the best things the Jews could do would be to dissolve in the rest of humankind, to blend in with the rest of humankind, so that Jewry as a people would simply cease to exist. That is what would be ideal."[17]

Curuppumullage Jinarajadasa (1875–1953), a leading Sinhalese Theosophist who later became the fourth president of the Theosophical Society, also expressed anti-Jewish sentiments. In an article he published in 1916, entitled "The Jewish People: A Letter to some Indian Jews," Jinarajadasa asserted that the Jews were not making the most of their lives because of certain characteristics in their tradition. The Jews, he claimed, "have not given any arts, or science, or law of a great constructive kind. . . . The Jews have been one of the proudest peoples of the world, and that pride continually narrowed their vision and made them the reverse of spiritual."[18] Similar to Annie Besant, Jinarajadasa accused the Jews of rejecting the Messiah (both in his reincarnation as Christ and in his previous and later incarnations) because of their self-righteousness, selfishness, and subscription to the letter of the law, rather than to its spirit. Because of their insistent hostility and persecution of the early Christians, he says, the karma of the Jews was enduring the suffering that they afflicted on others.[19] Jinarajadasa concludes that if the modern Jew wants to become the chosen of God, he should not bow down to the law and recognize that he must reform Judaism in the spirit of its ancient prophets.[20]

In later periods, Jinarajadasa expressed a more positive stance to Judaism. In a "A Message to Judaism," which he published in 1926 in *The Jewish Theosophist*, he said that the Jews should recognize the value of all other nations and religions and at the same time, proclaim to the world their moral heritage.[21] Following the rise of the Nazis to power in Germany, Jinarajadasa published in *The Theosophist* a condemnation of the persecution of the Jews in Germany. He noted that every intelligent man in Europe and America has heard the accusations against the Jews as individuals and as a race, "but no accusation whatsoever" he asserts "even if it be true in part—ever justifies hatred."[22]

Although most of the Theosophists shared Jinarajadasa's condemnation of the Nazis,[23] several German Theosophists joined the Nazi Party and defended its anti-Semitic policy.[24] Prof. Johannes Maria Verweyen (1883–1945), the former general secretary of the Theosophical Society in Germany, published in the September 1933 issue of *The Theosophist* a letter defending Hitler and the Nazi regime: "The so-called persecution of the Jews in Germany had not been a primary act, but in answer to the persecution of non-Jew by Jews, that means their predomination in theatres, literature, commerce, and so on."[25] Jutta Todtenhaupt, the leader of the Parsifal Lodge in Berlin, denied the persecution of the Jews and defended the Nazi regime: "There is no question whatever of a persecution, it is nothing but the driving back (*zurückdrängen*) of a block, which has pushed itself too far to the front, as well as a purification from elements which have swamped Germany since 1914, mostly coming from Galicia."[26] Hugo Vollrath (1877–1943), another prominent German Theosophist and the founder of the "Supernationale Theosophische Gesselschaft," also criticized Jinarajadasa for his stand against the Nazis and defended the latter's acts against the Jews: "In the interests of racial hygiene also, great care is being taken that this strange race may no longer hold a position, which does not belong to her, in a country not her own."[27]

Jewish Responses to Theosophical Antisemitism

Jewish Theosophists confronted and responded in different ways to the anti-Jewish prejudices and antisemitism they encountered within the Theosophical Society.

Some Theosophists of Jewish descent challenged the anti-Jewish stance of leaders and members of the Theosophical Society. Leonard Bosman contested the declaration of a Theosophist, whom he described as a student of comparative religion, that Judaism could not be reconciled with Theosophy. Bosman responded that Judaism and Theosophy can easily be reconciled through the "The Secret Doctrine of the Jews," the Kabbalah, which is essentially identical with Theosophy.[28] After the rise of the Nazis to power in Germany, S. S. Cohen, the Jewish Theosophist from India, responded to Johannes Maria Verweyen's approval of the Nazi antisemitic policies:

> It is beyond the comprehension of any right-thinking man, let alone a Theosophist, to read Professor Verweyen appealing for "Wisdom, Brotherhood and Justice" in *The Theosophist* for September . . . [I]t beats my "wisdom" to understand how predominance in theatres and literature can be called persecution—jealousy-provoking should be the appropriate term—and how can the one persecute the ninety-nine? I hope, in conclusion, that there will come about a change of attitude on the part of the Professor and his sympathizers, if any, to help the German nation to rise from its present perilous moral situation and to return to prosperity through the spiritual path of real "Wisdom, Brotherhood and Justice."[29]

However, it wasn't until later that Jewish Theosophists grappled with the anti-Jewish remarks made in the writings of Blavatsky. In 1977, Hans Zeuger, the president of Harmony Lodge in Tel Aviv and one of the founders of Theosophy in Israel, reported that he received from Franz E. Hirth, a Jewish Theosophist from Lichtenstein,[30] a list of "a rather astonishing number of anti-Semitic passage, very regrettably to be found in in Madame Blavatsky's various writings."[31] Zeuger asked to deliver this list to John Coats, the international president of the Theosophical Society, with the suggestion "that all these utterances should be eliminated in future editions and that Brother John Coats, the president, should issue a suitable statement to this effect."[32] A year later, during his visit to the London headquarters of the Theosophical Society, Zeuger mentioned Blavatsky's "offensive anti-Semitic remarks" to Boris de Zirkoff, the editor of Blavatsky's writings. According to Zeuger, de Zirkoff promised to take the matter up with the president, with the view of eliminating them in future editions of her works.[33]

As mentioned in the previous chapter, some Jewish Theosophists, such as Leonard Bosman and Alex Horne, accepted the negative image of Judaism as dogmatic, materialistic, and bereft of spirituality and vitality. However, Bosman, Horne, and other Theosophists of Jewish descent who criticized Orthodox Judaism did not accept the idea that Judaism concluded its historical mission and did not distance themselves from it. Rather they emphasized the spiritual and mystical resources of Judaism, called for its spiritual reform, and argued that it could enrich Theosophy with its spiritual resources.

As we have seen in previous chapters, many Jewish Theosophists gave lectures and published articles and books about Jewish mysticism and

Kabbalah. The purpose of these lectures and publications was not only to revive Jewish mystical knowledge among the Jews, but also to counter the negative image of Judaism within the Theosophical Society. Theosophists of Jewish background made efforts to present Kabbalah to non-Jewish Theosophists aiming to demonstrate its compatibility with Theosophy, while underscoring Judaism's contribution to occult and spiritual knowledge. The Association of Hebrew Theosophists declared that its aim was "to elevate Judaism to its rightful heritage and to enrich Theosophy, the Divine Wisdom, which underlies all religion, with the many treasures that are embodied in ancient and modern Judaism, and thus to be of greater service to humanity both as Jews and through Judaism, our cherished Faith."[34] Many Theosophists of Jewish descent presented themselves as experts in Kabbalah and used their Jewish origins and knowledge of Jewish tradition to enhance their cultural capital within the society. Some of the non-Jewish Theosophists accepted that Jewish members could contribute their knowledge of Kabbalah to the society. In a message to the Hebrew Theosophists (very different in its tone from the first message, discussed above), Annie Besant congratulated them for enriching Theosophy with the wisdom of their "occult treatises": "It is a great happiness to me to see members of the great Hebrew race enriching Theosophy with contributions from their ancient Faith. Much wisdom is enshrined in their occult treatises, and European philosophy and metaphysics own much to the subtle genius of the Hebrew Nation. Great have been its sufferings in the past, but the greater still will be its gifts in the future to the human race."[35] As we have seen in the last two chapters, Kabbalah played an important role in the response of Jewish Theosophists to Jewish criticizers of Theosophy, as well as in their confrontation with anti-Jewish biases within the Theosophical Society. The centrality of Kabbalah for Jewish Theosophists was mentioned many times also in previous chapters. I would like to turn now to the concluding chapter of this book, which will discuss in detail the interest of Theosophists of Jewish descent in Kabbalah and their contribution to modern Kabbalah.

Chapter 10

Qabbalah, the Theos-Sophia of the Jews
Jewish Theosophists and the Kabbalah

As we have seen in previous chapters, Kabbalah played a central role in the attempts of Jewish Theosophists to harmonize Judaism and Theosophy. Theosophists of Jewish descent regarded Kabbalah as "the secret doctrine of the Jews," a perennial knowledge essentially identical with other esoteric traditions and with the teaching of the Theosophical Society. Thus, for instance, Leonard Bosman responded to Theosophists that denied the possibility of reconciling Judaism and Theosophy: "Have they heard of the inner doctrine, the Received wisdom, the Qabalah or the Doctrine of the Heart, or the Theos Sophia of the Jews? But verily the Secret Doctrine of the Jews is Theos-Sophia and nothing but Theos-Sophia, and hence it is a matter of perfect simplicity to reconcile the two doctrines that emanate from one source."[1]

Kabbalah played an important role in Western esotericism in general and within Theosophy in particular. The Theosophical Society had been concerned with Kabbalah since its very beginning, and Kabbalistic ideas and concepts had an important place in the writing of Blavatsky and other leading Theosophists.

The interest and centrality of Kabbalah in the writings of Blavatsky and other Theosophists prompted Theosophists of Jewish origin to study Kabbalah, translate Kabbalistic texts, and present their understanding of Kabbalah. However, unlike the non-Jewish Theosophists, who expressed an ambivalent and sometimes disparaging stance toward Jewish Kabbalah, Jewish Theosophists valorized Kabbalah unequivocally and emphasized its Jewish nature and origins. They regarded Kabbalah as a highly significant component of Judaism and advocated its use in the spiritual reform of Judaism.

Several scholars have studied the place of Kabbalah in the writings of Blavatsky and other leaders of the Theosophical Society.[2] However, the contribution of Jewish Theosophists to modern perceptions and formations of Kabbalah received very little scholarly attention.[3] In the final chapter of this book, I offer a discussion of the Jewish Theosophists' interpretations of Kabbalah and analyze the contexts and significance of Jewish-Theosophical appropriations of Kabbalah.

In this framework, I will also examine the relations between Jewish Theosophy and the academic study of Kabbalah. I will argue that the Jewish Theosophists' interpretations were part of a wider current of modern-Jewish interest and that some of their basic assumptions about its nature and significance resemble and interconnect with the perceptions of modern scholars. I would like to open this chapter with a discussion of the interest of non-Jewish Theosophists, especially Blavatsky, in Kabbalah.

Theosophy and Kabbalah

The Hebrew word *Kabbalah*, derived from the verb stem *K.B.L.*, denotes something received, that is, tradition. Since the late Middle Ages, the term *Kabbalah* has come to describe specifically traditions concerning *Sefirot*, "divine powers," and the impact of prayer and performance of the Jewish precepts on the divine realm. The term *Sefirot*, derived from the Hebrew root, *S.F.R.*, which means both "to count" and "to tell," appeared for the first time in *Sefer Yetzirah* (The Book of Creation), a short and enigmatic text of unknown provenance attributed to the patriarch Abraham. In *Sefer Yetzirah*, the *Sefirot* refer to the ten primordial numbers, which, along with the twenty-two letters of the Hebrew alphabet, served as tools for God in the creation of the world. However, in the late twelfth century, the *Sefirot* came to be perceived as divine powers, or attributes, and were also described as the human-like form of God. The last *Sefirah*, Malkhut (Kingdom) or Schechina (Divine Presence) was perceived as the feminine aspect of the divine system. According to Kabbalistic texts, the relations between the divine powers, especially, between the male and female components of the divine system, are in disharmony. The way to repair the divine harmony and bring forth redemption is through meticulous performance of the divine precepts, according to Jewish religious law. Other topics discussed in

Kabbalistic literature are the emanation of the *Sefirot* from the transcendent Infinite (En-Sof), the human soul and its divine origin, and the doctrine of reincarnation.

The term *Kabbalah* was also used to refer to hermeneutics based on the combination, permutation, and numerical value of letters (*gematria, notarikon,* and *temura*) and to the knowledge and use of the power of divine names. In later periods, use of the divine names and the preparation of amulets was designated practical Kabbalah (*kabbalah maʾasit*).

During the thirteenth century, various schools of Kabbalah developed in Jewish communities in the Iberian Peninsula. It was probably in Castile during the late thirteenth and early fourteenth centuries that the different units of *Sefer ha-Zohar* (the Book of Splendor) were written. The *Zohar*, which was attributed to the second-century sage Rabbi Shimon Bar Yochai, gradually became the central text of most subsequent Kabbalistic schools. In the sixteenth century, new forms of Kabbalistic teaching were developed in Safed, in the upper Galilee, especially by Isaac Luria (1534–1572) and his disciples. Luria's innovative teachings, which were based to a large degree on his interpretation of the *Zohar*, were accepted by all later Jewish Kabbalistic schools.

From the late fifteenth century, some Christian scholars and theologians took an interest in Kabbalah. Prominent figures such as Giovanni Pico della Mirandola (1463–1494), Johann Reuchlin (1455–1522), Christian Knorr von Rosenroth (1636–1689), and many others translated Jewish Kabbalistic texts into Latin and developed Christian doctrines based on Kabbalistic concepts, ideas, and methods of interpretation. Christian Kabbalists believed in the antiquity of the Kabbalah (especially, the *Zohar*), assumed that Kabbalah was part of the perennial wisdom that contained Christological doctrines and aspired to use Kabbalah for missionary purposes.

In the nineteenth century, new forms of Kabbalah were developed within non-Jewish occult and esoteric circles. Occultist Kabbalah developed out of Christian Kabbalah. However, it did not emphasize so much the compatibility of Kabbalah with Christianity, but rather regarded Kabbalah as a perennial, universal esoteric-magical secret doctrine. The first prominent occult Kabbalist was Alphonse-Louis Constant (1810–1875), known as Éliphas Lévi. He was followed by many other occultists who found interest in Kabbalah, such as Helena Petrovna Blavatsky and other members of the nascent Theosophical Society.[4]

The Theosophical Society was concerned with Kabbalah since its very beginning. "Cabala" was indicated as one of the main topics (together with occultism) studied by the society at its foundational meeting in Blavatsky's apartment in New York on September 8, 1875. The evening before the meeting in which the Theosophical Society was founded, George H. Felt (1831–1895), a mechanical engineer and amateur Egyptologist, who became one of the two vice presidents of the Theosophical Society, gave a lecture titled "The Egyptian Cabala."[5]

Kabbalah played an important role in the writings of Blavatsky.[6] She discussed it in her first article on the occult, "A Few Questions to 'Hiraf,'" which was published in *The Spiritual Scientist* in July 1875, a few months before the foundation of the Theosophical Society. Blavatsky also discussed Kabbalah and integrated Kabbalistic concepts in her two major books, *Isis Unveiled* (1877) and *The Secret Doctrine* (1888). Her last work on the subject, "The Kabalah and the Kabalists at the Close of the Nineteenth Century," was published in *Lucifer* (1892) a few months after her demise.

Blavatsky derived her knowledge about Kabbalah from nineteenth-century occult and Masonic writings and from nineteenth-century scholarly works.[7] Her expositions were not always consistent, and some of her opinions changed with time. Notwithstanding her interest in it and the importance she gave it in her account of the transmission of perennial wisdom, her attitude of Jewish and Christian Kabbalah was ambivalent.[8]

In "A Few Questions to Hiraf," she defined Kabbalah as "the compound mystic textbook of all the great secrets of Nature" and distinguished between the "Primitive Oriental Cabala" and a corrupted "Western Cabala." According to Blavatsky, the Oriental Kabbalah was transmitted orally by the wise men of Chaldea, India, Persia, and Egypt. Moses, who was initiated in Egypt, altered and corrupted the original traditions: "While Oriental Cabala remained in its pure primitive shape, the Mosaic or Jewish one was full of drawbacks, and the keys to many of the secrets, forbidden by the Mosaic law—purposely misinterpreted."[9]

Blavatsky opened her book *Isis Unveiled*, which was first published in 1877, asserting the existence of an ancient text, of which only one original copy exists, from which "the most ancient Hebrew document of occult learning—the Siphra Dzeniouta," was compiled.[10] In a footnote on the same page, she mentions the "traditions of the Oriental Kabbalists." Blavatsky discussed the Oriental Kabbalah extensively, especially in the second volume of the book, which includes also kabbalistic diagrams of "the Hindu and the Chaldeo-Jewish cosmogonies."[11] She claimed that the Books of Ezekiel and Revelation had a Hindu kabbalistic derivation, equated the kabbalistic concept En-Soph (the Infinite) with Hindu and Buddhist concepts, and argued that the *Sefirot,* the ten divine emanations, were identical with the ten Hindu *prajapatis.*[12] According to Blavatsky, the idea of the emanation of the *Sefirot* from the first principal was shared by the Oriental and Jewish Kabbalists, and the idea that the first emanation was Wisdom was known to the Greeks, Persians, Gnostics, and early Christians: "The Kabbala—the Oriental as well as the Jewish—shows that a number of emanations (the Jewish Sephiroth) issued from the First Principal, the chief of which was Wisdom. This Wisdom is the Logos of Philo, and Michael, the chief of the Gnostic Eon; it is the Ormazd of the Persians; Minerva, goddess of wisdom of the Greeks, who emanated from the head of Jupiter; and the second Person of the Christian Trinity."[13] Blavatsky reiterated the notion that the "Oriental or the Universal Kabala" was much older and purer than the "Western Chaldeo-Jewish Kabbalah." Nonetheless, she wrote, little is known of the Oriental Kabbalah, whose adepts are few, but who can be met by travelers "on the shores of the sacred Ganges . . . in the silent ruins of Thebes, and in the mysterious deserted chambers of Luxor."[14] Following the British writer Charles William King, Blavatsky claimed that Buddhism was the ultimate source of Gnosticism and Kabbalah.[15] As Julie Chajes noted, "Blavatsky aspired to cleanse Kabbalah of its Jewish accretions, and return it its pure and essential Buddhist source."[16]

In "The Kabalists at the Close of the Nineteenth Century," Blavatsky emphasized again the universality of Kabbalah and disparaged the Jewish Kabbalah: "If Kabalah [*sic*] is a word in Hebrew, the system itself is no more Jewish than is sunlight; it is universal. On the other hand, the Jews can claim the Zohar, Sepher Yetzirah (Book of Creation), Sepher Dzeniuta, and a few others, as their own undeniable property and as Kabalistic works."[17] Although Blavatsky claimed that the Kabbalah extant in the West did not repay the trouble of a lifetime of study, she maintained that real, initiated Kabbalists still exist, especially in Germany and Poland. However, they do not publish what they know nor refer to themselves as Kabbalists.[18]

Other members of the early Theosophical Society were also interested in Kabbalah. I have already mentioned the lecture "The Egyptian Cabala" that George H. Felt, who became one of the two vice presidents of the Theosophical Society, presented on the eve of its foundation. According to Felt, Kabbalah was a geometrical figure, the perfect system of proportions, known to the Egyptians and Greeks, which provided the key to the Bible, human culture, and nature itself. Although Felt regarded Kabbalah as Greek and Egyptian and distinguished it from the "Hebraic style" of Kabbalah, he believed that the learned rabbis who made investigations into the Hebrew Kabbalah were also able to solve inexplicable mysteries.[19]

The other vice president of the nascent Theosophical Society, physician Seth Pancoast (1823–1889), was also interested in Kabbalah.[20] In 1883, he published a book entitled *The Kabbalah or the True Science of Light: An Introduction to the Philosophy and Theosophy of the Ancient Sages.* He also published two articles on Kabbalah ("Kabbalah" and "The Mystery of Numbers") in the April and May 1886 issues of *The Path.* Pancoast regarded the Kabbalah as an ancient Oriental system of Philosophy and Theosophy, the source of all known religions and philosophies.[21] According to Pancoast, the Kabbalah did not originate within Judaism: "The Kabbalah was formerly a tradition, as the word implies, and is generally supposed to have originated with the Jewish Rabbins. The word is of Hebrew origins, but the esoteric science it represents did not originate with the Jews; they simply recorded what had previously been traditional."[22] Although Kabbalah was not originally Jewish, Pancoast asserted that its first records were *Sepher Yetzirah* and *Sepher ha-Zohar.* He described the Kabbalistic *sephirot* in some detail[23] and asserted that the hidden secrets of the Oriental Kabbalah were about to be revealed and would enlighten present and future generations.[24] The distinction between Oriental Kabbalah and Jewish Kabbalah was also made by another founding member of the society, Emma Harding Britten (1823–1899), in her books *Ghost Land* and *Art Magic* (both 1876).[25]

Jirah Dewey Buck (1838–1916), the founder of the Theosophical lodge in Cincinnati, published an article in 1883 entitled "The Cabbalah," in which he claimed that Kabbalah was a secret wisdom embedded in the Hebrew scriptures, the Pyramids in Egypt and America, and the measures, motions, and space of the heavenly bodies.[26] However, the key to this wisdom was lost from Judaism, which became "a close corporation for commercial speculations and mutual protection."[27]

Theosophists in England also found interest in Kabbalah and published translations of Kabbalistic texts. William Wynn Westcott (1848–1925), the leading English esotericist, fellow of the Theosophical Society, and founder of Hermetic Order of the Golden Dawn, published a translation of *Sefer Yetzirah* in 1887, which was republished in 1893, by the Theosophical Publishing Society in London.[28] And in 1891 and 1893, he published articles on the Kabbalah in Blavatsky's journal, *Lucifer.*[29]

Westcott asserted that *Sepher Yetzirah* and the *Zohar* "contain a system of spiritual philosophy of clear design, deep intuition, and far-reaching cosmological suggestions."[30] He recognized that his "love and respect" for Kabbalah differed from the attitude of Blavatsky and other Theosophists, who valued Eastern wisdom more than Jewish Kabbalistic sources.[31] However, he said, although Blavatsky condemned the "modern vagaries" of Kabbalah, she implied that the pure and ancient version was a Western offshoot of prehistoric wisdom religion.[32] Notwithstanding his "love and respect" for Jewish Kabbalah, Westcott asserted that the ancient substratum and primal truths of the Kabbalah "have been obscured by generations of editors, by visionary and often crude additions, and by the vagaries of Oriental imagery."[33]

In 1887, Samuel Liddel MacGregor Mathers (1854–1918), a co-founder of the Hermetic Order of the Golden Dawn, who was also affiliated with the Theosophical Society, published *The Kabbalah Unveiled*, an English translation of three units from the *Zohar* (*The Book of Concealed Mystery*, *The Greater Holy Assembly*, and the *Lesser Holy Assembly*) based on Knorr von Rosenroth's seventeenth-century *Kabbalah Denudata*.[34] Mathers's *The Kabbalah Unveiled* was republished in 1912 by the Theosophical Society Publications in New York. Like Westcott, Mathers found more interest in the Kabbalah than Blavatsky and the early American Theosophists and presented a more positive view of Jewish Kabbalah, especially of *Sefer Yetzirah* and the *Zohar*. Mathers saw in the *Zohar* a means of unveiling the original message of Christianity, which was distorted by the church and hoped that his *Zohar* translations would advance a spiritual revolution of Christianity.[35]

Another British Theosophist interested in Kabbalah was Dr. Henry Pratt, a medical doctor and independent scholar who was described by Blavatsky as an "erudite Kabalist from England."[36] In 1899, Pratt published "About the Kabbalah" in *The Theosophist*.[37] Pratt, who asserted that the Hebrew Kabbalah could be studied only from original sources and not from translations,[38] declared, similar to Blavatsky, that Kabbalah was received by the Jewish rabbis from "Eastern mystics" during the Babylonian captivity and was applied by them, in an artificial way, to the Jewish Scriptures.[39]

During the late nineteenth and early twentieth centuries, other articles on Kabbalah were published in *The Theosophist*. In 1887 Montague R. Lazarus published an article entitled "Kabbalah and Microcosm," which was based on Knorr von Rosenroth's translation of Cordovero "de anima" in *Kabbala Denudata*.[40] Lazarus presented a positive view of Kabbalah and suggested that the Kabbalah and the Vedanta have a common source and are the same, "up to a certain point."[41] In 1902, D. Chamier published "The Kabbalah and Its Doctrine."[42] Chamier, who depends in his discussion mostly on Isaac Myers's *Qabbalah*, Arthur Waite's *The Doctrine and Literature of the Kabalah*, and the introduction to Kabbalah published by the Jewish Theosophist from Poona, A. D. Ezekiel, wrote that "a great deal of this doctrine of Kabalism is narrow and dogmatical and consequently uninteresting." However, he asserts, there are points of interest in its treatment of God and his relation to man and that there are similarities between Kabbalistic ideas and "Eastern Philosophy."[43]

Kabbalah played a central role in the writings and activities of the French occultist and medical doctor Gérard Encausse (1865–1916), known as "Papus," who was a active in the early French Theosophical Society, as well as in other French esoteric movements.[44] In 1887, Papus published a translation of *Sepher Yetzirah* in the journal of the French Theosophical Society, *Le Lotus*.[45] Papus asserted that the unique, common core of religion, from which all the different religious cults emanated, could be found "with a little bit of work" ("avec un peu de travail"), in the Kabbalah.[46] In 1892, after he resigned from the Theosophical Society and turned against it, he published *La kabbale, tradition secrete de l'occident*.[47] The book, which was inspired by the Christian-occultist ideas of Éliphas Lévi, Antoine Fabre d'Olivet, and Saint-Yves d'Alveydre, was introduced with a letter of praise written by the French Jewish scholar Adolphe Franck. Another article on the Kabbalah, by the Swiss esotericist and Freemason Oswald Wirth, was published in *Le Lotus* in 1889.[48] Wirth presented a positive appreciation of the Jewish Kabbalah, which he asserts, contains in the most masterful precision, the sublime secret of all initiations. However, he says, the ancient sublime truths contained in the secret doctrines of the Jewish Rabbis were tainted with errors and superstition.[49] In 1909, Albert Jounet (1863–1923), a Christian socialist and a member of the French Theosophical Society, published an anthology of translations from the *Zohar* entitled *La Clef du Zohar*. Jounet asserted that the *Zohar* contained ancient doctrines that concord with Christian esoteric teachings and with the Egyptian, Assyrian, Babylonian, Persian, Chinese, Indian, Celtic, and Greek mysteries.[50] He believed that knowledge of the *Zohar* would enable Christians to acknowledge the esoteric truths found in the Old Testament and help the Jews to understand the truths of Christianity.[51] Notwithstanding his admiration of the *Zohar*, he stated that it was chaotic, like most Oriental books, and did not adhere to Western logical methods.[52]

German Theosophists also found interest in Kabbalah. Rudolf Steiner, who was the secretary of the German Section of the Theosophical Society at the time, gave a short lecture on Kabbalah in 1904 in Berlin in which he presented his Theosophical-inspired understanding of the ten *Sefirot* (the lecture also included some Kabbalistic drawings).[53] Later, in 1910, Steiner presented a series of lectures, The Secrets of the Biblical Account of Creation," in which he presented his ideas concerning the esoteric spiritual notions of the ancient Hebrews, which he probably regarded as related to the Kabbalah (although he did not mention the term explicitly).[54] His most detailed discussion of the *Sefirot* was given after he left the Theosophical Society and founded Anthroposophy, in a lecture to the workers of the Goetheanum in 1924, which he also accompanied with drawings.[55]

Although Steiner referred to Kabbalah in his writings and lectures much less than Blavatsky did, his approach to Jewish Kabbalah was more favorable than hers. In his 1904 lecture on the Kabbalah, he said the Kabbalah, like other ancient secret doctrines, concurred with Theosophy: "I will say something about what is written in the Kabbalah. In my book Theosophy you will find that all such doctrines accord with what we learn in Theosophy."[56] Notwithstanding his positive appreciation of the Kabbalah, Steiner asserted that the deeper wisdom of the Kabbalah is scarcely known among Jews today. Remnants of the Kabbalistic wisdom, he said, can only be found among the "wonder Rabbis" who come from far off Galicia, whose outward appearance can be repulsive to the civilized men.[57]

Albrecht Wilhelm Sellin (1841–1933), a Freemason, Spiritualist, and Theosophist from Hamburg,[58] presented a lecture on "the spiritual-science significance of the Zohar" at the first general meeting of the Anthroposophical Society in Berlin, in 1913. In the lecture, which was published by the Philosophical-Theosophical press in Berlin,[59] Sellin asserted the antiquity of the *Zohar* and the Kabbalah and pointed out their similarities with Steiner's Theosophical teachings.[60] In the conclusion of his lecture, he said that while studying the *Zohar*, "I often sensed my soul being shaken by sacred shivers of awe, since much of what seemed to be the result of an occult experience actually corresponded with my own lived experiences."[61]

Jewish Theosophists' Interest in Kabbalah

The interest and centrality of Kabbalah in the writings of Blavatsky and other Theosophists prompted Theosophists of Jewish origin to study Kabbalah. Thus, for instance, A. D. Ezekiel, the Jewish Theosophist from Pune, related that he became interested in Kabbalah following his encounter with members of the Theosophical Society (to which he refers as the "Sufi Society") who were experts in Kabbalah: "The members of the Sufi Society that came to Bombay were not Jewish. I was very much astonished that foreign people were experts in our wisdom of Kabbalah, while we, the Jews, were barred from it. So, after much effort and sleepless nights, I studied a little of it and what I have studied, I will reveal to my brethren so that they can enter and study this knowledge, and this translation will help them to do so."[62] Similarly, the Anglo-Jewish Theosophist Leonard Bosman related that although he originally came from a "fairly Orthodox" Jewish family, he and his family were estranged from Jewish tradition. However, he wrote, "Through a study of the Divine Wisdom as explained by the Theosophical Teachers that the present writer was enabled to touch the deeper truths embodied in the teaching of orthodox Jewry."[63] These inner teachings of Judaism, he says, are the "Chichma (!) Nistorah, the secret wisdom, or Qabbalah."[64] Ré (Rebekka) Levie, a Jewish Theosophist from the Netherlands who initiated a Kabbalah study group in Amsterdam in 1905, wrote that the Theosophical Society's interest in comparative religion stimulated her to study "the Jewish religion, the Hebrew language, Hebrew scriptures, and most of all, the Kabbala."[65]

Following their interest in Kabbalah, Jewish Theosophists published articles, books, and translations of Kabbalistic writings that were intended for both Jewish and non-Jewish readers. Many of the Jewish Theosophists aspired to revive the knowledge of Kabbalah among the Jews through translating Kabbalistic texts to vernacular languages, as well as through lectures, articles, and books, in which they presented their Jewish-Theosophical interpretations of Kabbalah. As we have seen, Ezekiel related that following his studies of Kabbalah, he wanted to share his newly acquired knowledge with his Jewish brethren. Similarly, Bosman wrote that having found the light of Judaism through the Theosophical Society, he was anxious to share it with his compatriots.[66] As mentioned above, Levie initiated a Kabbalah study group for Jewish youth.

Some of the lectures and publications of the Jewish Theosophists on Kabbalah were aimed at a non-Jewish readership, intending to improve the image of Judaism and highlight the resemblance between Theosophy and Kabbalah. Thus, for instance, Ezekiel wrote that he published the *Introduction to Kabbalah* following the enquiries he received from fellow members of the Theosophical Society in India "with a view therefore to give the general reader some idea of the subject."[67] In the following years, many other Theosophists of Jewish origins presented lectures about the Kabbalah in different Theosophical lodges.[68]

The first Jewish Theosophist to publish books and articles about Kabbalah was A. D. Ezekiel. Between 1887 and 1888, Ezekiel translated several Kabbalistic texts into Jewish Arabic, which he published in the printing press he opened in Pune.[69] Ezekiel also published an *Introduction to Kabbalah* in English and a story, "The Kabbalist of Jerusalem," which appeared in *The Theosophist*.[70]

In the first decades of the twentieth century, other Jewish Theosophists followed suit and published extensively about Kabbalah. Leonard Bosman published several booklets in the series Esoteric Studies, Published by Dharma Press, which was owned by Bosman.[71] Elias Gewurtz, Bosman's teacher, also published several articles and books on Kabbalah, including "The Qabalah," in *The Theosophist* and *The Cosmic Wisdom as Embodied in the Qabbalah and in the Symbolical Hebrew Alphabet*, which he published together with Bosman. After he emigrated to the United States, he published *The Hidden Treasures of the Ancient Qabalah*, a book based on the lectures he gave in 1915 at the Krotona Lodge of the Theosophical Society.

Joshua Abelson, an English liberal rabbi and scholar who was affiliated with the Theosophical Society, discussed Kabbalah and Jewish mysticism in articles he published in *The Theosophical Review, The Theosophic Messenger*, and *The Jewish Chronicle*,[72] as well as in his first book, *The Immanence of God in Rabbinical Literature*. In 1913, he published a scholarly introduction to Kabbalah, entitled *Jewish Mysticism*, in the Quest series of G. R. S. Mead. Abelson also wrote the introduction to the first comprehensive translation of the *Zohar* into English, which was published by Soncino Press.[73]

Ernst Müller, the Jewish scholar and Zionist from Vienna who joined the Theosophical Society and became a follower of Rudolf Steiner, published translations of Kabbalistic texts, mostly from the *Zohar* into German,[74] as well as a monograph about the *Zohar*,[75] a book on the History of Jewish Mysticism,[76] a couple of academic articles on Jewish mysticism,[77] and an unpublished novel about the Kabbalist Rabbi Isaac Luria.[78]

Following the foundation of the Association of Hebrew Theosophists, several members, such as Pia Müller, Leonide Stambalchek, Bozena Brydlova, and H. Blumenfeld, published articles about Kabbalah and Hasidism in *The Jewish Theosophist*.[79] Alex Horne published a booklet called *An Introduction to Esoteric Judaism* and discussed Jewish mysticism in articles he published in *The Theosophist, The Jewish Theosophist*,[80] and in his book *Spiritualizing Unspiritual Judaism*.

THE HIDDEN TREASURES
OF THE
ANCIENT QABALAH

BY

ELIAS GEWURZ

"And cherish deep within thy heart the memory of those who have served as a channel of light to thy perplexed soul, and be thou grateful to them."
—From the Golden Precepts of Trismegistus.

VOL. I

THE TRANSMUTATION OF PASSION INTO POWER

YOGI PUBLICATION SOCIETY

Masonic Temple

Chicago, Ill.

Jewish Theosophists' Sources of Knowledge on Kabbalah

Most Theosophists of Jewish origin who lectured and published about Kabbalah did not receive a traditional Jewish education, and none of them studied in a traditional Jewish Kabbalah learning institute. Many of them had little or no knowledge of Hebrew and Aramaic and could not read Jewish Kabbalistic texts. It should be noted that knowledge of Kabbalah was limited among Jews in the late nineteenth and early twentieth centuries, especially in the modern Western-acculturated circles that most Jewish Theosophists came from. In many Jewish circles, especially in Western Europe and the United States, Kabbalah was rejected and disparaged.

As we have seen, the interest in Kabbalah of many of the Jewish Theosophists followed their interest in Theosophy. Hence, the writings of Blavatsky and other non-Jewish Theosophists and Esotericists, such as Fabre d'Olivet, Isaac Myers, and Rudolf Steiner were major sources for their knowledge of Kabbalah. Jewish Theosophists derived their knowledge of Kabbalah and Hasidism also from the writings of nineteenth- and twentieth-century scholars of Judaism, such as Adolphe Franck, Heinrich Graetz, Christian Ginsburg, Martin Buber, and Gershom Scholem, which were written in European languages and were accessible to them.

Some Jewish Theosophists who received traditional Jewish education may have had access to primary Jewish Kabbalistic sources. Elias Gewurtz claimed to have studied Talmud and Kabbalah in his youth and to have researched ancient manuscripts in the British Library.[81] However, his knowledge and perception of Kabbalah were based primarily on Western esoteric sources and contemporary scholarship and not on original Jewish Kabbalistic texts. Gewurtz brings many citations from the *Zohar* and other Kabbalistic sources in his writing, but most, if not all, of them, are false citations that cannot be found in the original texts.[82]

A. D. Ezekiel had access to original Jewish Kabbalistic texts and had sufficient knowledge of Hebrew and Aramaic to read and translate them. However, he admitted that he had difficulties understanding *Etz Hayyim*, the major source of Lurianic Kabbalah:[83] "Once I started reading it, I could not understand a word of it. At that time, one of my friends from our community, Rabbi Sassoon Abdullah Somekh, was here. When he saw me struggling to understand this book, he suggested that I consult his father in Baghdad. I wrote a letter to the famous sage Rabbi Abdullah Somekh in Baghdad and asked him to guide me how to understand this book."[84] Ezekiel also derived his knowledge of Kabbalah from nineteenth-century

Western European Jewish scholarship of Kabbalah. His *Introduction to the Kabbalah* was based on the English translation of an early nineteenth-century scholarly work by the Jewish scholar Peter Beer.

Joshua Abelson, an Anglo-Jewish scholar and rabbi, had good knowledge of Talmudic and Kabbalistic sources. Yet, he was not an expert on Kabbalah and relied mostly on secondary scholarly literature. In the preface to his *Introduction to Jewish Mysticism*, he acknowledged that "the translated extracts from the *Zohar* are only in some cases made by me from the original Hebrew-Aramaic. I owe many of them to the French and German translations to be found in the works of scholars from whom I have drawn much of my material."[85] Ernst Müller also had firsthand knowledge of Kabbalistic sources, especially, of the *Zohar*, from which he published translated passages. However, his writings on the *Zohar*, as well as his *History of Jewish Mysticism*, were dependent largely on academic scholarship (including, in his later work, on the studies of Gershom Scholem), as well as on Western-esoteric perceptions of Kabbalah, especially, those of Rudolf Steiner.[86]

Most of the Jewish Theosophists had no contact with traditional Jewish Kabbalists. A unique event was the meeting between the members of the New York branch of the Association of Hebrew Theosophists with Rabbi Hayim Yehuda Leib Auerbach, the head of the Kabbalistic Yeshiva Shaar ha-Shamaim in Jerusalem, during his visit in New York in 1932.[87]

In their writings, the Jewish Theosophists present a variety of different interpretations of Kabbalah. Yet, there are some shared perceptions that recure in their writings. Some of these perceptions are dependent on the Theosophical framework of their interest and on the major sources they used—Theosophical and esoteric writings on Kabbalah and the late nineteenth and early twentieth-century scholarly works on Kabbalah and Jewish mysticism. However, the Jewish identity of the Jewish Theosophists, as well as the interest and access some had to original Jewish Kabbalistic sources, shaped a unique Jewish-Theosophical perception of Kabbalah. In the following section, I examine the unique features of the perceptions and interpretations of Kabbalah, that were offered in the writing of Jewish Theosophists.

Jewish-Theosophical Perspectives on Kabbalah

A major assumption of Jewish Theosophists that inspired their interpretations of Kabbalah was that there was an identity between Kabbalah and Theosophy.

As mentioned earlier, Leonard Bosman asserted that "the Secret Doctrine of the Jews is Theos-Sophia and nothing but Theos-Sophia."[88] Similarly, Elias Gewurtz wrote, "What was once known to the few as the holy Qabalah is now proclaimed far and wide as Theosophy. It is all the same teaching and emanates from the same source."[89] Kadouri Ani, the leader of the Basra Jewish Theosophists wrote to the active chief rabbi of Basra, "Theosophy is not a religion, as you have alleged, but is a philosophical society—the Jewish Kabbalah itself."[90] The American Jewish Theosophist H. Blumenfeld asserted, "We recognize the Cabala and all pertaining to Theosophy as Twin sisters. We see all the ethics and wisdom of Theosophy interlaced with the highest aim of Cabala, both being the effort to make metaphysics subservient to the Brotherhood of men."[91]

The assumption concerning the similarity between Theosophy and Kabbalah shaped the ways Jewish Theosophists described and interpreted Kabbalah. In "The Kabbalist from Jerusalem," Ezekiel depicts the Kabbalist of Beth El and the hidden Kabbalists of Tunis similarly to the adepts and the mahatmas of the Theosophical Society. Sarah, the Jewish "seeress" in the story, performs supernatural phenomena, which are reminiscent of the phenomena performed by Blavatsky. In the conclusion of the story, the Jewish Kabbalist from Jerusalem asserts that Kabbalah and Theosophy are expressions of the same Universal Doctrine:

> "There is but one God and one truth," said he. "Whosoever may be the teacher, he can but teach the Universal Doctrine. There are such adepts in the Himalayas, as there are others of the same kind in Egypt and other parts of the world. God has not abandoned any family of his children to their own ignorance and weakness; He would not be a true Father, if that were so. These doctrines promulgated by the Theosophical Society are identical with those taught by the Kabbalists of our race; there is the same rule of life, the same goal to reach. The World has never been without such teachers, nor will ever be. In the darkest night of superstition and ignorance, in the deepest depths of social degradation, there are always living witnesses to the truth."[92]

It should be noted that Ezekiel's choice to translate the *Idra Zuta* was probably influenced by the interest of Theosophists and other Western esoteric circles in the text, which was translated at the same time into English, by Samuel Liddel MacGregor Mathers. Interestingly, the term *Idra Zuta* was translated on the English title page as "The Lesser Holy Assembly," the same term used by Mathers in *Kabbala Unveiled*. Possibly, Ezekiel's choice to translate *Sepher Yetzirah* was also influenced by the interest of esotericists and Theosophists in this text. As mentioned above, at the same period, William Wynn Westcott and Papus published English and French translations of *Sepher Yetzirah*. Ezekiel's Theosophical perspective on Kabbalah was probably the reason for his intriguing choice to reprint the *Sermon of True Faith*. This short text succinctly summarizes the unique Sabbatean Kabbalistic theology of Abraham Cardozo (described by Scholem as a "Gnostic dualism with a reversal of evaluation").[93] As a Theosophist, Ezekiel probably agreed with the assertion of the author of the *Sermon of True Faith*: "The true faith which I reveal to you [. . .] was forgotten amongst us, and for a thousand years nobody has known its essence and truth, and we have been, like the gentiles, misled in the knowledge of the Divine."[94]

Other Theosophists of Jewish descent also accepted the universalistic and perennial perception of Kabbalah. Alex Horne asserted, "The ancient Kabalah, the Gnosis, or traditional secret knowledge, was never without its representatives in any age or country." Hence, he speaks about Buddhist Kabbalists and asserts that Peter, James, and John were Kabbalists.[95] Louis Vet, the president of the Dutch Association of Jewish Theosophists, claimed that the Jews, who originally came from India, brought the ancient wisdom with them to Egypt. According to Vet, Moses incorporated the ancient Kabbalistic wisdom in the Bible in an encrypted way that could be deciphered through the numerical value of the Hebrew letters.[96]

The Jewish Theosophists who aspired to show that Kabbalistic doctrines were compatible with the teachings of the Theosophical Society emphasized Kabbalistic themes that were close to Theosophy (such as reincarnation, the divine origin of the human soul, etc.) and ignored Jewish Kabbalistic notions that were incompatible with Theosophy (such as the theurgic import of the Jewish commandments, the unique status of Jewish souls, etc.). In his article "Qabbalah," Elias Gewurtz wrote, "The principal textbook of the Kabbalah, the Zohar, contains a great variety of teachings on the inner life, the most prominent among them are the three doctrines of the Unity of God and the universe, the Law of Cause and Effect, and the Law of Spiritual Evolution by means of rebirth. [. . .] The immortal merit of the Kabbalistic writings is their freedom from dogma and from all sorts of limitations in regard to race, creed or color."[97] The three prominent teachings of the Kabbalah, specified by Gewurtz, are very close to central Theosophical teachings, and his claim that Kabbalah is nondogmatic and universalistic reflects the ideals of the Theosophical Society. Similarly, Bozena Brydlova asserted that the Kabbalah taught the Jews "the equality of all men, the emptiness of a material life and the doctrine of a God whom they need not fear."[98] Joshua Abelson's perception of Kabbalah was also influenced by his Theosophical interests. Following Annie Besant's remark that the belief in incarnation can be found in Kabbalah, Abelson presented a short summary of Kabbalistic ideas about the human soul and reincarnation and discussed the similarity between Theosophy and Judaism.[99] Abelson was interested in the similarities between Kabbalah and Western esotericism and published the articles "Swedenborg and the Zohar" and "Occult Thought in Jewish Literature."[100]

Rudolf Steiner's Theosophical ideas had a strong impact on Ernst Müller's interpretations of the *Zohar* and on his understanding of Jewish Mysticism. Müller recounted in his memoirs that he consulted with Steiner about the truth value of the *Zohar* and Kabbalah, and the later confirmed their correspondence with Anthroposophical "spiritual science."[101] Müller's integration between a Jewish national approach that emphasized the central role of Kabbalah in Judaism and the Theosophical/Anthroposophical perception of Kabbalah as primordial universal esoteric nature comes to the fore in the account of his spiritual quest through Judaism and Christianity, which he published in 1952: "And so, quite early, I recognized the Zohar text as a source of the Kabbalah, into which I gradually plunged myself. Here I saw—in an "occult revelation"—the primordial esoteric wisdom, however much transmitted in a confused way, but, nevertheless in constant connection with Jewish literature—half mystic, half popular, near-legendary—as well as with the occultism of other peoples and times."[102] In the framework of their Theosophically inspired interpretations of Kabbalah, Theosophists of Jewish descent adopted and developed the idea that Kabbalah represents the spiritual and mystical aspect of Judaism, which is essentially opposed to the legalistic aspects of Talmudic Judaism. Following this idea, which was first formulated by Christian Kabbalists and later adopted by Western esotericists and some modern Jewish thinkers and scholars,[103] Jewish Theosophists disparaged the Talmud and Jewish *halacha* (the Jewish legal tradition) as negative and unspiritual and valorized Kabbalah as the vital, spiritual essence of Judaism.

Bozena Brydlova wrote in her article "The Ancient Kabbalah" that while "the Kabbala and its principles are applicable admirably to our own times," the Talmud seems in our modern days "dreadfully useless and unpractical with its laws that were established to govern conditions which we have long outgrown." Brydlova asserted the social liberating power of the Kabbalah, which "made a strong appeal to the poor struggling creatures who were literally crawling along in the mud of despair under the yoke of oppression and sect tradition."[104]

Other Jewish Theosophists expressed similar ideas. According to Alex Horne, the Kabbalists "tried to draw religious life away from the dry and meaningless repetition of acts and formulas; they strove to inject religious devotion and true faith into observances that were fast becoming perfunctory."[105] Joshua Abelson asserted in his introduction to the English translation of the *Zohar*, that "the arid field of Rabbinism was always kept well-watered and fresh by the living streams of Cabbalistic lore."[106]

However, in some matters, Theosophists of Jewish origin held a different approach to Kabbalah from non-Jewish Theosophists. As we have seen, Blavatsky and other leading Theosophists expressed an ambivalent stance toward Jewish Kabbalah and regarded it as a late and distorted offshoot of the ancient universal secret doctrine. Jewish Theosophists held a different approach. They valorized the Kabbalah unequivocally, emphasized its Jewish nature and origins, and underlined the centrality of the Kabbalah in the universal secret doctrine that the Theosophical Society purported to reveal.

In his *The Music of the Spheres*, Leonard Bosman accepts the universality of the Kabbalah. Paraphrasing Blavatsky, he writes that "it should be understood that the Qabalah itself is Universal for it is no more Jewish than Pagan, as much Egyptian as Chaldean and Persian."[107] However, differently from Blavatsky, he emphasized the role of the Jews in the preservation and transmission of the ancient Kabbalah: "We claim here for the Jewish race the honor of being the recipient of such knowledge through their Wise Men."[108] Furthermore, Bosman challenged Blavatsky's ambivalent stance to Jewish Kabbalistic texts by asserting the identity of Jewish Kabbalah and the teaching of Blavatsky's magnum opus, *The Secret Doctrine*, and emphasizing the similarity in name, structure, and purpose between the mysterious Book of Dzyan, which Blavatsky's *Secret Doctrine* was allegedly based on, and the *Zoharic* text *Sifra Dezniuta*: "The Inner Teaching of Judaism is the same as that offered in the Secret Doctrine, the very name of the Book of Dzyan from which the Secret Doctrine was taken, and the Qabalistic work called the Book of Dzyaniouta(!) being similar in construction and purpose."[109] It is interesting to note that Gershom Scholem, the founder of the modern academic study of Kabbalah, accepted Bosman's suggestion and observed that the "bibliographical" connection between the fundamental writings of modern and Jewish Theosophy (i.e., Kabbalah) "seems remarkable enough."[110]

Other Jewish Theosophists also asserted and emphasized the antiquity and primacy of Jewish Kabbalah over other esoteric traditions. Bosman's colleague and teacher Elias Gewurtz claimed in his *Beautiful Thoughts of the Ancient Hebrews* that the Jewish Kabbalistic writings were "proved by the greatest scholars to antedate the most ancient teachings of the East. [. . .] Primitive humanity was not deprived of teachers, and to our earliest ancestors the doctrine of Unity was proclaimed."[111] Similarly, H. Blumenfeld asserted in his article "Theosophy and Cabala," that "according to my own absolute knowledge, Theosophy is a correct prototype of the Cabala of old; born in old Palestine and nursed at the breast of Zoroastric philosophy, and in former Talmudic days looked upon as a divine revelation.[112]

As mentioned above, a major source for Jewish Theosophists' knowledge of Kabbalah were the writings of Jewish scholars. During the nineteenth century, Jewish scholars, most of them affiliated with the Wissenschaft des Judentums (Science of Judaism) movement, studied Kabbalah from a modern academic perspective, using historical and philological methods. Many of these scholars researched Kabbalah from a critical, negative stance, which was prevalent in the Jewish enlightenment movement (the *haskalah*). These scholars regarded Kabbalah as backward and irrational, assumed that it was essentially alien to Judaism, and believed that it was introduced to Jewish culture from foreign sources in the late medieval period.[113] The negative stance toward Kabbalah was especially prominent in the scholarship of Heinrich Graetz (1817–1891), the most important Jewish historian of the time, who described it as "an ugly crust, a mushroom like structure, a fungus coating."[114]

Although many Jewish Theosophists derived their knowledge about Kabbalah from the writings of these scholars, they rejected their negative approach and their opinion concerning its origins and late provenance.

Joshua Abelson asserted in *The Immanence of God in Rabbinical Literature* that "it is therefore totally wrong to follow Graetz in regarding the medieval Kabbalah as a thing per se, as something quite apart from its Talmudic antecedents, as an unnatural child of the darkened intellects of the Jewish middle ages."[115] In his introduction to *Jewish Mysticism*, Abelson rejects Graetz's assumption that "Kabbalah is a false doctrine which, although new, styled itself as a primitive inspiration: although un-Jewish, called itself a genuine teaching of Israel."[116] Abelson, who like many other scholars at the time identified Kabbalah as Jewish mysticism asserted its antiquity and centrality in Jewish culture: "Jewish mysticism is as old as the Old Testament—nay, as old as some of the oldest parts of the Old Testament. . . . The current flowed on, uninterrupted, into the era covered by the Rabbinic period. The religious and philosophic literature, ritual, worship, of Jewish medievalism became heirs to it, developing and ramifying its teachings and implications."[117] Abelson begins his historical survey of the history of Jewish mysticism with a discussion of Essenism. He continues with chapters of Merkavah mysticism, Philo, *Sefer Yetzirah*, and *The Zohar*, as well as chapters on the *Schechina*, the ten *Sefirot*, and the Soul. Abelson did not discuss in detail the later developments of Jewish mysticism. However, he concluded his book with a short discussion of the "the great religious movement known as Hasidism." Its aim, he wrote, "was to revive the spiritual element in Judaism which had been largely crushed by the dead-weight of Rabbinical formalism."[118]

Other Theosophists of Jewish descent expressed similar ideas. Alex Horne claims that Jewish mysticism is as old as the some of the oldest parts of the Old Testament. He asserts the existence of a Jewish esoteric tradition that was kept from ancient times in the possession of Jewish adepts and transmitted orally from generation to generation.[119] The major schools of the Jewish esoteric philosophy were, according to Horne, the "Mercaba-riders," the Gnostics, the Essenes, the Therapeutae, the medieval Kabbalists, and the Hasidim.[120]

Ernst Müller, who refers several times to Abelson's book in his *History of Jewish Mysticism*, also asserts the antiquity of the Jewish mystical tradition. According to Müller, "The beginnings of Cabbalah are inseparably bound up with an ancient Jewish secret doctrine which had already existed previously under various designations."[121] In his introduction to the book, he says that while other works dealt in greater detail with various aspects of Jewish mysticism (probably, he is alluding to Gershom Scholem's *Major Trends in Jewish Mysticism*, which was published five years previously), his work "aims particularly at placing in their proper perspective the mystical spirit of the Bible itself, the mystical tendencies in the apocalyptic literature and the allegorical exegesis of the Bible, and the existence of an ancient esoteric lore closely connected with the popular Agada."[122]

Reviving Kabbalah

As we have seen in the previous chapters, Jewish Theosophists aspired to spiritualize contemporary Judaism. Many of them believed that the Theosophical-inspired revival of Judaism could be achieved through returning to Jewish mystical sources and reviving the spirit of the Kabbalah. As mentioned above, Bozena Brydlova called to resurrect the spirit of the Kabbalah, whose principals—in contradistinction to those of the Talmud—are "applicable admirably" to our time.[123] "It is high time" she wrote, "that someone resurrect its spirit and set it afloat over [the] cloudy-brained world."[124] Leonard Bosman asserted that the goal of the Jewish Theosophists is "to revivify Judaism by seeking to bring back to it the deeper truths so long overshadowed by materialistic wanderings."[125] Joshua Abelson suggested that in order to rectify modern Judaism, the Jews have to realize "how far we have traveled away from the true spiritual content of Judaism as represented in the Zohar and other similar text-books of mystical Judaism, which are ignored and forgotten."[126] Alex Horne, in his article "Theosophy and Modern Judaism," wrote:

> It is high time that the Theosophical spirit should be made to manifest itself in our religion as well, not as something new, not as something imposed from without, but as a resurrection of the spirit that breathed through the finer mysticism of old. It is time that Theosophically-minded Jews the world over banded themselves together for service to their co-religionists, for the purpose of bringing out the highest, the noblest, the most beautiful and inspiring truths that Judaism has to offer.[127]

Horne continued to suggest that "we ourselves would likewise witness a revival of spirituality in present day Judaism, if we only emulated the energy, the devotion, the love of knowledge, the yearning for spiritual communion, that the medieval Kabbalists exhibited on all sides."[128]

In their appeal to members of the Theosophical Society, the founders of the Association of Hebrew Theosophists declared, "The Association proposes to bring to light all the hidden spiritual riches of the Jewish Religion. A profound study of this last in the light of Theosophy will undoubtedly lead to the increase of Theosophical information in this field, while this same study will help the Jews to understand their own religion."[129] Although they did not state it explicitly, "the hidden spiritual riches of the Jewish religion" surely refers to Kabbalah.

Jewish Theosophy and Kabbalah Scholarship

The interest and appropriations of Kabbalah by Theosophists of Jewish origin were part of a larger current of modern Jewish interest in Kabbalah. Some of the basic assumptions of Jewish Theosophists concerning the nature and significance of Kabbalah resemble and interconnect with the perceptions of other modern Jewish intellectuals and scholars of Kabbalah. From the late nineteenth century, many Jewish intellectuals in both Western and Eastern Europe reaffirmed the value of Kabbalah and Hasidism, which were marginalized and disparaged by scholars of the Jewish Enlightenment and the Wissenschaft des Judentums movements. The positive reevaluation of the Kabbalah took place within the framework of neo-Romanticism and the Orientalist fascination with the "mystical East," as well as the emergence of Jewish nationalism.[130] Jewish intellectuals in the late nineteenth and early twentieth centuries often combined interest in mysticism and the occult with their Zionist ideology. In this framework, Jewish scholars, such as Hillel Zeitlin, Shmuel Abba Horodezky, and Martin Buber turned to the study of Kabbalah and Hasidism. Following these scholars, Gershom Scholem and his disciples established the modern academic research on Jewish mysticism.[131]

The relations between the academic study of Jewish mysticism and Jewish Theosophy are complex. The works of academic scholars of Jewish mysticism were an important source for the knowledge and understanding of Kabbalah of many Jewish (as well as non-Jewish) Theosophists, and some of the academic scholars of Jewish mysticism were familiar with the writings of Jewish followers of the Theosophical Society. Some scholars of Kabbalah, such as Moses Gaster, Joshua Abelson, and Ernst Müller were affiliated with the Theosophical Society and did not see a contradiction between the scholarly and the esoteric interest in Kabbalah. Abelson and Gaster were also affiliated with the Quest Society, which was founded by Blavatsky's former secretary, G. R. S. Mead. Not only Abelson and Gaster, but also Gershom Scholem, published in the Quest Society's journal and book series.[132]

Scholem's attitude to the Theosophical Society and Helena Blavatsky was ambivalent. Scholem dismissed the Theosophical Society as "pseudo-religion"[133] and lamented the "misuse or distortion" of Kabbalah in the writings of Blavatsky's circle.[134] However, in 1944, he wrote in a letter to the Jewish American scholar Joseph Blau, that the latter was too harsh in his judgment of Blavatsky:

> You are certainly too harsh on Madame Blavatsky, it is surely too much to say that the meaning of cabala has been forgotten in the "Secret Doctrine." After all, the Lady has made a very thorough study of Knorr von Rosenroth in his English adaption, and of Franck's "Cabale Juive." She certainly knew more about

cabalism than most of the other people you mention . . . I think
it might be rather interesting to investigate the cabalistical ideas
in their theosophical development. There is, of course, a big lot
of humbug and swindle [!], but, at least in Blavatsky's writings,
yet something more.[135]

Scholem was acquainted with the writings of some of the Jewish Theos-
ophists. He held in his library the writings of Ezekiel, Gewurtz, Bosman,
Müller, and Abelson, as well as the volumes of *The Jewish Theosophists*.
Scholem disparaged Gewurtz because of the dubious Kabbalistic citations
in his book.[136] He held Bosman in more esteem, and accepted his suggestion the Sifra Dezniuta was the source of Blavatsky's Book Dzyan.[137]
Scholem appreciated Abelson's book *The Immanence of God in Rabbinical
Literature*; however, he wrote that "this valuable monograph suffers from a
tendency for apologetic interpretations, that distort the meaning of several
sayings."[138] Scholem was acquainted with Ernst Müller and had corresponded
with him since the early stages of his career.[139] Scholem wrote a favorable
review of Müller's 1934 book on the *Zohar*, although he rebuked him for
adulterating the original meaning with Anthroposophical interpretations.[140]
Many years later, Müller rejected Scholem's criticism (without mentioning
him by name), asserting on the one hand that his own inner experiential
approach to Kabbalah was hardly accessible to a Kabbalah scholar, and on
the other hand, that he was careful not to refer to "theosophical realities"
(*theosophischen Gegebenheiten*) in his translations of the Zohar.[141]

Notwithstanding their different approaches and understandings of Kabbalah, academic scholars and Jewish Theosophists shared several assumptions
concerning its nature and significance and employed similar categories for
its interpretation.

A major category that is shared by scholars and Theosophists of Jewish
origin is the term *Theosophy* itself. The term was, evidently, central to Jewish Theosophists, who employed it in their interpretation of Kabbalah and
affirmed the fundamental identity between Theosophy and Kabbalah. The
term, however, holds also significant importance in the modern academic
discourse of Kabbalah.

The term denotes religious illumination and unmediated knowledge
of divine matters. Since the eighteenth century, Christian theologians, and
later, Jewish scholars, have characterized Kabbalah as Theosophy. Thus,
for instance, Christian Ginsburg, a prominent English scholar of Jewish
Eastern European descent, defined Kabbalah in his 1865 *The Kabbalah: Its*

Doctrines, Development and Literature as "a system of religious philosophy, or more properly of theosophy."[142] It is possible that the choice of the term *Theosophy* by Blavatsky and her colleagues for their nascent society was influenced by the identification of Kabbalah as Theosophy. Blavatsky's first use of the term, which appeared in her letter to Hiram Corson, from February 1875, is a paraphrase of Christian Ginsburg's description of Kabbalah as Theosophy.[143]

Gershom Scholem also accepted the identification of Kabbalah as Theosophy and asserted that Kabbalistic Theosophy "seeks to reveal the mysteries of the hidden life of God and the relationship between the divine life on the one hand and the life of man and creation on the other."[144] Although his understanding of the meaning of Theosophy, and of Kabbalah as Jewish Theosophy, is not far from that of the Theosophists, Scholem was careful to distinguish his use of the term from that of the Theosophical Society: "By theosophy I mean that which was generally meant before the term became a label for a modern pseudo-religion."[145] The centrality of the term in both the academic study of Kabbalah and in the Theosophical Society highlights the shared context and the connections between modern Jewish scholars of Kabbalah and Jewish followers of Theosophy. Paraphrasing Scholem's observation concerning the possible connection between *Sifra Dezniuta* and the Book of Dzyan, the similarity in the perspective of Jewish Kabbalah scholars and Jewish Theosophists is "remarkable enough."

Another central notion that is shared by Jewish Theosophists and scholars of Kabbalah is the interpretation of Kabbalah and Hasidism as "Jewish mysticism." As we have seen above, and in previous chapters, Jewish Theosophists frequently described Kabbalah as mysticism. The identification of Kabbalah (and Hasidim) as "mysticism," which was unknown to, or rejected by, traditional Jewish Kabbalists, became also fundamental in the modern academic study of Kabbalah.

The term *mysticism*, which during the enlightenment period denoted pathological religious enthusiasm, was redefined during the nineteenth century by American and European scholars and theologians. By the late nineteenth and beginning of the twentieth centuries, the positive perception of mysticism as a universal religious phenomenon whose essence is an encounter or union with the divine (or the "absolute") became prevalent. Thus, the American Quaker theologian Rufus Jones (1863–1948) defined mysticism as "the type of religion which puts the emphasis on immediate awareness of relation with God, on direct and intimate consciousness of the

Divine Presence. It is religion in its most acute, intense and living stage."[146] The Anglo-Catholic scholar Evelyn Underhill (1875–1941) characterized mysticism as "the expression of the innate tendency of the human spirit towards complete harmony with the transcendental order."[147]

Both Jewish Theosophists and Jewish academic scholars of Kabbalah accepted the new definition of mysticism and interpreted Kabbalah as a Jewish form of mysticism. The Jewish Theosophist Joshua Abelson, and the founder of modern Kabbalah studies, Gershom Scholem, relied on Rufus Jones and Evelyn Underhill's definitions of mysticism in their introductions to Jewish mysticism.[148]

Although mysticism was perceived, according to its modern definition, as a universal phenomenon, which exist in almost every religion, many Christian European scholars in the late nineteenth and early twentieth centuries denied that Judaism had a mystical tradition and argued that Judaism is fundamentally opposed to mysticism.[149] However, Jewish scholars of Kabbalah and Jewish Theosophists rejected the notion that Judaism was essentially incompatible with mysticism and lacked a mystical tradition. In 1906, Martin Buber, the Jewish philosopher and scholar of Hasidism, sent a copy of his new German translation of the stories of Rabbi Nachman of Breslov to the German publisher Eugen Diederichs. Buber added a note in which he wrote: "I am sending you a book, *The Tales of Rabbi Nachman*, which you may find interesting. Do you perhaps recall that once—a few years ago—we discussed the question of the existence of Jewish mysticism? You didn't want to believe it. With this book on Nachman I have opened up a series of documents that will expose its existence."[150] Similarly, Joshua Abelson opened his 1913 book on Jewish mysticism by noting that the prevailing opinion in his time, among theologians as well as the larger public, was that "Judaism and mysticism stand at the opposite poles of thought" and that the phrase *Jewish Mysticism*, is an indefensible contradiction in terms. The content of his introduction to Jewish mysticism, promised Abelson, "will show the utter falsity of this view."[151]

Most of the Jewish Theosophists and modern scholars of Kabbalah came from a Western-acculturated, "enlightened" Jewish background in which Kabbalah was marginalized and disparaged. However, both Jewish Theosophists and academic scholars developed great interest in Kabbalah and valorized it as a highly significant component of Jewish culture. As we saw above, Jewish Theosophists, who defined Kabbalah as Jewish mysticism, emphasized its important and vitalizing role in Jewish history and culture.

Often, they juxtaposed the spirituality and vitality of Jewish mysticism with the "stagnation" of Talmudic, legalistic Judaism.

The founders of the modern academic study of Jewish mysticism held similar notions.[152] In his 1906 essay on Jewish mysticism, Martin Buber claimed that Hasidism, which he perceived as the final and most advanced stage of Jewish mysticism, was a religious renewal movement that liberated the people from the dominance of Talmudic Law: "The proclamation of joy in God, after a thousand years of a dominance of law that was poor in joy and hostile to it, acted like a liberation. [. . .] [T]he people up till then had acknowledged above them an aristocracy of Talmud scholars, alienated from life. [. . .] [N]ow the people, by a single blow, were liberated from this aristocracy."[153] Similarly, Gershom Scholem juxtaposed Kabbalah to the *halacha* and regarded Jewish mysticism as the vital national force that enabled Judaism "to persist without degeneration over a period of thousands of years."[154]

Jewish Theosophists who accepted the negative image of rabbinic Judaism as dogmatic and materialistic advocated a spiritual renewal of contemporary Judaism through a return to Jewish mystical sources and a modern revival of Kabbalah and Hasidism. The founders of the modern academic study of Jewish mysticism also aspired for its renewal. In the conclusion of his second introduction to the *Tales of Rabbi Nachman*, Martin Buber expressed his hope for its resurrection, regarding it as essential to the destiny of Judaism: "It is not given to us to know whether a resurrection will be granted it, but the inner destiny of Judaism seems to me to depend on whether—no matter if in this shape or another—its pathos will again become deed."[155] Buber found in the Hasidic sources a potential for Jewish religious revival and wished to renew in his generation the vital force of the Hasidic tradition.[156] Gershom Scholem also regarded the study of Jewish mysticism as an important part of contemporary Jewish national revival.[157] Today, similar to the Jewish Theosophists, contemporary Kabbalah scholars emphasize the spiritual relevance of its study for the renewal and redemption of Jewish culture.[158] Thus, the senior Israeli Kabbalah scholar Yehuda Liebes, in his essay "The Religious Significance of Kabbalah Studies," asserts the centrality of the study of Kabbalah within Jewish national revival: "The secret doctrine (i.e., Kabbalah), has a particularly important role, because it surpasses the purely intellectual realm, and it includes also other layers of the soul and fullness of life."[159]

Conclusion

Kabbalah played a very central place in the thought of Jewish Theosophists and in their endeavors to negotiate between their Jewish identity and their alliance to the teachings and values of the Theosophical Society. Jewish Theosophists studied Kabbalah, translated Kabbalistic texts, and published articles and books about Kabbalah, in which they created Theosophical-inspired modern forms of Kabbalah.

The engagement of Jewish Theosophists in Kabbalah was prompted by the interest of Blavatsky and other leaders of the Theosophical Society. The Jewish identity of the Jewish Theosophists, as well as the interest and access some of them had to original Jewish Kabbalistic sources shaped the unique perceptions that characterized the Kabbalah of Jewish Theosophists.

Following Blavatsky and other non-Jewish Theosophists, the Jewish Theosophists regarded Kabbalah as an offshoot of the universal perennial ancient wisdom. However, in contrast to the ambivalent stance of Blavatsky and other occultists toward Jewish Kabbalah, Jewish Theosophists unequivocally valorized the Kabbalah and emphasized its Jewish nature and origins. They underlined its centrality in the universal secret doctrine that the Theosophical Society purported to reveal and claimed there was a similarity, even an identity, between Kabbalah and Theosophy. Furthermore, Theosophists of Jewish origin regarded Kabbalah as a highly significant component of Judaism and advocated its use for the spiritual renewal of Judaism.

The Jewish Theosophists regarded their mission both as bringing about a spiritual, Theosophical reform of Judaism and as enriching Theosophy with Jewish spirituality. Kabbalah played a central role in these twin missions to the Jews and Gentiles. The claim that Kabbalah and Theosophy are compatible served to counter allegations from Jewish opponents that Jewish Theosophists had distanced themselves from Judaism and to demonstrate that Theosophical ideas were not alien to Jewish knowledge. The perception of the compatibility of Kabbalah and Theosophy served also as means to defend Judaism, to improve the image of Judaism in the eyes of non-Jewish Theosophists, and to enhance the status of Jews in the Theosophical Society.

The centrality of Kabbalah within a modern Jewish liberal movement was a unique feature of Jewish Theosophy. By the late nineteenth century, knowledge of Kabbalah was restricted in westernized Jewish cultures and was prevalent mostly among traditional Jews in Eastern Europe, the Middle East, and North Africa. Kabbalah was largely rejected and despised among Western-acculturated Jewish circles from which most Jewish Theosophists came. Jewish Theosophy offered a unique attempt, at that time, to create a modern, westernized, universalistic form of Judaism that embraced Kabbalah and presented Jewish mysticism as the central component of the Jewish tradition. A similar stance was presented by some modern Jewish academic scholars who revalued Kabbalah from a neo-Romantic and Jewish national perspective. As we saw, some of the basic assumptions of the Jewish Theosophists concerning the nature and significance of Kabbalah resemble and interconnect with the interpretation of Kabbalah in academic scholarship.

The emphasis on the importance of Jewish Kabbalah in the history of the universal secret doctrine and the assertion that Jewish Kabbalah was essentially identical with the teachings of the modern Theosophists enabled Theosophists of Jewish origin to take part in the Theosophical Society and adopt its principals without abandoning their Jewish identity and Jewish national sentiments. The importance of Kabbalah in Theosophy also helped to augment their standing within the society. As we have seen, Jewish Theosophists lectured about Kabbalah in Theosophical lodges, published articles and books about Kabbalah, and translated Kabbalistic texts into European languages. Theosophists of Jewish descent were indeed perceived by other non-Jewish Theosophists as experts in Kabbalah. In her message to the Hebrew Theosophists, Annie Besant, the president of the Theosophical Society, congratulated them for enriching Theosophy with the wisdom of their "occult treatises" "It is a great happiness to me to see members of the great Hebrew race enriching Theosophy with contributions from their ancient Faith. Much wisdom is enshrined in their occult treatises, and European philosophy and metaphysics owe much to the subtle genius of the Hebrew Nation. Great have been its sufferings in the past, but the greater still will be its gifts in the future to the human race."[1]

However, the endeavor of Jewish Theosophists to spiritualize Judaism and to create a modern, liberal Jewish mystical movement did not find many followers within Jewish communities in the first half of the twentieth century. Nor were they able to stimulate much interest in Jewish Kabbalah or elevate the image of Judaism among the non-Jewish public. It was only in the last decades of the twentieth century that Kabbalah became appreciated in wider circles as an essential component of Judaism and valorized as a form of universal mystical knowledge. A spiritual liberal reform of Judaism, quite like that suggested by the Jewish Theosophists, was offered with considerable success by Jewish renewal and neo-Kabbalistic movements.[2] A positive image of Judaism as a treasure house of universal mystical knowledge, which the Jewish Theosophists attempted to advance in the early twentieth century, is today taken for granted in the Western world, and many non-Jews find much of interest in Jewish Kabbalah. The Jewish Theosophists who were discussed in detail in this book and their modern, Theosophical inspired interpretations of the Kabbalah can be seen as the early precursors and heralds of New Age Kabbalah.

Notes

Introduction

1. The three aims of the Association of Hebrew Theosophists appear in many sources. See, for instance, Gaston Polak, "Appeal to Members of the T.S.," *Theosophist* 47 (April 1926): 103–4.

2. Hayim Cohen, "Jewish Theosophists in Basra: A Symptom of the Struggle of the Generation of Enlightenment," *Ha-mizrah ha-Hadash* 15 (1965): 401–7 [Hebrew]; David Sagiv, *The Jewish Community in Basrah 1914–1952* (Jerusalem 2004), 73–88 [Hebrew].

3. Boaz Huss, "'The Sufi Society from America': Theosophy and Kabbalah in Poona in the Late Nineteenth Century," in *Kabbalah and Modernity*, ed. Boaz Huss, Marco Pasi, and Kocku von Stuckrad Kocku (Leiden and Boston: Brill, 2010), 167–93; Boaz Huss, " 'Qabbalah, the Theos-Sophia of the Jews': Jewish Theosophists and their Perceptions of Kabbalah," in *Theosophical Appropriations: Esotericism, Kabbalah, and the Transformation of Traditions*, ed. Julie Chajes and Boaz Huss (Beer Sheva: Ben-Gurion University of the Negev Press, 2016), 137–66; Boaz Huss, " 'To Study Judaism in Light of Theosophy and Theosophy in the Light of Judaism': The Association of Hebrew Theosophists and Its Missions to the Jews and Gentiles," *Theosophy across Boundaries*, ed. Hans Martin Krämer and Julian Strube (Albany: State University of New York Press, 2021), 253–78.

4. Shimon Lev, "Gandhi and His Jewish Theosophist Supporters in South Africa," *Theosophical Appropriations: Esotericism, Kabbalah and the Transformation of Traditions*, ed. Julie Chajes and Boaz Huss (Beer Sheva: Ben-Gurion University of the Negev Press, 2016), 245–71.

5. Alexandra Nagel, "The Association of Jewish Theosophists in the Netherlands: The Efforts of Louis Vet and Others to Revive Judaism," *Correspondences* 7, no. 2 (2019): 411–39.

6. Menahse Anzi, "Theosophy and Anti-Theosophy in Basra: Jews, the Indian Ocean and the British Empire," *Historia* 46–47 (July 2021): 123–66 [Hebrew];

Sasha Rachel Goldstein, "Baghdadi Jewish Networks in Hashemite Iraq: Jewish Transnationalism in the Age of Nationalism" (PhD dissertation, Leiden University, 2018), 176–87.

Chapter 1

1. Michael Gomes, "Studies in Early American Theosophical History, Pt. VI, Rev. Wiggin's Review of George Henry Felt's 1875 Lecture on the Cabala," *Canadian Theosophist* 71, no. 3 (1990): 63–69; James A. Santucci, "Blavatsky, Helena Petrovna," in *Dictionary of Gnosis and Western Esotericism*, ed. Wouter J. Hanegraaff et al.(Leiden: Brill, 2005), 177–85.

2. John Patrick Deveney, "D. E. de Lara, John Storer Cobb, and the New Era," *Theosophical History* 15, no. 4 (2011): 30.

3. Maria Carlson, *No Religion Higher than the Truth: A History of the Theosophical Movement in Russia, 1875–1922* (Princeton: Princeton University Press, 1993), 38–42; Santucci, "Blavatsky, Helena Petrovna," 177–85.

4. Bruce F. Campbell, *Ancient Wisdom Revived: A History of the Theosophical Movement* (Berkeley: University of California Press, 1980), 7; Michael Gomes, "Olcott, Henry Steel," in *Dictionary of Gnosis and Western Esotericism*, ed. Wouter J. Hanegraaff et al. (Leiden: Brill, 2005), 894–95.

5. Joscelyn Godwin, "Blavatsky and the First Generation of Theosophy," in *Handbook of Theosophical Currents*, ed. Olav Hammer and Mikael Rothstein (Leiden: Brill, 2013), 17–22.

6. On the early Theosophical Society, see Godwin, "Blavatsky and the First Generation of Theosophy," 15–31; John Patrick Deveney, "The Two Theosophical Societies: Prolonged Life, Conditional Immortality, and the Individualized Immortal Monad," in *Theosophical Appropriations: Esotericism, Kabbalah and the Transformation of Traditions*, ed. Julie Chajes and Boaz Huss (Beer Sheva: Ben-Gurion University Press, 2016), 93–114; Wouter Hanegraaff, "Western Esotericism and the Orient in the First Theosophical Society," in *Theosophy across Boundaries: Transcultural and Interdisciplinary Perspectives on a Modern Esoteric Movement*, ed. Hans-Martin Krämer & Julian Strube (Albany: State University of New York Press, 2020), 29–64.

7. "Preamble of the T.S., dated October 30, 1875," *Theosophical Forum* (September 1947): 515–17.

8. Josephine Ransom, A Short History of the Theosophical Society (Adyar: Theosophical Publishing House, 1938), 5.

9. Julie Chajes and Boaz Huss, "Introduction," in *Theosophical Appropriations: Esotericism, Kabbalah and the Transformation of Traditions*, ed. Julie Chajes and Boaz Huss (Beer Sheva: Ben-Gurion University Press, 2016), 9–10.

10. Joscelyn Godwin, *The Theosophical Enlightenment* (Albany: State University of New York Press, 1994), 303–6; Hanegraaff, "Western Esotericism and the Orient," 38–46.

11. Godwin, *Theosophical Enlightenment*, 305–6; Godwin, "Blavatsky and the First Generation of Theosophy," 20–21.

12. Nicholas Goodrick-Clarke, "The Coming of the Masters: The Evolutionary Reformulation of Spiritual Intermediaries in Modern Theosophy," in *Constructing Tradition: Means and Myths of Transmission in Western Esotericism*, ed. Andreas Kilcher (Leiden: Brill, 2010), 113–60.

13. Erik Reenberg Sand, "The Marriage between the Theosophical Society and the Arya Samaj," in *Imagining the East: The Early Theosophical Society*, ed. Tim Rudbøg and Erik Reenberg Sand (New York: Oxford University Press, 2020), 253–72.

14. Godwin, "Blavatsky and the First Generation of Theosophy," 23; Julie Chajes, "Orientalist Aggregates: Theosophical Buddhism between Innovation and Tradition," in *Innovation in Esotericism from the Renaissance to the Present*, ed. Tim Rudbøg and Jo Hedesan (Cham: Palgrave Macmillan, 2021), 229–54.

15. Deveney, "The Two Theosophical Societies," 93–114.

16. Mriganka Mukopadhyay, "Occult's First Foot Soldier in Bengal: Peary Chand Mittra and the Early Theosophical Movement," in *The Occult Nineteenth Century*, ed. Lukas Pokorny and Franz Winter (Cham, Switzerland: Palgrave Macmillan, 2021), 269–86; Kenneth Paul Johnson, "Theosophy in the Bengal Renaissance," in *Imagining the East: The Early Theosophical Society*, ed. Tim Rudbøg and Erik Reenberg Sand (New York: Oxford University Press, 2020), 231–45.

17. Joscelyn Godwin, "The Mahatma Letters," in *Imagining the East: The Early Theosophical Society*, ed. Tim Rudbøg and Erik Reenberg Sand (New York: Oxford University Press, 2020), 133–40.

18. W. Travis Hanes Jr., "On the Origins of the Indian National Congress: A Case Study of Cross-Cultural Synthesis," *Journal of World History* 4, no. 1 (1993): 69–98; Isaac Lubelsky, "Allan Octavian Hume, Madame Blavatsky and the Foundation of the Indian National Congress," in *Imagining the East: The Early Theosophical Society*, ed. Tim Rudbøg and Erik Reenberg Sand (New York: Oxford University Press, 2020), 303–20.

19. Campbell, *Ancient Wisdom Revived*, 87–95; J. Barton Scott, "Miracle Publics: Theosophy, Christianity and the Coulomb Affair," *History of Religions* 49, no. 2 (2009): 172–96. In 1986, the Society of Psychical Research published a reexamination of the case, prepared by Vernon Harrison, who concluded that Hodgson ignored evidence that favored Blavatsky's case and that the society owed an apology to Blavatsky. See Vernon Harrison, "J'Accuse, an Examination of the Hodgson Report of 1885," *Journal of the Society of Psychical Research* 53, no. 803 (April 1986): 286–310.

20. Godwin, "Blavatsky and the First Generation of Theosophy," 26.

21. Godwin, "Blavatsky and the First Generation of Theosophy," 26–27.

22. Hanes, "On the Origins of the Indian National Congress," 69–98.

23. Kevin Tingay, "Madame Blavatsky's Children: Theosophy and Its Heirs," in *Beyond New Age: Exploring Alternative Spirituality*, ed. Steven Sutcliffe and Marion Bowman (Edinburgh: Edinburgh University Press, 2000), 40.

24. For summaries of the major tenets of the teachings of Blavatsky and the Theosophical Society, see Carlson, *"No Religion Higher than Truth": A History of the Theosophical Movement in Russia, 1875–1922* (New Jersey: Princeton University Press, 1993), 114–28; Nicholas Goodrick-Clarke, *The Western Esoteric Tradition: A Historical Introduction* (New York and Oxford: Oxford University Press, 2008), 211–28; Olav Hammer, "Theosophy," in *The Occult World*, ed. C. Partridge (London: Routledge, 2014), 250–59; Michael Gomes, "H. P. Blavatsky and Theosophy," in *The Cambridge Handbook of Western Mysticism and Esotericism*, ed. Glenn Alexander Magee (New York: Cambridge University Press, 2016), 248–59.

25. On the genealogy of the term *Theosophy*, see Tim Rudbøg, "Helena Petrovna Blavatsky's Esoteric Tradition," in *Constructing Tradition: Means and Myths of Transmission in Western Esotericism*, ed. Andreas B. Kilcher (Leiden: Brill, 2010), 163.

26. H. P. Blavatsky, *The Secret Doctrine: The Synthesis of Science, Religion and Philosophy* (London: Theosophical Society Press, 1888), vol. 1, xx.

27. Blavatsky, *The Secret Doctrine*, vol. 1, viii.

28. H. P. Blavatsky, *Isis Unveiled: A Master Key to the Mysteries of Ancient and Modern Science and Theology* (New York: J. W. Bouton, 1877), vol. 1, 613. On Blavatsky's concept of "wisdom religion" and it sources, see Tim Rudbøg, "H. P. Blavatsky's 'Wisdom Religion' and the Quest for Ancient Wisdom in Western Culture," in *Innovation in Esotericism from the Renaissance to the Present*, ed. Tim Rudbøg and Jo Hedesan (Cham: Palgrave Macmillan, 2021), 201–28.

29. Blavatsky, *The Secret Doctrine*, vol. 1, 268.

30. For a comprehensive study of the Septenary theory, see Julie Hall, "The Saptaparna: The Meaning and Origins of the Theosophical Septenary Constitution of Man," *Theosophical History* 8, no. 4 (October 2007): 5–38; Julie Chajes, *Recycled Lives: A History of Reincarnation in Blavatsky's Theosophy* (Oxford: Oxford University Press, 2019), 77–82.

31. H. P. Blavatsky, *The Key to Theosophy* (London: Theosophical Publishing House, 1889), 138.

32. Hammer, "Theosophy," 254–55; Chajes, *Recycled Lives*, 73–77.

33. Chajes, *Recycled Lives*, 45–64.

34. For a detailed discussion of Blavatsky's theory of reincarnation, see Chajes, *Recycled Lives*, 31–40, 65–86; Gomes, "H. P. Blavatsky and Theosophy," 256.

35. Blavatsky, *The Key to Theosophy*, 341.

36. Hammer, "Theosophy," 255–56.

37. For a detailed discussion of the construction and development of the masters in Theosophy and its offshoots, see Nicholas Goodrick-Clarke, "The Coming of the Masters: The Evolutionary Reformulation of Spiritual Intermediaries in Modern Theosophy," in *Constructing Tradition: Means and Myths of Transmission in Western Esotericism*, ed. Andreas Kilcher (Leiden: Brill 2010), 113–60.

38. Goodrick-Clarke, "The Coming of the Masters," 144; Hammer, "Theosophy," 257.

39. Godwin, "Blavatsky and the First Generation of Theosophy," 27.

40. Laurence Cox, *Buddhism and Ireland* (Bristol: Equinox 2013), 230–32.

41. Nicholas Goodrick-Clarke, "Western Esoteric Traditions and Theosophy," in *Handbook of Theosophical Currents*, ed. Olav Hammer and Mikael Rothstein (Leiden: Brill, 2013), 298–300.

42. H. C. Kumar, "T. S. Muslim League," in *The General Report of the Forty-Ninth Anniversary and Convention of the Theosophical Society* (Adyar: Theosophical Publishing House, 1924), 227–31; "T. S. Muslim Association," in *The General Report of the Fifty-Second Anniversary and Convention of the Theosophical Society* (Adyar: Theosophical Publishing House, 1928), 256–58.

43. "T. S. Muslim Association," 256–58.

44. "T. S. Muslim Association," 256–58.

45. On movements deriving from Theosophy, see Kevin Tingay, "Madame Blavatsky's Children: Theosophy and Its Heirs," in *Beyond New Age: Exploring Alternative Spirituality*, ed. Steven Sutcliffe and Marion Bowman (Edinburgh: Edinburgh University Press, 2000), 37–50.

46. Tim Rudbøg, "Point Loma, Theosophy, and Katherine Tingley," in *Handbook of Theosophical Currents*, ed. Olav Hammer and Mikael Rothstein (Leiden: Brill, 2013), 51–71.

47. Catherine Wessinger, "The Second-Generation Leaders of the Theosophical Society (Adyar)," in *Handbook of Theosophical Currents*, ed. Olav Hammer and Mikael Rothstein (Leiden: Brill, 2013), 36.

48. Marco Pasi, "Theosophy and Anthroposophy in Italy during the First Half of the Twentieth Century," *Theosophical History* 15, no. 2 (2012): 89–95.

49. Nicholas Goodrick Clarke and Clare Goodrick-Clarke, *G. R. S. Mead and the Gnostic Quest* (Berkely: North Atlantic Books, 2005), 19–27.

50. Katharina Brandt and Olav Hammer, "Rudolf Steiner and Theoshopy," in *Handbook of Theosophical Currents*, ed. Olav Hammer and Mikael Rothstein (Leiden: Brill, 2013), 113–33.

51. Helmut Zander, "Transformations of Anthroposophy from the Death of Rudolf Steiner to the Present Day," in *Theosophical Appropriations: Esotericism, Kabbalah and the Transformation of Traditions*, ed. Julie Chajes and Boaz Huss (Beer Sheva: Ben-Gurion University Press 2016), 273–308.

52. Sean O'Callaghan, "The Theosophical Christology of Alice Bailey," in *Handbook of Theosophical Currents*, ed. Olav Hammer and Mikael Rothstein (Leiden: Brill, 2013), 93–95.

53. Anita Stasulane, "The Theosophy of the Roerichs: Agni Yoga or Living Ethics," in *Handbook of Theosophical Currents*, ed. Olav Hammer and Mikael Rothstein (Leiden: Brill, 2013), 193–215; Alexandre Andreyev, *The Myth of the Masters Revived: The Occult Lives of Nikolai and Elena Roerich* (Leiden: Brill, 2014), 104–8.

54. Wessinger, "The Second-Generation Leaders of the Theosophical Society," 38–43.

55. Tingay, "Madame Blavatsky's Children," 44–45.

Chapter 2

1. Henry Steel Olcott, "Old Diary Leaves, Chapter 8," *The Theosophist* 14, no. 2 (November 1892): 74 (This passage was omitted from the later version of "Old Diary Leaves," published in 1895). De Lara is mentioned also, 71, and "Old Diary Leaves, Chapter 9," *The Theosophist* 14, no. 3 (December 1892): 131 (republished in Henry Steel Olcott *Old Diary Leaves: The True Story of the Theosophical Society* [New York and London: G. P. Putnam's Sons 1895], 121, 129). According to a report on the foundation of the Theosophical Society, published in the *Spiritual Scientist*, one of the founders was "a venerable Jewish scholar and a traveler of repute." See "A Theosophical Society," *Spiritual Scientist* 3, no. 2 (September 16, 1875): 21.

2. For information on D. E. de Lara, see John Patrick Deveney, "D. E. de Lara, John Storer Cobb, and the New Era," *Theosophical History* 15, no. 4 (2011): 27–33. I am grateful to Marc Demarest and Pat Deveney for providing me with additional information, documentation, and clarification on de Lara's biography.

3. *Manchester Courier* and *Lancashire General Advertiser*, November 10, 1838. De Lara was presented in a similar way at the speech he gave on the occasion of the foundation of the New Synagogue in Manchester in 1844: "D. E. de Lara, Ll.D Member of the literary and Philanthropic Society, and of the institute of natural and experimental science, Professor of continental literature in the Royal, the literary and scientific, and the mechanics institution." See Bill Williams, *The Making of Manchester Jewry 1740–1875* (Manchester: Manchester University Press, 1985), 138.

4. Bill Williams, *The Making of Manchester Jewry*, 137–38.

5. "The Termination of the Mosaic Economy, as Described by a Modern Jew," *The Voice of Israel* no. 9 (January 1, 1845): 76.

6. De Lara published himself as "D. E. de Lara, LL.D., formerly director of National education in Spain, and during thirteen years Professor of Continental Languages and literature in the Royal and the Mechanics Institute, the Library and Scientific Institution and the High school at Liverpool." *New York Tribune* (May 5, 1856): 2.

7. *Boston Post*, December 6, 1853, 2. According to the report on the lectures, de Lara "recently returned from St. Petersburgh, after a residence of two years."

8. *New York Tribune*, December 10, 1856, 6.

9. Jonathan D. Sarna, "From Necessity to Virtue: The Hebrew-Christianity of Gideon R. Lederer," *Iliff Review* 37 (Winter 1980): 27–33; Shulamit S. Magnus, "Wengeroff in America: On the Resonance of Conversion and Fear of Dissolution in Early Twentieth Century American Jewry," *Jewish Social Science* 21, no. 2 (2016): 142–87.

10. Deveney, "D. E. de Lara," 31.

11. John Thomas, *Phanerosis: An Exposition of the Doctrine of the Old and New Testaments* (Birmingham: R. Roberts, 1869), ii. Thomas published a letter that was sent to him by de Lara, dated May 9, 1856, in which the latter stated that although a devout Jew may perhaps agree to some Christian teachings, no Jew can accept Christian doctrines of the trinity: "[T]he moment . . . a Jew is told that God has a son, and that there are three persons, three essences, three somethings or anythings in the Godhead . . . the moment, I say, a Jew is told of this, he shrinks back, and stands sternly aloof," iii.

12. In July 1875, he lectured in the Liberal Club in New York on Pope Sixtus V. In a review of the lecture, the editor of *The New Era* wrote: "Mr. de Lara, who is well known, at any rate to the readers of *The New Era*, through his writings upon the school question and other subjects, is a gentleman who has for a period of nearly half a century been engaged with his pen in enriching English literature, though chiefly under a nom de plume, in consequence of a too great modesty, which being a part of his nature, cannot be eradicated." *New Era* 5, no. 9 (September 1875): 597 (cited by Deveney, "D. E. de Lara," 30). In November 1875, he lectured on "Art and Nature" at Temple Ahawath Chesed in New York. See *Jewish Messenger* 38, no. 18 (November 12, 1875): 2.

13. Deveney, "D. E. de Lara," 27–33.

14. I am grateful to Pat Deveney, who provided me with these citations from the *The New Era* 5, no. 1 (1875).

15. Olcott, "Old Diary Leaves, Chapter 8," 74.

16. Deveney, "D. E. de Lara," 30–33. On Charles Sotheran, see Alice Hyneman Sotheran, "Reminiscences of Charles Sotheran as Pioneer American Socialist," in Charles Sotheran, *Horace Greely and Other Pioneers of American Socialism* (New York: Haskell House, 1971) (first published 1915), xi–xxxix; Godwin, *The Theosophical Enlightenment*, 283–85. It is interesting to note the connection between *The New Era*, a Jewish Reform journal, and the early Theosophical Society. Apart from de Lara and Sotheran, John Storer Cobb, who became the first recording secretary of the Theosophical Society, also published in *The New Era* and was reported to be the editor of the journal. *The New Era* reviewed Olcott's *People from the Other World* and reported about the meeting at Blavatsky's residence, which led to the foundation of the Theosophical Society. See *New Era* 5, no. 10 (October 1875); Deveney, "D. E. de Lara," 32.

17. "He was brought to us by Mr. Southeran, as also his daughter, Mrs. Alice B. Rhyne, the poetess." Olcott, "Old Diary Leaves, Chapter 8," 74.

18. "TS Society General Register 1875–1942," https://tsmembers.org/_Book 1 A, 1.

19. See the notes of the second meeting, published by Olcott, in *The Path*, 9, no. 1 (April 1894): 2. See also Olcott, "Old Diary Leaves, Chapter 9," 131.

20. Victoria de Lara Fibel, registered as member no. 69, joined the society on June 7, 1876. See "TS Society General Register," book 1A, 2.

21. Henry Samuel Morais, *The Jews of Philadelphia: Their History from the Earliest Settlements to the Present Time* (Philadelphia: Levytype, 1894), 327–29; *The Jewish Encyclopedia* (New York and London: Funk and Wagnalls, 1901), vol. 6, 513; Robert P. Swierenga, *The Forerunners: Dutch Jewry in the North American Diaspora* (Detroit: Wayne State University Press, 1994), 122, 159, 161; Peter Lanchidi, "Jacob Norton and the Quest for Universal Freemasonry: Jewish Masonic Consciousness within a Christian Fraternity," *American Jewish History* 105, no. 4 (2021): 491–92.

22. Blavatsky, *Isis Unveiled*, vol. 2, 379–80.

23. "Is He Koot Hoomi, Blavatsky's Mahatma?" *New York Herald*, August 16, 1891, 10.

24. "TS Society General Register," book 1A, 3 (member no. 138 "Alice H. Rhine").

25. Morais, *The Jews of Philadelphia*, 345–46.

26. For a detailed discussion of A. D. Ezekiel, and his activities in the Theosophical Society and printing ventures, see Boaz Huss, "The Sufi Society from America": Theosophy and Kabbalah in Poona in the Late Nineteenth Century," in *Kabbalah and Modernity*, ed. Boaz Huss, Marco Pasi, and Kocku von Stuckrad (Leiden and Boston: Brill, 2010), 167–93. For a description of Olcott's stay at the Ezekiel residence in 1885, see Olcott, *Old Diary Leaves*, vol. 3, 307–8.

27. Nathan Katz, *Who Are the Jews of India?* (Berkely, Los Angeles, and London: University of California Press, 2000), 126–59.

28. See "TS Society General Register," book 1A, 34 (member no. 984).

29. N. D. Khandalvala, "Madame H. P. Blavatsky as I Knew Her," *Theosophist* 50 (June 1929): 214. For a picture of A. D. Ezekiel, with Blavatsky, Olcott, and other members of the Theosophical Society, which was taken during a convention in Bombay in 1882, see http://www.teosofiskakompaniet.net/DamodarKMavalankarPioneer_2003_.htm.

30. Olcott, *Old Diary Leaves*, vol. 3, 307–8.

31. K. H. is Mahatma Koot Hoomi. The shrine, which contained a portrait of Koot Hoomi, was in the society's headquarters in Adyar and was the scene of many of the supernatural phenomena reported by members of the Theosophical Society.

32. Richard Hodgson, "Report of the Committee Appointed to Investigate Phenomena Connected with the Theosophical Society," *Proceedings of the Society for Psychical Research* 3 (London: Kegan Paul, Trench & Trübner, 1885): 211. See also Richard Hodgson, "The Defence of the Theosophists," *Proceedings of the Society for Psychical Research* 9 (London: Kegan Paul, Trench & Trübner, 1893–1894): 141.

33. *Times of India*, September 15, 1884, 6. The letter is cited in Leslie Price, "First Report of the Committee of the Society for Psychical Research," the Blavatsky Archives Online http://www.blavatskyarchives.com/sprrpmaintext.htm. A more detailed letter by Ezekiel, in which he gives his account of the "Poona Telegram," was published in *The Times of India*, September 18, 1884, 8. Judge Khandalavala wrote to Blavatsky in December 1885 about the reactions of Sassoon and Ezekiel to the publication of the Coulomb letters:

You are scarcely aware what a difficult task we had when the alleged letters appeared. Poor Sassoon wavering and ready to side with the public. Ezekiel's brother impatient to rush into print with a lot of matter collected haphazard from the conversation they had with you and scarcely knowing whether he was going to do you or Sassoon harm. Ezekiel scarcely remembering all the details and I knowing nothing as to what actually happened during your two visits. In spite of all that, I made the best of the situation and sent two letters signed by Ezekiel to *The Times of India* which greatly restored the peace of mind of our fellows and sympathizers.

Alfred Trevor Barker, *The Letters of H.P. Blavatsky to A.P Sinnett and Other Miscellaneous Letters* (London: T. F. Unwin, 1925), 161.

34. Price, "First Report," appendix 37.

35. Hodgson, "Report," 249. According to Coulomb, Blavatsky, who heard of Ezekiel's suspicions, gave orders to Coulomb's husband to dismantle the device through which the letters were pulled down. In a later report of the events, Hodgson related that Ezekiel detected the location of the hole that existed behind the shrine and was blocked up, as well as the "screw-rings" on the ceiling, that were used to produce the spurious letter. Hodgson, "The Defence of the Theosophists," 143.

36. Hodgson, "Report," 249.

37. Hodgson, "The Defence of the Theosophists," 147.

38. *Times of India*, September 18, 1884, 8.

39. Emma Coulomb, *Some Account of my Intercourse with Madame Blavatsky from 1872 to 1884* (Madras: Higginbotham, 1884), 78.

40. Michael Gomes, "H. P. Blavatsky's Annotations in Madame Coulomb's Pamphlet," *Theosophical History* 1, no. 6 (1985): 151.

41. A. D. Ezekiel, *Shomer Emuneem (First Argument), a Kabbalistic Controversy, Translated from Hebrew in Arabic (in Hebrew Characters). For the Use of Students of Kabala* (Poona: A. D. Ezekiel's Press, 1888) (no page number). In a letter to the editor of the Judeo-Arabic newspaper *Jewish Gazette Paerah*, Ezekiel gives a similar account of his way to the Kabbalah. However, he does not mention the "Sufi Society," but rather, a Parsee friend, whose question about the Kabbalistic concept of Adam Kadmon, prompted Ezekiel to study Kabbalah. See *Jewish Gazette Paerah*, June 26, 1888, 27. The Parsee friend of Ezekiel is probably Judge N. D. (Navroji Dorabji) Khandalavala, the president of the Poona lodge of the Theosophical Society. I am grateful to Yaakov Zamir, who provided me with a photocopy of Ezekiel's letter, and to Avi-ram Tzoreff, who helped me to translate it.

42. Ezekiel says it was not his real name. In the copy of "The Kabbalist of Jerusalem" that the late Mary Anderson, the international secretary of the Theosophical Society, Adyar, has kindly sent me, I found a handwritten note: "Col's Diary for July 21st, at Bombay—1887 Visit from Mr. Moses, the original of Rabbi Jacob in Ezekiel's story in the July Theosophist 'The Kabbalist of Jerusalem.' "

43. A. D. Ezekiel, "The Kabbalist of Jerusalem," *Theosophist* 8 (July 1887): 600.

44. Ezekiel, "The Kabbalist of Jerusalem," 601.

45. Boaz Huss, *The Zohar: Reception and Impact* (Oxford and Portland: Littman Library of Jewish Civilization, 2016), 210–15.

46. Letters against Ezekiel's translation, by Rabbi Solomon Twena of Calcutta, were printed in later issues of *The Jewish Gazette Paerah*. See David S. Sassoon, *Ohel Dawid: Descriptive Catalogue of the Hebrew and Samaritan Manuscripts in the Sassoon Library* (London: Oxford University Press 1932), vol. 1, 429–30 [Hebrew]; Huss, "The Sufi Society," 178–79.

47. *Havazelet* 18, no. 18 (February 24, 1888) (12 Adar 5648), 138–39. For an English translation of the letter, see Huss, "The Sufi Society," 178–79.

48. The decree was published in *Havazelet* 18, no. 20 (March 11, 1888) (28 Adar 5648): 156–57.

49. Yosef Hayyim, *Responsa Rav Pe'alim* (Jerusalem: Frumkin, 1901), vol. 1, 71b–72b (Yoreh Deah 56) [Hebrew]. For a detailed discussion of Hayyim's response, see Avir-ram Tzoreff, "Acknowledging Loss, Materializing Language: Translation and Hermeneutics of Gaps in Nineteenth Century Baghdad," *Middle Eastern Studies* 59, no. 1 (2023): 1–21.

50. Sassoon, *Ohel Dawid*, 429–30. Ezekiel was supported by a person who signed his letter to the editor, which was published in *Paerah* on August 10, 1888, "the young one 77." I am grateful to Mr. Yaakov Zamir, the archivist of the Babylonian Jewry Heritage Center, who turned my attention to this letter.

51. The letter was printed from manuscript by Pinchas Grayevsky, "On the Translation of the Idrot to Arabic," *Meginzei Yerushalaim* 2 (1930): 15–16 [Hebrew]. See Huss, "The Sufi Society," 179–80.

52. Grayevsky, "On the Translation of the Idrot," 16; Huss, "The Sufi Society," 180.

53. Peter Beer, *Geschichte, Lehren, und Meinungen aller Bestandenen und noch Bestehenden Religiösen Sekten der Juden und der Geheimlehre oder Kabbala* (Brünn: J. G. Trassler, 1822–23).

54. A. D. Ezekiel, *Natural Philosophy, Matter and Motion (catechism) in Arabic (in Hebrew characters). For the use of schools* (Poona: A. D. Ezekiel's Press, 1888). The book is dedicated to Moshe Avi Aziz of Calcutta.

55. Abraham David Ezekiel, *Cabticum Canticorum, or the Song of Solomon, Interlineary Translation from the Herbrew into Arabic (in Hebrew Characters)* (Poona: A. D. Ezekiel's Press, 1888); *Sepher Yesirah or the Book of Creation, Interlineary Translation from the Hebrew into Arabic (in Hebrew Characters)* (Poona: A. D. Ezekiel's Press, 1888).

56. Abraham David Ezekiel, *Dewan El Rahban: An Arabic Tale in Arabic (in Hebrew Characters)* (Poona: A. D. Ezekiel's Press, 1888); Abraham David Ezekiel, *Dewan El Mathee, an Arabic Tale in Arabic (in Hebrew Characters)* (Poona: A. D. Ezekiel's Press, 1888). I have not seen the last two publications, which are

mentioned in Brad Sabin, *Hebrew, Judeo-Arabic and Marathi Jewish Printing in India, Rare Printed Books from the Valmadonna Trust Library* (Leiden: Brill 2006), https://docplayer.net/54659768-Title-list-hebrew-judeo-arabic-and-marathi-jewish-printing-in-india.html.

57. The sermon was first published at the end of Isaac Lupis's *Kur Mezraf ha-Emunot u-Mareh ha-Emet* (Metz, 1847).

58. *Lucifer: A Theosophical Magazine* 9 (1891–92): 1.

59. *Theosophist* 18 [supplement] (June 1897): 35.

60. "TS Society General Register," book 1A, 64 (member no. 2535). S. A. Ezekiel published in 1885 in Bombay a lithography entitled *The Life of Moses in Egypt*, in Judeo-Arabic cursive handwriting. As mentioned above, Judge Khandalavala mentioned Ezekiel's brother in his letter to Blavatsky, in which he tells of the reaction of Sassoon and the Ezekiel brothers to the publication of the Coloumb letters. Other Baghdadi Jews who joined the Theosophical Society were Solomon Elias David, Moses Joseph Jacob, and Jacob Nissim Isaac (an employee of the Elias David Sassoon Company), who joined the society in 1884, and Aaron Nissim Ezekiel Judah and Aaron Raphael Joshua, who joined in 1885 ("TS Society General Register," book 1B, 77, 88).

61. "TS Society General Register," book 1A, 3 (member no. 115).

62. Júlia Gyimesi, "The Institutionalization of Parapsychology in Hungary in the 20th Century," in *Okkultismus im Gehäuse: Institutionalisierungen der Parapsychologie im 20. Jahrhundert im internationalen Vergleich*, ed. Anna Lux and Sylvia Paletschek (Berlin, Boston: De Gruyter), 202–3; Júlia Gyimesi, "Between Religion and Science: Spiritualism, Science and Early Psychology in Hungary," *International Psychology* 5 (2014): 6–8. A book of his essays on Spiritualism, magnetism, and somnambulism was published posthumously. See Adolf Grünhut, *Tanulmányok a spiritizmus köréből: Magnetizmus, szomnambulizmus, mediumizmus* (Budapest: A Szellemi Buvárok Pesti Egylete, 1921).

63. In *Isis Unveiled*, Blavatsky mentioned "the gentle Baronesse Adelma von Vay from Austria" as a noble example of a pure medium. See Blavatsky, *Isis Unveiled*, vol. 1, 325. Later, Blavatsky mentioned a crystal from the Gastein Mountains that Olcott exhibited in his lectures, which was sent to him by "our very esteemed friend and fellow, the Baroness Adelma von Vay." See H. P. Blavatsky, "Visions in the Crystal," *Theosophist* 3, no. 11 (August 1882): 287.

64. "TS Society General Register," book 1B, 106 (member no. 4208).

65. Karl Baier, "Occult Vienna: From the Beginnings until the First World War," in *Religion in Austria*, ed. Hans Gerald Hödl, Astrid Mattes, and Lukas Pokorny (Vienna: Praesens Verlag, 2020), vol. 5, 9–11.

66. On Eckstein's friendship with Freud, see Sibylle Mulot-Déri, "Alte Ungenannte Tage," in Friedrich Eckstein, *Alte unnennbare Tage* (Wien: Edition Atelier, 1992), 302. Freud, who has learned about Yoga from Eckstein, refers to him as "another friend of mine, whose insatiable craving for knowledge has led him to

make the most unusual experiments and has ended by giving him encyclopedic knowledge." Sigmund Freud, *Civilization and its Discontents* (New York: W. W. Norton, 1962), 19. See Karl Baier, "Yoga within Viennese Occultism: Carl Kellner and Co.," in *Yoga in Transformation*, ed. Karl Baier, Philip A. Mass, Karin Preisendanz (Göttingen: Vienna University Press, 2018), 403.

67. Baier, "Occult Vienna," 27–29; Sibylle Mulot-Déri, "Alte Ungenannte Tage," in Friedrich Eckstein, *Alte unnennbare Tage* (Wien: Edition Atelier, 1992), 298–300. Nicholas Goodrick-Clarke, *The Occult Roots of Nazism: Secret Aryan Cults and Their Influence on Nazi Ideology* (New York: New York University Press, 1992), 28; Helmut Zander, *Anthroposophie in Deutschland: Theosophische Milieus und gesellschaftliche Praxis, 1884 bis 1945* (Göttingen: Vandenhoeck and Ruprecht, 2007), vol. 1, 221–22. For Eckstein's memories of his connections with the Theosophical Society and its leaders, see Friedrich Eckstein, *Alte unnennbare Tage* (Wien: Edition Atelier, 1992), 64–66, 237–41.

68. Zander, *Anthroposophie in Deutschland*, vol. 1, 224–25; Baier, *Occult Vienna*, 27–29. Steven Beller, *Vienna and the Jews 1867–1938: A Cultural History* (Cambridge: Cambridge University Press, 1989), 31.

69. Zander, *Anthroposophie in Deutschland*, vol. 1, 224. Helmut Zander, *Rudolf Steiner: Die Biographie* (München: Piper Verlag, 2011), 63–64, 78–80. For correspondences between Steiner and Eckstein, see Rudolf Steiner, *Briefe, Band 1, 1881–1890* (Dornach: Rudolf Steiner Verlag, 1985), 186 (letter 169); Rudolf Steiner, *Briefe, Band 2, 1890–1925* (Dornach: Rudolf Steiner Verlag, 1987), 27–28 (letter 260), 29–30 (letter 262), 49–52 (letter 269). For Eckstein's impressions of Steiner, see Eckstein, *Alte unnennbare Tage*, 122–23. For Steiner's impressions of Eckstein, see Rudolf Steiner "Mein Lebensgang," GA b, Rudolf Steiner Online Archiv, 388–89, http://anthroposophie.byu.edu/schriften/028.pdf.

70. Steiner, *Briefe, Band 2*, 50 (letter 269).

71. Steiner, *Briefe, Band 2*, 27–28 (letter 259). Mayreder related that Eckstein was so furious by the Kosher restrictions demanded by the future in-laws of his sister, that he threatened to abandon his vegetarianism and eat ham in the wedding celebration.

72. Ernst Müller, "Erinnerungen an Friedrich Eckstein," *Blätter für Anthroposophie* 2 (1950): 418–21; a shorter and different version of this text was published in *Der Europäer* 15, no. 5 (2011): 11.

73. Robert S. Ellwood, *Islands of the Dawn: The Story of Alternative Spirituality in New Zealand* (Honolulu: University of Hawaii Press, 1993), 101. Mrs. M van Staveren and Mr. H. van Staveren are registered as members nos. 5284/5 of the Theosophical Society (joined 1.8.1889), "Theosophical Society General Register," book 1B, 133.

74. Nigel Isaacs, "Staveren, Herman van," *Dictionary of New Zealand Biography*, https://teara.govt.nz/en/biographies/2s40/staveren-herman-van/related-biographies (accessed September 10, 2021).

75. Rabbi Max Samfield, obituary, *Jewish Voice* (October 8, 1915): 4–5; Matthew Hicks, Rabbi Max Samfield Collection—Manuscript Collection Finding Aids—Dig Memphis—the Digital Archive of the Memphis Public Library & Information Center (oclc.org); Samfield, Max (jewishvirtuallibrary.org).

76. "Theosophical Society General Register," book A3, 159 (member no. 6348); *Path* 5, no. 2 (March 1891): 397.

77. Jewish fellows that appear in the Theosophical Society General Register include Benjamin Cohen d'Azevedo, from St. Thomas, British West Indies, who joined the society in 1881 ("TS Society General Register," book 1A, 19); Solomon Elias David, Moses Joseph Jacob, Jacob Nissim Isaac, Aaron Nissim Ezekiel Judah, and Aaron Raphael Joshua from India, who joined in 1884–1885 ("TS Society General Register," book 1B, 77, 88); John M. Cohen, from Philadelphia, who joined in 1887 ("TS Society General Register," book 1B, 105); and Henry Cohen, from Fort Wayne, Indiana, who joined in 1890 ("TS Society General Register," book 1B, 149).

78. For Imber's biography, see Jacob Kabakoff, *Master of Hope: Selected Writings of Naphtali Herz Imber* (London and Toronto: Associated University Press, 1985), 4–21. For a detailed discussion of Imber and his interest in occultism, Theosophy, and Kabbalah, see Boaz Huss, "Forward, to the East: Naphtali Herz Imber's Perception of Kabbalah," *Journal of Modern Jewish Studies* 12, no. 3 (2013): 398–418.

79. Margaret Oliphant, *Memoir of the Life of Laurence Oliphant and of His Wife Alice Oliphant* (Edinburgh and London: W. Blackwood, 1891), vol. 2, 343–44. Oliphant published a satire on the book, entitled "The Sisters of Tibet" in *Nineteenth Century*. See T. H. Meyer, *Laurence Oliphant: When a Stone Begins to Roll* (Great Barrington, MA: Lindisfarne Books, 2011), 99–123.

80. Judge Robert W. McBride was a member of the Indianapolis Theosophical Society and was later elected as a member of its executive committee. See *Theosophical Quarterly* 12 (1914): 96. Dr. Atkinson is probably Dr. W. J. Atkinson, who wrote in occult periodicals in the 1870s. I am grateful to Philip Deslippe and Janet Kerschner for this information.

81. On George Ayers, see Kurt Leland, "Alarums and Excursions: William James and the Theosophical Society, Theosophical History," *Theosophical History* 19, no. 4 (October 2018): 140–43.

82. Naphtali Herz Imber, ed., *Uriel: A Monthly Magazine Devoted to Cabbalistic Science* (Boston, MA: Cabbalistic, 1895): 19. Elsewhere, he said that he was offered $2,000 to translate the Zohar but refused. See *San Francisco Call*, April 19, 1896, 21.

83. Imber, *Uriel*, 58–59.

84. *San Francisco Call*, April 8, 1896, 7.

85. Imber, *Uriel*, 54. See also Naphtali Herz Imber, *Treasures of Two Worlds* (Los Angeles: Citizens, 1910), 93.

86. Imber, *Uriel*, 58–59.

87. *San Francisco Call*, April 7, 1896, 16; April 8, 1896, 7; April 12, 1896, 17; April 19, 1896, 21.

88. Imber, *Uriel*, 4.

89. Imber, *Uriel*, 57.

90. Imber, *Uriel*, 57.

91. Imber, *Treasures*, 10–11.

92. Imber, *Treasures*, 11.

93. Imber, *Uriel*, 60.

94. Imber, *Uriel*, 61. In his lectures in San Francisco, Imber juxtaposed the false mahatmas of Blavatsky to the thirty-six hidden Jewish masters: "The thirty-six masters of the Cabbala are not like the mahatmas of the Theosophists, sitting in idleness on the top of Thibet's Rocky Mountains meditating like fools." *San Francisco Call*, April 19, 1896, 21.

Chapter 3

1. *Theosophical Review* 34, no. 204 (July 15, 1904): 468.

2. On Benamozegh life and thought, see Alessandro Guetta, *Philosophy and Kabbalah: Elijah Benamozegh and the Reconciliation of Western Thought and Jewish Esotericism* (Albany: State University of New York Press, 2009); Clemence Boulouque, *Another Modernity: Elia Benamozegh's Jewish Universalism* (Redwood City, CA: Stanford University Press, 2021).

3. Boulouque, *Another Modernity*, 109–13.

4. Élie Benamozegh, *Bibliothèque de l'Hébraïsm* (Livourne: S. Belforte, 1897), vol. 2, 14. In a booklet dedicated to Kabbalah titled "Theosophy," Benamozegh asserted that "all the theosophical schools all over the world regard Jewish Kabbalah as the key of their philosophy." Élie Benamozegh, *Théosphie* (Livourne: S. Belforte, 1897), 6–7.

5. A year after Benamozegh's demise, Guglielmo Lattes published his biography: *Guglielmo Lattes, Vita e Opere di Elia Benamozegh: Cenni, considerazioni, note con ritratto dell'illustre rabbino* (Livorno: S. Belforte, 1901). Arrigo's uncle, Prof. Dante Lattes (1876–1965), was a prolific author, professor of Hebrew, and Zionist activist, and his brother, Rabbi Aldo Lattes (1880–1944), served as the chief rabbi of the Jewish community in Libya, under the Italian fascist regime and during World War II. See Bruno di Porto, "The Jewish Press in Livorno," *Kesher* 17 (1995): 68–69 [Hebrew].

6. See Arrigo Lattes, "In memoriam. Elia Benamozegh," *Vessilio Israelitico* 48 (1900): 47–48.

7. *General Report of the Twenty-Ninth Anniversary and Convention of the Theosophical Society*, 1904, 117.

8. Salvatore Attal, *Esoterismo Biblico* (Firenze: Salvadore Landi, 1908). The book was recently translated to French by Anne-Marie Baron, *Salvatore Attal, Ésotérisme Biblique* (Paris: L'Âge d'homme, 2015).

9. Anne-Marie Baron, "Présentation," in *Esoterismo Biblico*, Salvatore Attal, *Ésotérisme Biblique*, 11–34.

10. Decio Calvari, "Resumé du Mouvement Théosophique en Italie," *Transactions of the First Annual Congress of the Federation of the European Sections of the Theosophical Society, Held in Amsterdam, June 19th, 20th and 21st, 1904*, ed. Johan Van Manen (Leiden: Brill, 1906), 382. I follow the translation of Marco Pasi, "Theosophy and Anthroposophy in Italy," 92–93.

11. One of the early Theosophical journals in Italian, published 1897 through 1898 was entitled *Nova Lux*. See Pasi, "Theosophy and Anthroposophy in Italy," 95.

12. Di Porto, "The Jewish Press in Livorno," 71–72. The articles in the magazine refer many times to Benamozegh's thought and include several previously unpublished articles by him. The magazine's Zionist inclination is reflected in its title page, as well as in articles such as Salvatore Attal, "Il Sionismo in Italia," *Lux* 1, no. 5 (July 1904): 153–56; *Lux* 1, no. 7 (September 1904): 189–96; and Guglielmo Lattes's article on Theodore Herzl, *Lux* 1, no. 5 (July 1904): 159–61.

13. *General Report of Thirtieth Anniversary and Convention of the Theosophical Society*, 1905, 54.

14. Pasi, "Theosophy and Anthroposophy in Italy," 92.

15. See *General Report of the Twenty-Ninth Anniversary and Convention of the Theosophical Society*, 1904, 117; *General Report of Thirtieth Anniversary and Convention of the Theosophical Society*, 1905, 145; *General Report of the Thirty-First Anniversary and Convention of the Theosophical Society*, 1906, 149. Among his many publications are Cesare Augusto *Levi, Navi da guerra costruite nell'arsenale di Venezia dal 1664 al 1896* (Venezia: C. A. Levi, 1896); Cesare Augusto *Levi, Il Simon Mago ed altre leggende e visioni* (Firenze, Bemporad, 1900); Cesare Augusto *Levi, Dante e Sionne, o, la Città santa del premio divino e del lavoro umano, dall'antico Egitto ad oggi, traverso la Bibbia, il Vangelo e la Divina commedia* (Pisa: F. Mariotti, 1907). On Levi's interest in dreams, see E. Turba, C. Brillante, S. Arieti, "I sogni di Cesare Augusto Levi: Un' Interpretazione, Prefreudiana," *Medicina Nei Secoli Arte e Scienza* 19, no. 1 (2007) 305–13.

16. Pasi, "Theosophy and Anthroposophy in Italy," 116, n. 79; Hakl, *Eranos*, 29–30. Francesco Baroni, "Roberto Assagioli and Parapsychology," in Roberto Assagioli, *Psychosynthesis and Parapsychology*, ed. Kenneth Sørensen (Oslo: Kentaur, 2023), 13–20. I am grateful to Marco Pasi and Francesco Baroni, who turned my attention to Assagioli and provided me with information about him.

17. Oz Bluman, "The Moment of Worldwide Renewal: Hillel Zeitlin and the Theosophical Activity in Warsaw 1917–1924," *Modern Judaism* 41, no. 2 (2021): 142–55.

18. Aaron Zeitlin, "Mayn foter," in *Nakhmen Bratslaver: Der zeer fun Polodye*, *ed.* R. Hillel Zeitlin (New York: Farlag matones, 1952), 38 (I am indebted to Sam Glauber-Zimra for this reference). On Stabrowski, see Karolina Maria Hess and

Małgorzata Alicja Dulska, "Kazimierz Stabrowski's Esoteric Dimensions: Theosophy, Art, and the Vision of Femininity," *La Rosa di Paracelso* 1 (2017): 41–65.

19. Bluman, "The Moment of Worldwide Renewal," 155.

20. Bluman, "The Moment of Worldwide Renewal," 159, n. 56.

21. Marc Silverman, *A Pedagogy of Humanist Moral Education* (New York: Palgrave Macmillan, 2017), 82, 94.

22. Hanna Rudniańska and Krystyna Shmeruk, *Korczak, Tokarzewski i my* (Kraków: Rabid, 2005), 73–113. I am grateful to Karolina Maria Kotkowska (Hess) who turned my attention to Rudniańska's memoires.

23. See Apa B. Pant, "Maurice Frydman," in *The Mountain Path*, vol. 28, no. 1–2 (1991): 31–37; N. K. Srinivasan, "Maurice Frydman—Jnani and a Karma Yogi: A Biography," https://www.scribd.com/doc/97304328/3/Chapter-3-The-Karma-Yogi.

According to Apa Pant, Frydman was born in Krakow and became a Theosophist in 1926. David Godman, the archivist of Sri Ramana ashram, kindly informed me (private e-mail, June 4, 2015) that he was able to ascertain that Frydman was born in Warsaw and that in a letter in his possession, Frydman relates that he had read a book by Krishnamurti when he was sixteen (1917).

24. See "The TS in Poland," *The General Report of the Forty-Eighth Anniversary and Convention of the Theosophical Society* (Adyar: Theosophical Publishing House, 1924), supplement cxciv; "The TS in Poland," *The General Report of the Forty-Ninth Anniversary and Convention of the Theosophical Society* (Adyar: Theosophical Publishing House 1925), supplement cc. According to these reports, the secretary of the lodge was T. Bochensky, and the address of the lodge was Nawrot 8/29. In 1925, the address of the lodge changed to 199 Piotrowska street, flat 2, and its new secretary was M. Steinberg. See "The TS in Poland," *The General Report of the Fiftieth Anniversary and Convention of the Theosophical Society* (Adyar: Theosophical Publishing House, 1926), supplement cxcvi.

It is interesting that in her report of the activities of the Theosophical Society in Poland in 1924, Wanda Dynowska noted that the Action Lodge in Warsaw collected evidence concerning the Jewish question and wanted to "organize a platform for men of good will beyond the T.S. to discuss and to study this difficult problem of our country." See *The General Report of the Forty-Ninth Anniversary and Convention of the Theosophical Society*, 18, 157.

25. "W Łodzi wśród członków wielu Żydów. Ruch odrodzeńczy wśród nich żywy. Powstają dwa koła: żydowskie dla Polaków chcących znać Żydów, polskie (widocznie o studiach nad Polską) dla Żydów pragnących poznać Polaków. Jest poza tym koło wewnętrzne stojące ponad narodami." The document was published by Monika Rzeczycka and Izabela Trzcińska, *Polskie tradycje ezoteryczne 1890–1939. Tom. 1, "Teozofia i antropozofia"* (Gdańsk: Wydawnictwo Uniwersytetu Gdańskiego, 2019), 92. I am grateful to Karolina Maria Kotkowska (Hess) and Agata Świerzowska, who turned my attention to the document and translated it for me.

26. The information concerning the "Judaizm Istotny" lodge appears in the journal of the Polish Theosophical Society, *Przegląd Teozoficzny* 14, no. 2 (1928): 38–39. I am grateful to Karolina Maria Kotkowska (Hess), who supplied me with a photocopy of the list of Polish lodges from the journal. The address of the Judaizm Istotny Lodge and the names of its' president and secretary are the same as those of the Sattva Lodge, according to the 1925 report of the Polish Section (*The General Report of the Fiftieth Anniversary and Convention of the Theosophical Society*, cxcvi).

27. According to the directory of the Association of Hebrew Theosophists published in January 1930, the national representative in Poland was Mr. Steinberg, from Łodź, whose address was Piotrkowska 199. See *The Jewish Theosophist* (A Newer Magazine) (January 1930), 23.

28. The announcement was published in the Jewish Polish newspaper *Nasz Przegląd*, 19.4.1927, 7. The lecture took place at the hall of the teachers' union. I am grateful to Sam Glauber-Zimra, who found the announcement and informed me about it.

29. S. L. Bensusan, "How I Became a Member of the T.S.," *Theosophical Review*, vol. 1 (New Series) (1925): 210–13.

30. He published his first article that year in the *Herald of the Star*. For a description of his "conversion" to Theosophy, see Bensusan, "How I Became a Member of the T.S."

31. His last article was published in 1952, See S. I. Bensusan, "A Wild Life Day," *The Theosophist* 73 (1952): 96.

32. See A. E. Waite, *Shadows of Life and Thought* (London: Selwyn and Blount, 1938), 233–34. On Bensusan's relations with Waite, see R. A. Gilbert, *A. E. Waite: Magician of Many Parts* (Wellingborough: Crucible, 1987), 152.

33. See "Obituary: The Rev. Dr. J. Abelson, Leeds's Religious Leader," *Jewish Chronicle* (January 3, 1941): 17; "Abelson, Joshua," in *The Palgrave Dictionary of Anglo-Jewish History*, ed. William D. Rubinstein (New York: Palgrave Macmillian, 2011); Benjamin J. Elton, "Conservative Judaism's British Trailblazers," *Conservative Judaism* 63, no. 4 (2012): 64–65; Huss, "Academic Study of Kabbalah and Occultist Kabbalah," 116–18.

34. Joshua Abelson, "Talmud and Theosophy," *Theosophical Review* 37 (September 1905): 9–27. The paper was first read at the Bristol Lodge of the Theosophical Society.

35. Abelson writes that Theosophy is a "branch of knowledge in whose domain I am a comparative stranger." Abelson, "Talmud and Theosophy," 9.

36. Joshua Abelson, "Rabbinical Mysticism," *Theosophic Messenger* 13 no. 8 (May 1912): 503–7. The article is a reprint of Joshua Abelson, "Mysticism and Rabbinical Literature," *Hibbert Journal* 10 (1911–1912): 426–43.

37. Joshua Abelson, *Jewish Mysticism: An Introduction to the Kabbalah* (London: G. Bell & Son, 1913).

38. See *The Portsmouth Evening News*, December 6, 1913, 4; *Hampshire Telegraph*, December 12, 1913, 7; *Bath Chronicle and Weekly Gazette*, March 7, 1915, 7.

39. *Jewish Theosophist* 1, no. 5 (1927): 7.

40. See Mentor, "Missions to the Jews," *Jewish Chronicle*, March 25, 1927; Mentor, "Two Matters," *Jewish Chronicle*, February 24, 1929. See Liz Green, *Magi and Maggidim: The Kabbalah in British Occultism 1860–1940* (Ceredigion, Wales: Sophia Center Press), 297.

41. However, he published also on other topics. See his article "Maimonides on the Jewish Creed," *JQR* 19, no. 1 (1906): 24–58, and his article on the prohibition to wear a garment of wool and linen mixture, "A Garment of Divers Sorts," *The Jewish Chronicle Supplement*, August 1922, v–vi (interestingly, in this article, he refers to Éliphas Lévi as "the greatest occult philosopher on the nineteenth century." vi).

42. Joshua Abelson, *The Immanence of God in Rabbinical Literature* (London: Macmillan 1912).

43. *Jewish Chronicle Supplement*, May 1924, vii–viii.

44. *Jewish Chronicle Supplement*, January 1921, v–vi.

45. Joshua Abelson, " 'The Tree of Life: A Study in Magic,' by Israel Regardie," *Jewish Chronicle*, May 24, 1933, 21; Joshua Abelson, "The Kabbalah," *Jewish Chronicle*, May 24, 1935, 26.

46. M. Simon, H. Sperling, and P. P. Lavertoff, *The Zohar* (London: Soncino, 1931–1934), vol. 1, ix–xxvii. On the translation and Abelson's introduction to it, see Boaz Huss, "Translations of the Zohar: Historical Contexts and Ideological Frameworks," *Correspondences* vol. 4 (2016): 108–9.

47. On Elias Gewurz and his works that found their way to Gershom Scholem's private library, see Zvi Leshem, "Boldness of Invention and Falsification: Gershom Scholem on Elias Gewurz," the Librarians, *The Blog of the National Library of Israel,* May 1, 2023, https://blog.nli.org.il/en/gershom-scholem-elias-gewurz/.

48. Elias Gewurz's forefathers, Shmuel Henig and Elias, were the rabbis of the town in the first half of the nineteenth century. The son of Rabbi Elias, Rabbi Daniel, Elias Gewurz's grandfather, was a wealthy businessman. See N. M. Gelber, "The History of the Jews in Dembitz," in *Dembitz Book*, ed. Daniel Leibel (Tel Aviv: Ahdut, 1960), 14–34 [Hebrew]; Mendel Wilner, "The Jews of Dembitz," in *Dembitz Book*, ed. Daniel Leibel (Tel Aviv: Ahdut, 1960), 49–50 [Yiddish]. Wilner relates that Elias's father (whom he names Alter) lost all the fortunes of the family in an unsuccessful business venture. Gewurz mentions that he was born in a small town near Krakow, Galicia, and that his great grandfather was a rabbi and head of a Yeshiva and that his family was "one of the wealthiest and best known in Poland." Elias Gewurz, *Beautiful Thoughts of the Ancient Hebrews* (New York: Bloch, 1924), 3.

49. Wilner, "The Jews of Dembitz," 49. Gewurtz relates that at the age of twenty he left Poland and "traveled on the Continent of Europe and in the British Colonies." Gewurz, *Beautiful Thoughts*, 3.

50. Elias Gewurz, *The Coronation of King Edward VII and the Jews, in Three Languages, English, German, and Yiddish* (London: P. Meczyc, 1902).

51. Gewurz's baptism is registered in the Church of London Births and Baptisms, 1813–1916 (accessed through Ancestry.com). According to Wilner ("The Jews of Dembitz," 49), it was rumored in Dembitz that Gewurz went to the missionaries in London, and became a great priest (א גרויעסער גלח). Gershom Scholem wrote on the copy of Gewurz's *Beautiful Thoughts of the Ancient Hebrews*, which can be found in his library, that he heard from Daniel Leibel, who came from Dembitz, that Gewurz converted to Christianity, but he doubted this rumor.

52. Elias Gewurz and L. A. Bosman, *The Cosmic Wisdom as Embodied in the Qabbalah and in the Symbolical Hebrew Alphabet* (London: Dharma, 1914), 2.

53. The book was published as the second volume of the Esoteric Studies series by Gewurz and Bosman. The first book was Bosman's *The Mysteries of Qabalah*, published in 1913 and dedicated to Gewurz. Both books were republished by the Yogi Publication Society in 1922 under the title *The Mysteries of Qabalah*. Dharma Press announced the forthcoming publications by Gewurz—"The Restoration of the Hebrew Language," in two volumes (described as an "epoch making work based upon the research of Fabre d'Olivet), and "Atlantis: The Submerged Continent and Its Present Day Descendants"—neither of which was ever published.

54. Elias Gewurz, "The Qabalah," *Theosophist* vol. 36 (November 1914): 172.

55. In the preface to *The Cosmic Wisdom*, published by Bosman and Gewruz in 1914, the authors say that they met three years before in the headquarters of the Theosophical Society. See Gewurz and Bosman, *The Cosmic Wisdom*, 7.

56. See R. A. Gilbert, "Introduction," in Leonard Bosman, *The Meaning and Philosophy of Numbers* (Berwick, Main: Ibis, 2005), viii. According to the 1911 census, his occupation was "clock manufacturer."

57. See *International Theosophical Year Book* (Adyar: Theosophical Publishing House, 1937), 191; *General Report of the Forty-Ninth Anniversary and Convention of the Theosophical Society* (Adyar: Theosophical Publishing House, 1925), xxxi; Gilbert, "Introduction," ix.

58. Gilbert, "Introduction," x–xi.

59. The Dharma Press address was 16 Oakfield Road, Clapton, the home address of Bosman. The press published mostly books by Bosman and Gewurz.

60. Leonard Bosman, *A Plea for Judaism* (Adyar: Association of Hebrew Theosophists, 1926), 16–17.

61. Leonard Bosman, *The Music of the Spheres or Cosmic Harmony* (London: Dharma Press, 1914), 5.

62. Bosman, *Music of the Spheres*, 5. See also Leonard Bosman, *Mysteries of the Qabbalah* (London: Dharma, 1913), 31. Interestingly, in a short note on Blavatsky and the Theosophical Society, Gershom Scholem refers to Bosman's suggestion that Sifra Dezniuta is the "true etymology" of the Book of Dzyan. See Scholem, *Major Trends in Jewish Mysticism*, 398.

63. See Samuel Glauber-Zimra and Boaz Huss, " 'No Religion Could Be More Spiritual than Ours': Anglo-Jewish Spiritualist Societies in the Interwar Period," *Jewish Historical Studies* 53, no. 5 (2021): 89–97.

64. Hurst joined the Astrological Lodge in London in April 1920. See Joscelyn Godwin, "Beyond the Cosmic Ladder: The Ultimate State, according to Julius Evola and Paul Brunton," *Theosophical History 30, no.* 3 (2020): 262.

65. Michael Juste, *The White Brotherhood: An Occult Autobiography* (London: Rider 1927), 12–19.

66. During this period, Hurst published a couple of articles in the *Occult Review.* See Raphael Hurst, "The Occult Value of Scientific Attitude," *Occult Review* 34 (November 1921): 274–77; Raphael Hurst, "The Two Faces of Man," *Occult Review* 35 (May 1922): 286–98. On Brunton's ambivalent appreciation of Theosophy and of Blavatsky in later years, see Annie Cahn Fung, "Paul Brunton: A Bridge between India and the West" (doctoral thesis, Department of Religious Anthropology, Sorbonne, 1992), 18–22.

67. In later years, Brunton wrote about his Jewish background: "The narrow matrix in which heredity attempted to mold my nature, I early broke and discarded, for my whole thought and temperament were of another cast." *The Hidden Teaching beyond Yoga* (London: Rider, 1941), 29

68. Lewis writes this in a letter that he sent to Gershom Scholem in March 1948. See Boaz Huss and Jonatan Meir, " 'The Light Is Burning Pretty Low': The 1948 Correspondence between Samuel Lewis and Gershom Scholem," *Correspondences* 8, no. 1 (2020): 63–64.

69. On the Yogi Publication Society, see Philip Deslippe, *The Kybalion: The Definitive Edition* (East Rutherford: Penguin Random House, 2011), 17. Although the address of the society, which appears also in the title page of Gewurz's books, is "Masonic Temple, Chicago," the publishing society did not have anything to do with the Freemasons (the building, Chicago's first skyscraper, received the name because the Freemasons occupied the top of the building).

70. Elias Gewurz, "Comments on Light on the Path," *Messenger* 4, no. 4 (September 1916): 100–101; Elias Gewurz, "The Valley of Judgement," *Messenger* 4, no. 10 (March 1917): 297–98; Elias Gewurz, "The Occult Hierarchy & Its Messengers to the Outer World," *Theosophist* 44 (August 1923): 603–7.

71. On Martin A. Meyer, see Louis I. Newman, "Martin A. Meyer," *Publication of the American Jewish Historical Society* 29 (1925): 179–81.

72. Gewurz, *Beautiful Thoughts*, 10.

73. Huss and Meir "The Light Is Burning Pretty Low," 68. Much earlier, in a short review on Gewurz's *Beautiful Thoughts of the Ancient Hebrews*, Scholem observed that the source cited in the book "are somewhat odd, and the vast majority of the beautiful thoughts are not thoughts of the ancient Hebrews, but rather, those of the author." *Kiryat Sefer* 1, no. 4 (1925): 262. See Leshem, "Boldness of Invention and Falsification."

74. I am grateful to Philip Deslippe, who provided me with the information about Gewurz's death, as well as some other documents concerning his life.

75. See Meir and Huss, "The Light Is Burning Pretty Low," 57. Samuel Lewis mentions Gewurtz also in a letter he sent to Ada Martin, dated March 21, 1925: "Over your bed there is a quotation: 'The light eternal according to the Kabbalah,' and I have felt that where Gewurz failed, I have succeeded: That I might bring joy to your heart both as Mureed and a son of Israel. I saw Gewurz handwriting on the wall of the front room and felt it was 'handwriting on the wall.'" Murshid Samuel Lewis Archives website, http://www.ruhaniat.org/index.php/other-writing/other-papers/2290-initiation?highlight=WyJnZXd1cnoiLCJnZXd1cnonIl0=.

76. Bowen, *A History of Conversion*, 22, 215–18, 220–24; Mark Sedgwick, *Western Sufism*, 159–60.

77. *San Francisco Call* 111, no. 3 (December 3, 1911): 68.

78. Partrick Bowen, *A History of Conversion to Islam in the United States* (Leiden: Brill, 2015), vol. 1, 353–54; Mark Sedgwick, *Western Sufism: From the Abbasids to the New Age* (New York: Oxford University Press, 2017), 222–23, 225–28; Meir and Huss, "The Light Is Burning Pretty Low," 55–56.

79. Samuel Lewis, *Introduction to Spiritual Brotherhood: Science, Mysticism and the New Age* (San Francisco: Sufi Islamia/Prophecy, 1981), 48.

80. Lewis, *Spiritual Brotherhood*, 48.

81. Lewis, *Spiritual Brotherhood*, 48.

82. Jacob Rader Marcus, *The American Jewish Woman: A Documentary History* (New York: Ktav, 1981), 698; Gloria Steinem, "Pauline Perlmutter Steinem," *The Shalvi/Hynam Encyclopedia of Jewish Women*, https://jwa.org/encyclopedia/article/steinem-pauline-perlmutter.

83. *Theosophical Messenger* 19, no. 8 (august 1931): 476.

84. Marcus, *The American Jewish Woman*, 699.

85. I am grateful to Sam Glauber-Zimra, who turned my attention to Pedro Sprinberg's affiliation with Theosophy. On Sprinberg, see Zalman Rejzen, *Leksikon fun der Yiddisher literature, Prese un Filologye* (Vilne: B. Kletskin, 1929), vol. 4, 875–76; Javier Diaz, "El anarquismo en el movimiento obrero judio de Buenos Aires (1905–1909)," *Archivos* 4, no. 8 (2016), 131.

86. *General Report of the Fifty First Anniversary and Convention of the Theosophical Society* (Adyar: Theosophical Publishing House, 1927), 137; *Revista Teosofica Argentina* 10, no. 10 (1944): 284–85, 329; *Rejzen, Leksikon fun der Yiddisher literature*, vol. 4, 876. The publication of the special issue of *Theosofia en el Plata* by Sprinberg was announced in the Buenos Aires Yiddish newspaper *Di Idishe tsaytung* (December 2, 1925): 7.

87. Rejzen, *Leksikon fun der Yiddisher literature*, vol. 4, 876. I was not able to locate any of these articles.

88. *Ninetieth Annual General Report of the Theosophical Society* 1965 (Madras: The Theosophical Society 1966), 96.

89. *Israel Messenger*, May 6, 1927, 17.

90. On the foundation and activities of the Saturn Lodge, see Chuang Chienhui, "Theosophical Movements in Modern China," in *Theosophy across Boundaries: Transcultural and Interdisciplinary Perspectives on a Modern Esoteric Movement*, ed. Hans-Martin Krämer and Julian Strube (Albany: State University of New York Press, 2020), 155–56.

91. See *General Report of the Forty-Eighth Anniversary and Convention of the Theosophical Society* (Adyar: Theosophical Publishing House, 1923), 455; *International Theosophical Yearbook* 1937, 211; *North China Herald* (June 30, 1923): 900; Chienhui, "Theosophical Movements in Modern China," 156.

92. The names of Frieda Horne and Dora Stone are included in the list of members of the lodge that was sent by the Saturn Lodge to the recording secretary of the Theosophical Society in Adyar, on December 21, 1920. Mrs. D. S. Horne is listed among the members of the Shanghai Lodge in a letter sent to the recording secretary on March 27, 1924 (both documents are found in the China Files, Adyar Library). According to the report on the anniversary gathering of the Shanghai Lodge published on *North China Herald*, June 30, 1923, 900, Mr. A. Horne served as the book steward of the lodge. Frieda, who later married Jacob Beerbrayer, died at a young age. Some information of Horenstein/Horne family can be found on Geni and MyHeritage websites.

93. *The General Report of the Forty-Ninth Anniversary and Convention of the Theosophical Society* (Adyar: Theosophical Publishing House, 1925), 179.

94. *North China Herald*, May 26, 1923, 536.

95. *Theosophist* 46 (July 1925): 459–67.

96. A. Horne, "The Chinese Jews of K'ai-Feng-Fu," *Theosophist* 46 (July 1925): 466.

97. A. Horne, "Theosophy in Modern Judaism," *Theosophist* 47 (April 1926): 106.

98. Alex Horne, *Spiritualizing Unspiritual Judaism* (Seattle, WA: Association of Hebrew Theosophists, American Section, 1926).

99. On Reiss's life and career, see Fredrick's Reiss obituary, *New York Times*, November 22, 1981, 44; Kasuke Ito, "Fredrick Reiss (1891–1981)," *Bulletin of the New York Academy of Medicine* 61, no. 4 (1985): 378–84; Mátyás Mervay, "Dr. Frederick Reiss, Austro-Hungarian Master of the Shanghai Freemason Lodge Lux Orientis," *Refugees of Habsburgia in China*, https://wp.nyu.edu/habsburgiainchina/dr-frederick-reiss-austro-hungarian-master-of-the-shanghai-freemason-lodge-lux-orientis; *Refugees of Habsburgia in China*, "A Hungarian Old China Hand and the End of Empire: Loyalty Struggles in Interwar Shanghai's Migrant Community," *Austrian History Yearbook* (2024): 9, n. 129. I am grateful to Mátyás Mervay for providing me with information and materials concerning Reiss.

100. Dr. F. Reiss is listed among the members of the Shanghai Lodge in a letter sent to the recording secretary on March 27, 1924 (China Files, Adyar Library). According to the 1923 through 1924 annual report of the Shanghai Lodge, Brother

Reiss represented the lodge as a physician to the Jewish Communal Association. See *General Report of the Forty-Ninth Anniversary and Convention of the Theosophical Society* (Adyar: Theosophical Publishing House, 1925): 180.

101. Mervay, "Dr. Frederick Reiss, Austro-Hungarian Master of the Shanghai Freemason Lodge Lux Orientis."

102. "Dr. F Reiss Interviewed—Enchanted with Eres Yisrael," *Israel's Messenger* (November 3, 1933): 10. I am grateful to Matyas Mervay, who provided me with a copy of the article.

103. For information on David Gubbay and his family, see the Geni website (https://www.geni.com/people/David-Gubbay/6000000011181451861) and the Jewish Historical Society of Hong Kong website (https://jhshk.org/community/the-jewish-cemetery/burial-list/gubbay-david-sassoon/).

104. The letter, dated June 9, 1910, is found in the China Files, Adyar Library. In the letter, Gubbay mentions that "it is over a year ago since I last wrote you, and you were kind enough to answer my letter."

105. See *Far Eastern Theosophical Society Notes*, vol. 1, no. 6 (November–December 1924): 5 (I am grateful to Chuang Chienhui, who provided me with a photocopy of the Far Eastern Theosophical Society notes). Gubbay is registered as the vice president in the 1925 list of members of the Hong Kong Lodge, found in the China Files, Adyar Library. Gubbay is mentioned as a committee member of the lodge in the *General Report of the Fifty Second Anniversary and Convention of the Theosophical Society* (Adyar: Theosophical Publishing House, 1927), 179.

106. C. S. Gubbay, "Our Local Gubbay-ism, a Reply," *Israel's Messenger*, April 1932, 9. See Maisie J. Meyer, "Nissim Ezra Benjamin Ezra (1880–1936)," in *Shanghai's Baghdadi Jews*, ed. Maisie J. Meyer (Hong Kong: Blacksmith Books, 2015), 238.

107. These include N. E. David, "Universal Brotherhood & Love in Israelitism," *Theosophist* 28 (July 1907): 760–67 (August 1907): 820–28; N. E. David, "The Meaning of 'Gentiles' and 'Israel,'" *Theosophist* 29 (December 1907): 239–44 (January 1908): 317–21; N. E. David, "Karma and Reincarnation in Israelitism," *Theosophist* 29 (July 1908): 908–15 (August 1908): 998–1007 (September 1908), 1100–07. The last series of articles were republished as a booklet by the Indian Section of the Association of Hebrew Theosophists: N. E. David, *Karma and Reincarnation in Israelitism* (Karachi: L. Solomon 1928).

108. N. E. David, "Judaism" *The Proceedings of the Convention of Religions in India 1909* (Calcutta: Nababibhakar, 1910), 52–59. I am grateful to Okamato Yoshiko, who informed me of David's participation in the convention.

109. David, "The Meaning of Gentiles and Israel," 317. David argues that as such, "they were not intended to have a political independence or earthly kingdom of their own."

110. David, "The Meaning of Gentiles and Israel," 318–19.

111. David, "Karma and Reincarnation in Israelitism," 908.

112. David, "Karma and Reincarnation in Israelitism," 910.

113. David, "Universal Brotherhood in Israelitism," 767.

114. David, "Universal Brotherhood in Israelitism," 826.

115. On the Bene Israel community, see Katz, *Who Are the Jews of India?*, 90–125.

116. *International Theosophical Year Book* (Adyar: Theosophical Publishing House, 1937(, 237; D. D. Kanga, "The Passing of Prominent Theosophists, Dr. Solomon," *Theosophist* 62 (February 1941): 431–32; Shirley Berry Isenberg, *India's Bene Israel: A Comprehensive Inquiry and Sourcebook* (Bombay: Popular Prakashan), 1988, 184; Joan Roland, *Jews in British India: Identity in a Colonial Era* (Waltham, MA: Brandeis University Press, 1989), 97–98. In 1920, Solomon wrote a memorandum called "The Problem of the Minor Communities," which was forwarded to the national convention of the Home Rule League by Annie Besant. See Isenberg, *India's Bene Israel*, 250–51; Roland, *Jews in British India*, 97–98.

117. C. Jinarajadasa, "The Persecution of Hebrew Theosophists: Forward," *Theosophist* (June 1931): 363; *Jewish Advocate* (May 1931): 183; D. D. Kanga, "The Passing of Prominent Theosophists, Dr. Solomon," *Theosophist* 62 (February 1941) 431–32.

118. C. Jinarajadasa, "The Persecution of Hebrew Theosophists," *Theosophist* 52 (June 1931): 363.

119. Margaret Chatterjee, *Gandhi and His Jewish Friends* (London: Macmillan, 1992), 111. Chatterjee does not give a reference for this information.

120. J. E. Solomon, "My Experience in Healing," *The Theosophist* 57 (September 1936): 515–20.

121. On S. S. Cohen, see V. Ganesan, *The Human Gospel of Ramana Maharshi* (PDF file for personal sharing via eBook readers): 459–60; David Godman, "Talks on Sri Ramana Maharshi: Narrated by David Godman—Tales from Palakottu (Part I)," https://www.youtube.com/watch?v=yxCuGtCvkcg; Boaz Huss, " 'A Jew Living in an Ashram': The Spiritual Itinerary of S. S. Cohen," *Journal of Indo-Judaic Studies* 15 (2015): 20–29.

122. On Verweyen, see Helmut Zander, "Johannes Maria Verweyen (1883–1945) als Theosoph," in *Gaesdoncker Blätter* 7 (2005): 37–70; Peter Staudenmaier, *Between Occultism and Nazism* (Leiden: Brill, 2014), 226–27. Notwithstanding his initial support of the Nazi regime, Vereweyn was later arrested by the Nazis and died in Bergen-Belsen concentration camp.

123. S. S. Cohen, "The Jews and Poland," *Theosophist* 64 (December 1942): 263.

124. S. S. Cohen, "Hindu View on Dignity of Labour: A Jew in an Ashram Replies," *India and Israel* 4, no. 13 (1952): 37. I am grateful to Shimon Lev, who brought this letter to my attention.

125. On the Jews of Cochin, see Katz, *Who Are the Jews of India?* (Berkeley, Los Angeles, and London: University of California Press, 2000), 9–89.

126. On A. B. Salem's life and political activity, see James Chiriyankandatha, "Nationalism, Religion and Community: A. B. Salem, the Politics of Identity and the

Disappearance of Cochin Jewry," *Journal of Global History* 3 (2008): 21–42; Edna Fernandes, *The Last Jews of Kerala* (New York: Skyhorse, 2008), 123–27; Bala Menon and Essie Sassoon, *The "Jewish Gandhi" of Cochin* (Toronto: Tamarind Tree, 2020).

127. A. B. Salem, *Eternal Light: or, Jew Town Synagogue* (Ernakulam: S.D. Printing Works, 1929).

128. On Ritch, his activities in the Theosophical Society and his relations with Gandhi, see Chattarjee, *Gandhi and His Jewish Friends* (London: Macmillan, 1992), 39–42; Shimon Lev, "Gandhi and His Jewish Theosophist Supporters in South Africa," in *Theosophical Appropriations: Esotericism, Kabbalah and the Transformation of Traditions*, ed. Julie Chajes and Boaz Huss (Beer Sheva: Ben-Gurion University of the Negev Press, 2016), 247–52.

129. Lewis W. Ritch, "Letter," *The Theosophist* 18 (April 1897): 432. See also Ritch's memoirs of Gandhi in L.W. Ritch, "His Days in South Africa," in *Incidents of Gandhijis's Life*, ed. Chandrashanker Shukla (Bombay: Vora, 1949), 287–91.

130. Louis Ritch, *The South African Jewish Chronicle* (October 10, 1908): 248. Cited by Lev, "Gandhi and His Jewish Theosophist Supporters," 267.

131. Chatterjee, *Gandhi and His Jewish Friends*, 174; Shimon Lev, "Gandhi and His Jewish Theosophist Supporters," 248.

132. Herbert Kitchin (d. 1916), who later became the secretary of the Johannesburg lodge, was also close to Gandhi and was one of the first to reside at Gandhi's communitarian settlement, Phoenix Farm, near Durban. In 1906, he was briefly the editor of *Indian Opinion*. See Lev, "Gandhi and His Jewish Theosophist Supporters," 247, n. 5.

133. Lewis Ritch, "Africa," *Lucifer* 17 (September 1895): 83. On the activities of the circle, see also Lewis W. Ritch, "Letter," *Theosophist* 18 (April 1897): 433–34.

134. On Gandhi's relationship with the Theosophical Society in England, and later, in South Africa, see Chatterjee, *Gandhi and His Jewish Friends*, 172; Lev, "Gandhi and His Jewish Theosophist Supporters," 258–63.

135. M. Gandhi, *The Collected Works of Mahatma Gandhi* (Electronic Book) (New Delhi: Publications Division Government of India, 1999), vol. 11, 394, http://www.gandhiashramsevagram.org/gandhi-literature/mahatma-gandhi-collected-works-volume-11.pdf.

136. *General Report of the Thirty-Eighth Anniversary and Convention of the Theosophical Society* (Adyar: Theosophical Publishing House, 1914), 70 (the other two mentioned are Mr. and Mrs. Polak, who will be discussed below). In 1914, Gandhi distanced himself from Ritch because of the latter's misuse of funds. However, Ritch continued to be a supporter of Gandhi and the Indian cause. See Lev, "Gandhi and His Jewish Theosophist Supporters," 248.

137. On Kallenbach and his relationship with Gandhi, see Lev, "Gandhi and His Jewish Supporters," 255–56; Shimon Lev, *Soulmates: The Story of Mahatma Gandhi and Hermann Kallenbach* (Hyderabad: Orient Blackswan, 2012).

138. Lev, "Gandhi and His Jewish Supporters," 257–58; Shimon Lev, "Gabriel Isaac, Gandhi's Forgotten Lieutenant," *Jerusalem Report*, February 19, 2020, 34–36.

139. I am grateful to Victor Lal, who provided me with a draft of the chapter "The Polaks and World Jewry," from his forthcoming biography of H. S. L. Polak, in which he discusses Polak's family background.

140. On Polak and on his activities in South Africa, see Chatterjee, *Gandhi and His Jewish Friends*, 41–44; Lev, "Gandhi and His Jewish Supporters," 252–55.

141. Henry S. L. Polak, *The Indians of South Africa: Helots within the Empire and How They Are Treated* (Madras: G. A. Natesan, 1909).

142. Henry S. L. Polak, *M. K. Gandhi: A Sketch of His Life and Work* (Madras: G. A. Natesan, 1917); Millie Graham Polak, *Mr. Gandhi: The Man* (London: G. Allen & Unwin, 1931).

143. In an autobiographical essay entitled "Who's Who: An Essay in World Consciousness," Polak related that he heard Annie Besant lecture in 1903 and that he was greatly impressed by her dynamic personality. He says that he joined the Theosophical Society in Johannesburg under the influence of a Jewish friend, despite his strong disinclination to identify himself with any organization. I am grateful to Victor Lal, who provided me with a photocopy of the typescript of the article, which was written during World War II. However, in his article "Towards Practical Theosophy and Inter-religious Understanding," *Theosophist* 78 (February 1957): 324, Polak wrote that he joined the Theosophical Society ("unwillingly at first,") under Gandhi's persuasion. In a passage cited by Lev, Polak wrote that Isaac tried to persuade him to join, but he refused because he did not want to become a member of any religious organization. When he mentioned this to Gandhi, the latter urged him to become a member and told him that as a good Theosophist, he would become a better Jew. See Lev, "Gabriel Isaac, Gandhi's Forgotten Lieutenant," 34.

144. H. S. L. Polak, "Brotherhood as Understood in South Africa," *Theosophist* 31, no. 8 (May 1910): 987; Lev, "Gandhi and His Jewish Supporters," 255 (in later years, Polak related that he resigned in protest from the Johannesburg lodge, with the approval of Gandhi and Annie Besant. See: H. S. L. Polak, "Towards Practical Theosophy & Inter-Religious Understanding," *Theosophist* 78 [February 1957]: 327). In the editorial of the issue in which Polak's article was published, Annie Besant wrote that his strictures were already becoming out of date, as the officers of the South African Section and the Johannesburg lodge had spoken against the action of the Transvaal government. Besant noted that several officials of the lodge, including Kallenbach, Ritch, and Isaac, were working for Mr. Gandhi. See Annie Besant, "The Watchtower," *Theosophist* 31, no. 8 (May 1910): 959.

145. *The International Theosophical Year Book* (1937), 231; Information of his activities in the St. John's Wood lodge are found in the Adyar Archive.

146. *Jewish Theosophist* 1, no. 3 (1927): 25.

147. Glauber-Zimra and Huss, "No Religion Could be More Spiritual than Ours," 89–97.

148. Polak, "Towards Practical Theosophy," 328.

149. Cited by Lev, "Gandhi and His Jewish Theosophist Supporters," 267.

150. On the foundation of the Egyptian Section, see *The General Report of the Forty-Second Anniversary and Convention of the Theosophical Society* (Adyar: Theosophical Publishing House, 1918), 107–12; *The General Report of the Forty-Third Anniversary and Convention of the Theosophical Society* (Adyar: Theosophical Publishing House, 1919), 12, 99–108.

151. See Samir Raafat, "The Cairo Bourse," *Cairo Times*, October 30, 1997, http://www.egy.com/landmarks/97-10-30.php.

152. *The General Report of the Forty-Second Anniversary and Convention of the Theosophical Society* (Adyar: Theosophical Publishing House, 1918), 109; *The General Report of the Forty-Third Anniversary and Convention of the Theosophical Society* (Adyar: Theosophical Publishing House, 1919), 103, 105–6; "Rapport du Secretaire General" *Papyrus* vol. 3, no. 8 (June 1924): 5; *The General Report of the Forty-Ninth Anniversary and Convention of the Theosophical Society* (Adyar: Theosophical Publishing House, 1925), 123–24; Perez, "T. S. Federation in Egypt," *The General Report of the Fifty-Second Anniversary and Convention of the Theosophical Society* (Adyar: Theosophical Publishing House, 1928); *The Theosophical Yearbook* (1937), 20. In a letter to Annie Besant dated May 3, 1923, Perez spoke of his election as general secretary. The letter can be found in the Adyar Archive, Egypt file.

153. Joel Beinin, The Dispersion of Egyptian Jewry Culture: Politics and the Formation of Modern Diaspora (Cairo & New York: American University in Cairo Press, 2005), 68.

154. Perez letter, dated July 29, 1948, and Jinarajadasa's response, dated August 9, 1948, can be found in Adyar Archive, Egypt file.

155. One of them was probably Theo Levi. Perez mentions another Jewish Theosophist from Cairo in his letter: Isaac Cohen.

156. I am grateful to Raphi Levi, Theo's great-grandson, who supplied me with information about Theo Levi and provided me with photocopies of some of the book reviews written by him, especially in *L'Aurore: Journal D'information Juives*, which was published in Cairo (interestingly, one of these reviews was on the book on Zionism by Dante Lattes, the uncle of the Italian Jewish Theosophist Arrigo Lattes. See Theo Levi, "Il Sionismo par Dante Lattes," *Laurore* [October 18, 1928]: 3).

157. *The General Report of the Forty-Seventh Anniversary and Convention of the Theosophical Society* (Adyar: Theosophical Publishing House, 1923), 125–27 (A letter Levi sent to the recording secretary of the Theosophical Society, with the annual reports of 1920–1921 and 1921–1922, dated November 2, 1922, is in the Egypt file, Adyar Archives). Levi is listed as the secretary of the Hikmat-el-Kadim lodge in *The General Report of the Forty Ninth Anniversary and Convention of the Theosophical Society* (Adyar: Theosophical Publishing House, 1925), clxi.

158. *The Sixty Eighth Anniversary and Convention of the Theosophical Society* (Adyar: Theosophical Publishing House, 1944), 106.

Chapter 4

1. Maria (Cioata) Haralambakis, "Representations of Moses Gaster (1856–1939) in Anglophone and Romanian Scholarship," *New Europe College Yearbook* (2012–2013): 90–91; Simon Rabinovitch, "Jews, Englishmen, and Folklorists: The Scholarship of Joseph Jacobs and Moses Gaster," in *The Jew in Late-Victorian and Edwardian Culture: Between the East End and East Africa*, ed. Eitan Bar-Yosef and Nadia Valman (Basingstoke, NY: Palgrave Macmillan, 2009), 121–22.

2. Moses Gaster, "The Divine Name and the Creative Word," *Theosophical Review* 1 (new series) (1925): 4.

3. These included "The Alchemy of Alphabet," as well as book reviews of E. Kautsch, *Die Heilige Schrift des Alten Testaments*; William Barrett, *The Divine Rod*; Montague Summers, *The History of Witchcraft*; and S. L. MacGregor Mathers, *The Kabbalah Unveiled*. See Boaz Huss, " 'The Quest Universal': Moses Gaster's Interest in Kabbalah and Western Esotericism," *Kabbalah* 40 (2018): 264.

4. A letter from the president of the Jewish lodge, Samuel I. Heiman, dated May 23, 1928, inviting Gaster to lecture at the Jewish lodge can be found in Gaster Papers, UCL Special Collections, 56/459. The archives also include a flyer for the Jewish lodge, announcing its winter 1928 activities, which was probably attached to Heiman's letter. For information on the Gaster paper's collection, see https://www.ucl.ac.uk/library/special-collections/a-z/gaster.

5. A letter from Bensusan to Gaster (dated February 18, 1926) seems to address Gaster's reservations. In the letter, Bensusan explained to Gaster the current debates regarding Krishnamurti and his role as world teacher and advised him not to take anything he read about the Theosophical Society too seriously. Gaster Papers, 56/432.

6. Moses Gaster, "A Gnostic Fragment from the Zohar," *Quest* 14 (1923): 452–69.

7. This is mentioned in the leaflet of the Quest Society open meetings in the spring session of 1925, Gaster Papers, 97/422.

8. See Huss, "The Quest Universal," 255–56; Huss, "Academic Study of Kabbalah and Occultist Kabbalah," in *Occult Roots of Religious Studies*, ed. Yves Mühlematter and Helmut Zander (De Gruyter: Oldenbourg, 2021), 113–16.

9. Ronald Templeton, "Adolf Arenson," *Forschungsstelle Kulturimpuls*, https://biographien.kulturimpuls.org/detail.php?&id=24.

10. Ansgar Martins, *Hans Büchenbacher: Erinnerungen 1933–1949* (Frankfurt am Main: Mayer Info3, 2014), 390–93.

11. Andrej Belyi, *Verwandeln des Lebens: Errinnerugen an Rudolf Steiner* (Basel: Zbinden, 1975), 274; Martins, *Hans Büchenbacher*, 391.

12. Renatus Ziegler, "Carl Unger," https://biographien.kulturimpuls.org/detail.php?&id=724.

13. For information on Richard and Hilda Pollak, see Elisabeth Bessau, "Richard Pollak-Karin," https://biographien.kulturimpuls.org/detail.php?&id=1184; See also the website of the Jewish museum in Prague, https://www.jewishmuseum.cz/en/collection-research/on-line-collection/object-of-the-month/274/hilda-pollak-2-11-1874-viden-po-19-10-1942-treblinka-expressionen-i-xii-kolem-roku-1920-kopie/; On Richard Pollak's stigmata see, Sergei O. Prokofieff, *The Mystery of the Resurrection in the Light of Anthroposophy* (Forest Row: Temple Lodge, 2010), 138–39, 177–78.

14. On Berta Fanta, her salon, and her activities in the Theosophical Society, and later, in the Anthroposophical Society, see Wilma Iggers, *Women of Prague: Ethnic Diversity and Social Change from the Eighteenth Century to the Present* (Providence: Berghahn, 1995), 142–63; Georg Gimpel, *Weil de Boden selbst hier brennt: Aus dem Prager Salon der Berta Fanta (1865–1918)* (Vitalis: Praha, 2001); Maja Rehbein, " 'Könnte mam als Freier unter Freien leben . . .': Berta Fanta, Ida Freund und der Prager Salon," in *Anthroposophie und Judnetum*, ed. Ralf Sonnenberg (Frankfurt am Main: Info3-Verlag, 2009), 103–16.

15. See Else Bergmann, "Familiengeschichte," published in Gimpl, *Weil der Boden selbst hier brennt*, 257–58.

16. Berta Fanta mentions in her diary that she started reading the Bhagavad Gita in 1903. See Gimpl, *Weil der Boden selbst hier brennt*, 164. According to Else Bergmann, her aunt, Ida, was a medium. See Gimpl, 257–58.

17. On the Bohemian Section of the Theosophical Society and the Theosophical activities in Prague, see I. M. Kozlovsky, "Background and History of the Theosophical Society in Bohemia," *Theosophical History* 5, no. 4 (1994): 130–36; Zdeněk Vaňa, "Rudolf Steiner in Prague: Zur Geschichte der tschechischen anthroposophischen Bewegung," *Beiträge zur Rudolf Steiner Gesamtausgabe Eröffentlichungen aus dem Archiv der Rudolf Steiner-Nachlassverwaltung* (Dornach, 1992), 3–12. On the foundation of the German-speaking lodge, see the letters of Berta Fanta to Rudolf Steiner and Marie von Sievers, "Vaňa, "Rudolf Steiner in Prague," 51–52.

18. Gimpl, *Weil der Boden selbst hier brennt*, 257; Iggers, *Women of Prague*, 151–52.

19. *The General Report* 1912, 111–14.

20. Gimpl, *Weil der Boden selbst hier brennt*, 259; Iggers, *Women of Prague*, 152.

21. Vaňa, "Rudolf Steiner in Prague," 13; June O. Leavitt, *The Mystical Life of Franz Kafka: Theosophy, Cabala, and the Modern Spiritual Revival* (New York: Oxford University Press, 2012), 21–22.

22. Vaňa, "Rudolf Steiner in Prague," 17; According to Hugo Bergmann, who invited him to the lecture, Einstein did not have any understanding for it ("aber, leider, hatte er dafür kein Verständnis"). Bergman, *Tagebücher and Briefe*, vol. 2, 196. Ruth Mosiman related that when she met Bergmann in 1990, he told her that he went to hear Steiner's lecture in Prague, with two of his friends, Franz Kafka and

Albert Einstein. He said, "Franz Kafka burst out laughing when Dr. Steiner said one shouldn't eat too many eggs (Kafka ate a lot of eggs), and Albert Einstein became bored with the lecture." "Anthroposophical History in Israel," *Anthroposophical Life in Israel 2* (Spring–Summer 2001), 20.

23. Printed in Gimpl, *Weil der Boden selbst hier brennt*, 178–79. I follow the translation of Iggers, *Women of Prague*, 144.

24. Bergmann related that he received "certain exercises" from Steiner during their first meeting but that he stopped performing them after a few weeks. See Hugo Bergmann, "Parapsychologie und Anthroposophie: Rudolf Steiner Kritik der Parapsychologie," in *Studies in Mysticism and Religion Presented to Gershom G. Scholem on His Seventieth Birthday by Pupils, Colleagues and Friends*, ed. E. E. Urbach, R. J. Zwi Werblowsky, and Ch. Wirszubski (Jerusalem: Magnes, 1967), 40.

25. Samuel Hugo Bergmann, "On Rudolf Steiner," *Gazit* 26, no. 15 (1957): 93 [Hebrew]; Benjamin Ben-Zadok, *Judaism and Anthroposophy, Prof. S.H Bergmann's Encounter with Dr. Rudolf Stiener* (Tel Aviv: Humany, 2009), 27–29 [Hebrew].

26. Bergman, *Tagebücher and Briefe*, vol. 2, 452. Ben-Zadok, *Judaism and Anthroposophy*, 83–84.

27. Rudolf Steiner, *Gesamtausgabe Vorträge, Vorträge für Die Arbeiter Am Goetheanumbau* (GA353); Rudolf Steiner Verlag (Dornach, 1988), 201–2 (GA353. pdf [fvn-archiv.net]). See Udi Levy, "Samuel Hugo Bergmann, Pioneer, Scholar, Researcher—and an Anthroposoph?" *Adam/Olam* 3 (2013): 39.

28. Ben-Zadok, *Judaism and Anthroposophy*, 34–39. Ben-Zadok relates that Bergmann told the members of the Israeli Anthroposophical circle in Jerusalem that after he was wounded in the war, Steiner helped him to be transferred to a better hospital and thus saved his life. Else Bergmann gave a different account of Bergmann's hospitalization during the war. See Gimpl, *Weil der Boden selbst hier brennt*, 260.

29. Ben-Zadok, *Judaism and Anthroposophy*, 41–42.

30. Ben-Zadok, *Judaism and Anthroposophy*, 43. I am grateful to Enrico Lucca, who gave me a copy of the letter, dated July 28, 1919.

31. See Bergmann's epilogue to Else Bergmann's family history, in Gimpl, *Weil der Boden selbst hier brennt*, 272–73; Vaňa, "Rudolf Steiner in Prague," 33.

32. On Bergmann's acquaintance and attitude to Steiner and to the Anthroposophical Society, see Koren, "S. H. Bergmann's Attitude to the Teachings of Rudolf Steiner," *Iyyun* 49 (2000): 429–50 [Hebrew]; Benjamin Ben-Zadok, *Judaism and Anthroposophy: Prof. S. H. Bergmann's Encounter with Dr. Rudolf Stiener* (Tel Aviv: Humany, 2009), 26–45 [Hebrew]; Levy, Samuel Hugo Bergmann, 38–41; Boaz Huss, " 'There Are So Many Ways of Spiritual Development': Shmuel Hugo Bergmann's Interests in Western Esoteric and Alternative Spiritual Currents," in Shmuel Hugo Bergmann: A Life between Prague and Jerusalem, ed. Olaf Glöckner, Boaz Huss, and Marcela Menachem Zoufalá (Oldenburg: De Gruyter, 2024), 97–99.

33. Hugo Bergmann, "Introduction," in Rudolf Steiner, *Wie erlangt man Erkentnisse der höhern Welten*, ed. Samuel Hugo Bergmann, trans. Nachman Bar Shalom (Jerusalem: Rashbani, 1960), 5–11 [Hebrew].

34. See for instance his letter to Ernst Müller, dated August 17, 1944 (Bergman, *Tagebücher and Briefe*, vol. 1, 637) and the entry in his diary, February 24, 1958 (Bergman, *Tagebücher and Briefe*, vol. 2, 272).

35. Hugo Bergmann, "Introduction," 11.

36. On Müller's biography and on his interest in Theosophy, Anthroposophy, and Kabbalah, See Hans-Jürgen Bracker, "The Individual and the Unity of Humankind—an Account of the the Zionist and Anthroposophist Ernst Ernst Müller," in *Judaism and Anthroposophy*, ed. Fred Paddok and Mado Spiegler (Great Barrington, MA: SteinerBooks, 2003), 99–107; Binyamin Ben-Zadok, *Judaism and Anthroposophy: Prof. S. H. Bergmann's Encounter with Dr. Rudolf Steiner* (Tel Aviv: Humany, 2009), 89–94; Andreas Kilcher, "Kabbalah and Anthroposophy: A Spiritual Alliance according to Ernst Müller," in *Theosophical Appropriations: Esotericism, Kabbalah and the Transformation of Traditions*, ed. Julie Chajes and Boaz Huss (Beer Sheva: Ben-Gurion University Press 2019), 199–202; Martins, *Hans Büchenbacher* 386–90; Gerold Necker, "Ernst Müller's Encounter with Jewish Mysticism and Gershom Scholem," *Kabbalah* 40 (2018): 201–9; Nathaneal Riemer, "Ein Wanderer Zwischen den Welten—Zum 50sten Todesjahr von Ernst Müller," *David: Jüdische Kulturzeitschrift* 62 (2004) (available online at http://david.juden. at/kulturzeitschrift/61-65/62-Riemer.htm); Dianne Ritchey, "Guide to the Papers of Ernst Müller," Center for Jewish History, http://findingaids.cjh.org/?pID=481725.

37. *Vom Judentum: Ein Sammelbuch* (Leipzig: K. Wolff, 1913), 274–84.

38. Eleonore Lappin, *Der Jude 1916–1928* (Tubingen: Mohr Siebeck, 2000), 362.

39. Ernst Müller, *Der Sohar und Seine Lehre: Einleitung in die Gedankenwelt der Kabbalah* (Wein, Berlin: R. Löwit, 1920) [The third edition of the book was published in 1959, with an introduction by Hugo Bergmann]; Ernst Müller, *Der Sohar: Das Heilige Buch Der Kabbalah, Nach dem Urtext* (Wien: Heinrich Glanz, 1932). On Müllers *Zohar* translations, see *Kilcher*, "Kabbalah and Anthroposophy," 208–11; Huss, "Translations of the Zohar: Historical Contexts and Ideological Frameworks," *Correspondences* 4 (2016), 104; Necker, "Ernst Müller's Encounter with Jewish Mysticism," 215–16.

40. Ernst Müller, "Die Drei Sabbatischlieder des Jizchak Luria," *Menorah* 10 (1928): 601–3.

41. Ernst Müller, "Von Wort und Sinn der biblischen Schöpfungsgeschichte," *Der Jude* 8 (1924): 531–40. See Kilcher, 204–5; Necker, "Ernst Müller's Encounter with Jewish Mysticism," 210–13.

42. See Kilcher, "Kabbalah and Anthroposophy," 204–5.

43. See Bracker, "The Individual and the Unity of Humankind," 104; Martins, *Hans Büchenbacher*, 388.

44. Ernst Müller "Mein Weg durch Judentum und Christentum" (My way through Judaism and Christianity), *Judaica: Beiträge zum Verständnis des jüdischen Schicksals in Vergangenheit und Gegenwart* 4, no. 8 (1952). Müller further discussed the interrelationship between Judaism and Christianity as well as their connection with Anthroposophy in his article, "Wandlungen des jüdischen Bewusstseins in den letzten Jahrhunderten" (Changes of the Jewish consciousness in the last century), *Judaica: Beiträge zum Verständnis des jüdischen Schicksals in Vergangenheit und Gegenwart* 10 (1954): 129–54.

45. Stasulane, "The Theosophy of the Roerichs," 193–96; Andreyev, *The Myth of the Masters Revived*, 42–54.

46. Andreyev, *The Myth of the Masters Revived*, 71.

47. I am grateful to Sam Glauber, who first turned my attention to this circle. On the Jewish members of the inner circle of Nicholas and Helena Roerich followers, see Alexandre Andreyev, *The Myth of the Masters Revived: The Occult Lives of Nikolai and Elena Roerich* (Leiden: Brill, 2014), especially, 80–85, 121–23. On Ruth Grant, see also Fernanda Perrone, "Inventory to the Papers of Frances R. Grant," Special Collections and University Archives, Rutgers University Libraries, http://www2.scc.rutgers.edu/ead/manuscripts/grantf.html.

48. Some of her articles were published in Nicholas K. Roerich, *Himalaya: A Monograph* (New York: Brentano's, 1926).

49. Frances Ruth Grant, *Oriental Philosophy: The Story of the Teachers of the East* (New York: Dial, 1936).

50. Nicholas Roerich, *Leaves of Morya's Garden*, trans. Louis L. Horch (New York: Agni Yoga Society, 1923). The Russian original was published, also in 1923, in Paris.

51. Andreyev, *The Myth of the Masters Revived*, 334–35, 408–16.

52. Andreyev, *The Myth of the Masters Revived*, 421–22.

53. "Diaries of Helena Roerich," notebook 5, February 15, 1922, http://lebendige-ethik.net/index.php/english/47-notebooks/610-notebook-5.

54. "Diaries of Helena Roerich," notebook 11, December 17, 1922, http://lebendige-ethik.net/index.php/english/47-notebooks/628-notebook-11 (previously, Master Morya affirmed that the book can be translated to Hebrew and to German and that Yenta, that is, Esther Lichtman, can translate the book. See the entries of December 8 and December 11.

55. *Bleter Fun M's Gorten*, 1926, Steven Spielberg Digital Yiddish Library, no. 06412. Although the book was published without the name of its author, translator, and publisher, it appears under Maurice Lichtman's name in *The Library of Congress Catalogue of Copyright Entries*, New Series 23, no. 1 (Washington: Government Printing Office, 1926), 615. According to the catalogue, the book was published by the International Art Center in New York. I am grateful to Sam Glauber, who found the book and the information about its translator.

56. *Nature and Miracle* 1, no. 5 (April 14, 1922): 7–8.

57. *Nature and Miracle* 1, no. 5 (April 14, 1922): 8.

58. *Nature and Miracle* 1, no. 6 (April 14, 1922): 7–8. The English version of the article, which was first published in Russian in 1919, was published in *New Republic* 29 (December 21, 1921): 97–99.

59. *Nature and Miracle* 1, no. 6 (April 14, 1922): 3.

60. On March 14, Master Morya suggested that Nina Selinova (who later wrote the first biography of Roerich in English) should approach Rivkin to contact Sosnets (possibly, Isaac Sossnitz, the translator of Adolphe Frank's *The Kabbala or the Religious Philosophy of the Hebrew* [New York: Kabbalah Publishing, 1926]). "Sosnets" is mentioned also in Morya's communication from February 27. See "Diaries of Helena Roerich," notebook 5. On March 28, Morya said that Roerich was right in suggesting approaching the Hebrews, possibly, referring to the connection made with Rivkin. "Diaries of Helena Roerich," notebook 6.

61. "Diaries of Helena Roerich," notebook 6 (April 30).

62. See the English translation of the letter in https://www.roerich.org/correspondence/images/corr/203902_01.jpg. I am grateful to Sam Glauber, who turned my attention to this letter.

63. Markus Osterrieder, "From Synarchy to Shambhala: The Role of Political Occultism and Social Messianism in the Activities of Nicholas Roerich," in *The New Age of Occult and Esoteric Dimensions*, ed. Birgit Menzel, Michael Hagemeister, and Bernice Glatzer Rosenthal (Munchen, Berlin: Otto Sagner, 2012), 101–34.

64. Andreyev, *The Myth of the Masters Revived*, 190–91 (based on entries from Zina's diary, from October 1924). According to Helena Roerich's diary, Master Morya informed the group, on December 21, 1922, that Avirach (Maurice Lichtman) will come out to meet the "envoys" holding a Torah scroll and will greet the "Light of the East" on behalf of the Jewish people. "Diaries of Helena Roerich," notebook 11, December 21, 1922, http://lebendige-ethik.net/index.php/english/47-notebooks/628-notebook-11; see Andreyev, *The Myth of the Masters Revived*, 162.

Previously, on May 22, Helena wrote in her diary that "the view of Kamenets-Podolsk was painted" and "an image of a Hebrew, holding the Torah and menorah." See "Diaries of Helena Roerich," notebook 6, https://lebendige-ethik.net/index.php/english/47-notebooks/611-notebook-6.

65. Andreyev, *The Myth of the Masters Revived*, 347.

Chapter 5

1. Gaston Polak (1874–1970) was a mining engineer who joined the society in 1897 and became the general secretary of the Belgian section in 1913. Polak published many articles in Theosophical journals, especially *Le Lotus Bleu*, the journal of the French section of the society. See *The General Report of the Forty-Ninth Anniversary and Convention of the Theosophical Society* (Adyar: Theosophical Publishing

House, 1925), 110; *International Year Book*, 1937, 231; Theosophy World Resource Center, https://www.theosophy.world/encyclopedia/belgium-theosophy.

2. J. H. Perez, "A Short History of the Foundation of the AHT," *Jewish Theosophist* 1, no, 2 (February 1927, second and revised edition): 6.

3. Perez, "A Short History of the Foundation of the AHT."

4. I am grateful to James Chiriyankandatha, who kindly sent me the relevant passage from Salem's diary. Interestingly, Perez did not mention that it was Salem who finally gave the lecture.

5. Perez, "A Short History of the Foundation of the AHT," 7.

6. The names of the founders of the Association of Hebrew Theosophists appear in the caption of a group photo, which was taken after the ceremony of laying the foundation stone of the Adyar synagogue, published in *Jewish Theosophist* 1, no. 3 (April 1927): 13. A. Isaac was a "deputy superintendent of Telegraphs" in Poona. See *Jewish Theosophist* 1, no. 3 (April 1927): 26.

7. Perez, "A Short History," 7.

8. Gaston Polak "Association of Hebrew Theosophists: Appeal to Members of the TS," *Theosophist* 47 (April 1926): 103 (reprinted in *Jewish Theosophist* 1, no. 1 [September 1926]: 5). S. I. Heiman, of Southampton, England, replaced Cohen as international secretary. See *Jewish Theosophist* 1, no. 5 (December 1927): 9.

9. According to all the other reports on the foundation of the Association of Hebrew Theosophists, including the reprint of Besant's message in the Jewish Theosophist, the treasurer was J. H. Perez.

10. Annie Besant, "On the Watch Tower," *Theosophist* 47, no. 5 (February 1926): 553 (reprinted in *Jewish Theosophist*, vol. 1, no. 1 [September 1926]: 9).

11. G. Polak, "Association of Hebrew Theosophists: Appeal to Members of the TS," *Theosophist* 47 (April 1926): 103–4 (reprinted in *Jewish Theosophist* 1, no. 1 [September 1926]: 4–5); "Association of Hebrew Theosophists," *Messenger* 13, no. 11 (April 1926): 246.

12. Polak, "Association of Hebrew Theosophists," 103, 246.

13. Polak, "Association of Hebrew Theosophists," 103.

14. *Theosophist* 47, no. 2 (April 1926): 6. This passage was published in a report entitled "Theosophists Create a New Jewish Sect," published by the Jewish Telegraphic Agency (JTA) on February 17, 1927.

15. *Messenger* 14, no. 6 (November 1926): 128.

16. S. S. Cohen, "Adyar Synagogue: An Appeal," *Adyar Bulletin* 19 (April 1926): 64–66. The appeal was republished in Bosman, *A Plea for Judaism*, 22–23; *Jewish Theosophist* 1, no. 1 (September 1926): 5. The president of the committee was Gaston Polak; the chairman, A. B. Salem; the secretary, S. S. Cohen; and the treasurer, A. Schwartz. The members of the committee included the founders of the association, mentioned above, as well as J. Samsan, from Mhow, India, who may have also been present at the Jubilee convention.

17. *Jewish Theosophist* 1, no. 2 (February 1927): 10–11; 1, no. 3 (April 1927): 26–27; 1, no. 4 (July 1927): 13; 1, no. 5 (December 1927): 7.

18. *Jewish Theosophist* 1, no. 4 (July 1927): 4.

19. *Jewish Theosophist* 1, no. 4 (July 1927): 5, 14, 19, 26.

20. *Jewish Theosophist* 1, no. 3 (April 1927): 24–25; 1, no. 4 (July 1927): 10; 1, no. 5 (December 1927): 3.

21. S. S. Cohen, "Association of Hebrew Theosophists," *The General Report of the Fifty Second Anniversary and Convention of the Theosophical Society* (Adyar: Theosophical Publishing House, 1928), 260.

22. Bosman, *A Plea for Judaism*, 16–17.

23. Polak, "Association of Hebrew Theosophists," 104.

24. Polak, "Association of Hebrew Theosophists," 104.

25. *Jewish Theosophist*, 1, no. 3 (April 1927): 22.

26. *Jewish Theosophist* 1, no. 5 (December 1927): 7; Cohen, "Association of Hebrew Theosophists," 259.

27. *Jewish Theosophist* 1, no. 5 (December 1927): 9.

28. She was replaced by Stephan Polak. See *Jewish Theosophist: A Newer Magazine* (January 1930): 23.

29. Leon Benzimbra (1889–1962), born in Oran, Algeria was an engineer of public works. He served as the general secretary of the French section of the Theosophical Society between 1945 and 1946. He was also active in the French Association for the Study of Paranormal Phenomena (Groupe d'Études des Phénomènes Paranormaux) and served as its president until his death in 1962. See https://www. jbmarylafon.com/accueil/le-gepp/.

30. *Jewish Theosophist: A Newer Magazine* (January 1930), 23.

31. Roland, *Jews in British India*, 99–100. Samson published articles in the Bene-Israel journal the *Israelite* and the pamphlet *High Handedness at the Gate of Mercy Synagogue* (Bombay: Bahadur Printing Works, 1919).

32. *Jewish Theosophist* 1, no. 4 (July 1927): 27. Reuben Ani (whose brother, as we shall see in the next chapter, founded a Theosophical lodge in Basra, Iraq) had an import and export company in Bombay. Reuben's daughter, Rachel Menashe, wrote a memoire of the life of her family in Bombay. See Rachel Menashe, *Baghdadian Jews of Bombay, Their Life and Achievements: A Personal and Historical Account* (New York: Midrash Ben Ish Hai, 2013), 8–28. Rachel Menashe does not mention that her father was active in the Theosophical Society. However, she mentions that her father was a vegetarian and discusses a family visit in Adyar. See Menahse Anzi, "Theosophy and Anti-Theosophy in Basra: Jews, the Indian Ocean and the British Empire," *Historia* 46–47 (July 2021): 135, n. 50.

33. *Jewish Theosophist* 1, no. 4 (July 1927): 27.

34. *Jewish Theosophist* 1, no. 5 (December 1927): 7.

35. Wolfgang Von Weisl, "Indian Travel Sketches," *Reform Advocate* (August 24, 1929): 79.

36. In September 1931, Reuben Ani sent a letter to the editor of *Israel Messenger*, written on the stationary of "The Association of Hebrew Theosophists, Indian Section." See *Israel Messenger* (September 4, 1931): 20.

37. *Jewish Advocate* (July 1931): 190.

38. S. S. Cohen, "Association of Hebrew Theosophists," *The General Report of the Fifty-Second Anniversary and Convention of the Theosophical Society* (Adyar: Theosophical Publishing House, 1928), 260.

39. These were B. Samuel Goel and I. S. David. *Jewish Theosophist* 1, no. 3 (April 1927): 25.

40. N. E. David, *Karma and Reincarnation in Israelitism*, Bible Study (Karachi Centre) series no. 1, Association of Hebrew Theosophists (Indian Section) (Karachi: L. Solomon, 1928). The article was originally published in *Theosophist* in 1908.

41. *Jewish Theosophist: A Newer The* Magazine 1 (January 1930): 23.

42. Samuel Isaac Heiman (born 1896) was a teacher, and later the principal, of the Leicester College of Arts and Crafts. Apart from his activities in the Association of Hebrew Theosophists, he was also active in the Southampton Group of the Young Theosophists. *Canadian Theosophist* 7, no. 10 (December 15, 1926): 220; *Theosophist* 48 (January 1927), 491.

43. *Jewish Theosophist* 1, no. 1 (September 1926): 19.

44. S. I. Heiman, "News from England," *Jewish Theosophist* 1, no. 2 (December 1926): 13.

45. I am grateful to Leslie Price, who kindly provided me with a photocopy of the 1927 through 1928 list of charters of the Theosophical Society in England.

46. Their names appear on the letterhead of the Jewish Lodge. See the letter sent to Moses Gaster on May 23, 1928, Gaster Papers, UCL Special Collections, 56/459.

47. Cohen, "Association of Hebrew Theosophists," 259.

48. *Jewish Theosophist* 1, no. 5 (December 1927): 7.

49. Gaster Papers, UCL Special Collections, 56/459.

50. Regina Miriam Bloch (1889–1938) was a Jewish writer and poet who was interested in mysticism and esotericism. She published frequently in many periodicals, including the *Occult Review* and *Bnai Brith Magazine*, and served as the subeditor of *Sufi: A Quarterly Review*, between 1911 and 1915. She authored *The Confessions of Inayat Khan* (London: Sufi Publishing Society, 1915), *The Swine Gods and Other Visions* (London: John Richmond, 1917), and *The Book of Strange Loves* (London: John Richmond, 1918). She founded the children's museum in London in 1929 and (together with two other Jewish Theosophists, Leonard Bosman and H.S.L. Polak) the Jewish Society of Psychical Research in 1930. See "Jews and Theosophists: From Miss R. M. Bloch," *Jewish Chronicle* (March 9, 1928): 28; "Obituary: Miss R. M. Bloch," *Jewish Chronicle* (March 4, 1938): 12; Douglas A. Anderson, "Regina Miriam Bloch," *Lesser-Known Writers* blog, posted April 22, 2021, Lesser-Known Writers: Regina Miriam Bloch (desturmobed.blogspot.com); Glauber-Zimra and Huss, "No Religion Could Be More Spiritual than Ours," 89–97, http://desturmobed.blogspot.com/2021/04/regina-miriam-bloch.html?m=0.

51. Rabbi Louis Mendelsohn (c. 1868–1948) was an Orthodox rabbi and a member of the London Beth Din. In 1910, he wrote a master's thesis at the University of London on "Jewish Beliefs and Customs Connected with the Taboo." William D. Rubinstein, ed., *The Palgrave Dictionary of Anglo-Jewish History* (Chippenham and Eastbourne: Palgrave Macmillan, 2011), 662.

52. Letter dated May 23, 1928, Gaster Papers, UCL Special Collections, 56/459.

53. *Jewish Theosophist: A Newer Magazine* (January 1930): 23.

54. Mentor, "Strange Faiths," *Jewish Chronicle* (February 10, 1928): 9.

55. Mentor, "Strange Faiths."

56. Heiman's letter to the editor of *The Jewish Chronicle* is cited by Mentor, "Two Matters," *Jewish Chronicle* (February 24, 1928): 9.

57. According to Dutch scholar Alexandra Nagel, at least one hundred Jews joined the Dutch section of the society between 1893 and 1938. Alexandra Nagel, "The Association of Jewish Theosophists in the Netherlands: The Efforts of Louis Vet and Others to Revive Judaism," *Correspondences* 7, no. 2 (2019): 417.

58. I am grateful to Renger Dijkstra and Alexandra Nagel, who provided me with information and sources about the Dutch Section of the Association of Hebrew Theosophists. My discussion of the Dutch Section is largely based on Alexandra Nagel's study, "The Association of Jewish Theosophists in the Netherlands," 411–39.

59. "Vereeniging voor Joodsche Theosophen," *De Theosofische Beweging* 22, no. 10 (1926): 183–84.

60. "Vereeniging voor Joodsche Theosophen," 183. I follow the translation of Alexandra Nagel, "The Association of Jewish Theosophists in the Netherlands," 416.

61. Louis Vet, "Boodschap van Dr. Annie Besant, aan Joodsche Theosofen." *De Theosofische Beweging* 23 (1927): 73.

62. *Jewish Theosophist* 1, no. 4 (July 1927): 12, 16.

63. Nagel, "The Association of Jewish Theosophists in the Netherlands," 419.

64. Ré Levie, "Studie in Kabalah c.a.," *De Theosofische Beweging* 1, no. 12 (1905): 192–93; "Derde Congres van de Federatie der Theosophische Secties in Europa," *Algemeen Handelsblad*, June 9, 1906; *De Theosofische Beweging* 2, no. 7/8 (1906): 154. See also Nagel, "The Association of Jewish Theosophists in the Netherlands," 419.

65. "Vereeniging voor Joodsche Theosophen," 183–84.

66. Henri van Praag, "Weer een nieuwe secte?," *De Theosofische Beweging* (1926), 214; Nagel, "The Association of Jewish Theosophists in the Netherlands," 422–23.

67. Louis Vet, "De Theosofie een Secte?," *De Theosofische Beweging* (1926): 239–40; Nagel, "The Association of Jewish Theosophists in the Netherlands," 423.

68. J. H. Kengen, "Geachte Redactie!" *De Theosofische Beweging* 22 (1926): 238–39. Nagel, "The Association of Jewish Theosophists in the Netherlands," 423–24.

69. Louis Vet, "Samenwerken van Joodsche Theosofen," *De Theosofische Beweging* 23 (1927): 36–37, 98–99.

70. *Jewish Theosophist: A Newer Magazine* (January 1930): 23.

71. Louis Vet, "Vervolging van Joodsche Theosofen," *De Theosofische Beweging* 27 (1931): 369–71.

72. Nagel, "The Association of Jewish Theosophists in the Netherlands," 428.

73. Perez. "A Short History of the Foundation of the AHT," 7.

74. According to the Association of Hebrew Theosophists directory, published in January 1930, which was mentioned above, the national representative of the Association of Hebrew Theosophists in Poland was Mr. Steinberg, from Łódź. *The Jewish Theosophist: A Newer Magazine* (January 1930): 23. It is possible that the Jewish lodge in Warsaw, which was mentioned in the Jewish Polish newspaper *Nasz Przegląd*, on April 19, 1927, was also related to the Association of Hebrew Theosophists.

75. *Messenger* 13, no. 12 (May 1926): 265. The announcement was reprinted in the *The Theosophist* 47 (August 1926): 623–24.

76. A. Horne, "Theosophy in Modern Judaism," *Theosophist* 47 (April 1926): 106.

77. Janet Kerschner found such a letter sent to the Washington lodge on May 20, 1926, and kindly provided me with a copy.

78. In the first issue of *The Jewish Theosophist*, the American section of the Association of Hebrew Theosophists published "an appreciation," thanking Theosophical lodges for furnishing names of Jewish members and friends. *Jewish Theosophist* 1, no. 1 (September 1926): 16.

79. *Jewish Theosophist* 1, no. 2 (December 1926): 20–21.

80. *Jewish Theosophist* 1, no. 2 (December 1926): 10–11. Their election was announced in the *Jewish Theosophist* 1, no. 3 (April 1927): 23.

81. For biographical details, documents, and pictures of Samuels, see the Ryan Waller family tree at ancestry website https://www.ancestry.com/family-tree/person/tree/23516300/person/1398324860/facts. I am grateful to Janet Kerschner who provided me with further information on the life of Henry C. Samuels and of his activities in the Theosophical Society.

82. Henry C. Samuels, "A History of the Jewish People," *Theosophist* 71 (August 1950): 331.

83. Samuels mentions that he joined the Theosophical Society in 1919 in a letter he published in *The Jewish Theosophist* 2, no. 1 (April–June 1932): 5, and in a letter he published in *The Israel Messenger*, May 1, 1932, 8. On March 1926, Samuels gave a public lecture on Judaism and Christianity in the women's twilight tea at the Besant Lodge (*Seattle Daily Times*, March 8, 1926: 47), and on November 13, he led a round-table discussion at the lodge. I am grateful to Janet Kerschner for this information.

84. Dora was the sister of Vita, Samuels's first wife, who died at childbirth in 1918. Samuels married Dora in 1921, and they divorced in 1938. See Ryan Waller family tree, https://www.ancestry.com/family-tree/person/tree/23516300/person/1398324860/facts.

85. I am grateful to Janet Kerschner for this information. Janet Kerschner has also informed me that Samuels's daughter Vinita's marriage ceremony, in 1945, took place at the home of Ray. M. Wardall, a prominent Seattle Theosophist and a priest of the LCC.

86. Henry C. Samuels, "A Message to the Jewish Press," *Jewish Theosophist* 1, no. 3 (April 1927): 17.

87. Samuels, "A Message to the Jewish Press," 17.

88. Henry C. Samuels, *Morning Prayer: a Modern, Comprehensive and Applicable Order of Service, for Individual and Congregational Jewish Worship* (Seattle: New Synagogue Press, 1928).

89. Samuels, *Morning Prayer*, 33.

90. Henry C. Samuels, *Krishnamurti the Jew: A Presentation from the Jewish Point of View* (Seattle: New Synagogue Press, 1929).

91. See the following by Henry C. Samuels: "The Jews—Race or Nationality?," *Theosophist* 67 (December 1945): 120; *Palestine and Judea* (Seattle, Washington: Henry C. Samuels Publications, 1946); "Hebrew—Not Jew," *Theosophist* 68 (June 1947): 187–89; *Our Hebrew Faith* (Seattle, WA: Henry C. Samuels Publications, 1949); "History of the Jewish People," *Theosophist* 71 (August 1950): 328–33; "Concerning Studies in Religion—A Picture of the Great Hebrew Faith," *Theosophist* 75 (October 1953): 33–43; "Bible Translations," *Theosophist* 76 (May 1955): 105–12; *Understanding Our Holy Bible: An Hebraic View* (Seattle, Washington: Henry C. Samuels Publications, 1960).

92. Henry C. Samuels, "Hebrew—Not Jew," *The Theosophist* 68 (June 1947): 188–89.

93. Samuels, *Palestine and Judea*, 6. Samuels criticized the Zionists, who he claimed represent only the Judaic national group, and not the Hebrew faith and Jewish religion: "If the Zionist group would see this more clearly, or perhaps not ignore that fact, and not try to embrace the entire Hebraic or even Jewish following, which is totally inconsistent and impossible, they would make more progress in their efforts." Samuels, "The Jews—Race or Nationality?" 120.

94. For information on Bozena Brydlova, see https://theosophy.wiki/en/Bozena_Brydlova and the biography written by her great-grandson Lev Gross-Comstock, published on https://www.wikitree.com/wiki/Brydlova-1.

95. Bozena and Charles Grotte had a daughter, Alice, who inherited Grotte's estate ($125,000) after his death in 1927, when she was twelve years old. The large inheritance gained the attention of the press and was also reported in *The Jewish Theosophist* 1, no. 3 (April 1927): 24.

96. See Brydlova's letter to Shri Yogendra, dated July 24, 1922, published in Santan Rodriguez, *The Householder Yogi: The Life of Shri Yogendra* (Yoga Institute, 1997), 118.

97. Bozena Brydlova, *10 Unveiled: The Brydlovan Theory of the Origin of Numbers* (New York: Macoy, 1922). See also her article entitled "A Woman Scientist's Startling New Theory about Numbers," *Ogden Standard Examiner* (March

19, 1922): 2. Brydlova also wrote a play in three acts entitled "This Is My Body," which is mentioned in the *Catalogue of Copyright Entries* 19, no. 1 (1922): 963.

98. On William Rubin and his political and literary activities, see "William Benjamin Rubin Papers, 1908–1950" at the Archival Resources in Wisconsin website, http://digicoll.library.wisc.edu/cgi/f/findaid/findaid-dx?c=wiarchives;view=reslist; subview=standard;didno=uw-whs-mil0000p;focusrgn=bioghist;cc=wiarchives;byte=851 63699.

99. Bozena Brydlova, "Why Every Jew Should Join the Association of Hebrew Theosophists," *Jewish Theosophist* 1, no. 1 (September 1926): 7; Bozena Brydlova, "The Ancient Kabbalah," *Jewish Theosophist* 1, no. 2 (December 1926): 27–28; Bozena Brydlova, "A Plea for the Humble," *Jewish Theosophist* 1, no. 3 (April 1927): 30–31. Brydlova also presented a lecture titled "Hebrew Mysticism," under the auspices of the Association of Hebrew Theosophists. See *Wisconsin Jewish Chronicle*, November 12, 1926, 3.

100. Brydlova, "The Ancient Kabbalah," 27.

101. Brydlova, "A Plea for the Humble," 30–31.

102. Bozena Brydlova, *Flame of the Fog* (Wheaton, IL: Theosophical, 1927); Bozena Brydlova, *A Sinner's Sermons* (Wheaton, IL: Theosophical, 1927). In the *Catalog of Copyright Entries*, part 1. [B] Group 2. Pamphlets, Etc. New Series (1930), 128, there is a reference to a book Brydlova published in 1929, in Hollywood, California, together with the actor Bylek Rudolph, entitled *Lost Word, or the Chosen People*. I have not been able to locate this book.

103. For biographical information on Ball, see the obituary published in *Independent* (Long Beach, CA) (March 25, 1965): 34, and the Hoffaman family tree on the Ancestry website, https://www.ancestry.com/family-tree/person/tree/161053850/person/422189069610/facts?_phsrc=aKk1399&_phstart=successSource.

Louis's wife, Gertrude, who was president of the Long Beach section of the Council of Jewish Women, was also active in the Association of Hebrew Theosophists (see her report of her impressions of Annie Besant in *The Jewish Theosophist* 1, no. 3 [April 1927]: 22). One of Gertrud and Louis's children, born in 1925, was named "Halcyon" (probably, to commemorate Krishnamurti's famous pseudonym). Bert M. Ball, probably Louis's brother, also contributed funds for the Association of Hebrew Theosophists. See *Jewish Theosophist* 1, no. 4 (July 1927): 10.

104. Among his articles are "A Study in Races and Half-Castes," *Theosophist* 53 (September 1932): 794–95, and "A History of the Jewish People," *Theosophist* 70 (August 1949): 337.

105. *American Theosophist* 53, no. 1 (1965): 10.

106. I am grateful to Janet Kerschner, who kindly shared with me the information on Silberman and his family. Gene Wilder was the son of William (Velvel) Silberman, Franck's younger brother.

107. Tom Leonard, "Torment Willy Wonka Star Hid behind Those Twinkling Blue Eyes: How Gene Wilder's Clownish Characters Concealed a Life Battered by Tragedy," *Daily Mail*, August 31, 2016, https://www.dailymail.co.uk/news/

article-3766152/Torment-Willy-Wonka-star-hid-twinkling-blue-eyes-Gene-Wilder-s-clownish-characters-concealed-life-battered-tragedy.html#ixzz4Iv7aJBi3.

108. On Blochman's life and activities, see David F. Hoexter and Mary R. Hoexter, "Lazar E. Blochman of San Francisco, Santa Maria and Berkely," *Western States Jewish Historical Quarterly* 13, no. 1 (1980): 53–62. Passages from Blochman's memoires and diary concerning his childhood in San Francisco were published in Ava Fran Kahn, ed., *Jewish Voices of the California Gold Rush: A Documentary History 1849–1880* (Detroit, MI: Wayne State University Press, 2002), 299–301. Lazar's father, Emanuel Blochman, was a scholar who translated and published Elijah Benamozegh's *Jewish and Christian Ethics* in 1873. See Mary H. Hoexter, "Emanuel Blochman: French Born Orthodox Activist of San Francisco," *Western States Jewish Historical Quarterly* 20, no. 2 (1988): 99–108.

109. On Blochman's interests in Spiritualism, see Hoexter and Hoexter, "Lazar E. Blochman," 61. Blochman was also interested in astrology, and in 1902 he published "The Esoteric Philosophy of Life" in *The Adept: The American Journal of Astrology*. Blochman was a follower of the Esotericist and spiritual teacher Santa Onfa de Santos, or Sister Onfa (1856–1914), the founder of the Uranian Mission. Blochman, who probably funded the Uranian Mission, published a letter praising Sister Onfa's mystical powers in the *Journal of the American Society of Psychical Research* 7, no. 8 (August 1913): 458. See John Buescher, "Sister Onfa: Uranian Missionary to Messilla," *Southern New Mexico Historical Review* 23 (January 2021), 44–48.

110. See *Pacific Theosophist* 4, no. 10 (May 1894): 158.

111. See the following by L. E. Blochman: "Heaven an Evolutionary Conception," *Jewish Theosophist* 1, no. 2 (December 1926): 24–27; *Jewish Theosophist* 1, no. 3 (April 1927): 27–28; *Jewish Theosophist* 1, no. 4 (July 1927): 7–10; "A Prayer," *Jewish Theosophist* 1, no. 5 (December 1927) (inside cover); "Occult Conceptions of Heaven," *The Jewish Theosophist: A Newer Magazine* (January 1930): 9–10; "The Aura," *Jewish Theosophist* 2, no. 2 (July–December 1932): 4–5.

112. Blochman, "Heaven an Evolutionary Conception," *Jewish Theosophist* 1, no. 2, 27. For his discussion of Kabbalah see Blochman, "Heaven an Evolutionary Conception," *Jewish Theosophist* 1, no. 4, 8–10.

113. A. Horne, "Judaism and Theosophy," *Jewish Theosophist* 1, no. 4 (1927): 23–24.

114. *Jewish Theosophist* 1, no. 2 (December 1926): 13–16 (reprinted in *Jewish Theosophist* 1, no. 3 [April 1927]: 19–21).

115. A. Horne, *Spiritualizing Unspiritual Judaism* (Seattle, WA: Association of Hebrew Theosophists, American Section, 2016).

116. *Theosophist* 48 (February 1927): 613.

117. *Theosophist* 47 (April 1926): 105–106.

118. Horne published a review on Nina H. Adlerblum's *A Study of Gersonides in His Proper Perspective"* in the *Theosophical Messenger* 15 (May 1928): 282, and a review on the English translation of Adolphe Franck's *The Kabbalah*, in the *Theosophical Messenger* 17 (June 1929): 137.

119. Alexander Horne, *An Introduction to Esoteric Judaism* (Wheaton: Theosophical Press, 1928). The book was based on a lecture he presented to the Pacific Lodge in September 1926. Another book that Horne published in this period was *Theosophy and the Fourth Dimension* (London: Theosophical Publishing House, 1928). He also compiled and edited Blavatsky's *Alchemy and the Secret Doctrine* (Wheaton, IL: Theosophical Press, 1927).

120. Alexander Horne, "Is Persecution the Plan?," *Theosophist* 60 (August 1939): 489–90.

121. A. Horne, "After Two Thousand Years," *American Theosophists* 36 (March 1948): 62.

122. *Jewish Theosophist* 1, no. 4 (July 1927): 4. The secretary of the committee was Louis B. Ball, and its members were the officers of the section (Samuels, Silberman, and Rubin). Other members were Rubin Rose B. Angle, from Richmond Virginia; Louis Zalk, from Duluth, Minnesota; Solomon L. Flatow, from Brooklyn, New York; and Fanny S. Pritzker from Worcester Massachusetts. In the late 1950s, Solomon L. Flatow, who was the chairperson of the Brooklyn Lodge of the Theosophical Society donated the book to the Israeli society. See *Theosophie in Israel*, 4.

123. *Jewish Theosophist* 1, no. 2 (December 1926): 19.

124. *Jewish Theosophist* 1, no. 2 (December 1926): 19; *Jewish Theosophist*, 1, no. 5 (December 1927): 7.

125. *The Jewish Theosophist* 1, no. 2 (December 1926): 3, 31; *Jewish Theosophist* 1, no. 3 (April 1927): 22; *Jewish Theosophist* 1, no. 5 (December 1927): 7.

126. *Jewish Theosophist: A Newer Magazine* (January 1930): 23.

127. Jonatan Meir, *Kabbalistic Circles in Jerusalem* (1896–1948) (Leiden: Brill, 2016), 76.

128. *Jewish Theosophist* 2, no. 1 (April–June 1932): 7.

129. Jennie Wilson, "The Ancient Wisdom in Palestine," *World Theosophist* 2 (1932): 317.

130. *Jewish Theosophist* 1, no. 1 (September 1926): 9; *Jewish Theosophist* 1, no. 2 (April 1927): 35–36.

131. *Jewish Theosophist* 1, no. 4 (July 1927): 6–7; *Jewish Theosophist* 2, no. 2–3 (July–December1932): 1–2, 5.

132. *Jewish Theosophist* 2, no. 1 (April–June 1932): 1.

133. *Jewish Theosophist* 2, no. 1 (April–June 1932): 1, 7.

134. *Jewish Theosophist* 1, no. 4 (July 1927): 4, 13; *Jewish Theosophist* 2, no. 2–3 (July–December 1932): 4.

135. *Jewish Theosophist* 1, no. 1 (September 1926): 7.

136. *Jewish Theosophist* 1, no. 1 (September 1926): 20–21.

137. *Jewish Theosophist* 1, no. 3 (April 1927): 4–5.

138. *Jewish Theosophist* 1, no. 4 (Jul 1927): 23–24.

139. *Jewish Theosophist* 1, no. 2 (December 1926): 4; *Jewish Theosophist* 1, no. 3 (April 1927): 2.

140. *Jewish Theosophist* 1, no. 2 (December 1926): 29–30.

141. *Jewish Theosophist* 1, no. 1 (September 1926): 13.

142. *Jewish Theosophist* 1, no. 2 (December 1926): 27–28.

143. *Jewish Theosophist* 1, no. 3 (April 1927): 5–8.

144. *Jewish Theosophist* 1, no. 4 (July 1927): 3–4.

145. *Jewish Theosophist* 1, no. 4 (July 1927): 22–23.

Chapter 6

1. A. J. Brawer, *Avak Derakhim* (Tel Aviv: Am Oved, 1945), 252–53 [Hebrew].

2. The Jewish Theosophists in Basra were discussed by Hayim Cohen, "Jewish Theosophists in Basra: A Symptom of the Struggle of the Generation of Enlightenment," *Ha-mizrah ha-Hadash* 15 (1965): 401–7 [Hebrew]; Abraham Ben Yaakov, *Rabbi Sassoon Shandoch* (Haktav Institute: Jerusalem 1994), 70–72 [Hebrew]; David Sagiv, *The Jewish Community in Basrah 1914–1952* (Jerusalem: Carmel, 2004), 73–88 [Hebrew]; Menahse Anzi, "Theosophy and Anti-Theosophy in Basra: Jews, the Indian Ocean and the British Empire," *Historia* 46–47 (July 2021): 123–66 [Hebrew]; Sasha Rachel Goldstein, "Baghdadi Jewish Networks in Hashemite Iraq: Jewish Transnationalism in the Age of Nationalism" (PhD dissertation, Leiden University, 2018), 176–87.

3. See the letter of Reuben E. Ani published in *The Jewish Advocate* (May 1931): 167, and the letter of Kadouri Ani, published in "The Persecution of Hebrew Theosophists," *Theosophist* 52 (June 1931), 365 (according to Kadouri Ani, the lodge was active from 1916 through 1917). See also C. Jinarajadasa's message in *Theosophist* 52 (June 1931): 363 and Dr. Jacob E. Solomon's obituary, *Theosophist* 62 (February 1941): 431, and the report published by Ezekiel Zvi Kalzel, "Theosophy and Kosher Meat," *Ha-Doar Hayom* (January 21, 1936) [Hebrew]. According to a letter from the assistant general secretary of the Indian Section to the recording secretary of the Theosophical Society, dated October 31, 1928 (found in the Adyar Archive, Basra file), a Theosophical group was founded in Basra by Theosophists who had arrived from Bombay in 1911.

4. This was reported by Kalzel, "Theosophy and Kosher Meat." The headmaster of the AIU school (his name was not mentioned in Kalzel's report) was Moise Itach. See Sagiv, *The Jewish Community in Basrah*, 155.

5. "The Persecution of Hebrew Theosophists," *Theosophist* 52 (June 1931): 365.

6. See Cohen, "Jewish Theosophists in Basra," 402.

7. According to "The Crisis in Iraq Jewry," in *Israel's Messenger* (August 1, 1931): 7, Ani was "the worshipful master of the Freemasonry Lodge of Mesopotamia." According to Lane's Masonic Records (1717–1894) (dhi.ac.uk), three lodges operated in Basra: Lodge Mesopotamia (3820), named in 1917; Lodge Babylonia (4326), named in 1921; and Lodge Basra (5105), named in 1929. According to

the memoire of Yossef Kivity, whose father, Yaakov Kivity, was active in the Basra Lodge, there were two lodges in Basra, the English-speaking Lodge Basra and the Arabic-speaking Lodge Fayha. Most of the Basra Freemasons (which also included Moslems, Christians, and Indians) were Jewish. See http://www.mastermason.com/ GLIsrael/L1Reuven/IrakiFreemasons-E.html. For partial lists of Jewish Freemasons in Basra, see Sagiv, *The Jewish Community in Basra*, 87–88.

8. Letter from the assistant general secretary of the India Section to the recording secretary of the Theosophical Society, October 31, 1928, Adyar Archives, Basra File.

9. Kalzel, "Theosophy and Kosher Meat."

10. Sagiv, *The Jewish Community in Basrah*, 54.

11. "Although the Theosophical Lodge in Iraq consists of about 30 members only, they are very influential . . . [T]hese thirty members are more powerful than the 9970 Jews of Basra, who are powerless to do anything." "The Crisis in Iraq Jewry," *Israel's Messenger* (August 1, 1931): 9. For a partial list of the members and supporters of the Basra Theosophical group, see Sagiv, *The Jewish Community in Basrah*, 86–87.

12. According to a report from 1931, signed by "Observer": "This movement started three years ago after consultations with the 'chief Rabbi' of Basra, Heskel Sassoon . . . our leading Rabbi was actually instrumental in fostering it and giving it his official weight and countenance. His first blunder was by failing to report the society's activities to the Chief Rabbi of Iraq, until I am sorry to say its breeches of our law had attracted his attention and made him wake up." "Jews in Iraq Face a New Crisis," *Israel's Messenger* (June 1, 1931), 18, 23. The "Observer" who signed the report was probably Rahamim Sion, a Zionist activist from Basra, who later, following the contacts he made with Rabbi Jung, traveled to New York and studied at Yeshiva University. On Rahamim Sion, see Shulamith Z. Berger, "Pumbeditha Traveled West! Yeshiva College's First Iraqi Student," *Yeshiva University* blog, April 5, 2004. Anzi, "Theosophists and Anti-Theosophists," 149–50, n. 105.

13. Cohen, "Jewish Theosophists in Basra," 403; Anzi, "Theosophy and Anti-Thosophy,"135–36. According to Kalzel (who was informed by Ani), a substantial sum disappeared from the community's fund. When Ani appointed an investigation committee, the lay committee council resigned, and the decree against the Theosophists was issued by the office of the Baghdadi rabbinate. Kalzel, "Theosophy and Kosher Meat." S. S. Cohen claimed in a letter to the editor of *Israel's Messenger* that a commission appointed by the government found that the Rabbinical Party in Basra was guilty of misappropriating 450,000 Rs., out of the community funds. S. S. Cohen, "Rabbi Jung and Theosophy," *Israel's Messenger* (October 1, 1932): 19 (The editor commented that "this is a liable that we must not pass unchallenged.")

14. According to Reuben Ani (Kaduri's brother), the person who approached Rabbi Jung was the "Observer," who wrote the report against the Theosophists that was published in *Israel's Messenger* on June 1, 1931. Reuben Ani, "Basra Jews and

Theosophy," *Israel's Messenger* (September 4, 1931): 20. As mentioned above, the Observer was probably Rahamim Sion. On the connection between Sion and other members of the Basra community with Rabbi Jung, which began in 1928, see Anzi, "Theosophy and Anti-Theosophy," 148–49.

15. Hertz's reply was cited in a report in the *Times of Mesopotamia* (April 13, 1931); "Jews in Iraq Face a New Crisis," *Israel's Messenger* (June 1, 1931): 18, 23; and "The Persecution of the Jewish Theosophists," *Theosophist* 52 (June 1931): 368.

16. The cable, which was published in the *Times of Mesopotamia*, was cited by Reuben. E. Ani, "Theosophy in Iraq," *Jewish Advocate* (August 1931): 215.

17. Cited in "Jews in Iraq Face a New Crisis," *Israel's Messenger* (June 1, 1931): 18; and "The Persecution of the Jewish Theosophists," *Theosophist* 52 (June 1931): 369–70. See also Jung's letter to the editor, dated October 1931, which was published in *Israel's Messenger* (January 1, 1932): 26.

18. The English translation of the Hebrew circular was published in "The Persecution of Hebrew Theosophists." *Theosophist* 52 (June 1931): 363–64. Reuben Ani cited parts of the circular in his letter to the editor in "Theosophy and Jews," the *Jewish Advocate*, May 1931, 167.

19. An English translation of the letter was published in "The Persecution of Hebrew Theosophists," *Theosophist* 52 (June 1931): 365–68.

20. "Jews in Iraq Face New Crisis," *Israel's Messenger* (June 1, 1931): 18; "The Persecution of Hebrew Theosophists," *Theosophist* 52 (June 1931): 369–70 (reprinted from *Times of Mesopotamia*, April 13, 14, 1931); Reuben Ani, "Theosophy in Iraq," *Jewish Advocate*, August 1931, 215.

21. "Jews in Iraq Face New Crisis," *Israel's Messenger*, June 1, 1931, 18.

22. "The Persecution of Hebrew Theosophists." *Theosophist* 52 (June 1931): 375–76. (Reprinted from the *Times of Mesopotamia*, Basrah, May 5.) On the appeals of the detractors of the Jewish Theosophists to the Iraqi authorities, see Anzi, "Theosophy and Anti-Theosophy in Basra," 140.

23. On Isaac Nathan Said, see Anzi, "Theosophy and Anti-Theosophy in Basra," 143–45.

24. For a translation of the pamphlet, see Anzi, "Theosophy and Anti-Theosophy in Basra," 162–66.

25. Anzi, "Theosophy and Anti-Theosophy in Basra," 146–51, 163–64.

26. Sagiv, *The Jewish Community in Basra*, 80; Anzi, "Theosophy and Anti-Theosophy in Basra," 148.

27. The decree is cited by Reuben Ani, "Theosophy and Jews," *Jewish Advocate*, May 1931, 167; "The Crisis in Iraq Jewry," *Israel's Messenger*, August 1, 1931, 9.

28. The Arabic Section of the paper was الوقات العراقيه, the *Times of Iraq*. See Anzi, "Theosophy and Anti-Theosophy in Basra," 150. On the *Times of Mesopotamia*, see also Goldstein, "Baghdadi Jewish Networks in Hashemite Iraq," 179, n. 13.

29. *Israel's Messenger*, published in Shanghai, was edited by N. E. B. Ezra. *The Jewish Advocate*, published in Bombay, was founded and edited by Joseph Sargon

(Ezra's nephew) and subsidized by the Jewish National Fund. See Joan. G. Roland, "Baghdadi Jews in India and China in the Nineteenth Century: A Comparison of Economic Roles," in *The Jews in China*, ed. Jonathan Goldstein (New York and Armonk, NY: M. E. Sharpe, 1999), vol. 1, 151; Roland, *Jews in British India*, 129–30, 167.

30. "Jews in Iraq Face a New Crisis," *Israel's Messenger* (June 1, 1931): 18.

31. See the letter of A. Menashe, *Jewish Advocate* (June 1931): 184.

32. Nayim B. Samuel, "Theosophy and the Jews," *Jewish Advocate* (July 1931): 202.

33. *Jewish Advocate* (June 1931): 182–83.

34. "The New Crisis in Iraqian Jewry," *Israel's Messenger* (August 1931): 1. In his response to a letter of Reuben Ani, published in the September issue, Ezra repeated his accusations of the Jewish Theosophists, "who had donned the costumes of beggars in the home of aliens, in the hope of snatching crumbs of bread from other tables when their own table lacks nothing by way of satisfying their hungry souls," but he also repeated his condemnation of the excommunication and expressed his hope that it would be removed. *Israel's Messenger* (September 4, 1931): 20, 22.

35. *Jewish Advocate* (August 1931): 215.

36. Reuben E. Ani, "Basra Jews and Theosophy," *Israel's Messenger* (September 1931): 20.

37. Reuben E. Ani, "Theosophy and Jews," *Jewish Advocate* (October 1931): 237. Ani published this article as a response to Ben Nee's (the pseudonym of Benjamin Sargon) article, published in the September issue of *The Jewish Advocate*. Ben Nee, who defended Rabbi Jung's claims that he did not intend that his references to the biblical verses be taken literally, wrote: "It is a pity that the Jewish Theosophists have not seen it fit to explore in the mines of Judaism where they will discover priceless treasures rather than go to seek doctrines outside their religion" Ben Nee, "Jews and Theosophy," *Jewish Advocate* (September 1931): 226.

38. "The Persecution of Hebrew Theosophists." *Theosophist* 52 (June 1931): 363–77.

39. "The Persecution of Hebrew Theosophists," 377.

40. Louis Vet, "Vervolging van Joodsche Theosofen." *De Theosofische Beweging* 27 (1931): 369–71.

41. "Fighting the Light (the Story of a Modern Excommunication—Herem)," *Jewish Theosophist* 2, no. 1 (April–June 1932): 3–4.

42. "Fighting the Light," 4.

43. Henry C. Samuels, "An Open Letter," *Jewish Theosophist* 2, no. 1 (April–June 1932): 5. N. E. B. Ezra responded to this letter in an editorial published in *Israel's Messenger*, June 1932. Ezra's editorial was reprinted, with a response by Samuels in *The Jewish Theosophist* 2, no. 2–3 (July–December 1932): 7–8.

44. S. S. Cohen, "Excommunication in Modern Synagogue," *Jewish Advocate* (June 1931): 184.

45. Cohen, "Excommunication in Modern Synagogue," 185.

46. The letter can be found in AIU archive, Iraq I C 6003. See Anzi, "Theosophy and Anti-Theosophy in Basra," 136, n. 53. I am grateful to Menashe Anzi, who provided me with a copy of this letter, which he received in turn from Guy Bracha. Kadouri mentions in the letter that Mr. and Mrs. Menda, the principals of the AIU school in Basra, were active in the anti-Theosophic movement.

47. This was reported in a letter sent to C. Jinarajadasa, published in "The Persecution of Hebrew Theosophists." *Theosophist* 52 (June 1931): 377.

48. Sagiv, *The Jewish Community in Basra*, 82–83; Anzi, "Theosophy and Anti-Theosophy in Basra," 139. See also *Israel's Messenger* (September 4, 1931): 20; "The Persecution of Hebrew Theosophists," 376; *Jewish Theosophist* 2, nos. 2–3 (July–December 1932): 2.

49. Sagiv, *The Jewish Community in Basra*, 83; Anzi, "Theosophy and Anti-Theosophy in Basra," 141.

50. Sagiv, *The Jewish Community in Basra*, 82; Anzi, "Theosophy and Anti-Theosophy in Basra," 140.

51. *Israel's Messenger* (January 1, 1933): 6.

52. Anzi, "Theosophy and Anti-Theosophy in Basra," 148–51. I am grateful to Menashe Anzi, who provided me with a photocopy of the pamphlet.

53. Cohen published another letter condemning the rabbis who opposed the Jewish Theosophists in *The Jewish Messenger* (March 1, 1932): 13. Rabbi Jung's reply to Cohen, in which he repeated his strong condemnation of the Jewish Theosophists and Cohen's reply to Jung, "Mr. S.S Cohen Defends His Flock," were printed in *Israel's Messenger* (January 1, 1933): 21–22.

54. *Israel's Messenger* (March 3, 1933): 15; (April 1, 1933): 17–18.

55. Yehuda Fetaya, *Minhat Yehuda* (Baghdad: Elisha Shochat, 1933), 9b. (For an English translation, see Rabbi Yehuda Fetaya, *Minhat Yehduda*, trans. Avraham Leader [Jerusalem: Machom Haktav, 2010], 85–87.) See Anzi, "Theosophy and Anti-Theosophy in Basra," 137–39. I am grateful to Menashe Anzi for turning my attention to Fetaya's reference to the Jewish Theosophists.

56. Gershom Scholem recognized this and noted in his copy of Minhat Yehuda that Fetaya is probably referring to the Theosophists in Basra. See Scholem's digitized copy on the Hebrew National Library website, ‏ספר מנחת יהודה‏: (nli.org.il), 9b; Anzi, "Theosophy and Anti-Theosophy in Basra," 139, n. 62. In a short discussion of the Jewish Theosophists in Basra, published in 1945, Theosophy is described as a religion that originated in India, and its followers worship the Serpent. See A. B., "On the Condition of the Jews in Iraq," *Hed Ha-Mizrah* (October 5, 1945): 10.

57. Fetaya, *Minhat Yehuda*, 10a.

58. *Israel's Messenger* (June 1, 1934): 4.

59. Cohen, "Jewish Theosophists in Basra," 405. Sagiv, *The Jewish Community in Basra* 83–84; Anzi, "Theosophy and Anti-Theosophy in Basra," 141.

60. According to a 1945 article on the condition of Jews in Iraq, Kadouri Ani resided in Jerusalem at the time, and the number of the Jewish Theosophists in Basra dwindled. A. B., "On the Condition of the Jews of Iraq," 10.

Chapter 7

1. *Seventy-Eighth Annual General Report of the Theosophical Society* 1953 (Madras: Theosophical Society, 1954), 75 [hence, *AGR* 1953].

2. I. S. Cohen, "A Message from Tel Aviv," *The Canadian Theosophist* 32, no. 5 (July 15, 1951): 71. I have not been able to find any biographical details about Dr. Isaac S. Cohen.

3. *AGR* 1953, 75.

4. The official documents, in Hebrew, were published by Isaac Lubelsky, "Theosophy and Anthroposophy in Israel: An Historical Survey," in *Contemporary Alternative Spiritualties in Israel*, ed. S. Feraro and J. R. Lewis (New York: Palgrave Macmillan, 2017), 150–51. The registration of the "Theosophical Society, Israel branch," was announced in the daily newspaper *Haaretz*, August 31, 1954, 4.

5. *In Remembrance: The Things That Hath Been Is That Which Shall Be* (Safed: Theosophical Society, 1976), 66.

6. *In Remembrance*, 66–67.

7. *In Remembrance*, 7.

8. *In Remembrance*, 7.

9. *Mitteilung, Theosophische Gesselschaft Adyar, Israel* 1, no. 8 (June 1954): 7 (I was not able to locate earlier issues of the newsletter).

10. *Eightieth Annual General Report of the Theosophical Society* 1955 (Madras: Theosophical Society, 1956), 75 [hence, *AGR* 1955]

11. *Mitteilung, Theosophische Gesselschaft Adyar, Israel* 2, no. 2 (December 1954): 7; *AGR* 1955, 75. See also *Eighty Eighth Annual General Report of the Theosophical Society* 1963 (Madras: Theosophical Society 1964), 92 [hence, *AGR* 1963].

12. *Theosophie in Israel* (April 1957): 4.

13. See the interview with Zeuger in Tikva Weinstock, "Old People and Women Are Attracted to Theosophy," *Ma'ariv* (March 6, 1963) [Hebrew].

14. *Eighty First Annual General Report of the Theosophical Society* 1956 (Madras: Theosophical Society 1957), 76–77 [hence, *AGR* 1956]; *Theosophie in Israel* (February 1957): 2; (July–December 1959): 4.

15. *Eighty Second Annual General Report of the Theosophical Society* 1957 (Madras: Theosophical Society 1958), 79 [hence, *AGR* 1957]; *Theosophie in Israel* (October–November–December 1957): 4; (April–September 1958): 4; (July–December 1959): 4.

16. *AGR* 1956, 77.

17. Ilse Belilowsky, *Graphologie, Parapsychologie, Kabbalah: Die Handschrift greift Hinüber* (Zurich: W. Classen, 1974). I am grateful to Hans-Jürgen Bracker for providing me with the information on Ilse Fischer-Hahn Belilowksy.

18. *Eighty Third Annual General Report of the Theosophical Society* 1958 (Madras: Theosophical Society, 1959), 84; see *Theosophie in Israel* (April–September 1958): 4; (July–December 1959): 4.

19. For biographical information on Heinrich Srebrow, see his Mandatory Naturalization file, at the Israel State Archive, ISA-MandatoryOrganizations-Naturalization-000f83v, https://www.archives.gov.il/archives/Archive/0b07170680034dc1/File/0b071706808a96c.3. Srebrow was one of the founders of the Romema neighborhood in Haifa, and after he died, a square in the neighborhood was named after him.

20. *AGR* 1963, 92. Later, Kudjoe Mawudeku became the organizing secretary of the West African Theosophical Society in Accra, Ghana, See *Ninetieth Annual General Report of the Theosophical Society* 1965 (Madras: Theosophical Society, 1966), 99 [hence, *AGR* 1965].

21. Weinstock, "Old People and Women Are Attracted to Theosophy."

22. *AGR* 1965, 95–96. According to Zeuger's report, the international president of the Theosophical Society held back the granting of the federation certificate "because of the acute differences among the members in Israel." These differences were related to Zeuger's withdrawal of the charter of Lodge Galilea, presided by Chana Mor. In 1974, Zeuger tried again "to re-unite both members as well as Lodge here in Israel, after a ten year period of regretful separation." *Ninety-Ninth Annual General Report of the Theosophical Society* 1974 (Madras: Theosophical Society, 1975), 109 [hence, *AGR* 1974].

23. *AGR* 1965, 95; *Ninety-First Annual General Report of the Theosophical Society* 1966 (Madras: Theosophical Society 1967), 99 [hence, *AGR* 1966]; Ninety-Third Annual General Report of the Theosophical Society 1968 (Madras: The Theosophical Society, 1969), 87.

24. *AGR* 1966, 99.

25. *Ninety-Seventh Annual General Report of the Theosophical Society* 1972 (Madras: Theosophical Society, 1973), 117–118. The lodge was divided into a Hebrew-speaking group and Hungarian-speaking group.

26. *AGR* 1977, 19, 87–88.

27. *Ninety-Eighth Annual General Report of the Theosophical Society* 1973 (Madras: Theosophical Society, 1974), 119 [hence, AGR 1973].

28. *Hundred and Fifth Annual General Report of the Theosophical Society* 1980 (Madras: Theosophical Society, 1981), 47.

29. *Hundred and Ninth Annual General Report of the Theosophical Society* 1984 (Madras: Theosophical Society, 1985), 61–62. According to a journal report from 1989, there were about a hundred members of the Theosophical Society in

Israel at the time, and their center was in Ramat Gan. See Yoram Harpaz, "The Theosophists versus Krishnamurti," *Kol Hair* (August 4, 1989): 51.

30. For the current activities of the Israeli Theosophical Society, see its website, http://www.theosophia.co.il/.

31. See *Theosophie in Israel* (October–December 1958): 4; *Eighty-Fourth Annual General Report of the Theosophical Society* 1959 (Madras: Theosophical Society 1960), 76–77 [hence, *AGR* 1959]; *AGR* 1973, 119. Salomon also taught a course in Radiesthesia to Israeli students in the late 1950s. See the obituary published by the student of the course, *Davar* (February 23, 1959): 4.

32. *One Hundred and Third Annual General Report of the Theosophical Society* 1978 (Madras: Theosophical Society, 1979), 98 [hence, *AGR* 1978].

33. *One Hundredth Annual General Report of the Theosophical Society* 1975 (Madras: Theosophical Society 1976), 95 [hence, *AGR* 1975]; *Davar* (October 21, 1981): 7. Lissod published an edited volume on Gandhi, on the occasion of his one hundredth birthday, *Mahatma Gandhi: His Life and His Message to the World* (Rishpon: Yedidim, 1971) and translated to Hebrew (from Yiddish) Jospeh Luden's *A Short History of the Anarchist Idea* (Tel Aviv: Problemen, 1985). Lissod was a member of the Israel Section of the War Resisters International, which was founded in 1947. See Marcella Simoni, " 'Hello Pacifist'—War Resisters in Israel's First Decade," *Quest* 5 (2013): 77.

34. Yehuda Carmeli, "Benno Wolkowitz Obituary," *Anthroposophical life in Israel* 1 (Winter 2000/2001): 11.

35. See *In Remembrance*, 15–25; *Eightieth Annual General Report of the Theosophical Society* 1955 (Madras: Theosophical Society, 1956), 75 [hence, *AGR* 1955]; *AGR* 1956, 77.

36. *AGR* 1971, 165.

37. *AGR* 1956, 77; *AGR* 1957, 79; *AGR* 1963, 93; *AGR* 1965, 96; *AGR* 1970, 95; *AGR* 1976, 91.

38. See *AGR* 1974, 109; *AGR* 1975, 96.

39. *AGR* 1959, 77.

40. *AGR* 1976, 89.

41. *AGR* 1978, 97.

42. *In Remembrance*, 6, 10.

43. *In Remembrance*, 6, 11; *AGR* 1970, 95; *AGR* 1971, 106.

44. *In Remembrance*, 6,12; *AGR* 1973, 120; *AGR* 1974, 110. Summary of the lectures held at the 1974 convention in Amirim, which was published by the Bsorat ha-Galil Lodge, can be found in the Theosophical Library in Amsterdam. I am grateful to Alexandra Nagel and Renger Dijkstra, who sent me a copy of the booklet.

45. The first newsletter was published in June 1953. See *In Remembrance*, 7.

46. I am grateful to Jaishree Kanan, who located some issues of the newsletter at the Adyar Library and brought them to my attention. Copies of some of the issues are found also in the National Library of Israel.

47. *In Remembrance*, 7. I was able to locate only one issue of this journal.

48. In 1977, the Moriah and Covenant lodges participated in the publication of the journal.

49. *AGR* 1971, 105.

50. As far as I know, the only Theosophical texts published in Hebrew before the foundation of the Israeli lodges were lectures and conversation by Krishnamurti, which were translated to Hebrew by Rinah Mordechai and edited by Abraham Regelsohn. See Jido Krishnamurti, *Al Ha-Ikar* (Ein-Harod: Ha-Kibutz ha-Meuhad, n.d.; the book was probably published in the late 1930s).

51. *AGR* 1953, 75.

52. Jidu Krishnamurti, *Leraglei ha-Raban* (Kiryat-Shmona: Lishkat Bestorat Ha-Galil, 1971).

53. Charles W. Leadbeater, *Me'ever Lamavet* (Safed: Lishkat Bestorat Ha-Galil, 1970); Geoffrey Hodson, *Yoga Shel Or* (Kiryat-Shmona: Lishkat Bestorat Ha-Galil, 1972); Mabel Collins, *Or Al ha-Shvil* (Kiryat-Shmona: Lishkat Bestorat Ha-Galil, 1974).

54. Ernst Wood, *Concentration and Character Building—Practical Course* (Haifa: Ha-Aguda ha-Ben-Leumit le-Pituah ha-Mudaut, 1981).

55. H. P. Blavatsky, *Maphteah le-Teosophia* (Savion: Ha-Aguda ha-Teosophis Be-Israel, 1998); H. P. Blavatsky, *Torat ha-Nistar ha-Ma'asit* (Savion: Ha-Aguda ha-Teosophit be-Israel, 2005); Annie Besant, *Hidat ha-Hayim* (Savion: Ha-Aguda Ha-Teosophit be-Israel, 1998); Annie Besant, *Torat ha-Karma* (Savion: Ha-Aguda Ha-Teosophit be-Israel, 2000).

56. *The Seventy-Eighth Annual General report of the Theosophical Society* 1953 (Madras: The Theosophical Society 1954), 75 [hence, *AGR* 1953].

57. "Unsere Aufgaben in Israel sind gewaltige. Wir haben Teil an einem sehr schweren Karma des Judischen Volkes. So wie es eine der Ziele der Theosophischen Geselschaft ist, die noch ungerklarten Naturgesetze und die im Menschen verborgen liegenden Seelenkrafte zu erforschen, so betrachte ich es als eine der Theosophen in diesem Land, die Pflichten und den Platz der Juden in dem Grossen Plan der Entwicklung zu erforschen und mit Hilfe dieser erkenntnis das Karma der Juden zu heben." *In Remembrance*, 14.

58. *In Remembrance*, 52–56.

59. *In Remembrance*, 55.

60. *Mittelungsblatt* 2, no. 3 (February 1955): 4–7; 2, no. 4 (March 1955): 1, 5–7.

61. *AGR* 1974, 111; *AGR* 1976, 89.

62. See the index of *Or* magazine, http://www.theosophia.co.il/web/8888/nsf/web/6632/or-magazin.doc.

63. *AGR* 2005, 69.

Chapter 8

1. *Messenger* 13, no. 12 (May 1926): 265. The announcement was reprinted in *The Theosophist* 47 (August 1926): 623–24.

2. Gaston Polak, "Appeal to Members of the T.S.," *Theosophist* 47 (April 1926): 103–4.

3. Henry C. Samuels, "Basic Information of the Association of Hebrew Theosophists," *Jewish Theosophist* 1, no. 2 (1926): 8.

4. *Jewish Theosophist* 1, no. 5 (1927): 4.

5. Boaz Huss, " 'A Jew Living in an Ashram': The Spiritual Itinerary of S. S. Cohen," *Journal of Indo-Judaic Studies* 15 (2015): 20–29.

6. Typed letter, addressed to the Washington lodge, Theosophical Society, with the letterhead "Association of Hebrew Theosophists, American Section," sent from Milwaukee, Wisconsin, on May 20, 1926. I am grateful to Janet Kerschner, who located this letter and kindly sent it to me.

7. Lila B. Allebach, "Our Task as Hebrew Theosophists," *Jewish Theosophist* 1, no. 3 (1927): 4.

8. Alex Horne, "A Glorious Opportunity," *Jewish Theosophist* 1, no. 2 (1926): 7.

9. *AGR* 1971, 105.

10. Levie, "Studie in Kabalah c.a.," 192. I follow the translation of Nagel, "The Association of Jewish Theosophists in the Netherlands," 419.

11. Polak, "Appeal to Members of the T.S.," 103–4.

12. Bozena Brydlova "Why Every Jew Should Join the Association of Hebrew Theosophists." *Jewish Theosophist* 1, no. 1 (1926): 7.

13. *In Remembrance*, 14.

14. As far as I know, the only Theosophical texts published in Hebrew (probably, in the late 1930s), before the foundation of the Israeli lodges, were lectures and conversation by Krishnamurti, which were translated to Hebrew by Rinah Mordechai and edited by Abraham Regelsohn. Jido Krishnamurti, *Al Ha-Ikar* (Ein-Harod: Ha-Kibutz ha-Meuhad, n.d).

15. *AGR* 1953, 75.

16. H. P. Blavatsky, *Maphteah le-Teosophia* (Savion: Ha-Aguda ha-Teosophis Be-Israel, 1998); H. P. Blavatsky, *Torat ha-Nistar ha-Ma'asit,* trans. Anva Kantor (Savion: Ha-Aguda ha-Teosophit be-Israel), 2005.

17. Annie Besant, *Hidat ha-Hayim,* trans. Anva Kantor (Savion: Ha-Aguda Ha-Teosophit be-Israel, 1998); Annie Besant, *Torat ha-Karma,* trans. Anva Kantor (Savion: Ha-Aguda Ha-Teosophit be-Israel, 2000) [Hebrew].

18. Jidu Krishnamurti, *Leraglei ha-Raban.* Excerpts from *At the Feet of the Master,* translated to Hebrew, were published previously in the volumes of *Theosophie in Israel.*

19. Charles W, Leadbeater, *Me'ever Lamavet* (Safed: Lishkat Bsorat Ha-Galil, 1970) [Hebrew].

20. Ernst Wood, *Concentration and Character Building—Practical Course* (Haifa: Ha-Aguda ha-Ben-Leumit le-Pituah ha-Mudaut, 1981) [Hebrew]; Geoffrey Hodson, *Yoga Shel Or* (Kiryat-Shmona: Lishkat Bsorat Ha-Galil, 1972) [Hebrew]; Mabel Collins, *Or Al ha-Shvil* (Kiryat-Shmona: Lishkat Bsorat Ha-Galil, 1974) [Hebrew].

21. *Messenger* 13 (April 1926): 246.

22. *Jewish Theosophist* 1, no. 1 (1926): 5; 1, no. 4 (1927): 5, 14, 19, 26. In 1953, Isaac S. Cohen, the first presidential agent of the Theosophical Society in Israel, called to reestablish the Association of Hebrew Theosophists and to renew the plans to construct a synagogue in Adyar. See *AGR* 1953, 75.

23. S. I. Heiman, "Correspondence," *Jewish Theosophist* 1, no. 1 (1926): 20.

24. S. S. Cohen, "Correspondence," *Jewish Theosophist* 1, no. 1 (1926): 19.

25. Heiman, "Correspondence," 20.

26. Samuels, *Morning Prayer: A Modern, Comprehensive and Applicable Order of Service, for Individual and Congregational Jewish Worship* (Seattle: New Synagogue Press, 1929), 4.

27. Samuels, *Morning Prayer*, 33.

28. Samuels, *Morning Prayer*, 15–17. The passage was first published in the *International Star Bulletin*, in January 1928.

29. Samuels, *Morning Prayer*, 31.

30. Samuels, *Morning Prayer*, 6–7.

31. "For the Beauty of the Earth," by Folliot Stanford Pierpoint (1835–1917); Samuels, *Morning Prayer*, 22–23; and Rev. George Matheson (1842–1906), "Gather Us In, Thou Love That Fillest All"; Samuels, *Morning Prayer*, 38–39.

32. Samuels, *Morning Prayer*, 29–30.

33. Samuels, *Morning Prayer*, 33.

34. Leonard Bosman, *A Plea for Judaism* (Adyar: Association of Hebrew Theosophists, 1926), 16.

35. Bozena Brydlova, "The Ancient Kabbalah." *Jewish Theosophist* 1, no. 2 (1926): 28.

36. Alex Horne, *Spiritualizing Unspiritual Judaism* (Seattle, WA: Association of Hebrew Theosophists, American Section 1928), 10.

37. Alex Horne, "Theosophy and Modern Judaism," *Theosophist* 47 (April 1926): 105–6.

38. Horne, "Theosophy and Modern Judaism," 105.

39. Horne, "Theosophy and Modern Judaism," 14.

40. Horne, *Spiritualizing Unspiritual Judaism*, 10.

41. Horne, "A Glorious Opportunity," 8.

42. Allebach, "Our Task as Hebrew Theosophists," 4.

43. "A Message to Jews in India," *Jewish Theosophist* 1, no. 4 (1927): 27.

44. Horne, *Spiritualizing Unspiritual Judaism*, 5.

45. *In Remembrance*, 14.

46. The rabbis were misinformed. Ezekiel printed only the *Idra Zuta.*

47. *Havazelet* 18, no. 18 (February 24, 1888) (12 Adar 5648): 138–39; Huss, "The Sufi Society," 178–79.

48. *Havazelet* 18, no. 18 (February 24, 1888) (12 Adar 5648): 138–3.

49. *Havazelet* 18, no. 20 (March 11, 1888) (28 Adar 5648): 156–57; Yosef Hayyim, *Responsa Rav Pe'alim* (Jerusalem: Frumkin 1901), vol. 1, 71b–72b (Yoreh Deah 56). Letters denouncing Ezekiel and his translation by rabbis of Baghdad and Rabbi Solomon Twena of Calcutta were published in *The Jewish Gazette Paerah.* See Sassoon, *Ohel Dawid*, vol. 1, 429–30.

50. Huss, "The Sufi Society," 178–91.

51. Solomon's testimony was cited by C. Jinarajadsa in an article published in *The Theosophist* 52 (June 1931): 363. I have not found any other information concerning the excommunication of Solomon or of the existence of a separate community of Jewish Theosophists in Ahmedabad.

52. *Israel Messenger* (April 1, 1927): 14.

53. *Israel Messenger* (May 6, 1927): 17.

54. Cited in the *Jewish Daily Bulletin* (March 3, 1927): 2.

55. *Jewish Daily Bulletin* (March 3, 1927): 2.

56. Cited in the *Jewish Daily Bulletin* (March 10, 1927): 2.

57. Mentor, "Strange Faiths," *Jewish Chronicle* (February 10, 1928): 9.

58. Mentor, "Two Matters," *Jewish Chronicle* (February 24, 1928): 9.

59. "Jewish Defection," *Modern View* (May 1, 1931): 4–5.

60. "Jewish Defection," *Modern View* (May 1, 1931): 5.

61. Anzi, "Theosophy and Anti-Theosophy in Basra," 162–66.

62. Anzi, "Theosophy and Anti-Theosophy in Basra," 163.

63. Anzi, "Theosophy and Anti-Theosophy in Basra," 163.

64. Anzi, "Theosophy and Anti-Theosophy in Basra," 164.

65. Cited in *Theosophist* 52 (June 1931): 368–68; *Israel Messenger* (June 1, 1931): 18.

66. *Theosophist* 52 (June 1931): 368–68; *Israel Messenger* (June 1, 1931): 18. See also the cable sent by Rabbi Jung and Rabbi David de Sola Pool cited by Reuben. E. Ani, "Theosophy in Iraq," *Jewish Advocate* (August 1931): 215.

67. The English translation of the Hebrew circular was published in "The Persecution of Hebrew Theosophists." *The Theosophist* 52 (June 1931): 363–64. Reuben Ani cited parts of the circular in his letter to the editor of *The Jewish Advocate*, "Theosophy and Jews," *The Jewish Advocate* (May 1931): 167.

68. "Jews in Iraq Face New Crisis," *Israel's Messenger* (June 1, 1931): 18; "The Persecution of Hebrew Theosophists," *Theosophist* 52 (June 1931): 369–70 (reprinted from *The Times of Mesopotamia*, April 13, 14, 1931); Reuben Ani, "Theosophy in Iraq," *The Jewish Advocate* (August 1931): 215.

69. The decree is cited by Reuben Ani in a letter published in *The Jewish Advocate* (May 1931): 167.

70. "See "Jews in Iraq Face a New Crisis," *Israel's Messenger* (June 1, 1931): 18; *Jewish Advocate* (June 1931): 184.

71. *Jewish Advocate* (July 1931): 202.

72. *Israel Messenger* (September 4, 1931): 20.

73. Harth, "The Theosophists versus Krishnamurti," 51.

74. In the letters, Ezekiel cited from the works of Hayim Vital to defend his venture, gave instances of earlier translations of Kabbalistic works, relied on the translation of the Talmud into French, and threatened one of his correspondents with an action according to the Indian Penal Code. See David S. Sassoon, *Ohel Dawid: Descriptive Catalogue of the Hebrew and Samaritan Manuscripts in the Sassoon Library* (London: Oxford University Press 1932), vol. 1, 429.

75. Pinchas Grayevsky, "On the Translation of the Idrot to Arabic," *Meginzei Yerushalaim* 2 (1930), 16 [Hebrew].

76. Ezekiel, *Somer Emuneem.*

77. Sofia, "The Jewish Theosophist—A Paradox," *Jewish Theosophists* 1, no. 1 (1926): 21.

78. Heiman's letter to the editor of the *Jewish Chronicle* is cited by Mentor, "Two Matters," *Jewish Chronicle* (February 24, 1928): 9.

79. S. S. Cohen, "Excommunication in a Modern Synagogue," *Jewish Advocate*, June 1931, 184.

80. Henry C. Samuels, "Fighting the Light (the Story of a Modern Excommunication)." *Jewish Theosophist* 2, no. 1 (1932): 3–4.

Chapter 9

1. Brydlova, "Why Every Jew Should Join the Association of Hebrew Theosophists," *Jewish Theosophist* 1, no. 1 (1926): 7.

2. Brydlova, "Why Every Jew Should Join the Association of Hebrew Theosophists," 7.

3. See Olav Hammer, *Claiming Knowledge: Strategies of Epistemology from Theosophy to the New Age* (Leiden: Brill, 2004), 121–22; Peter Staudenmaier, "Rudolf Steiner and the Jewish Question," *Leo Baeck Institute Yearbook* 50, no. 1 (2005): 136–37; Karen Swartz, "Views from the Great White Brotherhood" (Dissertation, Linnaeus University, 2009), 60; Isaac Lubelsky, *Celestial India: Madame Blavatsky and the Birth of Indian Nationalism* (Sheffield and Oakville: Equinox 2012), 150, 153; J. D. Lavoie, "Theosophical Chronology in the Writings of Guido von List (1849–1919): A Link between H. P. Blavatsky's Philosophy and the Nazi Movement," in *Innovation in Esotericism from the Renaissance to the Present*, ed. G. D. Hedesan and T. Rudbøg (Cham: Palgrave Macmillan, 2021), 272–74.

4. H. P. Blavatsky, *The Secret Doctrine* (Theosophical Universal Press Online Edition), vol. 1, 230. http://www.theosociety.org/pasadena/sd/sd1-1-11.htm.

5. Blavatsky, *The Secret Doctrine*, vol. 2, 471.

6. Blavatsky, *The Secret Doctrine*, vol. 2, 471.

7. H. P. Blavatsky, *The Key to Theosophy* (London: Theosophical Publishing Company 1889), 45.

8. Lavoie, "Theosophical Chronology in the Writings of Guido von List," 273–74.

9. Coulomb, *Some Account of my Intercourse with Madame Blavatsky*, 78. It should be noted that Blavatsky denied this. See Gomes, "H. P. Blavatsky's Annotations in Madame Coulomb's Pamphlet," 151.

10. J. D. Buck, "The Cabbalah." *Theosophist* 5 (1883): 44–45.

11. *Jewish Daily Bulletin* (February 17, 1927): 2.

12. On Steiner's racial theories and his negative perception of Judaism, see Helmut Zander, "Rudolf Steiners Rassenlehre," in *Völkisch und National*, ed. Uwe Puschner and G. Ulrich Grossman (Darmstadt: Wissenschaftliche Buchgesellschaft 2009), 145–55; Ansgar Martins, *Rassismus und Geschichtsmetaphysik: Esoterischer Darwinismus und Freiheitsphilosophie bei Rudolf Steiner* (Frankfurt: Info3, 2012); Ansgar Martins, *Hans Büchenbacher: Erinnerungen 1933–1949* (Frankfurt am Main: Mayer Info3, 2014), 190–97, 369–75; Staudenmaier, "Rudolf Steiner and the Jewish Question"; Staudenmaier, *Between Occultism and Nazism*, 25–63, 166–67; Jan-Erik, Ebbestad Hansen, "The Jews—Teachers of the Nazis? Anti-Semitism in Norwegian Anthroposophy," *Nordeuropa-Forum* 17 (2015): 161–65.

13. I follow the translation of Staudenmaier, "Rudolf Steiner and the Jewish Question," 132. The review was first published in *Deutsche Wochenschrift* 6, nos. 16, 17 (1888). Republished in Rudolf Steiner's, online archive, http://anthroposophie. byu.edu/aufsaetze/l104.pdf, 152. The review was published in Hebrew by Koren, *Judaism and Anthroposophy* 2: 981–87.

14. Rudolf Steiner, "Die Sehnsucht der Juden nach Palästina," *Magazine für Literature* 66, no. 38 (1897); republished in Rudolf Steiner's, online archive, https://www.anthroposophie.net/steiner/bib_steiner_juden_palaestina.htm I follow the translation of Staudenmaier, "Rudolf Steiner and the Jewish Question," 134. A Hebrew translation of the article was published in the Israeli Anthroposophical journal Adam/Olam, Rudolf Stiener, "The Longing of the Jews to Palestine," translated by Isabel Cohen, *Adam/Olam* 33 (2015): 34–35. However, according to Ernst Müller, Steiner held Zionists in high esteem because, he said, they were open-minded concerning spirituality. See Necker, "Ernst Müller's Encounter with Jewish Mysticism," 216.

15. Rudolf Steiner, *Die Geschichte der Menchheit und die Weltanschauungen der Kulturvölker* (Dornach: Rudolf Steiner Nachlassverwaltung, 1988): 78, http://fvn-archiv.net/PDF/GA/GA353.pdf#view=Fit). For the English translation, see Rudolf Steiner, *From Beetroot to Buddhism* (London: Rudolf Steiner Press, 1999), 59.

16. Staudenmaier, "Rudolf Steiner and the Jewish Question," 38–139.

17. Steiner, *Die Geschichte der Menchheit*, 202. This lecture is not included in the lectures translated to English in *From Beetroot to Buddhism*. I follow the

translation of Staudenmaier, "Rudolf Steiner and the Jewish Question," 143 (and Staudenmaier, *Between Occultism and Nazism*, 167).

18. C. Jinarajadasa, "The Jewish People: A Letter to Some Indian Jews," *Adyar Bulletin* 9 (February 1916): 43.

19. Jinarajadasa, "The Jewish People," 47.

20. Jinarajadasa, "The Jewish People," 49–50.

21. C. Jinarajadasa. "The Message of Judaism," *Jewish Theosophist* (December 1926): 29–31.

22. *Theosophist* (June 1933): 257. Jinarajadasa reported that the organizers of the 1933 Theosophical Congress in Budapest removed the swastika from the Theosophical seal stamped on the badges of the delegates so that the Theosophists would not be construed as Jew haters and that he himself removed the swastika that appeared in recent photographs of Annie Besant.

23. Thus, for instance, the St. Catharine group of the Toronto Theosophical Society shared Jinarajadasa's denunciation of the Nazi regime. They protested the boycott and injustice perpetuated against the Jews in Germany. *Theosophist*, September 1933, 617.

24. The Theosophical Society was active in Germany until 1937. On the movements of the Theosophical Society in Nazi Germany, see Helmut Zander, *Anthroposophie in Deutschland: Theosophische Milieus und gesellschaftliche Praxis, 1884 bis 1945* (Göttingen: Vandenhoeck and Ruprecht, 2007), vol. 1, 210–19; Staudenmaier, *Between Occultism and Nazism*, 225–27.

25. *Theosophist* (September 1933): 724. See also Johannes Maria Verweyen, "Zur Frage der Adyar Gesellschaft," *Theosophie* 21 (1933): 240–41. On Verweyen and his activities within the Theosophical Society and his support of Hitler and National Socialism, see Helmut Zander, "Johannes Maria Verweyen (1883–1945) als Theosoph," *Gaesdoncker Blätter* 7 (2005): 37–70; Zander, *Anthroposophie in Deutschland*, vol. 1, 210; Staudenmaier, *Between Occultism and Nazism*, 226–27; Martins, *Büchenbacher*, 333. Notwithstanding his initial support of the Nazi regime, Verweyen was arrested in 1941 and died of typhus in Bergen-Belzen in 1945.

26. *Theosophist* (September 1933): 727–28. An unsigned letter, which admitted the persecution of Jews and expressed sympathy to German Theosophists who suffered from it (yet objected to Jinarajadasa' s accusations of the German people) was published in *The Theosophist* (September 1933): 726.

27. *Theosophist* (October 1933): 111. In his response to Vollrath, Jinarajadasa wrote: "What is one a Theosophist for, except to denounce such crimes against the root principles of humanity? I for one am not disposed to keep my Wisdom in one pocket and my Brotherhood in another." *Theosophist* (October 1933): 111. On Vollrath and his activities in the German Section of the Theosophical Society and other esoteric movements and on his nationalistic and pro-Nazi stance, see Zander, *Anthroposophie in Deutschland*, vol. 1, 320–31; Staudenmaier, *Between Occultism and Nazism*, 226.

28. Bosman, *The Music of the Spheres*, 5.

29. *Theosophist* (October 1933): 110.

30. Franz Eduard Hirth was born in 1913 in Vukovar and later resided in Prague, Belgrad, Tanger, and finally, Lichtenstein. He published a few articles in Theosophical journals in the late 1970s. See Erinnerungen Österreichischer Juden, *Namenliste* 17 on the *Institute für jüdische Geschichte Österreich* webpage, http://www.injoest.ac.at/media/namensliste.pdf. Hirth published an article titled "Solidarity," in *The Theosophist* 100 (January 1979): 110.

31. Hans Zeuger, "Harmony Lodge, Tel Aviv," *AGR* 1977, 88.

32. Zeuger, "Harmony Lodge, Tel Aviv," *AGR* 1977, 88.

33. Zeuger, *AGR* 1978, 99. Previously, in 1961, Zeuger reported that he was invited by Josephine Ransom, the vice president of the Theosophical Society, to correct the Hebrew quotations in Blavatsky's *The Secret Doctrine*. See Zeuger, "Israel, General Report," *AGR* 1961, 86.

34. *Jewish Theosophist* 1, no. 5 (December 1927): 9.

35. "A Message from Annie Besant to Hebrew Theosophists," *Jewish Theosophist* 1, no. 3 (1927): 2.

Chapter 10

1. Leonard Bosman, *The Music of the Spheres* (London: Dharma, 1914), 5.

2. Marco Pasi, "Oriental Kabbalah and the Parting of East and West in the Early Theosophical Society," in *Kabbalah and Modernity* ed. Boaz Huss, Marco Pasi, and Kocku von Stuckrad (Leiden and Boston: Brill, 2010), 150–66; Julie Chajes, "Construction through Appropriation: Kabbalah in Blavatsky's Early Works," in *Theosophical Appropriations: Esotericism, Kabbalah and the Transformation of Traditions*, ed. Julie Chajes and Boaz Huss (Beer Sheva: Ben-Gurion University of the Negev Press, 2016), 33–72; Julie Chajes, "Seth Pancoast and the Kabbalah: Medical Pluralism and the Reception of Physics in Late-Nineteenth Century Philadelphia," *Kabbalah* 40 (2018): 141–45.

3. Boaz Huss, " 'Qabbalah, the Theos-Sophia of the Jews': Jewish Theosophists and Their Perceptions of Kabbalah," in *Theosophical Appropriations: Esotericism, Kabbalah, and the Transformation of Traditions*, ed. Julie Chajes and Boaz Huss (Beer Sheva: Ben-Gurion University of the Negev Press, 2016), 137–66. This chapter is based to a large degree on this article.

4. See Wouter J. Hanegraaff, "Jewish Influences V: Occultist Kabbalah," in *Dictionary of Gnosis & Western Esotericism*, ed. Wouter J. Hanegraaff (Leiden: Brill, 2006), 644–47.

5. The lecture was based on a book he wrote but never published entitled "The Kabbalah of the Egyptian and the Greek Canon of Proportions." See James Santucci, "George Henry Felt: The Life Unknown," *Theosophical History* 6 (1967): 243–61; Godwin, *The Theosophical Enlightenment*, 286–87; Pasi, "Oriental Kabbalah,"

158; Hanegraaff, "Western Esotericism and the Orient," 33–38; Marc Demarest, "The Felt Working Group Progress Report," March 11, 2011, http://www.ehbritten. org/docs/felt_working_group_status_report_7-18-12.pdf.

6. See Nicholas Goodrick-Clarke, *Helena Blavatsky* (Berkley: North Atlantic Books, 2004), 75–85; Pasi, "Oriental Kabbalah," 150–66; Chajes, "Construction through Appropriation," 33–72; John Patrick Deveney, "The Two Theosophical Societies," 97–98.

7. Chajes, "Construction through Appropriation," 44–47.

8. Marco Pasi, "Oriental Kabbalah," 150–66; Chajes, "Construction through Appropriation," 33–72.

9. Helena Petrovna Blavatsky, "A Few Questions to "Hiraf," *Spiritual Scientist* (July 15, 22, 1875): 224. See Pasi, "Oriental Kabbalah," 159. Chajes, "Construction through Appropriation," 37–43.

10. Helena Petrovna Blavatsky, *Isis Unveiled: A Master Key to the Mysteries of Ancient and Modern Science and Theology* (New York: J. W. Bouton 1877–1878), vol. 1, 1. Goodrick-Clarke, *Helena Blavatsky*, 75. In *The Secret Doctrine*, Blavatsky identifies the ancient book that she mentioned in *Isis Unveiled* as the *Book of Dzyan*, which was written in the ancient language Senzar and was dictated by divine beings to the sons of light, in central Asia, at the beginning of the present (fifth) race. Blavatsky asserts that the *Book of Dzyan*, on whose stanzas *The Secret Doctrine* is based, is the source not only of *Sifra Dezniuta* but also of *Sepher Yetzirah*, as well as the Pentateuch and the sacred writings of China, India, Egypt, and Chaldea. See Blavatsky, *The Secret Doctrine*, vol. 1, 26.

11. Blavatsky, *Isis Unveiled*, vol. 2, 264–65.

12. Blavatsky, *Isis Unveiled*, vol. 2, 212, 451; Chajes, "Construction through Appropriation," 51.

13. Blavatsky, *Isis Unveiled*, vol. 2, 36; Chajes, "Construction through Appropriation," 51.

14. Blavatsky, *Isis Unveiled*, vol. 1, 17. Chajes, "Construction through Appropriation," 50.

15. Blavatsky, *Isis Unveiled*, vol. 2, 143; Chajes, "Construction through Appropriation," 54.

16. Chajes, "Construction through Appropriation," 52.

17. Helena Petrovna Blavatsky, "The Kabalah and the Kabalists," *Lucifer* 10, no. 57 (May 1892): 196.

18. Blavatsky, "The Kabalah and the Kabalists," 191, 195–96.

19. Demarest, "The Felt Working Group Progress Report," 18.

20. On Pancoast and his knowledge and perception of Kabbalah, see Julie Chajes, "Seth Pancoast and the Kabbalah: Medical Pluralism and the Reception of Physics in Late-Nineteenth Century Philadelphia," *Kabbalah* 40 (2018): 141–45.

21. Seth Pancoast, *The Kabbalah or the True Science of Light: An Introduction to Philosophy and Theosophy of the Ancient Sages* (Philadelphia: J. M. Stoddart, 1883), 11, 17; Seth Pancoast, "Kabbala" *Path* 1, no. 1 (1886): 8.

22. Pancoast, "Kabbala," 8.

23. Pancoast, *The Kabbalah or the True Science of Light*, 21–25.

24. Pancoast, "Kabbala, 13.

25. Julie Hall, "The Concept of Reincarnation in Theosophy: Modernity, Globalization and Western Esotericism" (unpublished doctoral thesis, University of Exeter, 2012), 215.

26. As Julie Hall (Chajes) noted, Buck relied on the ideas of his fellow Cincinnatian, the lawyer and freemason James Ralston Skinner (1830–1893). See Hall, "The Concept of Reincarnation," 213. In 1886, Skinner presented his ideas concerning Kabbalah in the journal of the American Section of the Theosophical Society, *The Path*. Skinner claimed that Kabbalah is the rational foundation of the Hebrew Scriptures and the "sublime science" upon which Masonry is based. See J. Ralston Skinner, "Notes on the Cabbalah of the Old Testament," *Path* 1, no. 4 (1886): 104. On Skinner's connections and influence on Blavatsky, see Malin Fitger, "The Tetractys and Hebdomad: Blavatsky's Sacred Geometry," *Correspondences* 8, no. 1 (2020): 103.

27. J. D. Buck, "The Cabbalah," *Theosophist* 5 (November 1883): 44.

28. William Wynn Westcott, *Sepher Yetzirah: The Book of Formation, and the Thirty Two Paths of Wisdom* (Bath: Robert H. Fryar 1887). In the introduction to the second edition of his translation of *Sepher Yetzirah*, Westcott asserted, "The late Madame Blavatsky, my esteemed teacher of Theosophy and my personal friend . . . expressed to me her recognition of the value of the 'Sepher Yetzirah' as a mystical treatise on cosmic origin, and her approval of my work in its translation, and of my notes and explanations." William Wynn Westcott, *Sepher Yetzirah* (London: Theosophical Publishing House 1893), 13.

29. William Wynn Westcott, "The Kabbalah," *Lucifer* 3 (August 1891): 465–69; 9 (September 1891): 27–32. William Wynn Westcott, "A Further Glance at the Kabbalah," *Lucifer* 12 (April–May 1893): 147–53, 202–8.

30. Westcott, "A Further Glance at the Kabbalah," 150.

31. Westcott, "A Further Glance at the Kabbalah," 150.

32. Westcott, "A Further Glance at the Kabbalah," 147.

33. Westcott, "A Further Glance at the Kabbalah," 152.

34. S. L. MacGregor Mathers, *The Kabbalah Unveiled* (London: George Redway), 1887. Mathers dedicated his *Zohar* translation to Anna Kingsford and Edward Maitland, the British esotericists who seceded from the Theosophical Society and founded the Hermetic Society.

35. Mathers, *The Kabbalah Unveiled*, 2. Another cofounder of the Hermetic Order of the Golden Dawn, who found much interest in Kabbalah, was the British poet, independent scholar, and occultist Arthur Edward Waite. Waite, who presented a more scholarly and erudite approach to Kabbalah (although he did not know Hebrew or Aramaic), dedicated one of the chapters in his first book on the Kabbalah to "The Kabalah and Modern Theosophy." See Arthur Edward

Waite, *The Doctrine and Literature of the Kabalah* (London: Theosophical Publishing Society, 1902), 433–37. Waite criticized Blavatsky's distinction between Jewish and Oriental Kabbalah, "her manifest errors" and the "singular assertions which rest more or less exclusively on the good authority of Madame Blavatsky" (437). Waite, also criticized "Mr, Mathers, who has a certain erudition but is devoid of critical judgement" (446). See also Waites's review of Mathers's "Kabalah Unveiled," *Occult Review* 7, no. 1 (1908): 1–5. On Waite's perceptions of the Kabbalah, see Wouter Hanegraaff, "Mysteries of Sex in the House of the Hidden Light: Arthur Edward Waite and the Kabbalah," *Kabbalah: The Journal for the Study of Jewish Mystical Texts* 40 (2018): 163–82.

36. Helena Petrovna Blavatsky, "Theosophical and Mystic Publications," *Lucifer* 1, no. 1 (September 1889): 77.

37. Henry Pratt, "About the Kabbalah," *Theosophist* 10 (August 1889): 649–61. See Hall, "The Concept of Reincarnation," 213. According to the front page of *New Aspects of Life and Religion* (1886), Pratt was preparing for publication of a book entitled "The Primitive, Spiritual, Occult and Natural Kabbalah."

38. Pratt, "About the Kabbalah," 650.

39. Pratt, "About the Kabbalah," 656.

40. Montague R. Lazarus, "The Kabbalah and the Microcosm," *The Theosophists* 8 (September 1887): 767–74; 9 (October–December 1887): 45–52, 119–24, 167–71; Lazarus, "The Kabbalah and the Microcosm," 168.

41. Montague R. Lazarus, "The Kabbalah and the Microcosm," *Theosophists* 8 (September 1887): 767–74; 9 (October–December 1887): 45–52, 119–124, 167–171.

42. D. Chamier, "The Kabbalah and Its Doctrine," *Theosophist* 24 (November 1902): 90–97.

43. Chamier, "The Kabbalah and Its Doctrine," 90.

44. On Papus and his involvement with the Theosophical Society, see Joscelyn Godwin, *The Beginnings of Theosophy in France* (London: Theosophical History Centre, 1989), 13–26.

45. Papus [Gerard Encausse], "Le Sepher Jesirah," *Le Lotus* 2 (October 1887): 11–27. Papus signed the article with the abbreviation *MST* (Membre de la Société Théosophique).

46. Papus, "Le Sepher Jesirah," 12.

47. Papus, *La Kabbale, tradition secrète de l'Occident, résumé méthodique, précédé d'une lettre d'Adolphe Franck* (Paris: George Carré, 1892).

48. Oswald Wirth, "Qabbalah," *Le Lotus* 3 (January 1889): 625–32. The article concludes with a long and positive review of Isaac Myer, *Qabbalah: The Philosophical Writings of Solomon ben Yehudah Ibn Gebirol* (Philadelphia: Isaac Myer, 1888).

49. Wirth, "Qabbalah," 629.

50. Albert Jounet, *La Clef du Zohar* (Paris: Bibliothèque Chacornac, 1909), 1.

51. Jounet, *La Clef du Zohar*, 3–4.

52. Jounet, *La Clef du Zohar*, 2. See Huss, "Translations of the Zohar," 101–2.

53. See Rudolf Steiner, "Über die Kabbala," in *Rudolf Steiner Gesamtausgabe* (GA 089) (Dornach: Rudolf Steiner Verlag, 2001) 273–79, https://odysseetheater. org/GA/Buecher/GA_089.pdf#view=Fit. Steiner mentioned the *Sefirot* also in a lecture he gave in Leipzig on January 12, 1908, Rudolf Steiner, "Über die Sephirot," *Beiträge Zur Rudolf Steiner Gesamtausgabe Heft* 32 (Dornach: Rudolf Steiner Verlag, 1970), 30–31, https://odysseetheater.org/GA/Beitraege/D32.pdf#page=&view=Fit.

54. Rudolf Steiner, "Die Geheimnisse der biblischen Schöpfungsgeschichte" (Rudolf Steiner Online Archive, 2010) (GA 122), 2–190, http://anthroposophie. byu.edu/vortraege/122.pdf. See Kilcher, "Kabbalah and Anthroposophy," 202–3.

55. Rudolf Steiner, "Die Geschichte der Menscheit und die Weltanschauungen der Kulturvölker (Zwölfter Vortrag, Dornach 10 Mai 1924)," in *Rudolf Steiner Gesamtausgabe Vortrage* (GA 353) (Dornach: Rudolf Steiner Nachlassverwaltung, 1988), 210–27, http://bdn-steiner.ru/cat/ga/353.pdf; Kilcher, "Kabbalah and Anthroposophy," 211.

56. Steiner, "Uber die Kabbala," 273; Kilcher, "Kabbalah and Anthroposophy," 203.

57. Steiner, "Uber die Kabbala," 273.

58. See: Zander, *Anthroposophie in Deutschland*, vol. 2, 964–66; Kilcher, "Kabbalah and Anthroposophy," 208–9; Peter Tradowsky, "Albrecht Sellin," *Kulturimpuls*, http://biographien.kulturimpuls.org/detail.php?&id=1230.

59. A. W. Sellin, *Die geisteswissenschaftliche Bedeutung des Sohar* (Berlin: Philosophische-Theosophische Verlag, 1913).

60. Kilcher, "Kabbalah and Anthroposophy," 208–9.

61. A. W. Sellin, *Die geisteswissenschaftliche Bedeutung des Sohar*, 46. I follow the translation of Kilcher, "Kabbalah and Anthroposophy," 209.

62. Ezekiel, "Introduction," *Idra Zuta.*

63. Bosman, *A Plea for Judaism*, 18.

64. Bosman, *A Plea for Judaism*, 20.

65. Levie, "Studie in Kabalah c.a.," 192; Nagel, "The Association of Jewish Theosophists in the Netherlands," 419.

66. Bosman, *A Plea for Judaism*, 17.

67. Ezekiel, *Introduction to the Kabbalah.*

68. Ré Levie presented a lecture of Kabbalah at the European congress of the Theosophical Society in Paris in 1906 (Nagel, "The Association of Jewish Theosophists in the Netherlands," 419). Joshua Abelson gave lectures on Jewish mysticism in several Theosophical lodges in England (*Portsmouth Evening News*, December 6, 1913, 4; *Hampshire Telegraph*, December 12, 1913, 7; *Bath Chronicle and Weekly Gazette*, March 7, 1915, 7).

Elias Gewurtz presented a series of lectures on Kabbalah at the Krotona Lodge in Hollywood in 1915 (Gewurtz, *The Hidden Treasures of the Ancient Qabalah*, 2); Alex Horne lectured on Jewish mysticism at the Pacific lodge of the Theosophical Society in San Francisco in 1926 (Horne, *An Introduction to Esoteric Judaism*, 1).

Bozena Brydlova lectured on Jewish mysticism at the Milwaukee lodge of the Theosophical Society (*Wisconsin Jewish Chronicle*, November 12, 1926, 3). Louis Vet presented a lecture on the Kabbalah at Theosophical lodge in The Hague in 1932 (Nagel, "The Association of Jewish Theosophists in the Netherlands," 428).

69. Ezekiel, *Idra Zuta, or the Lesser Holy Assembly*; Ezekiel, *Sepher Yesirah or the Book of Creation*; Ezekiel, *Shomer Emuneem (First Argument): A Kabbalistic Controversy*; Ezekiel, *A Sermon on True Faith, Copied from "Kor Musref."*

70. Ezekiel, *Introduction to Kabbalah*; Ezekiel, "The Kabbalist of Jerusalem" 597–601.

71. Bosman, *The Mysteries of the Qabbalah*; Bosman, *The Key to the Universe*; Bosman, *The Book of Genesis Unveiled*.

72. Abelson, "Talmud and Theosophy"; Abelson, "Rabbinical Mysticism"; Abelson, "Swedenborg and the Zohar"; Abelson, "Occult Thought in Jewish Literature."

73. Simon, Sperling, and Lavertoff, *The Zohar*, vol. 1, ix–xxvii. See Huss, "Translations of the Zohar," 108–9.

74. *Kilcher*, "Kabbalah and Anthroposophy," 208–11; Huss, "Translations of the Zohar"; Necker, "Ernst Müller's Encounter with Jewish Mysticism," 215–16.

75. Müller, *Der Sohar und Seine Lehre*.

76. Müller, *A History of Jewish Mysticism*.

77. Müller, "On Sepher Yetzirah"; Müller, "On Mysticism in Scripture."

78. See Kilcher, "Kabbalah and Anthroposophy," 207.

79. Müller, "The Chassidim"; Stambalchek, "Hasidism—One of the Jewish Aspects of Theosophy"; Brydlova, "The Ancient Kabbalah"; H. Blumenfeld, "Theosophy and Kabbalah."

80. Horne, "Theosophy and Modern Judaism"; Horne, "Judaism and Theosophy."

81. Gewurtz, *Beautiful Thoughts of the Ancient Hebrews*, 3.

82. As Gershom Scholem observed in a letter he wrote to Samuel Lewis in 1948: "I have never understood the mind of this author in putting out this book [i.e., *Beautiful Thoughts of the Ancient Hebrew*], not a single quotation of which is authentic. His quotations have nothing to do with what is contained actually in the source he mentions." Scholem, *Briefe*, vol. 2, 6: Huss and Meir, "The Light Is Burning Pretty Low," 68.

83. Ezekiel probably studied the version edited by Shmuel Vital, titled *Shmonah Shearim*, as he refers to it as "Etz Hayyim with Shmonah Shearim."

84. Ezekiel, "Introduction," *Shomer Emuneem*.

85. Abelson, *Introduction to Jewish Mysticism*, vi.

86. Kilcher, "Kabbalah and Anthroposophy," 207.

87. Henry C. Samuels, "Editorial Notes," *Jewish Theosophist* 2, no. 1 (April–June 1932): 7; Jennie Wilson, "The Ancient Wisdom in Palestine," *World Theosophist* 2 (1932): 317.

88. Bosman, *The Music of the Spheres*, 5.

89. Elias Gewurtz, "The Qabbalah," *Theosophist* 36 (November 1914): 172.

90. "The Persecution of Hebrew Theosophists," *Theosophist* 52 (June 1931): 365.

91. Blumenfeld, "Theosophy and Cabala," 3.

92. Ezekiel, "Kabbalist of Jerusalem," 601.

93. Scholem, *Kabbalah*, 399.

94. Ezekiel, *A Sermon on True Faith, Copied from "Kor Musref,"* 4.

95. Horne, "An Introduction to Esoteric Judaism," 3. And see Blavatsky, *Isis Unveiled*, vol. 2, 38.

96. Nagel, "The Association of Jewish Theosophists in the Netherlands," 428.

97. Gewurtz, "The Qabalah" 168–70; Gewurtz, *Beautiful Thoughts of the Ancient Hebrews*, 21–26.

98. Brydlova, "The Ancient Kabbalah," 28.

99. Abelson, "Talmud and Theosophy," 19–21.

100. *Jewish Chronicle Supplement*, May 1924, vii; *Jewish Chronicle Supplement*, January 1921, v–vi.

101. Kilcher, "Kabbalah and Anthroposophy," 207.

102. Müller, "Mein Weg durch Judentum und Christentum," 34–235 (see also Müller, 243). I follow Kilcher's translation, "Kabbalah and Anthroposophy," 209–10, 214.

103. See Boaz Huss, "For the Letter Kills, but the Spirit Gives Life: Halakha Versus Kabbalah in the Study of Jewish Mysticim," *Modern Judaism* 41, no. 1 (2022): 47–70.

104. Brydlova, "The Ancient Kabbalah," 28.

105. Horn, *An Introduction to Esoteric Judaism*, 22–23.

106. Joshua Abelson, "Introduction," In *The Zohar*, ed. Maurice Simon, Harry Sperling (London: Soncino, 1931), vol. 1, xiv.

107. Bosman, *The Music of the Spheres*, 5–6.

108. Bosman, *The Music of the Spheres*, 5–6.

109. Bosman, *The Music of the Spheres*, 6. See also Bosman, *Mysteries of the Qabbalah*, 31: "The Sepher Dzyaniouta (!) must be mentioned, especially for its likeness to the Stanzas of Dzyan, of the Secret Doctrine." As mentioned earlier, Blavatsky asserted that the Book of Dzyan was the source of *Sifra Dezniuta* as well as of *Sepher Yetzirah*, the Pentateuch, and the sacred writings of China, India, Egypt, and Chaldea. See Blavatsky, *The Secret Doctrine*, vol. 1, 26.

110. See Scholem, *Major Trends in Jewish Mysticism*, 399, n. 2. For other suggestions concerning the source and etymology of the Book of Dzyan, see Wouter Hanegraaff, *New Age Religion and Western Culture* (Albany: State University of New York Press, 1998), 453; Goodrick-Clarke, *Helena Blavatsky*, 75.

111. Gewurtz, *Beautiful Thoughts of the Ancient Hebrews*, 25.

112. Blumenfeld, "Theosophy and Cabala," 3.

113. On Kabbalah scholarship in the nineteenth century, see David Biale, *Gershom Scholem, Kabbalah and Counter-History* (Massachusetts and London: Harvard University Press, 1979), 13–32; Moshe Idel, *Kabbalah, New Perspective* (New Haven:

Yale University Press, 1988), 7–10; George Y. Kohler, *Kabbalah Research in the Wissenschaft des Judentums (1820–1880)* (Oldenburg: De Gruyter, 2019).

114. Heinrich Graetz, "Einer häßlichen Kruste, einem pilzartigen Gebilde, einem Schimmelüberzug," *Geschichte der Juden*, vol. 10 (Leipzig: Oscar Leiner, 1868), 124. See Peter Schäfer, "'Adversum Cabbalam' oder: Heinrich Graetz und die Jüdische Mystik," in *Heinrich Graetz und die jüdische Mystik, Reuchlin und seine Erben. Forscher, Denker, Ideologen und Spinner*, ed. P. Schäfer and I. Wandrey (Ostfildern: Jan Thorbecke, 2005), 204; Kohler, *Kabbalah Research*, 202.

115. Abelson, *The Immanence of God in Rabbinical Literature*, 1.

116. Heinrich Graetz, *History of the Jews* (New York: George Dobsevage, 1927), vol. 3, 547. Cited by Abelson, *Jewish Mysticism*, 10.

117. Abelson, *Jewish Mysticism*, 8.

118. Abelson, *Jewish Mysticism*, 174.

119. Horne, "An Introduction to Esoteric Judaism," 4–8.

120. Horne, "An Introduction to Esoteric Judaism," 10–30.

121. Müller, *History of Jewish Mysticism*, 61.

122. Müller, *History of Jewish Mysticism*, 7.

123. Brydlova, "The Ancient Kabbalah," 28.

124. Bozena Brydlova, "The Ancient Kabbalah," *Jewish Theosophist* 1, no. 2 (December 1926): 28.

125. Bosman, *A Plea for Judaism*, 17.

126. Abelson, "Swedenborg and the Zohar," viii.

127. Horne, "Theosophy and Modern Judaism," 106.

128. Horne, "An Introduction to Esoteric Judaism," 17–18. Nonetheless, Horne is also critical of the "extremes" to which he says many of the Kabbalists were carried in their "unregulated enthusiasm."

129. Polak, "Association of Hebrew Theosophists: Appeal to Members of the TS," 103–4.

130. Mendes-Flohr, *Divided Passions*, 77–132.

131. Huss, "Admiration and Disgust," 212–19; Huss, Mystifying Kabbalah, 50–55.

132. Huss, "The Academic Study of Kabbalah and Occultist Kabbalah," in *Occult Roots of Religious Studies*, ed. Yves Mühlematter and Helmut Zander (Oldenburg: De Gruyter, 2021), 113–24.

133. Scholem, *Major Trends*, 206.

134. Scholem, *From Berlin to Jerusalem*, 133.

135. Scholem, *Briefe*, 294; Burmistrov, "Gershom Scholem und das Okkulte," 28–30.

136. In a letter to Samuel Lewis, he wrote about Gewurtz and his book *Beautiful Thoughts of the Ancient Hebrews*: "I have never met this gentleman and have been quite puzzled about his personality on account of a book of his which I have in my collection. . . . I have never understood the mind of this author in

putting out this book, not a single quotation of which is authentic." See Huss and Meir, "The Light Is Burning Pretty Low," 67–68. See also Zvi Leshem, "Boldness of Invention and Falsification: Gershom Scholem on Elias Gewurz," *The Librarians, The Blog of the National Library of Israel,* May 1, 2023, https://blog.nli.org.il/en/gershom-scholem-elias-gewurz/.

137. Scholem, *Major Trends in Jewish Mysticism,* 398.

138. Gershom Scholem, *Elements of the Kabbalah and Its Symbolism* (Jerusalem: Mosad Bialik, 1976) [Hebrew], 266.

139. Necker, "Ernst Müller's Encounter with Jewish Mysticism," 217.

140. Gershom Scholem, "E. Müller: Der Sohar," *Orientalische Litteraturzeitung* 37 (1934): 743. See Kilcher, "Kabbalah and Anthroposophy," 212; Necker, "Ernst Müller's Encounter with Jewish Mysticism," 220.

141. Müller, "Mein Weg durch Judentum und Christentum," 233. See Kilcher, "Kabbalah and Anthroposophy," 212; Necker, "Ernst Müller's Encounter with Jewish Mysticism," 220–21.

142. Christian D. Ginsburg, *The Kabbalah, Its Doctrines, Development and Literature* (London: Routledge, 1865), 83.

143. See, Huss, "Qabbalah, the Theos-Sophia of the Jews," 160, n. 4.

144. Gershom Scholem, *Kabbalah* (Jerusalem: Keter), 1974, 4.

145. Scholem, *Major Trends,* 205–6. In case it was not sufficiently clear to what Scholem was referring when he mentioned a "modern pseudo-religion" (a term taken from René Guénon's 1921 *Le Théosophisme: Histoire d'une Pseudo-Religion*), he added a note in which he discussed the possible connection between Blavatsky's *Book of Dzyan* and the *Sifra Dezniuta* of the *Zohar.* See Scholem, *Major Trends,* 398.

146. Rufus M. Jones, *Studies in Mystical Religion* (London: MacMillan,1909), xv.

147. Evelyn Underhill, *Mysticism: A Study of the Nature and Development of Man's Spiritual Consciousness* (New York: Dutton, 1911), xiv.

148. Abelson, *Jewish Mysticism,* 9–10, 37, 87, 166. Scholem, *Major Trends,* 3–4.

149. Mendes-Flohr, *Divided Passions,* 89–90; Huss, *Mystifying Kabbalah,* 38–39.

150. Grete Schaeder, ed., *Martin Buber: Briefwechsel aus sieben Jahrzehnten,* I (1897–1918) (Heidelberg: Lambert Schneider, 1972), 253; Huss, *Mystifying Kabbalah,* 1.

151. Abelson, *Jewish Mysticism,* 1. Abelson argues against the denial of the existence of Jewish mysticism also in "Rabbinical Mysticism," 506–5, and included a chapter titled "The Compatibility of Mysticism and Rabbinic Theology," in *The Immanence of God in Rabbinical Literature,* 340–56. On the denial of the existence of mysticism in Judaism, see Boaz Huss, *Mystifying Kabbalah: Academic Scholarship, National Theology, and New Age Spirituality* (New York: Oxford University Press, 2020), 38–39.

152. See Huss, "For the Letter Kills, but the Spirit Gives Life," 59–61.

153. Martin Buber *The Tales of Rabbi Nachman* (Bloomington: Indiana University Press, 1956), 15.

154. Scholem, *On Jews and Judaism in Crisis*, 19; Huss, "For the Letter Kills, but the Spirit Gives Life," 60–61.

155. Martin Buber *The Tales of Rabbi Nachman*, 32.

156. Huss, *Mystifying Kabbalah*, 65.

157. Huss, *Mystifying Kabbalah*, 87.

158. Huss, *Mystifying Kabbalah*, 89.

159. Yehuda Liebes, "Thoughts of the Religious Significance of Kabbalah Research," in *The Path of the Spirit: Eliezer Schweid's Jubilee Volume*, ed. Yehoyada Amir (Jerusalem: Hebrew University, 2005), 203 [Hebrew].

Conclusion

1. Besant, "A Message from Dr. Besant to Hebrew Theosophists," 4.

2. Boaz Huss, "The New Age of Kabbalah: Contemporary Kabbalah, the New Age, and Postmodern Spirituality," *Journal of Modern Jewish Studies* 6 (2007): 107–25.

Bibliography

[n.a.]. 1875. "A Theosophical Society." *Spiritual Scientist* 3, no. 2 (September 16): 21–22.

[n.a.]. 1891. "Is He Koot Hoomi, Blavatsky's Mahatma?" *New York Herald*, August 16, 10.

[n.a.]. 1907. "France." *The Theosophist* 28 (September): 938–939.

[n.a.]. 1925. "T. S. in Austria." *The General Report of the Forty-Ninth Anniversary and Convention of the Theosophical Society*, clvii. Adyar: Theosophical Publishing House.

[n.a.]. 1926. "Association of Hebrew Theosophists." *The Messenger* 13, no. 11 (April): 246.

[n.a.]. 1926. "Announcements and News Items." *The Jewish Theosophist* 1, no. 2 (December): 18–22.

[n.a]. 1927. "A Message to Jews in India," *The Jewish Theosophist* 1, no. 4 (July): 27.

[n.a.]. 1928. "TS Muslim Association." *The General Report of the Fifty-Second Anniversary and Convention of the Theosophical Society*, 256–258. Adyar: Theosophical Publishing House, 1928,

[n.a.]. 1931a. "Jews in Iraq Face a New Crisis." *Israel's Messenger*, June 1, 18, 23.

[n.a.]. 1931b. "The Persecution of Hebrew Theosophists." *The Theosophist* 52 (June): 363–377.

[n.a.]. 1931c. "The New Crisis in Iraq Jewry." *Israel's Messenger*, August 1.

[n.a.]. 1931d. "Theosophy in Iraq." *TJA*, August, 214–215.

[n.a.]. 1931e. "Basra Jews and Theosophy," *Israel's Messenger*, September 4, 20.

[n.a.]. 1947. "Preamble of the TS, dated October 30, 1875." *The Theosophical Forum*, September, 515–517.

[n.a.]. 1960. "Haskalah and Zionism." In *Dembitz Book*, ed. Daniel Leibel, 33–34. Tel Aviv: Ahdut [Hebrew].

[n.a.]. 1976. *In Remembrance: The Things That Hath Been Is That Which Shall Be.* Safed: Theosophical Society Publication.

[n.a.]. 2011. "Abelson, Joshua." In *The Palgrave Dictionary of Anglo-Jewish History*, ed. William D. Rubinstein. New York: Palgrave Macmillan, 2011.

A. B. 1945. "On the Condition of the Jews in Iraq." *Hed Ha-Mizrah* (October 5): 10.

Abelson, Joshua. 1905. "Talmud and Theosophy." *Theosophical Review* 37 (September): 9–27.

Abelson, Joshua. 1906. "Maimonides on the Jewish Creed," *JQR* 19 (1): 24–58.

Abelson, Joshua. 1911–1912. "Mysticism and Rabbinical Literature." *The Hibbert Journal* 10: 426–443.

Abelson, Joshua. 1912a "Rabbinical Mysticism." *Theosophic Messenger* 13, no. 8 (May): 503–507.

Abelson, Joshua. 1912b. *The Immanence of God in Rabbinical Literature.* London: Macmillan.

Abelson, Joshua. 1913. *Jewish Mysticism: An Introduction to the Kabbalah.* London: G. Bell & Son.

Abelson, Joshua. 1921. "Swedenborg and the Zohar." *The Jewish Chronicle Supplement*, January, vii–viii.

Abelson, Joshua. 1922 "A Garment of Divers Sorts." *The Jewish Chronicle Supplement*, August, v–vi.

Abelson, Joshua. 1924. "Occult Thought in Jewish Literature." *The Jewish Chronicle Supplement*, May, vi.

Abelson, Joshua. 1931. "Introduction." In *The Zohar*, ed. Maurice Simon, Harry Sperling, vol. 1., ix–xxx. London: Soncino.

Abelson, Joshua. 1933. "The Tree of Life: A Study in Magic, by Israel Regardie." *The Jewish Chronicle*, May 12, 21.

Abelson, Joshua. 1935. "The Kabbalah (review of *The Mystical Qabalah*, by Dion Fortune." *The Jewish Chronicle*, May 24, 26.

Anderson, Douglas A. 2021. "Regina Miriam Bloch." *Lesser-Known Writers* blog, posted April 22. Lesser-Known Writers: Regina Miriam Bloch (desturmobed. blogspot.com).

Andreyev, Alexandre. 2014. *The Myth of the Masters Revived: The Occult Lives of Nikolai and Elena Roerich.* Leiden: Brill.

Ani, Reuben E. 1931. "Theosophy and Jews." *TJA*, October, 237.

Anzi, Menahse. 2021. "Theosophy and Anti-Theosophy in Basra: Jews, the Indian Ocean and the British Empire," *Historia* 46–47 (July 2021): 123–166 [Hebrew].

Attal, Salvatore. 1908. *Esoterismo Biblico.* Firenze: Salvadore Landi.

Attal, Salvatore. 2015. *Ésotérisme Biblique.* Paris: L'Âge d'homme, 2015.

Beer, Peter. 1e *religiösen Sekten der Juden und der Geheimlehre oder Kabbala.* Brünn: Trassler.

Baier, Karl. 2018. "Yoga within Viennese Occultism: Carl Kellner and Co." In *Yoga in Transformation*, ed. Karl Baier, Philip A. Mass, Karin Preisendanz, 389–438. Göttingen: Vienna University Press.

Baier, Karl. 2020. "Occult Vienna: From the Beginnings until the First World War." In *Religion in Austria*, ed. Hans Gerald Hödl; Astrid Mattes; Lukas Pokorny, vol. 5, 1–76. Vienna: Praesens Verlag.

Baron, Anne-Marie. 2015. "Présentation." In *Ésotérisme Biblique*, ed. Salvatore Attal, 11–34. Paris: L'Âge d'homme.

Barker, Alfred Trevor. 1925. *The Letters of H. P. Blavatsky to A. P Sinnett and Other Miscellaneous Letters*. London: T. F. Unwin, 1925.

Baroni, Francesco. 2023. "Roberto Assagioli and Parapsychology." In *Roberto Assagioli: Psychosynthesis and Parapsychology*, ed. Kenneth Sørensen, 9–32. Oslo: Kentaur.

Barton, Scott, J. 2009. "Miracle Publics: Theosophy, Christianity and the Coulomb Affair." *History of Religions* 49, no. 2: 172–196.

Bauduin, Tessel M. 2013. "Abstract Art as 'By Product of Astral Manifestation': The Influence of Theosophy in Modern Art in Europe." In *Handbook of Theosophical Currents*, ed. Olav Hammer and Mikael Rothstein, 429–449. Leiden: Brill.

Bauduin, Tessel M. 2015. "The Occult and the Visual Arts." In *The Occult World*, ed. Christopher Partridge. Abingdon: Routledge.

Begrunder, Michael. 2020. "Experiments with Truth: Gandhi, Esotericism, and Global Religious History." In *Imagining the East: The Early Theosophical Society*, ed. Tim Rudbøg and Erik Reenberg Sand, 345–374. New York: Oxford University Press.

Beinin, Joel, 2005. *The Dispersion of Egyptian Jewry: Culture, Politics and the Formation of Modern Diaspora*. Cairo and New York: American University in Cairo Press.

Belilowsky, Ilse. 1974. *Graphologie, Parapsychologie, Kabbalah: Die Handschrift greift Hinüber*. Zurich: W. Classen.

Beller, Steven. 1989. *Vienna and the Jews 1867–1938: A Cultural History*. Cambridge: Cambridge University Press.

Belyi, Andrej. 1975. *Verwandeln des Lebens: Errinnerugen an Rudolf Steiner*. Basel: Zbinden.

Benamozegh, Élie. 1897a. Bibliothèque de l'Hébraïsm. Livourne: S. Belforte.

Benamozegh, Élie. 1897b. *Théosphie*. Livourne: S. Belforte.

Bensusan, S. I. 1925. "How I Became a Member of the TS." *The Theosophical Review*, 1 (New Series): 210–213.

Ben-Yaakov, Abraham. 1994. *Rabbi Sasson Shandoch*. Jerusalem: Haktav Institute [Hebrew].

Ben-Zadok, Binyamin. 2009. *Judaism and Anthroposophy: Prof. S. H. Bergman's Encounter with Dr. Rudolf Steiner*. Tel Aviv: Humany.

Bergmann, Samuel Hugo. 1985. *Tagebücher and Briefe*, ed. Miriam Sambursky. Konigstein: Athenaum.

Besant. Annie. 1926a. "On the Watch Tower." *The Theosophist* 47, no. 5 (February): 551–558.

Besant. Annie. 1926b. "A Message from Dr. Besant to Hebrew Theosophists." *The Jewish Theosophist* 1 no. 2 (December): 4.

Blavatsky, Helena Petrovna. 1875a. "A Few Questions to 'Hiraf.' *Spiritual Scientist*, July 15 and 22, 217–18, 224, 236–37. http://www.theosociety.org/pasadena/bcw/b75-6-15.htm.

Blavatsky, Helena Petrovna. 1875b. "Some Unpublished Letters of H. P. Blavatsky." *Theosophical University Press Online Edition*. http://www.theosociety.org/pasadena/corson/cors-lt1.htm.

Blavatsky, Helena Petrovna.1877. *Isis Unveiled: A Master Key to the Mysteries of Ancient and Modern Science and Theology*. New York: J. W. Bouton.

Blavatsky, Helena Petrovna. 1882. "Visions in the Crystal." *The Theosophist* 3, no. 11 (August): 287–288.

Blavatsky, Helena Petrovna.1888. *The Secret Doctrine: The Synthesis of Science, Religion and Philosophy*. London: Theosophical Society Press.

Blavatsky, Helena Petrovna. 1889a. *The Key to Theosophy*. London: Theosophical Publishing House.

Blavatsky, Helena Petrovna. 1889b. "Theosophical and Mystic Publications." *Lucifer* 1, no. 1 (September): 77.

Blavatsky, Helena Petrovna. 1892. "The Kabalah and the Kabalists." *Lucifer* 10, no. 57 (May): 185–196.

Bloch, Regina Miriam. 1915. *The Confessions of Inayat Khan*. London: Sufi.

Blochman, L. E. 1927a. "Heaven an Evolutionary Conception." *The Jewish Theosophist* 1, no. 2 (December): 24–27; 1, no. 3 (April): 27–28; 1, no. 4 (July): 7–10.

Blochman, L. E. 1927b. "A Prayer." *The Jewish Theosophist* 1, no. 5 (December) (inside cover).

Blochman, L. E. 1930. "Occult Conceptions of Heaven." *The Jewish Theosophist: A Newer Magazine* (January), 9–10.

Blochman, L. E. 1932. "The Aura." *The Jewish Theosophist* 2, no. 2 (July–December): 4–5.

Bluman, Oz. 2021. "The Moment of Worldwide Renewal: Hillel Zeitlin and the Theosophical Activity in Warsaw 1917–1924." *Modern Judaism* 41, no. 2: 137–161.

Blumenfeld, H. 1927. "Theosophy and Cabala." *The Jewish Theosophist* 1, no. 4 (July): 3–4.

Bosman, Leonard. 1913. *The Mysteries of the Qabbalah*. London: Dharma.

Bosman, Leonard. 1914. *The Music of the Spheres or Cosmic Harmony*. London: Dharma.

Bosman, Leonard. 1923. *Amen: The Key to the Universe*. London: Dharma.

Bosman, Leonard. 1925. *The Book of Genesis Unveiled*. London: Dharma.

Bosman, Leonard. 1926. *A Plea for Judaism*. Adyar: Association of Hebrew Theosophists.

Bosman, Leonard. 2005. *The Meaning and Philosophy of Numbers*. Berwick, ME: Ibis.

Bosman Leonard, and Elias Gewurtz, Elias.1914a. *The Cosmic Wisdom as Embodied in the Qabbalah and in the Symbolical Hebrew Alphabet*. London: Dharma

Bosman Leonard, and Elias Gewurtz. 1914b. *The Teachings of Theosophy Scientifically Proved. Compiled from Various Sources by L. A. Bosman*. Arranged, edited and prefaced by Elias Gewurz. London: Dharma.

Boulouque, Clémence. 2021. *Another Modernity: Elia Benamozegh's Jewish Universalism*. Standford: Stanford University Press.

Bowen, Partrick. 2015. *A History of Conversion to Islam in the United States*. Leiden: Brill.

Brawer, Avrahan J. 1945. *Avak Derakhim*. Tel Aviv: Am Oved [Hebrew].

Brunton, Paul. 1934. *A Search in Secret India*. London: Rider.

Brydlova, Bozena. 1922. *10 unveiled: The Brydlovan Theory of the Origin of Numbers*. New York: Macoy Publishing and Masonic Supplies.

Brydlova, Bozena. 1926a. "Why Every Jew Should Join the Association of Hebrew Theosophists." *The Jewish Theosophist* 1, no. 1 (September): 7.

Brydlova, Bozena. 1926b. "The Ancient Kabbalah." *The Jewish Theosophist* 1, no. 2 (December): 27–28.

Brydlova, Bozena. 1927a. "A Plea for the Humble." *The Jewish Theosophist* 1, no. 3 (April): 30–31.

Brydlova, Bozena. 1927b. *A Sinner's Sermons*. Wheaton, IL: Theosophical Press.

Brydlova, Bozena. 1927c. *Flame of the Fog*. Wheaton, IL: Theosophical Press.

Buber, Martin. 1956. *The Tales of Rabbi Nachman*. Bloomington: Indiana University Press.

Buck J. D. 1883. "The Cabbalah." *The Theosophist* 5 (November): 44–45.

Buescher, John. 2021. "Sister Onfa: Uranian Missionary to Messilla." *Southern New Mexico Historical Review* 23 (January): 33–48.

Burmistrov, Konstantin. 2006. "Gershom Scholem und das Okkulte." *Gnostika: Zeitschrift für Wissenschaft & Esoterik* 33 (July): 23–34.

Calvari, Decio. 1906. "Resumé du Mouvement Théosophique en Italie." In *Transactions of the First Annual Congress of the Federation of the European Sections of the Theosophical Society, Held in Amsterdam, June 19th, 20th and 21st, 1904*, ed. J. Van Manen, Amsterdam, 1906.

Campbell, Bruce F. 1980. *Ancient Wisdom Revived: A History of the Theosophical Movement*. Berkeley: University of California Press.

Carlson, Maria. 1993. *No Religion Higher than the Truth: A History of the Theosophical Movement in Russia, 1875–1922*. Princeton: Princeton University Press.

Chajes, Julie. 2016. "Construction through Appropriation: Kabbalah in Blavatsky's Early Works." In *Theosophical Appropriations: Esotericism, Kabbalah and the Transformation of Traditions*, ed. Julie Chajes and Boaz Huss, 33–72. Beer Sheva: Ben-Gurion University of the Negev Press.

Chajes, Julie. 2018. "Seth Pancoast and the Kabbalah: Medical Pluralism and the Reception of Physics in Late-Nineteenth Century Philadelphia." *Kabbalah* 40: 131–161.

Chajes, Julie. 2019. *Recycled Lives: A History of Reincarnation in Blavatsky's Theosophy*. Oxford: Oxford University Press.

Chajes, Julie. 2021. "Orientalist Aggregates: Theosophical Buddhism between Innovation and Tradition." In *Innovation in Esotericism from the Renaissance to the Present*, ed. Tim Rudbøg and Jo Hedesan, 229–254. Cham: Palgrave Macmillan.

Chajes, Julie, and Boaz Huss. 2016. "Introduction." In *Theosophical Appropriations: Esotericism, Kabbalah and the Transformation of Traditions*, ed. Julie Chajes and Boaz Huss, 9–29. Beer Sheva: Ben-Gurion University Press.

Chamier. D. 1902. "The Kabbalah and Its Doctrine." *The Theosophist* 24 (November): 90–97.

Chatterjee, Margaret. 1992. *Gandhi and His Jewish Friends*. London: Macmillan.

Chienhui, Chuang. 2020. "Theosophical Movements in Modern China." In *Theosophy Across Boundaries: Transcultural and Interdisciplinary Perspectives on a Modern Esoteric Movement*, ed. Hans-Martin Krämer and Julian Strube, 149–178. Albany: State University of New York Press.

Chiriyankandatha, James. 2008. "Nationalism, Religion and Community: A. B. Salem, the Politics of Identity and the Disappearance of Cochin Jewry." *Journal of Global History*, 3: 21–42.

Cohen, Hayim. 1965. "Jewish Theosophists in Basra: A Symptom of the Struggle of the Generation of Enlightenment." *Ha-mizrah ha-Hadash* 15: 401–407 [Hebrew].

Cohen, I. S. 1951. "A Message from Tel Aviv." *The Canadian Theosophist* 32, no. 5 (July): 71.

Cohen, I. S. 1953. "State of Israel." *The Seventy-Eighth Annual General Report of the Theosophical Society*. Madras: The Theosophical Society, 75.

Cohen, S. S. [Samuel Suliman]. 1928. "Association of Hebrew Theosophists." *The General Report of the Fifty Second Anniversary and Convention of the Theosophical Society*, 259–260. Adyar: Theosophical Publishing House.

Cohen, S. S. 1931. "Excommunication in Modern Synagogue." *TJA*, June, 184–185.

Cohen, S. S. 1932. "Letter to the Editor." *Israel Messenger*, March 1, 13.

Cohen, S. S. 1933. "Mr. S. S. Cohen Defends His Flock." *Israel Messenger*, January 1, 21–22.

Cohen, S. S. 1942. "The Jews and Poland." *The Theosophist* 64: 263.

Collins, Mabel. 1974. *Or Al ha-Shvil* Kiryat-Shmona: Lishkat Bsorat Ha-Galil [Hebrew].

Coulomb, Emma. 1884. *Some Account of My Intercourse with Madame Blavatsky from 1872 to 1884*. Madras: Higginbotham.

Cox, Laurence. 2013. *Buddhism and Ireland*. Bristol: Equinox.

David, N. E. 1907. "Universal Brotherhood & Love in Israelitism." *The Theosophist* 28 (July): 760–767; (August) 820–828.

David, N. E. 1907–1908. "The Meaning of "Gentiles" and "Israel." *The Theosophist* 29 (December 1907): 239–244; (January 1908): 317–321.

David, N. E. 1908. "Karma and Reincarnation in Israelitism." *The Theosophist* 29 (July): 908–915; (August): 998–1007; (September): 1100–1107.

David, N. E. 1909. "Judaism." *The Proceedings of the Convention of Religions in India*. Calcutta: Nababibhakar Press, 52–59.

David, N. E. 1928. Karma and Reincarnation in Israelitism. Bible Study (Karachi Centre) Series no. 1, Association of Hebrew Theosophists (Indian Section) Karachi: L. Solomon.

De Lara, David E. 1823. *A Key to the Spanish Language*. London Boosey & Sons.

De Lara, David E. 1825. *A Key to the Portuguese Language*. London: Boosey & Sons.

De Lara, David E. 1845. "The Termination of the Mosaic Economy, as Described by a Modern Jew." *The Voice of Israel* 9 (January 1): 76.

Demarest, Marc. 2011. "The Felt Working Group Progress Report." http://www.ehbritten.org/docs/felt_working_group_status_report_7-18-12.pdf.

Deslippe, Philip. 2011. *The Kybalion: The Definitive Edition*. East Rutherford: Penguin Random House.

Deveney, John Patrick. 1997a. *Paschal Beverly Randolph: A Nineteenth-Century Black American Spiritualist, Rosicrucian, and Sex Magician*. Albany: State University of New York Press.

Deveney, John Patrick. 1997b. *Astral Projection or Liberation of the Double and the Work of the Early Theosophical Society*. Fullerton: Theosophical History Occasional Papers.

Deveney, John Patrick. 2011. "D. E. de Lara, John Storer Cobb, and The New Era." *Theosophical History* 15, no. 4: 27–33.

Deveney, John Patrick. 2016. "The Two Theosophical Societies: Prolonged Life, Conditional Immortality, and the Individualized Immortal Monad." In *Theosophical Appropriations: Esotericism, Kabbalah and the Transformation of Traditions*, ed. Julie Chajes and Boaz Huss, 93–114. Beer Sheva: Ben-Gurion University of the Negev Press.

Di Porto, Bruno. 1995. "The Jewish Press in Livorno." *Kesher* 17: 63–72 [Hebrew].

Diaz, Javier. 2016. "El Anarquismo en el Movimiento Obrero Judio de Buenos Aires (1905–1909)," *Archivos* 4, no. 8: 119–140.

Eckstein, Friedrich. 1992. *Alte unnennbare Tage*. Wien: Edition Atelier.

Ellwood, Robert S. 1993. *Islands of the Dawn: The Story of Alternative Spirituality in New Zealand*. University of Hawaii Press: Honolulu.

Elton, Benjamin J. 2012. "Conservative Judaism's British Trailblazers." *Conservative Judaism* 63, no. 4: 55–76.

Ezekiel, Abraham David. 1887a. *Idra Zuta, or the Lesser Holy Assembly, Translated from the Aramaic Chaldee into Arabic (in Hebrew Characters)*. Poona: A. D. Ezekiel's Press.

Ezekiel, Abraham David. 1887b. "The Kabbalist of Jerusalem." *The Theosophist* 8 (July): 597–601.

Ezekiel, Abraham David. 1888a. *A Sermon on True Faith, Copied from "Kor Musref" & Translated from Hebrew in Arabic (in Hebrew Characters). For the Use of Students of Kabalah*. Poona: A. D. Ezekiel's Press.

Ezekiel, Abraham David. 1888b. *Cabticum Canticorum, or the Song of Solomon, Interlineary Translation from the Herbrew into Arabic (in Hebrew Characters*. Poona: A. D. Ezekiel's Press.

Ezekiel, Abraham David. 1888c. *Dewan El Mathee, an Arabian Tale in Arabic (in Hebrew Characters)*. Poona: A. D. Ezekiel's Press, 1888.

Ezekiel, Abraham David. 1888d. *Dewan El Rahban: An Arabian Tale in Arabic (in Hebrew Characters)* Poona: A. D. Ezekiel's Press, 1888.

Ezekiel, Abraham David. 1888e. *Introduction to the Kabbalah*. Poona: A. D. Ezekiel's Press.

Ezekiel, Abraham David. 1888f. *Natural Philosophy, Matter and Motion (catechism) in Arabic (in Hebrew characters). For the use of schools*. Poona: A. D. Ezekiel's Press.

Ezekiel, Abraham David. 1888g. *Sepher Yesirah or the Book of Creation, Interlineary Translation from the Hebrew into Arabic (in Hebrew Characters)*. Poona: A. D. Ezekiel's Press.

Ezekiel, Abraham David. 1888h. *Sepher Yesirah or the Book of Creation: Interlinear Translation from the Hebrew into Arabic (in Hebrew Characters)*. Poona: A. D. Ezekiel's Press.

Ezekiel, Abraham David. 1888i. *Shomer Emuneem (First Argument), a Kabbalistic Controversy, Translated from Hebrew in Arabic (in Hebrew Characters). For the Use of Students of Kabala*. Poona: A. D. Ezekiel's Press.

Ezekiel, S. A. 1885. *The Life of Moses in Egypt*. Bombay: Indian.

Ferentinou, Victoria. 2016. "Light from Within or Light from Above? Theosophical Appropriations in Early Twentieth Century Greek Culture." In *Theosophical Appropriations: Esotericism, Kabbalah and the Transformation of Traditions*, ed. Julie Chajes and Boaz Huss, 273–308. Beer Sheva: Ben-Gurion University Press.

Fitger, Malin. 2020. "The Tetractys and Hebdomad: Blavatsky's Sacred Geometry." *Correspondences* 8, no. 1: 73–115.

Fung, Annie Cahn. 1992. *Paul Brunton: A Bridge between India and the West*. Doctoral thesis, Department of Religious Anthropology, Sorbonne. Online text, published by wisdomsgoldenrod http://www.paulbrunton.org/files/PBThesisPt1.pdf.

Fernandes, Edna. 2008. *The Last Jews of Kerala*. New York: Skyhorse.

Freud, Sigmund. 1962. *Civilization and Its Discontents*. New York: W. W. Norton.

Fetaya, Yehuda. 1933. *Minhat Yehuda*. Baghdad: Elisha Shochat [Hebrew].

Franck, Adolphe. 1926. *The Kabbalah or the Religious Philosophy of the Hebrews*. Translated by I. Sossnitz, New York: Kabbalah Publishing Company.

Gandhi, M. 1999. *The Collected Works of Mahatma Gandhi* (Electronic Book), New Delhi, Publications Division Government of India, 1999, volume 11. ttp://www.gandhiashramsevagram.org/gandhi-literature/mahatma-gandhi-collected-works-volume-11.pdf.

Ganesan, V. *The Human Gospel of Ramana Maharshi* PDF file for personal sharing via eBook readers.

Gaster, Moses. 1925. "The Divine Name and the Creative Word." *The Theosophical Review* 1: 4.

Gelber, N. M. 1960. "The History of the Jews in Dembitz." In Daniel Leibel, ed. Dembitz Book, 14–34. Tel Aviv: Ahdut [Hebrew].

Gewurtz, Elias. 1902. *The Coronation of King Edward VII and the Jews, in Three Languages, English, German, and Yiddish.* London: P. Meczyc.

Gewurtz, Elias. 1914. "The Qabalah." *The Theosophist* 36 (November): 168–172.

Gewurtz, Elias. 1916. "Comments on Light on the Path." *The Messenger* 4, no. 4 (September): 100–101.

Gewurtz, Elias. 1917. "The Valley of Judgement." *The Messenger* 4, no. 10 (March): 297–298.

Gewurtz, Elias. 1918. *The Hidden Treasures of Ancient Qabalah.* Chicago: Yogi Publication Society.

Gewurtz, Elias. 1922. *The Mysteries of the Qabala.* Chicago: Yogi Publication Society.

Gewurtz, Elias. 1923. "The Occult Hierarchy & Its Messengers to the Outer World." *The Theosophist* 44 (August): 603–607.

Gewurtz, Elias. 1924. *Beautiful Thoughts of the Ancient Hebrews.* New York: Bloch.

Gilbert, Robert A. 1987. *A. E. Waite: Magician of Many Parts.* Wellingborough: Crucible.

Gilbert, Robert A. 2005. "Forward." In Leonard Bosman, *The Meaning and Philosophy of Numbers*, vii–xiv. Berwick, Maine: Ibis.

Gimpel, Georg. 2001. *Weil de Boden selbst hier brennt: Aus dem Prager Salon der Berta Fanta (1865–1918).* Vitalis: Praha.

Ginsburg, Christian D. 1865. *The Kabbalah: Its Doctrines, Development and Literature.* London: Routledge.

Glas, Norbert. 1944. *The Jewish Question: A Problem of Mankind.* Sheffield: Sheffield Educational Settlement.

Glauber-Zimra, Samuel, and Boaz Huss. 2021. " 'No Religion Could Be More Spiritual than Ours': Anglo-Jewish Spiritualist Societies in the Interwar Period." *Jewish Historical Studies* 53, no. 5: 83–104.

Godman, David. "Talks on Sri Ramana Maharshi: Narrated by David Godman—Tales from Palakottu (Part I)." https://www.youtube.com/watch?v=yxCuGtCvkcg.

Godwin, Joscelyn. 1989. *The Beginnings of Theosophy in France* London: Theosophical History Centre.

Godwin, Joscelyn. 1994. *The Theosophical Enlightenment.* Albany: State University of New York Press.

Godwin, Joscelyn. 2013. "Blavatsky and the First Generation of Theosophy." In *Handbook of Theosophical Currents*, ed. Olav Hammer and Mikael Rothstein, 15–31. Leiden: Brill.

Godwin, Joscelyn. 2020a. "Beyond the Cosmic Ladder: The Ultimate State, according to Julius Evola and Paul Brunton." *Theosophical History* 30, no. 3: 261–278.

Godwin, Joscelyn. 2020b. "The Mahatma Letters." In *Imagining the East: The Early Theosophical Society*, ed. Tim Rudbøg and Erik Reenberg Sand, 133–155. New York, Oxford University Press,

Goldstein, Sasha Rachel. 2018. "Baghdadi Jewish Networks in Hashemite Iraq." PhD dissertation, Leiden University.

Gomes, Michael. 1985. "H. P. Blavatsky's Annotations in Madame Coulomb's Pamphlet." *Theosophical History* 1, no. 6: 144–156.

Gomes, Michael. 1990. "Studies in Early American Theosophical History, Pt. VI, Rev. Wiggin's Review of George Henry Felt's 1875 Lecture on the Cabala." *Canadian Theosophist* 71, no. 3: 63–69.

Gomes, Michael. 2005. "Olcott, Henry Steel." In *Dictionary of Gnosis and Western Esotericism*, ed. Wouter J. Hanegraaff, 894–895. Leiden: Brill.

Gomes, Michael. 2016. "H. P. Blavatsky and Theosophy." In *The Cambridge Handbook of Western Mysticism and Esotericism*, ed. Glenn Alexander Magee, 248–259. New York: Cambridge University Press,

Goodrick-Clarke, Nicholas. 1992. *The Occult Roots of Nazism: Secret Aryan Cults and Their Influence on Nazi Ideology.* New York: New York University Press.

Goodrick-Clarke, Nicholas. 2004. *Helena Blavatsky.* Berkley: North Atlantic Books.

Goodrick-Clarke, Nicholas. 2008. *The Western Esoteric Tradition: A Historical Introduction.* New York and Oxford: Oxford University Press.

Goodrick-Clarke, Nicholas. 2010. "The Coming of the Masters: The Evolutionary Reformulation of Spiritual Intermediaries in Modern Theosophy." In *Constructing Tradition: Means and Myths of Transmission in Western Esotericism*, ed. Andreas Kilcher, 113–160. Leiden: Brill.

Goodrick-Clarke, Nicholas. 2013. "Western Esoteric Traditions and Theosophy." In *Handbook of Theosophical Currents*, ed. Olav Hammer and Mikael Rothstein, 261–397. Leiden: Brill.

Goodrick-Clarke, Nicholas, and Clare Goodrick-Clarke. 2005. *G.R.S. Mead and the Gnostic Quest.* Berkeley: North Atlantic Books.

Graetz, Heinrich. 1868. *Geschichte der Juden*, vol. 10. Leipzig: Oscar Leiner.

Graetz, Heinrich. 1927. *History of the Jews.* New York: George Dobsevage.

Grant, Frances Ruth. 1938. *Oriental Philosophy: The Story of the Teachers of the East.* New York: Dial.

Grayevsky, Pinchas. 1930. "On the Translation of the Idrot to Arabic." *Meginzei Yerushalaim* 2: 15–16 [Hebrew].

Greene, Liz. 2012. *Magi and Maggidim: The Kabbalah in British Occultism 1860–1940.* Ceredigion, Wales: Sophia Center.

Grünhut, Adolf. 1921. *Tanulmányok a spiritizmus köréből: magnetizmus, szomnambulizmus, mediumizmus.* Budapest: Szellemi Buvárok Pesti Egylete.

Gubbay, C. S. 1932. "Our Local Gubbay-ism, a Reply." *Israel's Messenger* (April): 8–9.

Guénon, René. 1921. *Le Théosophisme: Histoire d'une Pseudo-Religion.* Paris: Nouvelle Librairie Nationale.

Guetta, Alessandro. 2009. *Philosophy and Kabbalah: Elijah Benamozegh and the Reconciliation of Western Thought and Jewish Esotericism.* Albany: State University of New York Press.

Gyimesi, Júlia. 2014. "Between Religion and Science: Spiritualism, Science and Early Psychology in Hungary." *International Psychology* 5: 1–23.

Gyimesi, Júlia. 2016. "The Institutionalization of Parapsychology in Hungary in the 20th Century." In *Okkultismus im Gehäuse: Institutionalisierungen der Parapsychologie im 20. Jahrhundert im internationalen Vergleich*, ed. Anna Lux and Sylvia Paletschek, 201–224. Berlin and Boston: De Gruyter.

Hall, Julie. 2012. "The Concept of Reincarnation in Theosophy: Modernity, Globalization and Western Esotericism." Unpublished doctoral thesis, University of Exeter.

Hammer, Olav. 2004. Claiming Knowledge: Strategies of Epistemology from Theosophy to the New Age. Leiden: Brill.

Hanegraaff, Wouter. 1998. *New Age Religion and Western Culture*. Albany: State University of New York Press.

Hanegraaff, Wouter. 2006. "Jewish Influences V: Occultist Kabbalah." In *Dictionary of Gnosis & Western Esotericism*, ed. Wouter J. Hanegraaff, 644–647. Leiden: Brill.

Hanegraaff, Wouter. 2018. "Mysteries of Sex in the House of the Hidden Light: Arthur Edward Waite and the Kabbalah." *Kabbalah: The Journal for the Study of Jewish Mystical Texts* 40: 163–182.

Hanegraaff, Wouter. 2020. "Western Esotericism and the Orient in the First Theosophical Society." In *Theosophy Across Boundaries: Transcultural and Interdisciplinary Perspectives on a Modern Esoteric Movement*, ed. Hans-Martin Krämer and Julian Strube, 29–64. Albany: State University of New York Press.

Hanes, Travis W. III. 1993. "On the Origins of the Indian National Congress: A Case Study of Cross-Cultural Synthesis." *Journal of World History* 4, no. 1: 69–98.

Hansen, Jan-Erik Ebbestad. 2015. "The Jews—Teachers of the Nazis: Anti-Semitism in Norwegian Anthroposophy." *Nordeuropa-Forum*: 161–216.

Haralambakis (Cioata), Maria. 2012–2013. "Representations of Moses Gaster (1856–1939) in Anglophone and Romanian Scholarship." *New Europe College Yearbook*: 89–128.

Harpaz, Yoram. 1989. "The Theosophists versus Krishnamurti." *Kol Ha-Ir* 4 (August): 51–53, 71.

Harrison, Vernon. 1986. "J'Accuse, An Examination of the Hodgson Report of 1885." *Journal of the Society of Psychical Research* 53, no. 803: 286–310.

Hayyim, Yosef. 1901. *Responsa Rav Pe'alim*. Jerusalem: Frumkin [Hebrew].

Hicks, Matthew. Rabbi Max Samfield Collection—Manuscript Collection Finding Aids—Dig Memphis—The Digital Archive of the Memphis Public Library & Information Center (oclc.org).

Hill, Brad Sabin. 2006. *Hebrew, Judeo-Arabic and Marathi Jewish Printing in India: Rare Printed Books from the Valmadonna Trust Library*. Leiden: Brill 2006. https://docplayer.net/54659768-Title-list-hebrew-judeo-arabic-and-marathi-jewish-printing-in-india.html.

Hodgson, Richard. 1885. "Report of the Committee Appointed to Investigate Phenomena Connected with the Theosophical Society." *Proceedings of the Society for Psychical Research* 3, 201–400. London: Kegan Paul, Trench & Trübner.

Hodgson, Richard. 1894. "The Defense of the Theosophists." *Proceeding of the Society for Psychical Research* 9, 129–159.

Hodson, Geoffrey. 1972. *Yoga Shel Or*. Kiryat-Shmona: Lishkat Bsorat Ha-Galil [Hebrew].

Hoexter David F., and Mary R. Hoexter. 1980. "Lazar E. Blochman of San Francisco, Santa Maria and Berkeley." *Western States Jewish Historical Quarterly* 13, no. 1: 53–62.

Hoexter, Mary R. 1988. "Emanuel Blochman: French Born Orthodox Activist of San Francisco." *Western States Jewish Historical Quarterly* 20, no. 2: 99–108.

Horne, Alex. 1925a. "The Chinese Jews of K'ai-Feng-Fu." *The Theosophist* 46 (July): 459–467.

Horne, Alex. 1925b. "Theosophy in China." *The Theosophist* 46 (July): 530–533.

Horne, Alex. 1926a. "A Glorious Opportunity." *The Jewish Theosophist* 1, no. 2 (December): 7–8.

Horne, Alex. 1926b. "Theosophy in Modern Judaism." *The Theosophist* 47 (April): 105–106.

Horne, Alex. 1926c. *Spiritualizing Unspiritual Judaism*. Seattle, Washington: Association of Hebrew Theosophists, American Section.

Horne, Alex. 1927a. "Judaism and Theosophy." *The Jewish Theosophist* 1 no. 4 (July): 23–24.

Horne, Alex. 1927b. "Association of Jewish Theosophists," *The Theosophist* 48 (February): 613.

Horne, Alex. 1928a. *An Introduction to Esoteric Judaism*. Wheaton: Theosophical Press.

Horne, Alex. 1928b. "Nina H. Adlerblum's *A Study of Garsonides in His Proper Perspective*. Review." *The Theosophical Messenger* 15 (1928): 282.

Horne, Alex. 1928c. *Theosophy and the Fourth Dimension*. London: Theosophical Publishing House.

Horne, Alex. 1929. "Adolphe Franck's 'The Kabbalah, or, The Religious Philosophy of the Hebrews.' Review." *The Theosophical Messenger* 17 (June): 137.

Horne, Alex. 1939. "Is Persecution the Plan." *The Theosophist* 60 (August): 489–490.

Horne, Alex. 1948. "After Two Thousand Years." *American Theosophists* 36 (March): 61–62.

Huss, Boaz. 2005. "Ask No Questions: Gershom Scholem and the Study of Contemporary Jewish Mysticism." *Modern Judaism* 25, no. 2: 141–158.

Huss, Boaz. 2006. "Admiration and Disgust: The Ambivalent Re-Canonization of the Zohar in the Modern Period." In *Study and Knowledge in Jewish Thought*, ed. Howard Kreisel, 203–237. Beer-Sheva: Ben-Gurion University of the Negev Press.

Huss, Boaz. 2007a. "Authorized Guardians: The Polemics of Academic Scholars of Jewish Mysticism Against Kabbalah Practitioners." In *Polemical Encounters: Esoteric Discourse and its Others*, ed. Olav Hammer and Kocku von Stuckrad, 81–103. Leiden and Boston: Brill.

Huss, Boaz. 2007b. "The New Age of Kabbalah: Contemporary Kabbalah, the New Age, and Postmodern Spirituality," *Journal of Modern Jewish Studies* 6: 107–125.

Huss, Boaz. 2010. " 'The Sufi Society from America': Theosophy and Kabbalah in Poona in the Late Nineteenth Century." In *Kabbalah and Modernity*, ed. Boaz Huss, Marco Pasi, and Kocku von Stuckrad Kocku, 167–193. Leiden and Boston: Brill.

Huss, Boaz. 2013. " 'Forward to the East': Naphtali Herz Imber's Perception of Kabbalah." *Journal of Modern Jewish Studies* 12: 398–418.

Huss, Boaz. 2015. " 'A Jew Living in an Ashram': The Spiritual Itinerary of S. S. Cohen." *Journal of Indo-Judaic Studies* 15: 20–29.

Huss, Boaz. 2016a. " 'Qabbalah, the Theos-Sophia of the Jews': Jewish Theosophists and their Perceptions of Kabbalah." In *Theosophical Appropriations: Esotericism, Kabbalah, and the Transformation of Traditions*, ed. Julie Chajes and Boaz Huss, 137–166. Beer Sheva: Ben-Gurion University of the Negev Press.

Huss, Boaz. 2016b. *The Zohar: Reception and Impact.* London: Liverpool University Press.

Huss, Boaz. 2016c. "Translations of the Zohar: Historical Contexts and Ideological Frameworks." *Correspondences* 4: 81–128.

Huss, Boaz. 2018. " 'The Quest Universal': Moses Gaster's interest in Kabbalah and Western Esotericism." *Kabbalah* 40: 255–266.

Huss, Boaz. 2020a. *Mystifying Kabbalah: Academic Scholarship, National Theology, and New Age Spirituality.* New York: Oxford University Press.

Huss, Boaz, and Jonatan Meir. 2020b. " 'The Light Is Burning Pretty Low': The 1948 Correspondence between Samuel Lewis and Gershom Scholem." *Correspondences* 8, no. 1: 45–72.

Huss, Boaz. 2020c. " 'The Qabbalah of the Hebrew and the Ancient Wisdom Religion of Asia': Isaac Myer and the Kabbalah in America." *Kabbala in America: Ancient Lore in the New World*, ed. Brain Ogren, 72–93. Leiden: Brill.

Huss, Boaz. 2021a. "Academic Study of Kabbala and Occultist Kabbala." In *Occult Roots of Religious Studies*, ed. Yves Mühlematter and Helmut Zander, 104–131. Oldenbourg: De Gruyter.

Huss, Boaz. 2021b. " 'For the Letter Kills, but the Spirit Gives Life': Halakha versus Kabbalah in the Study of Jewish Mysticism." *Modern Judaism* 41, no. 1: 47–70.

Huss, Boaz. 2021c. " 'To Study Judaism in Light of Theosophy and Theosophy in the Light of Judaism': The Association of Hebrew Theosophists and Its Missions to the Jews and Gentiles." In *Theosophy across Boundaries*, ed. Hans Martin Krämer and Julian Strube, 253–278. Albany: State University of New York Press.

Huss, Boaz. 2024. " 'There Are So Many Ways of Spiritual Development': Shmuel Hugo Bergmann's Interests in Western Esoteric and Alternative Spiritual Currents." In *Hugo Bergmann: A Life between Prague and Jerusalem*, ed. Olaf Glöckner, Boaz Huss, and Marcela Menachem Zoufalá. Oldenburg: De Gruyter, 2024, 97–117.

Hyneman Sotheran, Alice. 1971. "Reminiscences of Charles Sotheran as Pioneer American Socialist." In *Horace Greely and Other Pioneers of American Socialism*, ed. Charles Sotheran, xi–xxxix. New York: Haskell House Publishers.

Iggers, Wilma. 1995. *Women of Prague: Ethnic Diversity and Social Change from the 18th Century to the Present*. Providence: Berghahn.

Imber, Naphtali Herz, ed. 1895. *Uriel: A Monthly Magazine Devoted to Cabbalistic Science*. Boston, MA: Cabbalistic Publishing Company.

Imber, Naphtali Herz, ed. 1910. *Treasures of Two Worlds*. Los Angeles, CA: Citizens Printing Shop.

Isaacs, Nigel. 1990. "Staveren, Herman van." *Dictionary of New Zealand Biography*. https://teara.govt.nz/en/biographies/2s40/staveren-herman-van/related-biographies.

Isenberg, Shirley Berry. 1988. *India's Bene Israel: A Comprehensive Inquiry and Sourcebook*. Bombay: Popular Prakashan.

Ito, Kasuke. 1985. "Fredrick Reiss (1891–1981)." *Bulletin of the New York Academy of Medicine* 61, no. 4 (1985): 378–384.

Jinarajadasa, C. 1916. "The Jewish People: A Letter to Some Indian Jews." *Adyar Bulletin* 9 (February): 43–51.

Jinarajadasa, C. 1926. "The Message of Judaism." *The Jewish Theosophist* 1, no. 2 (December): 29–31.

Jinarajadasa, C. 1931. "The Persecution of Hebrew Theosophists: Forward." *The Theosophist* (June): 363.

Johnson, Kenneth Paul. 2020. "Theosophy in the Bengal Renaissance." In *Imagining the East: The Early Theosophical Society*, ed. Tim Rudbøg and Erik Reenberg Sand, 231–245.

Jounet, Albert. 1909. *La Clef du Zohar*. Paris: Bibliothèque Chacornac.

Jung, Leo. 1933. "Rabbi Jung and Theosophy." *Jewish Messenger*, January 1, 21.

Juste, Michael. 1927. *The White Brother: An Occult Autobiography*. London: Rider & Co.

Kabakoff, Jacob. 1985. *Master of Hope: Selected Writings of Naphtali Herz Imber*, London and Toronto: Associated University Press.

Kahn, Ava Fran, ed. 2022. *Jewish Voices of the California Gold Rush: A Documentary History 1849–1880*. Detroit MI: Wayne State University Press.

Kalzel, Ezekiel Zvi. 1936. "Theosophy and Kosher Meat." *Ha-Doar Hayom* (January 21) [Hebrew].

Kanga, D. D. 1941. "Dr. Solomon." *The Theosophist* 62 (February): 431–432.

Karppe, Sylv. 1901. *Etude sur les origines et la nature du Zohar, Précédée D'une Étude Sur L'Histoire de la Kabbale*. Paris: F. Alcan.

Katz, Nathan. 2000. *Who Are the Jews of India?* Berkeley, Los Angeles, and London: University of California Press.

Khandalvala, N. D. 1929. "Madame H. P. Blavatsky as I Knew Her." *The Theosophist* 50 (June): 213–222; (July): 309–318.

Kilcher, Andreas. 2016. "Kabbalah and Anthroposophy: A Spiritual Alliance according to Ernst Müller." In *Theosophical Appropriations: Esotericism, Kabbalah and the*

Transformation of Traditions, ed. Julie Chajes and Boaz Huss, 197–222. Beer Sheva: Ben-Gurion University Press.

Koren, Israel. 2000. "S. H. Bergman's Attitude to the Teachings of Rudolf Steiner." *Iyyun* 49: 429–450 [Hebrew].

Koren, Israel. 2019. *Judaism and Anthroposophy: Ancient Controversies in a Modern Garb*. Tel Aviv: Idra Press [Hebrew].

Kozlovsky, I. M. 1994. "Background and History of the Theosophical Society in Bohemia." *Theosophical History* 5, no. 4: 130–136.

Krishnamurti, Jido. 1935. *Al Ha-Ikar*. Ein-Harod: Ha-Kibutz ha-Meuhad.

Krishnamurti, Jido. 1971. *Leraglei ha-Raban*. Kiryat-Shmona: Lishkat Bsorat Ha-Galil [Hebrew].

Kumar, H. C. 1924. "T.S. Muslim League." *The General Report of the Forty-Ninth Anniversary and Convention of the Theosophical Society*, 227–231. Adyar: Theosophical Publishing House.

Lanchidi, Peter. 2021. "Jacob Norton and the Quest for Universal Freemasonry: Jewish Masonic Consciousness within a Christian Fraternity." *American Jewish History* 105, no. 4: 479–504.

Lanepart, Herbert Edward. 1925. "Hong Kong Lodge." In *The General Report of the Forty-Ninth Anniversary and Convention of the Theosophical Society*. Adyar: Theosophical Publishing House, 182.

Lattes, Arrigo. 1898. *Fantasie di un antisemite*. Livorno: S. Belforte.

Lattes, Arrigo. 1900a. "In Memoriam: Elia Benamozegh." *Vessilio Israelitico* 47: 47–48.

Lattes, Arrigo. 1900b. *Studio sulle cause della decadenza del culto israelitico*. Livorno: S. Belforte.

Lattes, Arrigo. 1968. "Altezza e divinità dell'Ebraismo." *La Rassegna Mensile di Israel* 34, no. 12: 668–674.

Lattes, Guglielmo. 1901. *Vita e opere di Elia Benamozegh: Ccenni, considerazioni, note con ritratto dell'illustre rabbino*. Livorno: S. Belforte.

Lavoie, Jeffrey D. 2021. "Theosophical Chronology in the Writings if Guido von List (1849–1919): A Link between H. P. Blavatsky's Philosophy and the Nazi Movement." In *Innovation in Esotericism from the Renaissance to the Present*, ed. Georgina D. Hedesan and Tim Rudbøg, 255–278. Cham: Palgrave Macmillan, 2021.

Lazarus, Montague R. 1887. "The Kabbala and the Microcosm." *The Theosophist* 8 (September): 767–774; 9 (October): 45–52; (November): 119–124; (December): 167–171.

Leadbeater, Charles W. 1971. *Me'ever Lamavet*. Kiryat-Shmona: Lishkat Bsorat Ha-Galil [Hebrew].

Leavitt, June O. 2012. *The Mystical Life of Franz Kafka: Theosophy, Cabala, and the Modern Spiritual Revival*. New York: Oxford University Press.

Leland, Kurt. 2018. "Alarums and Excursions: William James and the Theosophical Society." *Theosophical History* 19, no. 4 (October): 140–157.

Leshem, Zvi. 2023. "Boldness of Invention and Falsification: Gershom Scholem on Elias Gewurz." The Librarians, The Blog of the National Library of Israel, May 1. https://blog.nli.org.il/en/gershom-scholem-elias-gewurz/.

Lev, Shimon. 2012. *Soulmates: The Story of Mahatma Gandhi and Hermann Kallenbach*. Hyderabad: Orient Blackswan.

Lev, Shimon. 2016. "Gandhi and His Jewish Theosophist Supporters in South Africa." *Theosophical Appropriations: Esotericism, Kabbalah and the Transformation of Traditions*, ed. Julie Chajes and Boaz Huss, 245–271. Beer Sheva: Ben-Gurion University of the Negev Press.

Lev, Shimon. 2020. "Gabriel Isaac, Gandhi's Forgotten Lieutenant." *The Jerusalem Report*, February 19, 34–36.

Levi, Cesare Augusto. 1896. *Navi da guerra costruite nell'arsenale di Venezia dal 1664 al 1896*. Venezia: C. A. Levi.

Levi, Cesare Augusto. 1900a, *Il Simon Mago ed altre leggende e visioni*. Firenze: Bemporad.

Levi, Cesare Augusto. 1900b. *Le collezioni veneziane d'arte e d'antichità dal secolo XIV ai nostri giorni*. Venezia: F. Ongania.

Levi, Cesare Augusto. 1907a. *Dante e Sionne, o, la Città santa del premio divino e del lavoro umano, dall'antico Egitto ad oggi, traverso la Bibbia, il Vangelo e la Divina commedia*. Pisa: F. Mariotti.

Levi, Cesare Augusto. 1907b. *Venezia, Corfu ed il Levante: Relazione storico-archivistica*. Venezia: C. Ferrari.

Levi, Theo. 1923. "T.S. in Egypt." *The General Report of the Forty-Seventh Anniversary and Convention of the Theosophical Society*. Adyar: Theosophical Publishing House, 125–127.

Lewis, Samuel. 1981. *Introduction to Spiritual Brotherhood: Science, Mysticism and the New Age*. San Francisco: Sufi Islamia/Prophecy Pub.

Liebes, Yehuda. 2005. "Thoughts of the Religious Significance of Kabbalah Research." In *The Path of the Spirit: Eliezer Schweid's Jubilee Volume*, ed. Yehoyada Amir, 197–208. Jerusalem: Hebrew University [Hebrew].

Lubelsky, Isaac. 2017. "Theosophy and Anthroposophy in Israel: An Historical Survey." In Contemporary Alternative Spiritualties in Israel, ed. S. Feraro and J. R. Lewis, 135–154. New York: Palgrave Macmillan.

Lubelsky, Isaac. 2020. "Allan Octavian Hume, Madame Blavatsky and the Foundation of the Indian National Congress." In *Imagining the East: The Early Theosophical Society*, ed. Tim Rudbøg and Erik Reenberg Sand, 303–320. New York: Oxford University Press.

Luria, Maxwel. 1995. "Introduction." In *Elijah Benamozegh, Israel and Humanity*, ed. Maxwell Luria, 1–30. New York: Paulist.

Magnus, Shulamit S. 2016. "Wengeroff in America: On the Resonance of Conversion and Fear of Dissolution in Early Twentieth Century American Jewry." *Jewish Social Science* 21, no. 2: 142–187.

Marcus, Jacob Rader. 1981. *The American Jewish Woman: A Documentary History.* New York: Ktav.

Martins, Ansgar. 2014. *Hans Büchenbacher: Erinnerungen 1933–1949.* Frankfurt am Main: Mayer Info3.

Mathers, S. L. MacGregor. 1887. *The Kabbalah Unveiled.* London: George Redway.

Mathers, S. L. MacGregor. 1912. *The Kabbalah Unveiled.* New York: Theosophical Society.

Menashe, Rachel. 2013. *Baghdadian Jews of Bombay, Their Life and Achievements: A Personal and Historical Account.* Great Neck, NY: Midrash Ben Ish Hai.

Mendes-Flohr. Paul. 1991. *Divided Passions: Jewish Intellectuals and the Experience of Modernity.* Detroit: Wayne State University Press.

Menon, Bala, and Essie Sassoon. 2020. *The "Jewish Gandhi" of Cochin.* Toronto: Tamarind Tree.

Mervay, Mátyás. 2020. "Dr. Frederick Reiss, Austro-Hungarian Master of the Shanghai Freemason Lodge Lux Orientis." *Refugees of Habsburgia in China.* https://wp.nyu.edu/habsburgiainchina/dr-frederick-reiss-austro-hungarian-master-of-the-shanghai-freemason-lodge-lux-orientis/.

Mervay, Mátyás. 2024. "A Hungarian Old China Hand and the End of Empire: Loyalty Struggles in Interwar Shanghai's Migrant Community." *Austrian History Yearbook*: 1–21.

Meyer, Maisie J. 2015. "Nissim Ezra Benjamin Ezra (1880–1936)." In Shanghai's Baghdadi Jews, ed. Maisie J. Meyer, 224–251. Hong Kong: Blacksmith Books.

Meyer, T. H. 2011. *Laurence Oliphant: When a Stone Begins to Roll.* Great Barrington, MA: Lindisfarne Books.

Morais, Henry Samuel. 1894. *The Jews of Philadelphia: Their History from the Earliest Settlements to the Present Time.* Philadelphia: Levytype.

Mukopadhyay, Mriganka. 2021. "Occult's First Foot Soldier in Bengal: Peary Chand Mittra and the Early Theosophical Movement." In *The Occult Nineteenth Century*, ed. Lukas Pokorny and Franz Winter, 269–286. Cham, Switzerland: Palgrave Macmillan.

Müller, Ernst. 1920. *Der Sohar und Seine Lehre: Einleitung in die Gedankenwelt der Kabbalah.* Wein and Berlin: R. Löwit Verlag.

Müller, Ernst. 1924. "Von Wort und Sinn der biblischen Schöpfungsgeschichte." *Der Jude* 8: 531–540.

Müller, Ernst. 1928. "Die Drei Sabbatischlieder des Jizchak Luria." *Menorah* 10: 601–603.

Müller, Ernst. 1932. *Der Sohar: Das Heilige Buch Der Kabbalah, Nach dem Urtext.* Wien: Glanz.

Müller, Ernst. 1943. "On Sepher Yetzirah." *Metzudah* 2: 105–110 [Hebrew].

Müller, Ernst. 1945. "On Mysticism in Scripture." *Metzudah* 3–4: 110–115 [Hebrew].

Müller, Ernst. 1946. *History of Jewish Mysticism.* Oxford: East and West Library.

Müller, Ernst. 1950. "Erinnerungen an Friedrich Eckstein." *Blätter für Anthroposophie* 2: 418–421.

Müller, Ernst. 1952. "Mein Weg durch Judentum und Christentum." *Judaica: Beiträge zum Verständnis des jüdischen Schicksals in Vergangenheit und Gegenwart* 4, no. 8: 23–243.

Müller, Ernst. 1954. "Wandlungen des jüdischen Bewusstseins in den letzten Jahrhunderten." *Judaica: Beiträge zum Verständnis des jüdischen Schicksals in Vergangenheit und Gegenwart* 10 (1954): 129–154.

Müller, Ernst. 2011. "Erinnerungen an Friedrich Eckstein." Der Europäer 15, no. 5: 11.

Müller, Pia. 1927. "The Chassidim." *The Jewish Theosophist* 1, no. 4 (July): 22–23.

Mulot-Déri, Sibylle. (1992). "Alte Ungenannte Tage." In *Alte unnennbare Tage*, ed. Friedrich Eckstein, 298–300. Wien: Edition Atelier.

Myer, Isaac. 1888. *Qabbalah: The Philosophical Writings of Solomon ben Yehudah Ibn Gebirol.* Philadelphia: The Author.

Nagel, Alexandra. 2019. "The Association of Jewish Theosophists in the Netherlands: The Efforts of Louis Vet and Others to Revive Judaism." *Correspondences* 7, no. 2: 411–439.

Necker, Gerold. 2018. "Ernst Müller's Encounter with Jewish Mysticism and Gershom Scholem." *Kabbalah* 40: 201–223.

Nee Ben. 1931. "Jews and Theosophy." *TJA*, September, 225–226.

Newman, Louis I. Martin. 1925. "A. Meyer." *Publication of the American Jewish Historical Society* 29: 179–181.

Noblston, Lily. 1925. "Shanghai Lodge." In *The General Report of the Forty-Ninth Anniversary and Convention of the Theosophical Society*, 179–181. Adyar: Theosophical Publishing House.

O'Callaghan, Sean. 2013. "The Theosophical Christology of Alice Bailey." In *Handbook of Theosophical Currents*, ed. Olav Hammer and Mikael Rothstein, 93–112, Leiden: Brill.

Olcott, Henry Steel. 1892. "Old Diary Leaves, chapter 8." *The Theosophist* 14, no. 2 (November) pp. 67–75.

Olcott, Henry Steel. 1895. *Old Diary Leaves: The True Story of the Theosophical Society.* New York and London: G. P. Putnam's Sons.

Oliphant, Margaret. 1891. *Memoir of the Life of Laurence Oliphant and of His Wife Alice Oliphant.* Edinburgh and London: W. Blackwood.

Osterrieder, Markus. 2012. "From Synarachy to Shambhala: The Role of Political Occultism and Social Messianism in the Activities of Nicholas Roerich." *The New Age of Occult and Esoteric Dimensions*, ed. Birgit Menzel, Michael Hagemeister and Bernice Glatzer Rosenthal, 101–134. Munchen and Berlin: Otto Sagner.

Pancoast, Seth. 1883. *The Kabbalah, or the True Science of Light: An Introduction to Philosophy and Theosophy of the Ancient Sages.* Philadelphia: J. M. Stoddart.

Pancoast, Seth. 1886a. "Kabbala." *The Path* 1, no. 1: 8–14.

Pancoast, Seth. 1886b. "The Mystery of Numbers." *The Path* 1, no. 2: 37–41.

Pant, Apa B. 1991. "Maurice Frydman." In *The Mountain Path* 28, no. 1–2: 31–33.

Papus [Gerard Encausse]. 1887. "Le Sepher Jesirah." *Lotus* 2 (October): 11–27.

Papus [Gerard Encausse]. 1892. *La Kabbale, tradition secrète de l'Occident, résumé méthodique, précédé d'une lettre d'Adolphe Franck.* Paris: George Carré.

Partridge, Christopher. 2020. "Adventures in 'Wisdom Land': Orientalist Discourse in Early Theosophy." In *Imagining the East: The Early Theosophical Society*, ed. Tim Rudbøg and Erik Reenberg Sand, 15–16. New York: Oxford University Press.

Pasi, Marco. 2010. "Oriental Kabbalah and the Parting of East and West in the Early Theosophical Society." In *Kabbalah and Modernity*, ed. Boaz Huss, Marco Pasi, and Kocku von Stuckrad, 150–166. Leiden and Boston: Brill.

Pasi, Marco. 2012. "Theosophy and Anthroposophy in Italy during the First Half of the Twentieth Century." *Theosophical History* 15, no. 2: 92–93.

Perez. J. H. 1924. "Rapport du Secrétaire General." *Papyrus* 3, no. 8 (June): 5.

Perez. J. H. 1925. "T. S. in Egypt." In *The General Report of the Forty-Ninth Anniversary and Convention of the Theosophical Society*, 123–124. Adyar: Theosophical Publishing House, 123–124.

Perez. J. H. 1927. "A Short History of the Foundation of the A.H.T." *The Jewish Theosophist* 1, no. 2 (February) (second and revised edition): 6.

Perez. J. H. 1928. "T.S. Federation in Egypt." In *The General Report of the Fifty-Second Anniversary and Convention of the Theosophical Society*. Adyar: Theosophical Publishing House, 193–194.

Polak, Gaston. 1925. "T.S. in Belgium." In *The General Report of the Forty-Ninth Anniversary and Convention of the Theosophical Society*. Adyar: Theosophical Publishing House, 109–110.

Polak, Gaston. 1926. "Association of Hebrew Theosophists: Appeal to Members of the TS." *The Theosophist* 47 (April): 103–104.

Polak, Henry S. L. 1909. *The Indians of South Africa: Helots within the Empire and How They Are Treated.* Madras: G. A. Natesan.

Polak, Henry S. L. 1910. "Brotherhood as Understood in South Africa." *The Theosophist* 31 (May): 987–1000.

Polak, Henry S. L. 1917. *M. K. Gandhi: A Sketch of His Life and Work.* Madras: G. A. Natesan.

Polak, Henry S. L. 1957. "Towards Practical Theosophy and Inter-religious Understanding." *The Theosophist* 7 (February): 321–330.

Polak. Millie Graham. 1931. *Mr. Gandhi: The Man.* London: G. Allen & Unwin.

Pratt, Henry. 1889. "About the Kabbalah." *The Theosophist* 10 (August): 649–661.

Price, Leslie. "First Report of the Committee of the Society for Psychical Research." *The Blavatsky Archives Online* http://www.blavatskyarchives.com/sprrpmaintext.htm.

Raafat, Samir. 1997. "The Cairo Bourse." *Cairo Times*, October 30, 1997. http://www.egy.com/landmarks/97-10-30.php.

Rabinovitch, Simon. 2009. "Jews, Englishmen, and Folklorists: The Scholarship of Joseph Jacobs and Moses Gaster." In *The Jew in Late-Victorian and Edwardian Culture: Between the East End and East Africa*, ed. Eitan Bar-Yosef and Nadia Valman, 113–130. Basingstoke, NY: Palgrave Macmillan.

Ransom Josephine. 1938. *A Short History of the Theosophical Society.* Adyar: Theosophical Publishing House.Rehbein, Maja. 2009. " 'Könnte mam als Freier unter Freien leben . . .': Berta Fanta, Ida Freund und der Prager Salon." In *Anthroposophie und Judnetum*, ed. Ralf Sonnenberg, 103–116. Frankfurt am Main: Info3-Verlag.

Rejzen, Zalman. 1929. *Leksikon fun der Yiddisher literature, Prese un Filologye.* Vilne: B. Ḳletsḳin [Yiddish].

Riemer, Nathaneal. 2004. "Wanderer Zwischen den Welten—Zum50sten Todesjahr von Ernst Müller." *David: Jüdische Kulturzeitschrift* 62. http://www.david.juden. at/kulturzeitschrift/61-65/62-Riemer.htm.

Ritch, Lewis W. 1895. "Africa." *Lucifer* 17, no. 97 (September): 83.

Ritch, Lewis W. 1897. "Letter." *The Theosophist* 18 (April 1897): 431–433.

Ritch, Lewis W. 1899. "New Branch—South African Lodge." *The Theosophist* 20 (June): 42–43.

Ritch, Lewis W. 1949. "His Days in South Africa." In Incidents of Gandhijis's Life, ed. Chandrashanker Shukla, 366–370. Bombay: Vora.

Roerich, Nicholas, K. 1926. *Himalaya: A Monograph.* New York: Brentano's.

Roland, Joan G. 1989. *Jews in British India: Identity in a Colonial Era.* Hanover: Brandeis University Press.

Roland, Joan G. 1999. "Baghdadi Jews in India and China in the Nineteenth Century: A Comparison of Economic Roles." In *The Jews in China*, ed. Jonathan Goldstein, vol. 1, 141–156. New York: M. E. Sharpe.

Rousse-Lacordaire, Jérôme. 2016. "Bulletin d'histoire des ésotérismes." *Revue des sciences philosophiques et théologiques* 100: 517–532.

Rubinstein, William D. 2011. *The Palgrave Dictionary of Anglo-Jewish History.* New York: Palgrave Macmillan.

Rudbøg, Tim. 2010. "Helena Petrovna Blavatsky's Esoteric Tradition." In *Constructing Tradition: Means and Myths of Transmission in Western Esotericism*, ed. Andreas B. Kilcher, 161–177. Leiden: Brill, 2010.

Rudbøg, Tim. 2013. "Point Loma, Theosophy, and Katherine Tingley." In *Handbook of Theosophical Currents*, ed. Olav Hammer and Mikael Rothstein, 51–71. Leiden: Brill.

Rudbøg, Tim. 2021. "H. P. Blavatsky's 'Wisdom religion' and the Quest for Ancient Wisdom in Western Culture." In *Innovation in Esotericism from the Renaissance to the Present*, ed. Tim Rudbøg and Jo Hedesan, 201–228. Cham: Palgrave Macmillan.

Rudniańska Hanna, and Krystyna Shmeruk. 2005. *Korczak, Tokarzewski i my.* Kraków: Rabid.

Rzeczycka, Monika, and Izabela Trzcińska. 2019. *Polskie tradycje ezoteryczne 1890–1939. Tom. 1, Teozofia i anthropozofia*. Gdańsk: Wydawnictwo Uniwersytetu Gdańskiego.

Saelid, Ingvild, Lisbeth Mikaelsson. 2013. "Theosophy and Popular Fiction." In *Handbook of Theosophical Currents*, ed. Olav Hammer and Mikael Rothstein, 453–470. Leiden: Brill.

Sagiv, David. 2004. The Jewish Community in Basra 1914–1952. Jerusalem: Carmel [Hebrew].

Salem, A. B. 1929. *Eternal Light: or, Jew Town Synagogue*. Ernakulam: S. D. Printing Works.

Samuel, Nayim B. 1931. "Theosophy and the Jews." *TJA*, July, 202.

Samuels, Henry C. 1925. "The Jew & the World Teacher." *Herald of the Star* 14 (December): 466.

Samuels, Henry C. 1926. "A Message to the Jewish Press." *The Jewish Theosophist* 1, no. 3 (April): 15–19.

Samuels, Henry C. 1928. *Morning Prayer: A Modern, Comprehensive and Applicable Order of Service, for Individual and Congregational Jewish Worship*. Seattle: New Synagogue Press.

Samuels, Henry C. 1929. *Krishnamurti the Jew: A Presentation from the Jewish Point of View*. Seattle: New Synagogue Press.

Samuels, Henry C. 1932a. "Fighting the Light (the Story of a Modern Excommunication—Herem)." *The Jewish Theosophist* 2, no. 1 (April–June): 3–4.

Samuels, Henry C. 1932b. "An Open Letter." *The Jewish Theosophist* 2, no. 1 (April–June): 5–6.

Samuels, Henry C. 1932c. "Editorial Notes." *The Jewish Theosophist* 2, no. 1 (April–June): 7.

Samuels, Henry C. 1938. "Theosophy and Hebraism." *American Theosophist* 26 (July): 168.

Samuels, Henry C. 1945. "The Jews—Race or Nationality?" *The Theosophist* 67 (December): 120.

Samuels, Henry C. 1946. *Palestine and Judea*. Seattle, WA: Henry C. Samuels.

Samuels, Henry C. 1947. "Hebrew—Not Jew." *The Theosophist* 68 (June): 187–189.

Samuels, Henry C. 1949. *Our Hebrew Faith*. Seattle, WA: Henry C. Samuels.

Samuels, Henry C. 1950. "A History of the Jewish People." *The Theosophist* 71 (August): 328–333.

Samuels, Henry C. 1953. "Concerning Studies in Religion—A Picture of the Great Hebrew Faith." *The Theosophist* 75 (October): 33–43.

Samuels, Henry C. 1955. "Bible Translations." *The Theosophist* 76 (May): 105–112.

Samuels, Henry C. 1960. "Understanding Our Holy Bible: An Hebraic View." Seattle, WA: Henry C. Samuels.

Sand, Erik Reenberg. "The Marriage between the Theosophical Society and the Arya Samaj." In *Imagining the East: The Early Theosophical Society*, ed. Tim Rudbøg and Erik Reenberg Sand, 253–272. New York: Oxford University Press.

Santan Rodriguez. 1982. *The Householder Yogi: The Life of Shri Yogendra.* Bombay: Yoga Institute.

Santucci, James A. 1997. "George Henry Felt: The Life Unknown." *Theosophical History* 6: 243–261.

Santucci, James A. 2005. "Blavatsky, Helena Petrovna." In *Dictionary of Gnosis and Western Esotericism*, ed. Wouter J. Hanegraaff et al., 177–185. Leiden: Brill.

Sarna, Jonathan D. 1980, "From Necessity to Virtue: The Hebrew-Christianity of Gideon R. Lederer." *Iliff Review* 37: 27–33.

Sassoon, David S. 1932. *Ohel Dawid: Descriptive Catalogue of the Hebrew and Samaritan Manuscripts in the Sassoon Library.* London: Oxford University Press.

Schaeder, Grete, ed. 1972. *Martin Buber: Briefwechsel aus sieben Jahrzehnten*, I (1897–1918). Heidelberg: Lambert Schneider.

Schäfer, Peter. 2005. " 'Adversum Cabbalam' oder: Heinrich Graetz und die Jüdische Mystik." In *Heinrich Graetz und die jüdische Mystik, Reuchlin und seine Erben. Forscher, Denker, Ideologen und Spinner*, ed. P. Schäfer and I. Wandrey, 189–210. Ostfildern: Jan Thorbecke.

Scholem, Gershard/Gershom. 1934. "E. Müller: Der Sohar." *Orientalische Litteraturzeitung* 37: 742–744.

Scholem, Gershard/Gershom. 1961. *Major Trends in Jewish Mysticism.* New York: Schocken Books.

Scholem, Gershard/Gershom. 1976a. *Elements of the Kabbalah and Its Symbolism.* Jerusalem: Mosad Bialik [Hebrew].

Scholem, Gershard/Gershom. 1976b. *Explications and Implications: Writings on Jewish Heritage and Renaissance.* Tel Aviv: Am Oved [Hebrew].

Scholem, Gershard/Gershom. 1976c. *On Jews and Judaism in Crisis: Selected Essays.* New York: Schocken Books.

Scholem, Gershard/Gershom.1995. *Briefe (2), 1948–1970*, ed. Thomas Sparr. München: C. H. Beck.

Sedgwick, Mark. 2017. *Western Sufism: From the Abbasids to the New Age.* New York: Oxford University Press.

Sellin, Albrecht Wilhelm. 1913. *Die geisteswissenschaftliche Bedeutung des Sohar.* Berlin: Philosophisch-Theosophischer Verlag.

Silverman, Marc. 2017. *Pedagogy of Humanist Moral Education.* New York: Palgrave Macmillan.

Simon, Maurice, Harry Sperling, and Paul Levertoff. 1931–1934. *The Zohar.* London: Soncino.

Simoni, Marcella. 2013. " 'Hello Pacifist'—War Resisters in Israel's First Decade." *Quest* 5: 73–110.

Skinner, J. Ralston. 1876. *Key to the Hebrew Egyptian Mystery in the Source of Measures Originating the British Inch and the Ancient Cubit.* Philadelphia: David McKay.

Skinner, J. Ralston. 1886. "Notes on the Cabbalah of the Old Testament." *The Path* 1, no. 4: 103–108; 1, no. 5: 134–139.

Solomon, J. E. 1936. "My Experience in Healing." *The Theosophist* 57 (September): 515–520.

Srinivasan, N. K. 2012. "Maurice Frydman—Jnani and a Karma Yogi: A Biography." https://www.scribd.com/doc/97304328/3/Chapter-3-The-Karma-Yogi.

Stambalchek, Leonide. 1927. "Hasidism—One of the Jewish Aspects of Theosophy." *The Jewish Theosophist* 1, no. 3 (April): 5–8.

Stasulane, Anita. 2013. "The Theosophy of the Roerichs: Agni Yoga or Living Ethics." In *Handbook of Theosophical Currents*, ed. Olav Hammer and Mikael Rothstein, 193–215. Leiden: Brill.

Staudenmaier, Peter. 2005. "Rudolf Steiner and the Jewish Question." *Leo Baeck Institute Yearbook* 50, no. 1: 127–147.

Staudenmaier, Peter. 2014. *Between Occultism and Nazism: Anthroposophy and the Politics of Race in the Fascist Era.* Leiden and Boston: Brill.

Steinem, Gloria. 2009. "Pauline Perlmutter Steinem." *The Shalvi/Hynam Encyclopedia of Jewish Women.* https://jwa.org/encyclopedia/article/steinem-pauline-perlmutter.

Steiner, Rudolf. 1970. "Über die Sephirot," *Beiträge Zur Rudolf Steiner Gesamtausgabe Heft* 32 (Dornach: Rudolf Steiner Verlag, 1970), 30–31. https://odysseetheater.org/GA/Beitraege/D32.pdf#page=&view=Fit

Steiner, Rudolf. 1985. *Briefe, Band 1, 1881–1890.* Dornach: Rudolf Steiner Verlag.

Steiner, Rudolf. 1987. *Briefe, Band 2, 1890–1925.* Dornach: Rudolf Steiner Verlag.

Steiner, Rudolf. 1988. "Die Geschichte der Menscheit und die Weltanschauungen der Kulturvölker (Zwölfter Vortrag, Dornach 10 Mai 1924)" *Rudolf Steiner Gesamtausgabe Vortrage* (GA 353), Dornach: Rudolf Steiner Nachlassverwaltung, 210–27. http://bdn-steiner.ru/cat/ga/353.pdf.

Steiner, Rudolf. 2001. "Über die Kabbala." *Rudolf Steiner Gesamtausgabe* (GA 089), Dornach: Rudolf Steiner Verlag, 273–279. https://odysseetheater.org/GA/Buecher/GA_089.pdf#view=Fit.

Steiner, Rudolf. 2009. "Mein Lebensgang" (GA 28), Rudolf Steiner Online Archive, 388–389. http://anthroposophie.byu.edu/schriften/028.pdf,

Steiner, Rudolf. 2010. "Die Geheimnisse der biblischen Schöpfungsgeschichte." (GA 122), Rudolf Steiner Online Archive, 2–190. http://anthroposophie.byu.edu/vortraege/122.pdf.

Swierenga, Robert P. 1994. *The Forerunners: Dutch Jewry in the North American Diaspora.* Detroit: Wayne State University Press.

Templeton, Ronald. "Adolf Arenson." *Forschungsstelle Kulturimpuls.* https://biographien.kulturimpuls.org/detail.php?&id=24.

Thomas, John. 1869. *Phanerosis: An Exposition of the Doctrine of the Old and New Testaments.* Birmingham: R. Roberts.

Tingay, Kevin. 2000. "Madame Blavatsky's Children: Theosophy and Its Heirs." In *Beyond New Age: Exploring Alternative Spirituality*, ed. Steven Sutcliffe and Marion Bowman, 37–50. Edinburgh: Edinburgh University Press, 37–50.

Turba, E., C. Brillante, and S. Arieti. 2007. "I sogni di Cesare Augusto Levi: Un' Interpretazione, Prefreudiana." *Medicina Nei Secoli Arte e Scienza* 19, no. 1: 305–313.

Tzoreff, Avi-ram. 2023. "Acknowledging Loss, Materializing Language: Translation and Hermeneutics of Gaps in Nineteenth Century Baghdad." *Middle Eastern Studies* 59, no. 1: 1–21.

Underhill, Evelyn. 1911. *Mysticism: A Study of the Nature and Development of Man's Spiritual Consciousness.* New York: Dutton.

Vaňa, Zdeněk. 1992. "Rudolf Steiner in Prague: Zur Geschichte der tschechischen anthroposophischen Bewegung." *Beiträge zur Rudolf Steiner Gesamtausgabe, Eröffentlichungen aus dem Archiv der Rudolf Steiner-Nachlassverwaltung* 192: 1–40.

Verweyen, Johannes Maria. 1933. "Zur Frage der Adyar Gesellschaft." *Theosophie* 21: 240–241.

Von Weisl, Wolfgang. 1929. "Indian Travel Sketches." *The Reform Advocate* (August 24): 78–79.

Waite, Arthur Edward. 1902. *The Doctrine and Literature of the Kabalah* London: Theosophical Publishing Society.

Waite, Arthur Edward. 1938. *Shadows of Life and Thought.* London: Selwyn and Blount.

Waller, Ryan. 2011. Message Board Post, Katz-L Archives, Ancestry Rootsweb. http://archiver.rootsweb.ancestry.com/th/read/KATZ/2011-01/1295943370.

Weinstock, Tikva. 1963. "Old People and Women Are Attracted to Theosophy." *Ma'ariv* (March 6) [Hebrew].

Wessinger, Catherine. 2013. "The Second Generation Leaders of the Theosophical Society (Adyar)." In *Handbook of Theosophical Currents*, ed. Olav Hammer and Mikael Rothstein, 33–50. Leiden: Brill.

Westcott, William Wynn. 1887. *Sepher Yetzirah: The Book of Formation, and the Thirty Two Paths of Wisdom.* Bath: Robert H. Fryar (reprint, London: Theosophical Publishing House, 1893).

Westcott, William Wynn. 1891. "The Kabbalah." *Lucifer* 3 (August): 465–469; 9 (September): 27–32.

Westcott, William Wynn.1893. "A Further Glance at the Kabbalah." *Lucifer* 12 (April–May): 147–153, 202–208.

Williams, Bill. 1985. *The Making of Manchester Jewry 1740–1875.* Manchester: Manchester University Press.

Willson, Jennie. 1932. "The Ancient Wisdom in Palestine." *The World Theosophist* 2: 317.

Wilner, Mendel. 1960. "The Jews of Dembitz." In *Dembitz Book*, ed. Daniel Leibel, 49–50. Tel Aviv: Ahdut [Yiddish].

Wood, Ernst. 1981. *Concentration and Character Building—Practical Course.* Haifa: Ha-Aguda ha-Ben-Leumit le-Pituah ha-Mudaut [Hebrew].

Yehudai, Ori. 2014. "Displaced in the National Home: Jewish Repatriation from Palestine to Europe, 1945–1948." *Jewish Social Studies* 20, no. 2: 69–110.

Zander, Helmut. 2007. *Anthroposophie in Deutschland: Theosophische Milieus und gesellschaftliche Praxis, 1884 bis 1945*. Göttingen: Vandenhoeck and Ruprecht.

Zander, Helmut. 2009. "Rudolf Steiners Rassenlehre." In *Völkisch und National*, ed. Uwe Puschner and G. Ulrich Grossman, 145–155. Darmstadt: Wissenschaftliche Buchgesellschaft.

Zander, Helmut. 2011. *Rudolf Steiner, Die Biografie*. München: Piper Verlag.

Zander, Helmut. 2016. "Transformations of Anthroposophy from the Death of Rudolf Steiner to the Present Day." In *Theosophical Appropriations: Esotericism, Kabbalah and the Transformation of Traditions*, ed. Julie Chajes and Boaz Huss, 273–308. Beer Sheva: Ben-Gurion University Press.

Ziegler, Renatus. "Carl Unger." https://biographien.kulturimpuls.org/detail.php?&id=724.

Index